T0208329

VOICES WAITING TO BE HEARD

Nineteen Eyewitness Accounts of Arnold's 1775 March to Quebec.

Drawn by Sydney Adamson.   Halftone plate engraved by H. Davidson.
WORKING AGAINST THE FLOOD ON DEAD RIVER

STEPHEN DARLEY

authorHOUSE

AuthorHouse™
1663 Liberty Drive
Bloomington, IN 47403
www.authorhouse.com
Phone: 833-262-8899

Published by AuthorHouse 06/01/2021

ISBN: 978-1-6655-2609-8 (sc)
ISBN: 978-1-6655-2607-4 (hc)
ISBN: 978-1-6655-2608-1 (e)

Library of Congress Control Number: 2021909913

Print information available on the last page.

CONTENTS

FOREWORD

America's first historical editor, Ebenezer Hazard, wrote, "I wish to be the means of saving from oblivion many important papers which without something like this collection will infallibly be lost… [Some papers] are intimately connected with the liberties of the people; others will furnish some future historian with valuable materials." The same can be said of Stephen Darley with his fourth book, *Voices Waiting to be Heard,* which again focuses on Benedict Arnold and, more importantly, the soldiers who served under him. This time the subject is the event that first thrust Arnold into the public eye and made him a hero. Building upon Kenneth Roberts' classic *March to Quebec: Journals of the Members of Arnold's Expedition,* Darley offers thirteen more narratives of soldiers who participated in Benedict Arnold's famous trek through the Maine wilderness in 1775, along with six accounts from pension applications. This brings the number of known journals from this expedition to thirty-eight, the most of any Revolutionary War campaign. Through painstaking research in archives, newspapers, and other sources, Darley discovered some of these accounts as recently as 2018. Many of the journals compiled here have never been published previously or in limited editions only, making them virtually unknown to most students and scholars of the American Revolutionary War and therefore all the more valuable. Beyond this, the authors include not only officers, but also enlisted men and volunteers from different colonies, giving a diversity of perspectives.

Contemporaries compared Arnold's trek to Quebec with Hannibal's 218 BC march through the Alps, and the journals that Darley include provide a graphic view of the hardship that Arnold's men endured. From seasickness on the way to Maine to a late season hurricane that drowned the landscape, the soldiers faced difficult terrain and freezing temperatures in a wilderness bereft of provisions and shelter. Readers will get a deeper understanding of the bravery and determination these men demonstrated to survive, while sharing what little food they had. Arnold endured these conditions too, yet forged ahead to the French Canadian settlements with a small band to obtain provisions for his starving army.

Voices Waiting to be Heard offers far more than this, however. The journals also provide new insights into Arnold's crossing the St. Lawrence River, the siege of Quebec, and the failed December 31 assault upon the city. Most interestingly, the journals also offer readers a view of those soldiers captured in the attack. These accounts reveal new details about the American prisoners – the so-called "old country men" – who subsequently enlisted with the British and why they did so. Readers also learn of escape plans, interactions with British soldiers and residents of Quebec, and the prisoners' eventual parole and release in late Summer 1776. Taken as a whole *Voices Waiting to be Heard* provides an in-depth view of the Arnold expedition to Quebec, and it gives readers a greater understanding of those who participated in this epic event.

Stephen Darley has made an important contribution to our understanding of the Arnold Expedition to Quebec, and his efforts show that new sources about the Revolutionary War may be uncovered at any time.

Michael P. Gabriel, Kutztown University, editor, *Quebec During the American Invasion, 1775-1776: The Journal of François Baby, Gabriel Taschereau, and Jenkin Williams.*

LIST OF ILLUSTRATIONS AND MAPS

PORTRAITS

Portrait of Gen. Benedict Arnold. Drawn from Life at Philadelphia by Du Simitier. The European Magazine and London Review, March 1, 1783. Author's copy.

Portrait of Lieut. Col. Eleazer Oswald. Courtesy of the New York Public Library Digital Gallery. Emmet Collection of Manuscripts, Print Collection, Division of Arts, Prints and Photographs.

Portrait of Maj. Gen. Henry Dearborn (1872). Courtesy of the New York Public Library Digital Collection. Same as above.

Portrait of Dr. Isaac Senter, c. 1793. Oil on canvass painting by Samuel King. Courtesy of the Rhode Island Historical Society.

Silhouette Portrait of Matthias Ogden. Courtesy of Tim Abbott, *Walking the Berkshires blog.* http://greensleeves.typepad.com. Obtained from New Jersey Historical Society.

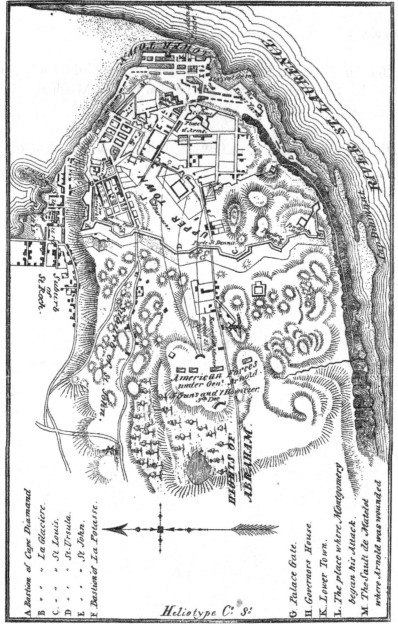

A Bastion of Cape Diamand.
B "   " La Glaciere.
C "   " St Louis.
D "   " St Ursula.
E "   " St John.
F Bastion of La Potasse.

G. Palace Gate.
H. Governors House.
K. Lower Town.
L. The place where Montgomery
   began his Attack.
M. The Sault de Matelot
   where Arnold was wounded

Heliotype C⁰ S:

COL. ARNOLD'S FORCES BEFORE QUEBEC, 1775.

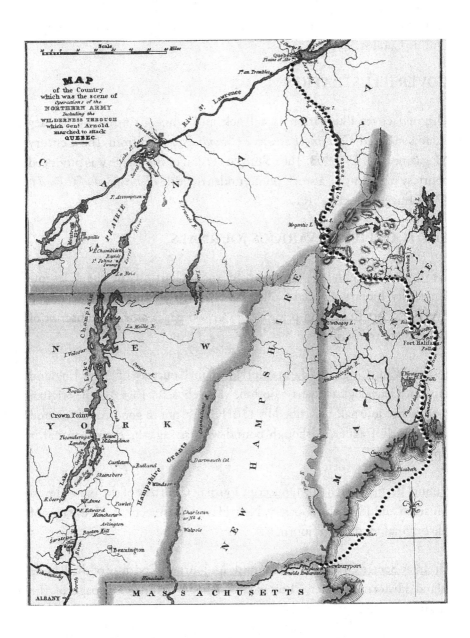

ILLUSTRATIONS

Working Against the Flood on the Dead River. Illustration by Sydney Adamson, 1903. Courtesy of Library of Congress, Prints and Photographs Online Catalog.

COVER ILLUSTRATION

Original cover illustration is a black and white painting by Sydney Adamson titled *Carrying Bateaux at Skowhegan Falls* from The Century Magazine, Vol. 43, 1903. The colorized version of the image was produced courtesy of Alamy as a stock photo under the title of *Invasion of Canada, 1775*, Image ID: HRP5RT.

PHOTOCOPIES OF VARIOUS JOURNALS

<u>Dearborn's Original Transcribed Journal</u>: Courtesy of the Glasgow University Library, Special Collections, Glasgow, Scotland. Transcribed by Dr. Robert Robertson prior to 1783. Two pages of the manuscript of Robertson's transcription.

<u>Joseph Ware Original Manuscript Journal</u>: Courtesy of New England Historic Genealogical Society, Boston, Massachusetts. Page 3 of the original manuscript journal. Described by HEHGS as "not in good condition and is extremely fragile...Although bound with string, the entire journal is ripped in half."

<u>Samuel Barney Original Manuscript Journal</u>: Courtesy of the New Haven Museum and Historical Society, New Haven, Connecticut. Two pages of the original manuscript journal.

<u>Dr. Isaac Senter Original First Manuscript Journal</u>: Courtesy of the Rhode Island Historical Society, Providence, Rhode Island. One page of the original manuscript journal.

<u>Eleazer Oswald Manuscript Journal</u>: Courtesy of National Archives and Records Administration, Continental Congress Papers, Washington, D.C. One page of the original manuscript journal.

<u>Matthias Ogden Original Journal</u>. Courtesy of Morristown National Historic Park, Park Collection, P23. One page of the original manuscript journal.

MAPS

Map of Arnold Expedition Route to Quebec. Prepared by my stepson, David Picton, from a Map published by R. Baldwin entitled "A View of the Rivers Kennebec and Chaudière, with Colonel Arnold Route to Quebec; Map of the Country which was the scene of Operations of the Northern Army Including the Wilderness Through which Gen'l Arnold marched to attack Quebec." This map was taken in an Atlas of John Marshall's biography *The Life of Washington,* published in 1805.

Map of Quebec City and Surrounding Landmarks during the Siege of Quebec in 1775. Prepared by my step son David Picton from Col. Arnold's Forces Before Quebec, 1775. Taken from Edwin Martin Stone. *The Invasion of Canada in 1775,* published by Knowles, Anthony & Co., Printers, 1867.

CHRONOLOGY OF THE EXPEDITION TO QUEBEC

<u>Sept 6, 1775</u>. Orders were given by General George Washington to Benedict Arnold to draft recruits and collect provisions, and orders to Rueben Colburn of Maine to build 200 bateaux.

<u>Sept. 13-15</u>. Troops who volunteered for the expedition began making their way in small groups to Newburyport, MA.

<u>Sept. 19.</u> Arnold's Army sailed out of the Newbury harbor on eleven transport vessels to go to the Kennebec River in Maine.

<u>Sept. 20.</u> Arrived at mouth of Kennebec River.

<u>Sept. 21.</u> Transports arrived at Rueben Colburn's shipyard in what is now Pittston, Maine. There they took possession of 200 plus bateaux.

<u>Sept. 23.</u> Bateaux reached Fort Western, now Augusta, Maine. Here a man killed another man which was the first casualty of the expedition.

<u>Sept. 24.</u> Arnold sent exploring party to mark the route to the Chaudière River in Canada under the command of Lieutenant Steele.

<u>Sept. 25</u>. First Division leaves Fort Western.

<u>Sept. 30.</u> Arnold portaged around Taconic Falls and arrived at Fort Halifax.

<u>Oct. 1.</u> Arnold arrived at Skowhegan Falls.

<u>Oct. 2.</u> Arnold arrived at Norridgewock Falls, which was the last English settlement.

<u>Oct. 10.</u> Arnold arrived at Caratunk Falls.

<u>Oct. 11.</u> Expedition arrived at the Great Carrying Place where they left the Kennebec River.

<u>Oct. 13.</u> Arnold sent a letter to "some Gentlemen in Quebec" informing them of his plan.

<u>Oct. 16.</u> Arnold arrived at Bog Brook, a tributary of the Dead River which was the end of the great carry. Dr. Senter erected a log hospital at this point to house the sick men.

<u>Oct. 22-23.</u> A hurricane surprised the men and the resulting rain completely changed the landscape.

<u>Oct 25.</u> Expedition reached the Chain of Ponds. Enos's Division of three companies with 233 men left the expedition to return to Boston.

<u>Oct. 26.</u> Arnold reached the Height of Land, crossing from Maine into Canada.

<u>Oct. 27.</u> Expedition arrived at Lake Megantic in Canada.

<u>Oct. 28.</u> Arnold ahead of main party begins to descend the Chaudière River.

<u>Oct. 30.</u> Arnold ahead of main party arrives at first French settlement, known as Sartigan.

<u>Nov. 2.</u> Arnold sends back food for his men. Included cattle and other provisions.

<u>Nov. 3.</u> Arnold's men began to arrive at Sartigan.

<u>Nov. 6.</u> Expedition men began arriving at Point Levis across St. Lawrence River from Quebec

<u>Nov. 14.</u> Expedition crossed the St Lawrence River at night and landed at Wolfe's Cove. Arnold then marched them to walls of Quebec.

<u>Nov. 19.</u> Arnold ordered expedition to Point aux Trembles.

<u>Dec 1.</u> General Montgomery meets up with Arnold at Point aux Trembles bringing equipment and supplies.

<u>Dec. 4-5.</u> Expedition marched back to Quebec.

<u>Dec. 31.</u> After four weeks of pressure on the city, the American Army under Montgomery mounted an assault on Quebec that ended up as a failure. Arnold was wounded and Montgomery was killed. Of Arnold's men, 40 were killed, 258 were not captured and 383 were taken prisoner.

<u>May 17.</u> Prisoners Major Meigs and Capt. Dearborn were allowed to leave early to go back to Boston.

<u>Aug. 7.</u> All officers and men who were prisoners and who were willing to sign a parole were released to sail to New York in British vessels. Their route was down the St Lawrence River to the Atlantic Ocean.

<u>Aug. 25.</u> Released prisoners were landed at Elizabethtown, New Jersey.

PREFACE

In 1938, after writing two historical novels about Benedict Arnold in the Revolutionary War, well-known Maine author, Kenneth Roberts, published *March to Quebec,* his compilation of journals regarding Benedict Arnold's epic and historic expedition to capture Quebec in 1775. In his compilation, Roberts included journals he thought were the most significant ones known at that time. He revised his book in 1940 to add the journal of the expedition surveyor, John Pierce, which he believed was second in importance only to Arnold's journal. Clearly not all historians agree with that assessment. The addition of the Pierce journal increased the number of American journals in his book to eleven. Roberts also included the journal of Lieutenant John Montresor, a British engineer, because Montresor was the first to make the journey from Quebec to Maine in 1761and his journal was used by Arnold. He also added several letters written by Benedict Arnold which covered both the expedition and the time when Arnold and his troops were in Canada.[1]

Roberts' notable book has received many positive reviews and comments since its publication. It has become one of the seminal works of the Arnold expedition because it allows readers access to the actual texts of the eleven selected journals in one book. Prior to Roberts, most of the expedition journals had been published only in limited editions or in historical journals of limited readership. The expedition journals included in Roberts' book were virtually unknown to the general public prior to its publication. He made them readily available to everyone and many people bought his book because of his reputation as an author of historical fiction.

Realizing how much attention has been focused on Roberts' compilation of expedition journals and given how many journals have been uncovered over the past fifty years, I felt it timely to compile this new and different collection of thirteen expedition journals. I realize that Roberts has already published eleven important journals that provide the participants detailed overview of the expedition's day to day experiences. However, more is better because there are so many other interesting journals that are still relatively unknown and should be available to the public.

The thirteen additional journals I have included in this book also provide a greater and more complete historical understanding of the expedition. Only one of them, written by Eleazer Oswald, can compare to the insights and details in Roberts' presentation of Arnold's journal. None of these journals contain the myriad of details that are included in John Joseph Henry's two hundred twenty four page recitation of his experiences trekking through the wilderness and being held prisoner in Quebec. However, all of the journals included in this book are authentic and contain very important personal impressions of the hardships and dangers encountered by their writers. I believe they should also be available to interested readers.

In 2011, I published my contribution to the journals of the expedition in *Voices from a Wilderness Expedition: The Journals and Men of Benedict Arnold's Expedition to Quebec in 1775*.[2] The primary purpose of that book was to compile a listing all known journals of the expedition and to provide a list of the names of the participant that went on the march. Since its publication, I have received a number of emails from people who provided me with new information about the expedition, including leads on possibly new journals. Most of these leads turned out to be positive and led me to previously unknown journals. The most recent lead was from Robert Stevens who identified a journal by William Preston from New Hampshire. These newly discovered journals stimulated my interest in writing a second book that would compile all of the new journals that I have reviewed, some of which are also mentioned in *Voices*. *Voices* also identifies some journals previously published in little known historical magazines and journals

There are many references throughout this book to my previous book on the Arnold expedition to Quebec, *Voices from a Wilderness Expedition: The Journals and Men of Benedict Arnold's Expedition to Quebec in 1775*. For ease of reference, throughout the introductory information for each journal, the General Notes and the endnotes on each journal, I will refer to that book as *Voices*.

In *Voices*, I included the typescript transcription of five significant journals which are also included in this book. I uncovered these journals during my research for the book. They are the original Henry Dearborn journal found in the University of Glasgow Library which is quite different from the Massachusetts Historical Society version; an anonymous journal also located in the same library; the second journal of Doctor Isaac Senter that I found in the Rhode Island Historical Society, which had never been transcribed or published; Private Samuel Barney's journal, which I found in the archives of the New Haven Museum and Historical Society; and the journal of Private Moses Kimball which was transcribed into a typescript around 1928 but never published.

I described one of the journals listed in Chapter One of *Voices* as the Anonymous Journal. It was published only once before in 1900 in a limited publication historical magazine titled *The American Antiquarian and Oriental Journal*. In 2013, primarily due to the research effort of my colleague, Stephen Burk, who contacted me about a relative who served in the expedition, we were able to identify the author of this journal as William Pierce of Massachusetts. We published an article about our research and findings as to the authorship of the journal in *Early America Review*. The William Pierce journal is included in this book and is being published for the first time since 1900.

This compilation also includes the Private Joseph Ware journal, which Roberts did not include in his book. He justified his decision saying it was similar to the Wild, Tolman, Stocking, Morison and Provincial journals and had no "individuality" so it was therefore, "unnecessary." Roberts did, however, acknowledge that Ware was the only journal containing a list of American prisoners taken at the failed assault on Quebec, and included that list in his book. In *Voices*, I called the journals of Ware, Tolman, Wild and Dorr the collaborative Ward Company journals. Justin Smith's 1903 book went into great detail analyzing why the journals of Joseph Ware and Ebenezer Tolman were similar. However, he then went on to explain his reasons for thinking Tolman was the original author. He also concluded that Ware was not even on the expedition.[3]

In Chapter Three of *Voices*, I provide my analysis of the two journals, and disagree with Smith about the Ware journal. My conclusion was as follows;

> There is ample evidence to conclude that Ware was the original author of the collaborative journals. The two pension applications cited above are sufficient proof to support this conclusion. None of the evidence favoring

Tolman is as persuasive as the pension applications that support Ware.[4]

Based on my research regarding the Ware journal, I have included it in this compilation because it is written by the original author and deserves to be included because of Ware's inclusion of the list of prisoners.

Thanks to a 2018 email from Robert Stevens of Maine, who recently participated in a reenactment of the entire route of the Arnold expedition headed by Hodding Carter, I was able to review an anonymous expedition journal that had been published in four editions of the *Pennsylvania Packet* newspaper in November of 1779.[5] Despite this early publication, no one had ever identified it as an expedition journal or published it. Although it only covers the period to the author's arrival at the first Canadian settlement on November 3, 1775, that journal is included in this book. It is a well-written and interesting narrative of the expedition traveling from Newburyport through the Maine wilderness.

In addition to the *Pennsylvania Packet* journal, Rob Stevens also alerted me to another previously unknown journal written by William Preston of New Hampshire. Preston's journal is also unknown even though a hand written transcription of his journal has been in the New Hampshire Historical Society Library since 1928, in the papers of his nephew, Charles Horace Herbert.

This book also features the "Journal of a Provincial," which is now accepted as the journal written by Sergeant William McCoy of Captain William Hendricks's Company of riflemen. In *Voices*, I explain why McCoy is the accepted author of the Provincial journal. I also conclude that Kenneth Roberts was not correct in his conclusion that McCoy's journal is in the same category as the Stocking, Ware, Wild and Tolman journals. I found that 'there is no entry in the McCoy journal that contains identical or even closely similar language to those found in the Ward Company collaborative journals, Ware, Wild and Tolman." [6]

Another expedition journal only published once before is the journal of Private Jeremiah Greenman. Greenman was from Newport, Rhode Island, and wrote a diary or journal covering his entire Revolutionary War experience. His journal begins in 1775 and ends in 1784. Any journal that records daily entries for that period of time is important because of its comprehensive look at the war. Greenman provides more detailed information about the march than most others. It is unlike any other journal and includes the author's personalized comments on his daily life. Although he served in Captain Samuel Ward's Company with five other journalists, his journal is unique and is not a copy of any others.

This book is a supplement to Roberts' book but is an equally important compilation because it offers thirteen journals in one source that either have not been previously published, previously published in limited distribution sources or in one instance published in a book. Most Revolutionary War readers and enthusiasts will unlikely to take the time and effort to find the previous publications of each of these journals. In both Roberts and this compilation, interested readers will find a diverse sample of the experiences of the men who made this extraordinary march to Quebec through an untamed wilderness.

The 1775 invasion of Canada is an unusual occurrence because of its timing so early in the war. At this time, which was even before the colonies had really got their feet wet and had come to grips with the reality of what course they had embarked upon, no one knew the outcome. Sometime in August of 1775, less than two months after taking command of the Continental Army, Commander-in-Chief George Washington made the decision to send two distinct detachments of men to invade Canada with the objective of making it the 14th colony, thus depriving the British of their existing North American base of operations. One of those detachments was the so-called secret expedition commanded by Colonel Benedict Arnold to take Quebec by marching through the untamed and unknown wilderness of Maine and Lower Canada.[7]

What is not well understood is how difficult the march to Quebec was for the men who agreed to go on it without any idea of what they would encounter. What most readers fail to appreciate is just how much the outcome of Arnold's expedition was affected by factors outside the control of its leaders or the endurance of the participants. Sickness, later including smallpox, unusual cold and rainy weather, and difficult terrain were three external factors that adversely influenced the detachment despite the exemplary leadership of Arnold. As if the afore mentioned factors were not enough, the expedition's food supply became badly depleted as the march went on. The food shortage was directly related to weather and topography. However, there were two other factors that affected the food supply and the ability of the men to complete the march.

The first of these factors was the green wood used to manufacture the 200 boats that were used to navigate the rivers and lakes along the route. The green wood made the boats heavier to carry and also resulted in the wood contracting as it dried making the boats subject to water leakage which ruined their food supply. The final factor was the return of Lieutenant Colonel Roger Enos's Division to Cambridge while the expedition was still in the wilderness.[8] There were 233 men in the Enos Division who left the expedition as a group leaving the survivors with a smaller share of the remaining food than would be expected. In addition to the Enos Division, there were an additional 156 men who returned home due to illness or died in the wilderness.

In addition to the thirteen journals, also included in this compilation are six pension applications from participants on the expedition. While the pension applications do not contain chronological experiences of the applicant, each one does contain some interesting details about various experiences or observations that add to our understanding of the expedition. These personal accounts provide additional information about, and a unique perspective to, the history of the expedition to Quebec. They have significant credibility because each one is a firsthand account. However, since most of the declarations were made more than fifty years after the march, they do not have the advantage of explaining a recent experience in the same way as the journals. It is to be expected that in remembering a personal experience that happened that long ago one might exaggerate his role or leave out important details. In my view, these applicants speak for themselves and are worth reading.

The expedition to Quebec cannot be thoroughly understood without recognizing the incredible leadership role and accomplishments of its commander, Colonel Benedict Arnold. Much of my writing and research on the Revolutionary War period has been about Arnold and the military adventures in which he was a key participant. His leadership skills are exemplified by his conduct at the head of the Quebec expedition.

Various military leaders and authors have said the following about Arnold's conduct during the expedition. In my opinion, none of these statements are exaggerated and I agree with all of them.

- Major General Philip Schuyler (1775). "Col. Arnold's march does him great honour. Some future historian will make it the subject of admiration to his readers."[9]
- Joseph Warren (1775). "A genius" who commanded "a march under such circumstances, and attended with such difficulties, as modern story can't equal."[10]
- George Washington, Commander-in-Chief (1975) The merits of this gentleman is certainly great... I heartily wish that fortune may distinguish him as one of her favorites."[11]
- Kenneth Roberts, Author (1938). "The cold truth is that his [Arnold's] journal is a marvel of accuracy greater even than that of trained engineer officer Montresor. His letters are models of clarity, comprehensiveness, vigor, simplicity and restraint; the intelligence conveyed in them is invariably reliable. Both together provide irrefragable proof that Arnold was a great soldier and a great leader."[12]
- John Codman, historian. (1901). "The Arnold of Ticonderoga and Quebec, whose name was a synonym for bravery, determination and patriotic fever, is not often remembered now, His good deeds are forever obscured by the shadow of his great crime. But it will help us to do full justice to that strange and unfortunate man, if we follow again the story of the gallant but ill-fated expedition which he led through the wilderness of Maine and Canada..."[13]

There are two authors whose writings were essential in compiling this book of unknown journals. First and foremost is Justin Smith who wrote two books on the expedition. His first book, titled *Arnold's March from Cambridge to Quebec,* was published in 1903 and became the standard for details about the Arnold expedition and the men who wrote journals known to him at that time. His second book was a two volume series, *Our Struggle for the Fourteenth Colony,* published in 1907. His second one has extensive details about both the Arnold expedition and the Montgomery expedition along with numerous paintings, maps, sketches and photos of people, places and land marks of the American patriot effort in 1775 and 1776 to invade Canada. It also includes information on subsequent attempts to bring Canada into the colonies.[14]

The second author is Stephen Clark, whose book, *Following Their Footsteps: A Travel Guide & History of the 1775 Secret Expedition to Capture Quebec*,[15] is a detailed guide book to the route that the expedition followed from Cambridge to Quebec. This route is now known as the Arnold Trail and one Maine organization, Arnold Expedition Historical Society (AEHS), has been working to preserve the trail since its formation in 1967. Steve Clark, a native and a long-time resident of Shapleigh, Maine, is an officer in Arnold Expedition Historical Society and has been involved in its efforts to identify and preserve the Arnold Trail. Clark is a past president of the Maine Appalachian Trail Club and has written numerous articles about the mountains and rivers of Maine. His detailed descriptions of the various landmarks along the Arnold trail were extraordinarily helpful in the preparation of the General Notes.

GENERAL ARNOLD.

ACKNOWLEDGEMENTS

The research for this book has extensively relied on the assistance and cooperation of many individuals and institutions that aided me in finding and reviewing the personal accounts of the participants in the Arnold expedition. The emphasis of this book on the compilation of the thirteen little known accounts and the need to identify the locations of those journals required an examination of the extant manuscript journals either in person at the institution where they are housed or by reviewing a photocopy of the journal provided by that institution. This objective could not have been achieved without the assistance of the librarians and research staff who generously gave time and attention to my requests.

Those institutions which house the journals included in this book are the following.

- The Special Collection librarians at the University of Glasgow library who provided me with copies of the "Durben" journal manuscript transcription as well as the Anonymous #2 journal. When I contacted them in 2009, they copied the journal transcriptions as well as the Appendices and comments by Hunter and Robertson.
- New England Historical and Genealogical Society Library which houses the original Joseph Ware journal, Judy Lucey, Archivist. NEHGS provided a photocopy of one page of the Ware journal that is in very bad condition.
- Rhode Island Historical Society which has the original draft of Dr. Isaac Senter's journal. In 2010, the library provided me with a copy of the manuscript journal in their possession, as well as information on the provenance of the manuscript.
- New Hampshire Historical Society for the William Preston journal transcription. Paul Friday, Reference Librarian, was very helpful in providing me with all of the documentation on the Preston journal that was in their library.
- Dartmouth College Library for the transcription of Moses Kimball's journal housed in the Kenneth Roberts Papers.

- New Haven Museum and Historical Society which has the original manuscript journal of the Samuel Barney journal and a transcription by his great grandson. Special appreciation is due to this institution which served as my home base in my research for my 2011 book *Voices*. Here I found new information on Benedict Arnold, many books and journals of the expedition, various family and town histories and a Roster of Arnold's men. Thanks to former Librarian and Curator, James W. Campbell, for his help and cooperation.
- The original Matthias Ogden Journal located in the Morristown National Historical Park which also has the transcription by the New Jersey Historical Society

The following institutions provided me with important documents regarding the Arnold expedition: the Massachusetts Historical Society, the Historical Society of Pennsylvania, the Boston Public Library Rare Books and Manuscripts Department, Houghton Library of Harvard University and the Manuscript Division of the Library of Congress.

In my research on the expedition to Quebec, I examined family histories and genealogy in the Connecticut State Library, the Connecticut Historical Society, Yale University Library and the Godfrey Memorial Library in Middletown, Connecticut. I also received help and information from Jean Loughlin of the Mifflin County Historical Society and David M. Rikes of the Cumberland County Historical Society and Hamilton Library.

The following institutions provided me with photocopies of important documents that helped me in my research: Donald Mennerich of the New York Public Library; Pennsylvania State Archives, Joy Werlink of the Washington State History Research Center; Wisconsin Historical Society; and Patrice N. Kane at the Archives and Special Collections of the Fordham University Library.

The journals in this book would not have been compiled without the involvement of Robert Stevens of Maine who in the past two years has identified two totally unknown journals of the Arnold expedition for me. Rob first informed me of a journal that had been published in the Pennsylvania Packet newspaper in 1779 which no one since that time had discovered. I was skeptical at first that a journal published in a well-known newspaper for that time had been completely ignored for two hundred and forty years. However, upon reviewing the pages of the Pennsylvania Packet it was the case. This seemed almost too good to be true and I wondered how I might make people aware of it. Less than a year later, I got an email from Rob telling me he had found another unknown expedition journal written by William Preston. Rob informed me how he found the journal and told me where it was located. Again I was skeptical as it seemed beyond belief that Rob could have discovered two unknown journals in less than two years. Upon verifying the existence of the Preston account, I knew I had to publish a new compilation of unknown or little known expedition journals similar to the one by Kenneth Roberts.

Thanks to Annette Lamb from Utah, a descendant of William Preston, for providing me with the information she had on Preston and his journal. It was Annette who first informed Rob Stevens about the Preston journal in response to his email when he viewed her comment to an expedition book on Amazon.

I recognize my colleague Stephen Burk for his work in researching the identity of the author of the anonymous journal initially published in *The American Antiquarian and Oriental Journal* in 1900. It is through his research that we now know that the journal was written by William Pierce of Hadley, Massachusetts.

Mark Sullivan from Indiana contacted me some months ago regarding a possible expedition journal written by Freeman Judd. I replied to him that I had no information on a Judd journal. Mark was so interested that he informed me that he was going to make every effort to find a copy of that journal. After doing extensive research, Mark concluded that there was no copy of the Judd journal existing anywhere in the public domain and gave up his search. He subsequently wrote an article in the *Journal of the American Revolution* on his efforts. In this compilation I refer to it as a lost journal which was added as a chapter as a direct result of Mark's effort.

I am indebted to Marie Blades, then a high school student, who in 1980 wrote a pamphlet for the Morris County Historical Society regarding her conclusions about the identity of the author of an Arnold expedition journal in the collection of the Rockaway Free Public Library. Blades publication identifies the author as Matthias Ogden and presents the results of her research which led her to identify its author. As a result of reading her pamphlet, I did my own research to confirm Ogden as the author.

Special thanks to Sarah Minegar, Archivist for the Morristown National Historical Park, who helped me obtain a microfilm of the Matthias Ogden journal which was located in the Lloyd W. Smith Archival Collection, Morristown National Historical Park. My previous attempts to locate the original had not worked out so this was an important breakthrough. In addition, Sarah sent me a photocopy of the first page of the Ogden journal which is included in this book.

I want to recognize the long standing efforts of the Arnold Expedition Historical Society of Pittston, Maine. Formed in 1973 in anticipation of the Bicentennial of the 1775 expedition, as a local Maine organization, it has consistently since then been the backbone of the efforts to publicize the historic nature of the expedition to the public largely without any significant financial help from the federal or state government. In addition to sponsoring a reenactment of the march in 1975, AEHS has placed markers at various significant locations on the Arnold Trail as well as marking the route of the original trail in rural Maine. When I found out about AEHS in 1776, I became a member and have found myself constantly amazed at how much they accomplish with only volunteers and limited financial resources. Their dedication and devotion to the expedition is well beyond any similar historical organization that I am aware of.

My primary contact person at the Society has been Steve Clark who wrote a very helpful guide book in 2003 to help interested readers follow the route of the Arnold expedition. Steve has always been available to assist me with questions and in finding further information regarding the expedition. His guide book was essential in my preparation of the General Notes for this compilation.

Thanks to my step son David Picton for his important help in producing maps, cover illustration and all images used in this book.

This book would not have been completed without the on-going assistance and support of my wife, Peggy Brennan. Not only did she encourage me at critical points in the development of the manuscript, she also served as my preliminary proof reader and then copy editor. Her suggestions were always helpful and made this a much better book by encouraging me to make the complex aspects of an event more to the point. I could not do this work without her assistance.

CHAPTER ONE

ABUNDANCE OF JOURNALS

Because of the unusually large number of journals written by its participants, the Arnold expedition to Quebec is unique. No other Revolutionary War military campaign or battle is as thoroughly documented with personal accounts. As far back as the early 1900's, expedition historian Charles E. Banks concluded that the Arnold expedition "was more thoroughly journalized" than any other campaign.[16] At that time, Banks was able to identify twenty such journals. In the intervening years new journals have been discovered, and now thirty-eight journals can be identified, including two journalists who each wrote two different versions of their journals and two known journals that are "lost." (See Chapter 15). While at first look, the actual number of journals may not seem to be a large number, however, compared to any other Revolutionary War campaign the numbers are extraordinary. For a Table containing information on all of the journals see Appendix A.

Historian Christopher Ward commented on the number of journals that made up the sources for the Arnold expedition. "Probably no other expedition of similar length made by so few men has produced so many contemporary records."[17] Ward was not confining his conclusion just to expeditions in the American Revolution, but to all wars. The only Revolutionary War campaign that even approaches the number of journals written by the men in Arnold's expedition was the Sullivan Expedition in 1779. Twenty-six extant journals were written by officers and NCO's from that expedition but none were written by privates. Most of these journals are included in the compilation of the Sullivan expedition journals.[18]

Several of the thirty-eight Quebec expedition journals were not published until recently, a few were published only once or twice in the past in limited circulation publications, others have been published in limited edition books and three have been lost. Oddly enough, however, new finds are still coming forward. The most recent discoveries are the journal by

1

an unnamed participant that was published in 1779 in the *Pennsylvania Packet* newspaper, and the journal of William Preston. Both were unknown until rediscovered in 2018 thanks to an alert amateur history buff, Robert Stevens. Those newly discovered journals are a welcome addition to the collection of personal reminiscences that remain the most important basis for understanding the expedition and its participants.

Every journal in every war contains the journalist's unique perspective and observations of the people, places and events that confronted him during the period covered by his journal. For the Arnold expedition, each journalist wrote his experiences when he, as part of the army, made his way through a wilderness never before seen by him or his fellow participants. A soldier's journal is a written record of how one person experienced a series of daily events that culminated in a battle or other significant event. These accounts are personal experiences that enliven the history of a battle or campaign. Each man on the Arnold expedition had a different reaction and view of the things he saw and experienced as he participated in the march. The totality of the expedition journals tells an unforgettable story of personal unrivaled hardship and adversity.

John Codman, who listed eighteen known journals in his book, summarized the expedition journals as follows.

> *They constitute a fairly large and invariably interesting body of historical material, which preserves unimpaired the quaint individuality of their widely diverse authors, and the unmistakable color and atmosphere of a period which must always be of particular importance to the student of American history. The reader will find much to entertain him in any of these journals...*[19]

All of the men on the expedition were volunteers. Some of them joined individually, and some in groups, that were then organized into companies. Given the nature of the mission, Arnold and Washington only wanted to take on those men who were willing to be part of the effort. Each man made his own choice and it is clear that many were eager to be part of it. One wonders what motivated them to agree to travel to a place none of them had ever been to and on a route which was not known to them.

For these volunteers, there was no one who had traveled the route and, therefore, could have enlightened them about the conditions and obstacles they would encounter.

Twelve of the thirty-eight journals were written by officers and the rest by enlisted men, including sergeants. No other Revolutionary War battle or campaign has this many accounts written by the enlisted ranks. These journals by the regular soldiers are important because they help us better understand what the Quebec expedition was really like to the regular soldier in the field. Of course with this many journals, there are disagreements about daily events, including dates specific incidents happened, and observations about distances of portages and when food ran short. But these are individuals reporting on their daily lives and they were not all in the same place at the same time. Some accounts were likely written after the events occurred when memories may have faded or become confused. Inconsistencies should be expected among the writers and, in my opinion, reconfirms the journals' authenticity.

Justin Smith appropriately summed up the nineteen personal accounts that he knew about as of 1903.

> *In short, the witnesses are many and their testimony is full, though it covers by no means every point. A satisfactory harmony of all these varying accounts, often confused and often inaccurate, is hard to secure; but the problem has to be faced.*[20]

The Quebec expedition journal that is the most published was written by Major Return J. Meigs of Middletown, Connecticut. His journal is reproduced in at least thirteen different publications starting in 1776, very soon after he completed his journal, and ending in 2010 in a biography of Meigs' life. The Meigs journal, which is included in Kenneth Roberts's compilation, stands out because it was published in the London Magazine in September of 1776, barely nine months after he completed writing it. Meigs was captured during the assault and likely had his journal with him at that time. The British most likely confiscated it and shipped it back to England on a vessel leaving Quebec in the early months of 1776. No doubt the London Magazine newspaper was very eager to publish a rebel journal that detailed Arnold's expedition to Quebec.[21]

The journals of Dearborn and Greenman in this compilation are in a special category because each of them wrote journals that covered the period between their release from a Quebec prison in 1776 and the end of the war. Greenman's is especially unique because it is one of only a handful of journals written by privates providing an account of the entire war. Both have been published as complete journals.

Including those published in this compilation, all of the extant expedition journals will have been published at least once. Given the number of journals, this is a notable accomplishment. The locations of thirteen surviving original journal manuscripts were identified in *Voices*, although two of these are questionable as originals. Four journals, Arnold, John Pierce, Haskell and one of Senter's, were not placed in public repositories until the first quarter of the twentieth century, over one hundred and fifty years after the expedition.

The unusual number and scope of the journals about this one significant event in an eight year war is "an extraordinary occurrence" and therefore cries out for further study. On September 9, 1938, well-known author Kenneth Roberts published the first, and prior to the publication of this compilation, the only compilation of Arnold expedition journals in *March to Quebec: Journals of the Members of Arnold's Expedition.* The following journals were included in Roberts' book, which was reprinted with an additional journal in 1940. All of these journals are explained in detail in Chapter One of *Voices from a Wilderness Expedition*.

- Col. Benedict Arnold's Journal.
- Captain Henry Dearborn's Massachusetts Historical Society Journal.
- Major Return J. Meigs' Journal.
- Dr. Isaac Senter's Historical Society of Pennsylvania Journal.
- Capt. Simeon Thayer's Journal.
- John Joseph Henry's Journal.
- Pvt. James Melvin's Journal.
- Pvt. Caleb Haskell's Journal.
- Pvt. George Morison's Journal.

- Pvt. Abner Stocking's Journal.
- Pvt. Simon Fobes' Journal.
- Pvt. Ephraim Squier's Journal.
- Surveyor John Pierce's Journal. Journal added by Roberts in 1940

An additional thirteen journals are provided to the reader in this new compilation. These additional journals are virtually unknown and each will provide an original voice to add to the accounts published by Roberts. The journals reproduced in this book include journals by a Connecticut private; a future Secretary of War; an anonymous journal from the University of Glasgow Library; a Rhode Islander whose journal covered the entire war; a New Hampshire blacksmith; a New Haven friend of Arnold; a school teacher from Pennsylvania; a New Jersey friend of Aaron Burr; a New Hampshire town political figure; a Massachusetts private; an anonymous journal from the Pennsylvania Packet newspaper; a second journal by a Rhode Island doctor; and a Bunker Hill veteran.

This book will provide any Revolutionary War enthusiast with a better understanding of the Arnold expedition to Quebec by providing thirteen first-hand accounts written by participants, both officers and enlisted men. None of these journals are widely known and only two, Ware and McCoy, are included in the different listings of journals by previous authors up to 1938. Three of the accounts, William Pierce, Pennsylvania Packet and Ogden, were published in long forgotten and now hard to obtain journals or newspapers and have not been readily available to the typical reader for many years.

Five of the journals, Dearborn, Anonymous #2, Kimball, Senter and Barney, were first published in *Voices* in 2011. Of the five, Dearborn, Anonymous #2 and Senter's second journal were discovered in the research leading up to the publication of that book and were transcribed by this author. Kimball and Barney had already been transcribed but had never been published. However, a few excerpts from the Kimball journal were provided by Kenneth Roberts in his chapter on the James Melvin Journal.

The experiences contained in three journals, Lieutenant William Heth, Lieutenant Francis Nichols and Sergeant Charles Porterfield, are not in this compilation because their entries only include the time that they were prisoners in Quebec in 1776 and, therefore, have no entries for the historic march that preceded it. Even though these journals have only been published one or two times, since they include nothing about the march they are not included in this compilation. Perhaps a future compilation will include only journals that cover the period of time the journalists were detained as prisoners at Quebec. Although some of the journals included in this book have entries describing when the author was in a Quebec prison, the emphasis is on the expedition through the wilderness and the period up to and including the assault on Quebec on December 31, 1775.

Each of the journals featured in this compilation has its own chapter. As an introduction to each journal, the following information will be provided. First, a description of the journal will be offered that contains interesting and little known facts about the journal. Second, each introduction will include a publishing history that lists all previous publications of the journal. Third, will be a short biography of the journalist, where the journalist's name is known.

The journals featured in this book have been edited with format changes and punctuation and spelling corrections as needed to make the journal easier to read and understand. The dates of the entries are provided in chronological order with each day starting a new paragraph. Many of the journals were not written in that format. Some reproductions of Revolutionary War journals have chosen to present the journal exactly as it was written by the participant author. In this compilation the choice was made to edit these journals to make them more readable.

Kenneth Roberts revealed how he determined the order in which the journals appear in his book. "The journals, with the exception of that of John Pierce, the surveyor of the expedition, are arranged in this book in the order of their importance as historical evidence, rather than according to their interest as narratives." Because it is believed that each of the thirteen journals in this book is important in its own right, these journals will be presented in alphabetical order beginning with the journal of Private Samuel Barney. No attempt has been made to evaluate their relative importance as historical evidence

CHAPTER TWO

DIARY OF SAMUEL BARNEY
OF NEW HAVEN

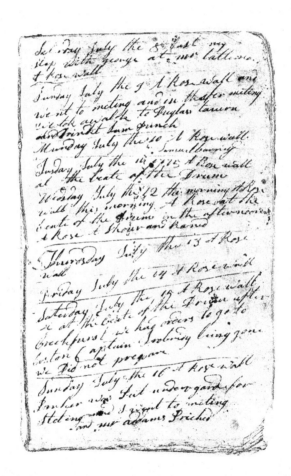

<u>DESCRIPTION</u>

Samuel Barney was a private in Captain Oliver Hanchett's Company and
is an example of accounts by an enlisted man. His journal is small, 3 ¾ X

6 ½ inches, composed of paper bound together without a cloth binding. While doing research for my book, *Voices*, I found his manuscript journal in the archives of the New Haven Museum and Historical Society, as well as a transcription of the journal by his great grandson, Francis Bishop Barney. He stated that "a few brief entries have been omitted, as adding nothing to the interest. But as may be seen, not even illness deterred the writer from making an entry in his much-valued Diary each day." The great grandson's transcription is used for this compilation.

Barney's account is interesting because he provides the names of a number of his fellow soldiers, mostly from Captain Hanchett's Company. His extensive use of names is different than any other journal, except for the journal of Surveyor John Pierce from Roberts' book. As a result, it is possible to verify the names of other participants in the march who were in Barney's company and what happened to them. He provides the names of men killed and sent back, which is also unique to his journal.

Based on the wording of the entries, this is an original manuscript that was written as he went along the route to Canada rather than after the expedition was over. Barney provides a different perspective because his entries include details on both him and his friends. It is an account of his personal experiences so it is much more than a record of his company or a general narrative of the expedition. He provides a written record of how the journey affected him physically and how he felt each day. This is not found in any other journal. Barney's journal was unknown until the publication of *Voices*. He deserves to be recognized and remembered.

PUBLICATION

The only previous publication of Barney's journal is in *Voices*, Chapter Seven, pp. 174-185.

AUTHOR.

Samuel Barney was born in New Haven, Connecticut in 1753. Very little is known about the details of Barney's life. He enlisted in Captain Caleb Trowbridge's Company in May of 1775 following the Lexington Alarm and went to Boston. On September 6, 1775, he enlisted in Captain

Oliver Hanchett's Company for the expedition to Quebec under Arnold. He was involved in the attack on Quebec but was not taken prisoner because he helped to carry the wounded Benedict Arnold from the field to the hospital. Barney continued to serve in Canada until May 27, 1776, when he was discharged by Arnold at Montreal and returned home.

In 1837, Barney's widow submitted a pension application that included a statement by their daughter describing his service on the march to Quebec. "He bore his part of the dreadful sufferings of that well remembered march through the woods … with an undaunted heart, although being among those who were destitute of shoes." In 1777, Barney attempted to get back wages and travel money that he argued he was owed from the Connecticut legislature. There is no evidence that he ever succeeded.

Barney joined the company of Captain Thomas Trowbridge in March 1779. Trowbridge's plan was to sail to the West Indies. On the fourth day out to sea, the ship was captured by the British and Barney and his shipmates were imprisoned on the infamous Jersey prison ship. While there, he contracted a serious fever from which he suffered for many weeks. He was exchanged in August of 1779 and returned home "in a very debilitated state." According to his daughter, his war experiences resulted in "almost unparalleled sufferings" that impaired him for the rest of his life.

Barney married Sarah Bassett on August 20, 1778, in New Haven and they had two children. After the war, he built a house on Church Street in New Haven where he lived the rest of his life. Barney died on July 17, 1805, and is buried in the Grove Street Cemetery. His grave stone is so weathered now that it is almost impossible to read the dates on the stone. His wife, Sarah, collected a pension for his service in the war in 1838 through a bill approved by the U.S. House of Representatives, which approved payments to her going back to a starting date of March 4, 1831.

JOURNAL

September the 16th, 1775. Had this book of one Mr. Jones of Newbury Porte [Newburyport]. This book cost nine copper.[22]

Samuel Barney

Roxbury, September 6th, 1775. Enlisted to go to Quebeck: Isaac George, Gabriel Hotchkiss, Samuel Barney, John Wise, Elijah Mix, Arch Blakeley, Roswell Ransom, Sherman Shattuck, Joseph Lewis, Daniel Jud[d], Freeman Jud[d], Allen Jud[d], Benjamin Warner, Isaac Knap, Samuel Barnes, Allen Ives.[23]

The 8th day went to Cambridge.

September the 9th [we] was reviewed.

September the 10th. There was five [st]raglers brought to Cambridge Guard House from Roxbury.

September, Tuesday the 13th, 1775. Isaac George, Gabriel Hotchkiss, John Wise and I washed at Inn at Cambridge where Jonathan Browne lives. Marched from Cambridge to Mistick about 3 or 4 miles and next morning we marched about 3 or 4 miles to Malden and went to breakfast at William Watts; and then went on to Newt's Tavern in Lynn, which is five miles, where we got some grog and then went to Howes Tavern in Denwitch which is seven miles; and to Meeting House is 2 miles and about 1 and a half [miles] to Benjamin Dealins in Danvers and left Salem on the right hand.

September the 14th, 1775. Went on seven miles to Beverley and to Wentham Meeting House is three miles and to Ipswich to landlord John Browne is two miles and to landlord Stainers is 5 miles.

September the 16th, Saturday. Got to Newbury Porte[24] *which is seven miles more.*

Sunday the 17th. I went to meeting at church.

Monday, September the 18th, 1775. Slept at Abraham Simmons and went on board the sloop Britania.[25]

Tuesday, September the 19th. Ate a breakfast of codfish and rum and got under way about six o'clock in the morning and steered about boat come off. The River runs about north westerly. Came to anchor about one o'clock. This day ate a dinner of herrings and then went east and by south. In the afternoon sailed by the Island of Oritage and was by Piscataqua Light House and passed by the Island of Sholes about three o'clock. Boon Island [was] about east and our course was northeast.[26]

Wednesday, September the 20th. Passed the Island of Seguin.[27] Our course was north east by that island. This morning entered the River's mouth and the pilot [went] up to a spring and got some water and made some grog, and [we] drank it with a good stomach. From Saguin to where we anchor is 30 miles, where George and I got some beer and made some flip. About eight o'clock we got under way and rode up the River five miles and then come to and stayed all night.

September, Tuesday [Thursday] the 21st. This morning arose well and got under way about seven o'clock. This morning had a good breakfast of chocolate and went up the River three miles and came to Broxby by Captain Christian. Got ashore at Gardiners Town[28] about one o'clock. From Newburyport to Gardners Town was two hundred miles. The people say this town is fifty-five miles from Quebeck.[29]

September, Friday the 22nd, 1775. This morning arose well but very cold; but last night we had a dance and last night there was a [illegible] brig launched here. This morning was whipped a man at Gardners Town, 10 stripes by verdict. Isaac George and I went up in a battow[30] eight miles and we beat anyone that was there, but I blistered my hands very bad.

September, Saturday the 23rd. This morning arose well but lay very hard upon the barrels and it is very cold. Isaac George and I went up the River three miles to Fort Western[31] and there we landed our barrels[32]; and then went down again and brought up all our things about five o'clock at night, and it was very cold.

September, Sunday the 24th. This morning arose well and all the rest of our mess and George & Blakeslee [did] too. Last night was shot a man, one [Rueben] Bishop, and is liked to die.[33] This day passed off with mending clothes, and a hard shower of rain, and we was in our tent. Bishop died today about five o'clock in the afternoon.

September, Monday the 25th. This morning arose well and went to prayers and some compani[es] marched off. This day was whipped one James Culverson ten stripes for taking a thirty shilling bit to change and never returned it again to one Biggs. This day had a good dinner of fish. This Culverson was drummed out of camp. This day Rueben Bishop was buried, of Captain Williams company.[34]

September, Tuesday the 26th. This morning arose not very well. A rainy day, and in the afternoon about three o'clock, one James McCormack was to be hung and [illegible] upon the scaffold and was reprieved, and at once.[35]

September, Wednesday the 27th. This morning arose well and went to prayers. John Love was whipped thirty nine stripes for stealing. About noon [there] was whipped a sailor for stealing, twenty stripes. Set out in battos and went up the River five miles and then come to and stayed all night.

September, Thursday the 28th, 1775. Arose well and ate chocolate for breakfast. Loaded our battows and went up about two miles and came to falls, Samuel Barnes, John Wise and I. From the falls to Vasselborough[36]*is forty miles. [At the falls]where we found a man and drinked some grog and ate a dinner of codfish; and to the next falls is one mile and a half. Went up the River about 8 miles and come to and stayed all night. Next morning went up to a man's house and got some milk. There is good land here.*

Friday, September the 29th. This morning arose well but I lay very cold, and Isaac George, Gabriel Hotchkiss and I went in the battows and went up the River five miles to Forte Halifax and had dam[n]ed bad work to get there, and had a damned bad boat.[37] *We got up to [from] Forte Halifax to the first Carrying place and we carried our boat and then pitched our tent and made a large fire, and I lay down by it and I slept well.*

Saturday, September the 30th. This morning arose well and got some chocolate and herrings, and then we loaded our battow, and Barnes, Wise and [Benjamin] Warner went in them about a mile, and come to a bad falls that lasted about a quarter of a mile; and then went about two miles and came to Three Mile Falls, that were very bad. Then George, Hotchkiss and I went to a house and had an ox killed; and then we had to go back a mile and pitched our tents and slept.

October, Sunday the 1st. This morning arose well and went up the River 13 miles. Had some bad falls, and the rest was good. This day George, Barnes and I has come to a good place.

October, Monday the 2nd. This morning arose well and it is liked to rain. George, Barnes and I goes in the boat. Went up the River one mile and a half, all bad falls, and then came to a carry where we had to carry our boats fifty rods, and set out again. Had good water [for] three miles and then we stopped. Slept very well this night.

October, Tuesday the 3rd. 1775. This morning arose well. George, Barnes and I in the batto set out and had some very good water and then had some very bad falls, and had a leaky boat.[38] *Came up the River 8 miles, and then came to a carrying place, where we had to carry one mile and a half. The name of this place is Norridgewock.*[39]

October, Wednesday the 4ᵗʰ, 1775. This morning arose well but George [was] out. The name of this place is Norridgewock. Is five miles back and wait. Today we carried our boats over this carrying place. No more English inhabitants upon this River after this; and then come to the Indians.

October, Thursday the 5ᵗʰ. This morning arose well and tarried here at the carrying place all this day; and mended my jacket. Had a wheat pudding for dinner. Loaded our batto about five o'clock and went up the River about one mile, and stopped and slept. Barnes, Hotchkiss and I. George is sick.

Friday, October the 6ᵗʰ, 1775. This morning arose well and slept. Had some chocolate for breakfast. In the afternoon we set out and went about three miles. Barnes, George and Wise, for I was sick. The best land I ever see. I feel better. I slept but little.

Saturday, October the 7ᵗʰ, 1775. Arose this morning but felt very poorly; but George, Barnes and I went in the boat and went twelve miles to the carrying place,[40] *where we carried our things seventy rod. Then we loaded our boats and went about one mile and a half; but I felt poorly all day and all night; but I stole pork and Warner stole some bread.*

Sunday, October the 8ᵗʰ. This morning, being very rainy, I lay very late, for I was poorly, and we did not move from here this day. We stayed here all day and [I] did not feel a bit well. Made no grains all day, and now Hotchkiss is making bread.

Monday, October the 9ᵗʰ, 1775. This morning arose a little better than I have been. This morning clear and cold and very windy; and Wise, Warner and Hotchkiss got into the battow and [then] there fell a storm. Then Barnes and Hotchkiss went in about seven miles and very bad going it was.

Tuesday, October the 10ᵗʰ. This morning arose well, and Hotchkiss, Warner and I went in the boat and went up the River five miles, and [had] a very hard way; and then came to the carrying place which is three miles and a quarter by the chain. Allen Ives and Allen [Judd] and Amasa Allen[41] *went home the 6ᵗʰ day of October.*

Wednesday, October the 11ᵗʰ. This morning arose well, but George is poorly yet. We ate a chocolate for breakfast without sugar, and carried over ten battows. Then we carried a barrel of flour and got almost across and left it; and then we laid by all night and then in the morning, we carried it up, then went back,

Thursday, October the 12ᵗʰ. *This morning arose up and carried over some pork, and then came back again and carried over the Major's boat and pitched a tent.*

Friday, October the 13ᵗʰ. *This morning arose well and carried our things over this place, which is two miles. The first pond is one mile and the next is two miles, where we encamped. James Taylor, Ichabod Swaddle and [Sylvanus] Hale came into our mess. Today it snowed.*

Saturday, October the 14ᵗʰ. *This morning arose well and we carried our things over this place, which is two miles; and it rained some but we got a good fire tonight and feel well.*

Monday, October the 16ᵗʰ, 1775. *This morning arose well and carried our provisions one mile and a quarter; and drived our boats into the creek which leads to Dead River⁴², and went up the River two miles. Wise and I pitched our tent and had some (illegible) for supper and felt well.*

Tuesday, October the 17ᵗʰ, 1775. *This morning arose well and got some breakfast and shaved, and hove away the shoes that Hill made us. We don't move from here today. We feel well and have cleaned our guns today.*

Wednesday, October the 18ᵗʰ. *This morning arose well. It is cold and pleasant, and there is twenty men a going to go back about two miles after fresh beef. Started late, but went up the River 10 miles and a half, and went by an Indian hut where the Ingen [Indian] spys was kept⁴³, and overtook two other companies and then stopped. Wise, Hale and I went in the boats. Good land here. We went six miles and had a carrying place about five rods, and the rest a good River.*

Thursday, October the 19ᵗʰ. *This morning arose well and it rained very hard here. We moved in the afternoon and went up the River five miles and had some bad falls.*

Friday, October the 20ᵗʰ. *This morning arose well and it rained very hard; but we moved and had our allowance shortened from three-quarters of a pound of pork to half a pound, and a final pint of flour⁴⁴; and we went up the River five miles and had a carrying place which was 15 rods, and then went up the River ten miles more. Rained all day. [John]Wise, [Ichabod] Swaddell and*

I in the boats. I have a bad boil and a sore shoulder. We had some bad falls. The Major's boat was overset.

Saturday, October 21ˢᵗ. This morning arose well but it had rained very hard and we went up the River four miles and then had a carrying place, which was 40 rods; then went up the River two miles and then had another [carrying place], which was 50 rods, and then stopped. It rained very hard.

Sunday, October the 22d. This morning arose well but lame with a boil. This morning it did let up, and we went up the River one mile and a half and had a carrying place of 80 rods; and then went up the River 100 rods and came to another carrying place and stopped. [We] were held up all the way by bushes. Taylor, Wise and I, [and] the Major and Captain got lost, but they found us in the night.

Monday, October the 23d. Arose well and stood guard. We went up the River. We carried our things over this place which is 100 rods, and then went up the River six miles, and had many bad falls, and George's boat was overset.

Tuesday, October the 24ᵗʰ, 1775. This morning arose well. [Isaac] George, [Name Not Readable], [Theophilus] Hyde, [Simon] Winter, [Roswell] Ransom & [David] Sheldon was sent forward and to (Not Readable). Was sent back [John] Cole, [Elijah] Mix, [Josiah] Remington, [Name Not Readable], [Abijah] Perry, [Joseph] Curtis. Then we all set out and went up the River three miles and it snowed. Barnes, [Mark] Lun and I in the boats. We had a good place.

Wednesday, October the 25ᵗʰ. This morning arose well and went up the River 4 miles and had a carrying place 10 rods, and then went up the River 100 rods and has another about 8 rods, and then went up the River two miles and had a very bad way. Then another carrying place and carried over that, which is a quarter of a mile, and then stopped. Barnes, Swaddell and I in a boat.

Thursday, October the 26ᵗʰ. This morning arose well and went up the River about half a mile and then went into a Pond and then had two more Ponds, and had a carrying place about 15 rods. We went twelve miles today, [Elijah] Marshall, Swaddel and I.

Friday, October the 27ᵗʰ. This morning arose well and slept on the top of a mountain and carried the boats into a Pond which is a mile, and then crossed the Pond. Then had another carrying place which is three quarters of a mile, and then went into another Pond which carried us into the great carrying place, which is four miles.

Saturday, October the 28*th*. This morning arose well, and left out battos and took seven days provisions on our backs, and went four miles to the creek that leads to Showdare.

Sunday, October the 29*h*. This morning arose well and it snowed but we marched ten miles and came to Showdare. This is not the Showdare Pond,[45] for we have been lost and have traveled in the swamp.

Monday, October the 30*th*. This morning arose well and traveled 15 miles in the woods.

Tuesday, October the 31*st*. his morning arose well and it was cold and snowed. We traveled seven miles and found Showdare River.[46] Traveled 8 miles and stopped.

Wednesday, November the 1*st*. This morning arose well and marched 20 miles. It snowed and our provisions was almost gone.

Thursday, November the 2d. This morning arose well and a fine day, and some of us marched off soon, and we traveled 24 miles and had news of provisions ahead; and we traveled one mile more and stopped and ate all our provisions up.

Friday, November the 3d. We rose early and marched 18 miles and found cattle and got some meat and ate hearty, and it stormed fierce.[47] Then we went about 10 miles and I gave an Indian a Pistareen[48] to carry us down five miles, and found houses. George gave us a loaf of bread and some butter and ate hearty, and built a house. It snowed and I had sentry guard.

Saturday, November the 4*th*. This morning arose well and was very lame, but went about two miles. We see two Frenchmen in a boat and they carried us 19 miles and we gave them six Pistareens for it.

Monday, November the 6*th*. This morning arose well and stayed here till about 4 o'clock and then marched about half a mile.

Tuesday, November the 7*h*. This morning arose well but very lame. We marched from Saint Maries[49] 16 miles through the woods and it snowed very hard.

Wednesday, November the 8*th*. This morning arose very unwell but marched about five miles and stopped.

Thursday, November the 9*th*. This morning very lame and stayed all day to a white house.

Friday, November the 10ᵗʰ, 1775. This morning arose very sick and stayed here at the white house and it snowed very fast all day. The regulars fired cannon all day and we had news that our men took a Lieutenant and a barge.⁵⁰ Our company marched off and left me for I was sick.

Saturday, November the 11ᵗʰ. This morning arose very sick and laid out a Pistareen fore butter and another for eggs. Stayed here all night.

Sunday, November the 12ᵗʰ. This morning arose, was better and marched 9 miles and found the Company.

Monday, November the 13ᵗʰ. This morning arose well and stayed here till night and then we went over the River Saint Lawrence and landed where General Wolfe did.⁵¹ Then a barge came along and we fired at them and killed three men.

Tuesday, November the 14ᵗʰ. This morning arose well and had an alarm, for the regulars [British] took one of our men. We marched up to the Fort and they fired at us.

Wednesday, November the 15ᵗʰ. This morning arose well and went on guard down by the River.

Thursday, November the 16ᵗʰ. This morning came off guard. The ship fired at us and came very near. This day Sergeant Dixon was shot in the leg and died.

Friday, November the 17ᵗʰ. This morning arose well but it is very cold.

Saturday, November the 18ᵗʰ. This morning arose well and went on guard at the sentry guard.

Sunday, November the 19ᵗʰ. This morning came off guard and all the rest were gone, but George and I overtook them. Marched 24 miles and went in my stocking feet and was very [illegible], lame and cold.

Monday, November the 20ᵗʰ. This morning arose well and marched one mile and a half and found the Company.

Tuesday, November the 21ˢᵗ. This morning arose well and got a pair of shoes and washed; and George cut my hair, and [we] made some pancakes. I laid out two pistareens and a half for rum and eggs.

Wednesday, November the 22d. This morning arose well. Isaac George, debtor, to one shilling that I paid to Salem on the way out, and to [buy] one shirt.

Thursday, November the 23d. This morning arose well but it snowed.

Friday, November the 24. This morning arose well and it snowed. But I went to the tavern and ate till I am sick.

Saturday, November the 25th. This morning arose well and [I] am going [illegible] miles and met Captain Grant. And went a [illegible] and found it near that [illegible] in some good [illegible]. Then I had a fit [?].

Sunday, November the 26th. This morning arose very well and John Wise and I went about two miles; and I got three pints of rum and got some bread and milk and paid for it. This day heard that Hull was dead.

Monday, November the 26. This morning arose. [The rest of the entry is cut off and unreadable.]

Friday, December the 1st. This morning arose well and we all slung our packs and marched over to the Captain's, and Major Meigs[52] came and talked to us. There were three vessels came down and we marched two miles to see General Montgomery.[53]

Tuesday, December the 5th. This morning arose well and marched to the review and went again to [the] other side of the creek, and [had] our mess. [Then we] went three or four miles and could not find no house. We loaded our guns and at last found a house where we stayed; and in the morning we drew lots to know who should eat milk.

Wednesday, December the 6th. This morning arose well and it snowed. Went over to the Captain's where we played for some wine and then found a house to go into.

Thursday, December the 7th. This morning arose well. Nothing strange happened today.

Friday, December the 8th. This morning arose well and [we] went to the review.

Saturday, December the 9th. This morning arose well and went about three miles and called the Quarter Master to our store; and went on fatigue, and we built a battery and have 26 guns.

Sunday, December the 10th. This morning not very well and the Regulars fired all this morning.

Monday, December the 11th. This morning came off fatigue. We built a gun battery. It was very cold.

Tuesday, December the 12th. This morning was on guard and our mess house burned and the Regulars fired all the while. Came off guard.

Wednesday, December the 13th. This morning arose not very well but ate breakfast of bread and milk, but was not well. This night ate a supper of turkey.

Thursday, December the 14th, 1775. This morning arose not well for I have lumbago, and this day there was a ball come through our breastwork and killed three men and wounded two more.

Friday, December the 15th. This morning arose not well. Our men fired 16 cannon and then sent in a flag of truce for them to resign, but they won't and our men went at it again.54 They have killed one man and wounded another.

Saturday, December the 16th. This morning arose not well. A fine day. Last night an Indian was killed and today a Soldier was killed and three of our cannon was dismantled. They fired all the while.

Sunday, December the 17th. This morning arose no better. A stormy day. This day passed and nothing done.

Friday, December the 22d. This morning arose well and we had orders to fasten a hemlock bush to our caps.

Sunday, December the 24th. This morning arose well, and this night we had a sermon preached by Mr. Spring; and he took his text on the 2d Book of Chronicals, the twenty second chapter and twenty 9 verse. "And the fear of God was on all the Kingdoms of those countries when they heard the Lord fought against the enemies of Israel".55

Monday, December the 25th. This morning arose very poorly and had orders to proceed to General Montgomery's at five o'clock in the afternoon.

Tuesday, December the 26th. This morning arose some better. We was asked who would scale the walls. There was [17]? turned out.

Wednesday, December the 27th. This morning arose well and it snowed, and we had orders to go into Quebec; and all paraded, but it cleared up and we did not go.

Saturday, December the 30th. This morning arose well and last night Sergeant Singleton deserted to the regulars. There they have been and fired cannon all day and all night.

Sunday, December the 31st. Last night we went to scale the walls. General Montgomery was killed and all our people that got into low[er] town are took prisoners.56 Major Meigs come out on parole of honor.

Monday, January the 1st. This morning it was very stormy and we had to retreat. The Colonel is wounded.57

Tuesday, January the 2d. Last night [we] was afraid that the regulars would come out and we lay on our arms all night. Major Meigs came out again on parole.

Wednesday, January the 3d. *This morning arose well. Lieutenant Cooper is dead and William Goodrich too. It is very warm and Sergeant Liman [Abner Lyman] and James Moore is gone home.*

Thursday, January the 4th. *This morning arose well and it is very warm and rainy. We heard that the Regulars was coming out.*

Friday, January the 5th. *This morning arose well. Last night we heard that Joseph Goff was dead. It is very warm and rainy. Major Meigs went into Quebec.*

Saturday, January the 6th. *This morning arose well and it is very cold, but nothing happened today.*

Sunday, January the 7th. *This morning arose well. Today very pleasant and we are going to send the soldiers' things into them. There was a hundred men killed and wounded. Nathaniel Gutridge [Goodrich] is dead.*

Monday, January the 8th. *This morning arose well. This day it snowed and this day George Hubbard of Bedford died with the small pox. Three French prisoners died. Borbo [Barbeau] for one.*

Tuesday, January the 9th. *This morning arose well and it snowed very hard all night and then cleared.*

Wednesday, January the 10th. *This morning arose well. It is very cold today and the old Flag o' truce died.*

Thursday, January the 11th. *This morning arose well. It snowed very hard and the old man was buried.*

The following statement by the author's great grandson has been placed at the end of the journal: "Here the diary ends abruptly but out of necessity, as the book was filled and probably no other was to be had."

CHAPTER THREE

ANNONYMOUS JOURNAL # 2

(INCLUDED AS APPENDIX I TO DURBEN'S JOURNAL)

DESCRIPTION.

This journal, written by an unknown author, is included in the Appendix to the Dearborn journal from the University of Glasgow Library that was discovered as I was writing *Voices*. It was among a number of different manuscripts from the personal library of William Hunter, a well-known Scottish book collector. His library was bequeathed to the Library of the University of Glasgow upon his death in 1783. According to the library, the Dearborn journal, which the library listed as the "Durben" journal, was in a bound volume entitled "Manuscripts from the Library of William Hunter."

This anonymous journal was edited and transcribed by Dr. Robert Robertson, who was in Quebec in 1776 as a doctor on a British vessel. Robertson took this journal and what he called the Durben journal as well as a much shorter third journal and gave them to his friend William Hunter. They were hiding in the Glasgow Library since 1783. Robertson's transcription contains fewer entries and less detail than the "Durben" journal. In his introductory note to the journal, he explains why.

"I think it proper to add the two following short journals as Appendix to the proceeding one because the obstacles and hardships which the Rebels met with & underwent between Cambridge & Quebec are more fully expressed in those than in it. Had there been a possibility of so doing, I would have united them with Durben's, but by their marching in different Parties they were seldom at any place in the same day. Repetitions of those occurances which are involved in the preceeding journal are carefully avoided; and it required much pains to amend the language of those, as it did to amend Durben's."

This journal, because of its brevity and its scrubbing by Robertson, does not contain sufficient information to identify the author, his rank or his company. However, the entries in the journal for Sept. 24, Oct. 8, Nov. 12, Nov. 14 and Nov. 21 seem to suggest that the author was a member of one of the Rifle Companies. The journal is presented below as it appears in the manuscript.

PUBLICATION

The only previously publication is in *Voices from a Wilderness Expedition*, pp. 127-133.

AUTHOR

Since the author is not known, no biography can be presented.

JOURNAL

On the 19th of September three Companies of Riflemen & eleven of Musket Men embarked & sailed on board of eleven Transports[58] to Kennebek River.[59]

22d. We found two hundred & twenty light Batteaux[60] ready for us; and got thirty miles up the River.

23d. As the Transports could go no further up, we put all our provision etc. in the Batteaux & rowed up to Fort Western.[61]

24th. We went up the River a mile and a half and encamped. Sixteen batteaux were allotted to every Company.

25th. We rowed seven miles up to Halfway Brook & encamped.

26th. We reached Fort Halifax[62] & encamped on the side of Sabasticook River[63]; it was a rainy day.

27th. We got our Batteaux over the portage about three hundred yards at the Falls of Taconmick[64]; & after rowing up four miles & a half further we encamped.

28th. At night we encamped after getting twelve miles up; in several places there was such a rippling & strong currents of the River that we were obliged to set the Batteaux up with poles.

29th. We found the River shallow & rapid in many parts; and our men by wading to track the boats & by setting them up were much fatigued & dejected. They had everything to carry across the Portage at the Falls of Shupigan[65], about 200 yards, and after all we advanced three miles only.

30th. The Batteaux were again tracked in many places, & we got up about ten miles to Norridgewalk Falls in Norrywok.[66]

October the 1st. We got the Batteaux etc. across the Portage, & encamped at night beyond all the Inhabitants. Many of our men were sick.

2d. We could only get two miles forward.

3d. By a mistake that we soon discovered, we rowed up the Seven Mile stream; & returned into the Kennebek & got seven miles up.

4th. The men were much dejected from the River's being full of rocks and shoals; but we advanced seven miles to Devils Falls[67]; & the Portage over which we transported the Batteaux was rocky & full of precipices. At night we encamped.

5th. We set the boats eight miles up through many rapid & shallow streams, & encamped.

6th. By setting up our Boats as usual we proceeded five miles.

7th. We reached the Portage which is said to be six miles over; & we cut down the brush for a mile upon it to render the carriage of our boats etc. easy. Then we encamped.[68]

8th. Captain Morgan[69] *return'd from measuring the Portage, which he found shorter than it was computed. By the different accounts of the way that we had still to go to Quebec, our expedition began to wear a gloomy aspect.*

9th. Here we left seven of our Batteaux, & began to carry the rest over a swampy country. Some of the men were unable to carry half a mile. Carrying fatigued them more than setting or tracking the Batteaux [up] the River. At night we cleared a place & encamped.

10th. Our flower [flour] was very inconvenient to carry; and for greater care in carrying, we unpack'd our pork, slung it with ropes & carried it on poles. After having carried it about two miles the men gave out with fatigue; then we encamped.

11th. We crossed about 140 rods over the end of a lake; proceeded then about half a mile, & encamped.

12th. Lieutenant Steele[70] *returned, who had been sent as a scout to the Chaudière to see if there [was] anything to oppose us; & to take prisoner an old remarkable villain of an Indian called Natanus*[71]*, whom Governor Carleton had honour'd with a Captain's commission. He had been on the Dead River all the summer; & there was found at his hut a draught of the River on birch bark, drawn with charcoal, in the cleft of a stick which was stuck in the ground. We crossed a second pond; and then after carrying everything a quarter of a mile came to a third.*

The 13th & 14th. We were employ'd in getting over the Portage.

15th. We paint[ed] the Batteaux, one of which was now allowed to every mess, & every Company was divided into eight messes. Sixteen days provisions were given to each mess-- all we had. Lieutenant Steele was dispatched with twenty four men to clear the Portages; & two Indians & one man were sent off with dispatches to Quebec to get intelligence in what manner the Inhabitants would receive us; they promis'd to meet us again in ten days.

16th & 17th. We got about nine miles up the Dead River[72]*. We passed two ripplings.*

On the 18th, we passed through three ripplings, & waded a little way to a Portage having the Morrishall River on our left. We had advanced about eleven miles. Then we came into a current that was very rapid a little way about half a mile from the Portage. After rowing about eight miles in very crooked still water, the River became shallow & rapid in many places, where we went up about four miles further. Our course was that day N. 26W.

19th. We had three Portages to cross, one of 18 poles; the second of 72; & the 3d of 74 poles, in getting about four miles up the River. The men complain'd of their short allowance of provisions, having only a pint lightly fill'd with flower [flour] & a less proportion of pork. And there were only remaining 12 days provisions, at that rate.[73]

20th & 21st. [We] Were [in heavy] rain.

22d. The River overflowed the place of our encampment; which obliged us to break up our camp, and embark. But the boats work'd up with so much difficulty that many preferred marching in an excessively, nay almost an incredibly bad way, from its swampiness & being full of thickets. We had taken the wrong, or the left branch of the River too; & had we not met two of our men who had been sent on a hunting the day before, & who put us in the right way, we must have perished. We gained about seven miles.

23d. We cross'd the eighth Portage. The River was exceedingly rapid from the rains. One boat with five muskets & some baggage was lost; & another was overset but all the men were sav'd.

24th. A Council of War[74] adjudged proper to send Captain Hanchet[75] forward with fifty men to conduct Colonel Arnold to the Inhabitants with all expedition to purchase provisions; & Captain Gotridge [Goodrich][76] had leave to march with them. That their boats might not detain them at the Portages, they left them all but two, & one cannon which they carried. We crossed the tenth Portage, having advanced seven miles.

25th. Our water was very bad. One of our boats sunk but nothing was lost. Another boat was drove back that detain'd me, & prevented me from getting up further. I therefore put ashore & with much difficulty could get a fire made.

26th. We cross'd three ponds. The Dead River now became very crook'd, narrow, & in many places extremely rapid. Then we cross'd another Pond & encamped near a sixth. We got sixteen miles.

On the 27th, we crossed the sixth & two other Ponds. The Portages were very difficult to get over, being quite swampy & covered with thickets. We now carried but three of our Batteaux with us.

28th. It was propos'd to make a common stock of our provisions, & to share *them equally; but Gotridge [Goodrich] refus'd to do it. We received a letter from Colonel Arnold*[77] *directing us to keep N by E or N.N.E. to avoid a large swamp; & recommending the bearer of the letter for our pilot.*

29th*. Colonel Green*[78] *having undertaken to pilot us, we came, after a march of six miles, to a large Pond & followed its winding course until dark, when we encamped; but I got over the Pond, determining to push forward to the Inhabitants.*

30th*. A large gutter arising from an extensive swamp & running into the lake stopped me. Colonel Green & a Major Bigelow*[79] *join'd me. Being now bewildered we agreed to go to a ridge that was in sight, south of us. From thence we cross'd the swamp, & kept about N.N.W. to hit Chaudière River, or lake. We waded to our waists in crossing the gutter & swamp, & cold it was. By keeping along shore then we came at last to Antijuntuck Lake, or the Chaudière Lake or Pond*[80]*, and March'd a mile in a track & encamped.*

31st*. We march'd twenty six miles. We heard that two of the Batteaux had been lost with one man, some rifle muskets, ammunition & baggage, & money.*

Nov'm 1st*. The men were quite feeble. We came to a River,*[81] *which by a map we suppos'd to be but eight miles from the Inhabitants; and marched in all twenty four miles.*

2d. I divided my last morsel with my friend. The men were greatly distressed; many of them not having eat for two days. I pass'd some the preceeding day who said that they had lived some time on dogs flesh; & that others had boiled their shoes, pouches, etc. to eat.[82] *After having march'd about ten miles we met some Frenchmen, & a Sergeant with some oxen & oat meal, with the husks on, which we thought was sumptuous fare.*[83]

3d. We met some more provisions, & with inexpressable joy we beheld the uppermost houses on the Chaudière.[84] *We waded a branch of the River which was very cold, & went into an Indians hut to warm ourselves. The Indian gave us some bread, butter & honey for which he made us pay extravagantly. At a house further down the River we found provisions [al]ready dress'd for us.*

4th*. The landlady where I lodged being told that we came from Boston sung a French song to the tune of Yankee Doodle Dandy. [We] Laughed very heartily.*

5th*. My cloaths [clothes] were so ragged that my breeches could not keep my shirt in. All the Inhabitants were kind to us.*

6th*. I appeared to be ably decent in Peter grubs brushes, & my boots. We* *march'd eleven miles to Tres Chemins Riviere without seeing a house. At night we got down, & quartered amongst the farmers.*

7ᵗʰ. It snow'd & was very cold.

8ᵗʰ. We march'd heartily, under orders, to within three miles of Point Levi[85]*; where we halted to prevent our being discover'd by the enemy. We hear that armed Indians came the night before from General Schyler*[86] *with an express to Colonel Arnold; & to our great mortification we were told that a hundred soldiers arrived at Quebec last Sunday from Newfoundland; it having been without any troops before, General Carleton having withdrawn them elsewhere. We were further told that there were but 150 Canadians embodied in the Garrison, & that even many of them had been forced to take up arms. It was suppos'd that the Indians whom Colonel Arnold dispatched with the letter from the Dead River must have betray'd him as he did not return with an answer, & as the Gentleman to whom he wrote is put on board of a Frigate that sailed up the River in the evening. P.M. We march'd near to a mill*[87] *on the side of St. Laurence River, in which it was said there were three hundred bushels of wheat. The enemy discover'd us.*

9ᵗʰ. We were alarm'd by a report that the Kings Troops were coming over to attack us, upon which we run out as fast as we could; but it proved to be only a boat that attempted to rob the mill or destroy a small vessel that lay ashore. We plac'd Sentinels along shore to prevent any boats from coming over, or crossing to Town.

10ᵗʰ. The Frigate fir'd at the mill.

11ᵗʰ. It was much talked of to storm the Town. Blacksmiths were employ'd to make the Spears & hooks, & carpenters to make ladders but everything was carried on in confusion. What better could be expected of them who were at the head of affairs having obtain'd their places only by Interest or Wealth. They could never boast of military geniuses, nor of their experience. The Commander in Chief [Benedict Arnold] indeed to do him justice was a clever, active, & sensible little man, and followed the sea sometimes I was told.[88] *However the scheme of scaling the walls of Quebec with 800 men, with not twenty rounds of ammunition, & their arms in bad order, to attack 400 well provided in everything plainly showed that he was no able General. P.M. a topsail schooner came down the River that was suppos'd to have General Carleton*[89] *on board and several vessels sail'd downwards. Some thought that the Tories were going off.*

12th. *Our little Army was divided into two battalions. The command of one was given to Colonel Green & the other to Major Meigs; & the Rifle Companies was equally divided under their command, which distressed our Corps much. Indeed we ought all to have laid down our commissions rather than to have serv'd under men who possess'd no one quality requisite to make them good officers.*[90]

13th. *It was reported that the Indians whom Colonel Arnold sent to General Schuyler were taken; that our plan would thereby be blown, & that the enemy who had hitherto supposed us to be 2000 strong would know our real force.*

14th. *As our Division cross'd the River Captain Morgan & others fir'd at a boat which got off from us; but as groans were heard some of the crew were probably wounded. Five hundred men were left to guard Point Levi side.*[91]

17th. *A merchant found means to slip out of the Garrison to us, & took a Memorandum of the necessaries we wanted to the amount of four hundred pounds; & we were told that there were great disputes between Colonel MacLean*[92], *who commanded [those] whom they called their regular Troops, & the Inhabitants.*

18th. *We learn'd that Colonel MacLean had taken all the marines & sailors out of the ships in the harbour; that he had prevail'd on the rabble of the Town to take up arms, which made them in all seven hundred strong; & that he was to sally out on us with Field Pieces on next day. Therefore as we were not more than seven hundred strong from our losses, & sickness, & as most of our ammunition was gone. The Riflemen having but two rounds each, & the Musketmen only two besides all the arms being bad condition, we march'd to Point aux Trembles*[93], *& took up our quarters. General Carleton left the Town, & went on board of a schooner which sail'd down to Quebec with two others a few hours before we arriv'd.*

20th. *By an express from Montreal, we heard that General Carleton had been forc'd to make his escape in a small birch canoe with two men.*

21st. *Major Bigelow presented two Gentlemen to Captain Morgan, who followed us from Quebec to beg protection, & that their property might be secure when the City fell into our hands. They were detained however as spies; it having an odd appearance that they should ask protection from an army that was running away. Neither of them understood a word of English; one of them was a German.*

CHAPTER FOUR

CAPTAIN HENRY DEARBORN'S ORIGINAL JOURNAL

MAJ. GEN HENRY DEARBORN.

DESCRIPTION.

The "Captain Durben" journal was discovered in 2010, while this author was writing *Voices,* in an online Americana exhibit by the Special Collections section of the University of Glasgow Library. The exhibit contained photos and information on books and manuscripts relating to America from the Library's collection. On page 4 was a photo of the first page of the journal with a description noting that the manuscript was a journal about Arnold's expedition to Quebec written by a Captain Durben. The description clearly indicated that this manuscript journal was about the Arnold expedition and had been in the Glasgow University Library since 1783. It was astonishing that this journal dated back to 1783 and was previously and completely unknown.

The Durben manuscript journal was among a number of different manuscripts from the personal library of William Hunter that was bequeathed to the University of Glasgow upon Hunter's death in 1783. The Library has referenced it as MS Hunter 608, entitled "Manuscripts from the Library of William Hunter." In order to make a determination as to the authenticity of the manuscript and the identity of Captain Durben, a copy was obtained from the University of Glasgow Library which was the hand written text transcribed by Dr. Robertson. It was turned it into typescript by this author.

After transcribing Robertson's text, an analysis of the contents of the journal convinced me that its author was Captain Henry Dearborn and that it was, in fact, his original journal.[94] In 1776 it was given to a Dr. Robert Robertson in Quebec by an unknown party and brought by him back to Scotland where he transcribed it from the original. Dr. Robertson was in Quebec in 1776 as the surgeon on H.M.S *Juno*, and he did return to Scotland sometime after 1777. He completed his transcription of the original sometime after that and then gave his transcription to William Hunter.

Robertson included the following note about his transcription with the journal.

An exact copy of A Journal of the Route, and Proceedings of 1100 Rebels, who marched from Cambridge, in Massachusetts Bay, under the Command of Colonel Arnold, in the fall of the year 1775; to attack Quebec: But providentially failed in their Rebellious Attempt to subdue it, Although there were not 100 Regular Troops in the Garrison, So bravely was it defended by the Seaman, the Militia & those few Regulars. I mean particularly that Body of the Militia called the British.

The Sense and Meaning of the Original--which was kept by a Captain Durben.-- are strictly adhered to in this copy; but the Orthography, Syntax,

& diction of it were so extremely deficient, and even barbarous, if I may be allowed the Exception, that it would have been highly ridiculous to have transcribed it verbatim.

Yet notwithstanding all the Pains I have taken to render it clear and intelligible, some Pages are still obscure, and perhaps indistinct. But I know of no method by which I could amend them, unless by Fiction; and that I would not adopt. However, in Order to elucidate those in some measure I have subjoined a few notes, that I flatter myself will not, at least, be entirely useless.

As to the proper Names, or even the Names of Places, should I unfortunately have mis-spelled them at times, I am hopeful the Error is venial.

The manuscript journal contains the following note in William Hunter's handwriting.

This was given to me by Mr. Robertson Surgeon of his Majesty's Ship Juno-- who procured a genuine copy of the Journal at Quebec. He assured me that I might depend on its being faithfully transcribed; and I know that I can depend on any thing he asserts.

William Hunter

(It is important to note that this journal is different from the Dearborn journal published in the Massachusetts Historical Society in 1885 and subsequently included in Kenneth Robert's compilation).

PUBLICATION

The only previous publication of the original Dearborn journal was in *Voices*, Chapter Two, pp. 95-127.

AUTHOR

Captain Henry Dearborn commanded a company of musket men on the expedition and was in the Battle of Saratoga in 1777, the Battle of Monmouth in June of 1778, Sullivan's expedition against the Iroquois Indians in the summer of 1779 and was Deputy Quartermaster in 1781 in the Battle of Yorktown. He rose to be a Major General in the Maine State Militia in 1783 and then served as Congressman from Maine from 1795-1797. He was appointed as Secretary of War under President Thomas Jefferson, where he served until 1808, and was appointed Senior

Major General of the Army during the War of 1812 by President James Madison. Madison subsequently nominated him as Secretary of War but his nomination was rejected by the Senate. Dearborn died on June 6, 1829 in Roxbury, Massachusetts. He became the highest ranking officer from the expedition and is one of the best known Arnold expedition alumni due to the various positions he held subsequent to the expedition. See bio of Dearborn in *Voices* on pages 16 and 17.

JOURNAL

On the 13th of September 1775, we marched from Cambridge to Mystick; on the 14th to Salem; on the 15th to Ipswich; and on the 16th to Newborough Port[95].

The 17th being Sabath we attended meeting.

On the 18th we embarked on board of ten vessels, and waited for a wind.

The 19th we sailed for the mouth of the Kennebek River[96].

Before noon of the 20th we got into that River.

21st. We sailed up as high as Gardiner's Town[97] and met with good entertainment at Doctor Gardiner of Boston's seat.

22nd. We got up to where the Bateaux[98] were built[99]; from thence we carried thirty three men of each Company in the Bateaux up to Fort Western[100]; That is about forty miles up from the mouth of the River; and at night all our men had mostly got up to the Fort.

23d. One of the men shot another.[101]

24th. The criminal was taken up.

On the 25th he was tried by a Court Martial, was found guilty & received Sentence of death.

26th The convict was carried to the place of Execution, and there reprieved by Colonel Arnold, [until] General Washington's pleasure could not be known.

27th. At three after noon we embarked on board the Bateaux with forty five days provisions; got four miles up the river; and encamped ashore.

28th. We encamped after getting two miles up.

The 29th before noon we got up four miles- to Fort Halifax[102]; and after staying there about half an hour we crossed the River to the Portage, ninety seven roods in length. When we had haled [hauled] our Bateaux, and carried everything else over the Portage, we encamped on the River's side.

On the 30th we went six miles up the River; it was extremely rapid with many little falls in it.

31st. We got up three miles; there Major Meigs[103] had got a Bullock killed for us; of which we eat heartily; and carried whatever [was] left along with us, three miles further up, & there encamped.

October 1st We reached ten miles up the River- the land that we passed was in general good, with a number of Inhabitants upon it.

2d. Before noon we got up to Sowegan Falls[104], there we hauled out Bateaux up, calked [caulked] them, [and] carried them over the Portage, that was forty roods long; then we reloaded the Bateaux, crossed the River, encamped on the other side of it. Our course so far up the River was generally from N. to NE.

3d. We got twelve miles up the River to Norrywok.[105] There was few

Inhabitants on the shore we passed by. Our first Division of Musket Men had marched from thence the preceeding day only. There, too, we found our three Companies of Riflemen; the former left Fort Western two days and the latter on a Day before us. At Norrywok are the Ruins of an Indian Fort; an appearance of some old Intrenchments; a Friars Grave with a cross at one end of it; and a good deal of cleared ground.[106]

4th. We haled [hauled] up our Bateaux at the Portage, and dried them. On the 5th we calked [caulked] them & paid [paint] them; & repaked [repacked] our Pork and Bread.

6th. We haled [hauled] & carried everything over the Portage, that was a mile across, launched & loaded the Bateaux, then we went two miles up the River, and encamped ashore.

The 7th we proceeded eight miles up the River, and then encamped.

On the 8th we reached up to Caratunkas[107]. *The River runs down there between two very high rocks, that are not above forty feet or under. After getting everything across the Portage, of eighty seven rods, we went up the River four miles, and encamped.*

9th .We advanced nine miles up the River; then we put ashore and encamped.

The 10th we proceeded six miles up and arrived at one afternoon at the great Portage[108] *whereupon there is water. The course of the River upwards from that was about NW between two mountains.*

11th .We began to carry our things across to the first pond that was about four miles distant from the River.

12th .A party of my men were set about building of a Block House[109]; *the rest of them assisted to carry everything to the Pond, to which we encamped at night.*

13th . It blowed so hard that we could not cross the Pond. There was plenty of fine trout in it.

The 14th we crossed the pond. It was about three quarters of a mile over. Then we carried our things about half a mile to a second Pond, & crossed it about a mile and a half over. Afterwards we carried our things about a mile & a half and encamped.

On the 15th we carried our things a mile & a quarter further before we reached a third Pond that was a very fine two miles wide. After crossing it we carried our things nine miles, and encamped.

16th .We had our things to drag & carry three miles further over a Spruce Heath that was knee deep of mire; after that we launched our Bateaux in the Dead River[110]; got up about half a mile and then put ashore, and encamped. The Dead River is only a continuation of the Kennebek and there makes the large flexure that employed us six days in crossing. In that great winding the River is almost on continued fall, and nowhere passable the Indians said. Where we encamped it was very deep & still; and most probably that occasioned its being called the Dead River. The land on the other side of it was, apparently, fine.

17th We reached ten miles up the River. The land seemed to be very good & pleasant. Then we crossed a Portage about eight rods over, and encamped by the River.

On the 18th we got fifteen miles up. There was found our first Division of Musket Men employed in making cartridges. My company filled some powder; and Joseph Thomas was appointed my Ensign. Each company had half a quarter of fresh Beef given to them.

19th. Our Division put off in their Bateaux and went about five miles up the River. There were three little falls in it; and in every other place the current was gentle. It rained all day.

[20th]. We got thirteen miles as we supposed. Up the River there were several little falls in it & we had one short Portage of about thirteen roods to cross. At night we encamped. It rained all day.

21st .We proceeded up the River about three miles, when we came to a Portage thirty five rods long, and carried our things across it. After getting up the River about two miles, we came to another Portage of thirty rods that we crossed, and then encamped. It rained hard all day.[111]

22nd .The River rose about eight feet in the night, overflowed its banks, hurt our Baggage considerably; and retarded us much. We only got three miles up and crossed a Portage of seventy four rods in length.

23d. We proceeded about nine miles up the River. Most of our advanced Foot, through a mistake, went up a River that runs into the Dead River. As we supposed that they had made the mistake, my Bateau was sent up the River after them; but before it had reached them, about four miles, they had found out their error, and were carrying their things over the land into the Dead River. When the Bateaux returned, we went on up the River until we joined those Foot at a Portage where we all encamped, and held a Council of War.[112]

The 24th. In consequence of the Council, I was ordered to proceed forward with fifty men up the River, to the Chaudière: and the sick were sent back under the care of an Officer and a Surgeon. At night I and my men put ashore and encamped.

25th. We got six miles up only but we have three Portages in the way to cross; two of them were about four rods each in length, and the other was ninety. It was squally with snow.

26th. We crossed a Pond two miles wide, and soon after a Gutter about four rods. Then we came to and passed over a second Pond about a mile in width; and went over a Portage of about a mile & a half in length. After that we had a third Pond about three miles wide to cross, & we got over a small Portage. We had a fourth Pond to cross 3 mile wide, before we got into a narrow River that we went up about four miles when we came to a small Portage of fifteen rods long, & crossed it. We came then to another pond half a mile in width; and after crossing over that we encamped very much fatigued.

27th. We crossed over the Portage of one mile; we crossed a Pond about fifty rods in width. We got over another Portage of about forty four roods long. Then we came to a Pond two miles wide and crossed it. We were now on the Portage of the Chaudière[113]*, where we left our Bateaux and went on, each man carrying his own share of the Provision. When we had walked about a mile we encamped. I found a Bark canoe left there by the Indians I imagined, which I took to be carried in, as I had been taken ill the preceeding night.*

28th. We got over the Portage; in all it was about four miles & a quarter long; and reached the Pond of Chaudière.[114] *On the east side of the Pond a River runs into it that my People could not ford; they therefore waded the Pond to an Island that before they thought had been the Continent. I joined them in my canoe, and took into it Capt. Goodrich*[115] *who had near perished on that Island after wading breast high to it, and breaking the ice before him as he waded. Before he did that he attempted in vain to wade the River already mentioned. When we had gone up along the Island a little way in the canoe, we came to a good Indian House with a fire in it.*[116] *One of our advanced Party was there, who had been obliged to stay behind for want of Provisions to carry him on. I sent my canoe to find out Captain Goodrich's Bateau that was gone, he knew not where, with a Sergeant & a man that were sick, but it being dark night the Bateau could not be found. The Island was low & swampy. We were both very uneasy about our men.*

On the 29th early in the morning we returned to our men & found them in better spirits than we expected. We had begun to carry them over in my canoe when Captain Smith's[117] Bateau arrived; the rest of them were carried over in that. After we had walked about sixty rods, we unexpectedly came to another River that we got over with great difficulty. Then we went as far as the Indian House that I had lodged at the night before, and encamped. Although my men were extremely fatigued they had got in all about thirteen miles. I was yet very ill.

The 30th my men marched early in the morning. I went down the Pond in my canoe, and met them at the lower end of it. When we found out the mouth of the Chaudière that looked less wild than it really proved to be. We got down that River about eighteen miles, but in going down many of the Bateaux run aground; some of them overset; and others filled. None except Colonel Arnold's Bateau, and my own canoe, lived. One man was drowned and many of our things was lost.

31st. My Party marched down along the River about twenty miles; and I went down the River in my canoe. The River was shallow, rocky, and very rapid; and besides I had two short Portages to cross over. At night we encamped.

November 1st. My men marched down about thirty miles; and I went down the River in my canoe; as the bottom of it was all worn and cut through from the rapidity and rockiness of the River, I resolved on using it no more. At night we encamped.

2nd. As we were journeying down we met five oxen, and two horses that Colonel Arnold had sent to meet us by some Canadians. The cattle were a very agreeable sight to us; for we had very near been starved through want of Provisions for some time.[118] After advancing about four miles further we came to a Portage of a mile long-- when I found a good canoe. The River has a great fall there. At the foot of the fall there were two Indians in a canoe with Provisions for us. I went with them down the River, and my own canoe followed us. About six miles below the fall we reached the first houses of the Inhabitants at three [in the] afternoon. It was very difficult to get down the River. At four o'clock Lieutenant Hutching[119], and Ensign Thomas with my men arrived where I was. Provisions had been got ready for us there by the Colonel- and we stayed all night.

3rd. My men went on & I hired an Indian to carry me down the River in his canoe about four miles where Colonel Arnold was. A number of Indians *gathered about us to be hired, and we engaged with twenty two of them for forty eight shillings a month. I stayed there all night by the Colonel's advice, as I was still very bad. The People were kind to me.*

4ᵗʰ. It rained hard all night, and snowed all day. I did not move.

5ᵗʰ. It was clear and moderate weather. I hired a horse & rode four miles, and put up at a tavern. Two of our Men were sent back with Horses to meet me. One of these men was Canadian born in Quebec, who spoke good French & tolerable English; he enlisted with us at Fort Western on the Kennebek River.

I hired an Indian on the 6ᵗʰ to carry me down the River eight miles in his canoe to one Pere St. Joses where I took lodgings as I yet continued ill. But my men marched on with the rest to Point Levi.

On the 7ᵗʰ, they arrived at St. Mary's[120]; and on the 8ᵗʰ they got to Point Levi[121].

9ᵗʰ. Nothing happened. The Canadians were very kind to our people.

On the 10ᵗʰ they took a Midshipman Prisoner; he belonged to the Hunter Sloop of War & was a brother of the Captain- his name's Mackenzie.[122]

11ᵗʰ & 12ᵗʰ. Nothing particular happened.

13ᵗʰ. At nine o'clock of the preceeding night our men began to embark on board of thirty-five canoes; and at four of the morning they landed safely on the other side of the River St. Laurence-- at the place where General Wolfe landed his army in the year 1759, now called Wolfe's Cove. From thence they Marched across the Heights of Abraham[123], & took possession of some Houses for their Quarters. The Colonel took up his quarters in Major Caldwell's[124] house.

14ᵗʰ. At noon the enemy surprised and took prisoner one of our sentinels. The Colonel drew up the men; marched them close to the Garrison; and gave the enemy three Hazzas; Then he marched our People in a circular form, full in their view, whilst they fired a number of cannon shot at them from the Garrison-- without hurting one of them, after that he carried them back to their Quarters. A number of the Houses in the suburbs were burnt by the enemy. The Inhabitants with what effects they could preserve were forced to go into the Country for shelter.

Captain Ogden[125] was sent with a flag of truce to demand the Town and Citadel in the name and behalf of the United Colonies; but they fired upon him and would not suffer him to approach the Citadel. In the evening our Men were informed by a Gentleman from Quebec that they might expect an attack that night, or the next day, from the Garrison. It was reported too that about two hundred Canadians belonging to the suburbs declared if the troops that were in the Garrison continued to burn their Houses, that they would apply to Colonel Arnold either for assistance or directions what to do. Our men were ordered to ly]lie] under arms to prevent their being surprised. The weather was fine for the season.

15th. An express was sent to General Montgomery[126]. Captain Ogden was again sent with a flag of truce to demand the Town & Garrison to be delivered up; but he only met with the same reception that he did the day before. At noon our Men were alarmed with a report that the enemy were coming to attack them; and they turned out to receive them; but the report proved to be false. The Canadians came in daily to pay their respects to Colonel Arnold, and to beg his protection.

16th. The Colonel received an address from the Inhabitants of Point au Tremble[127], and he had certain advice that Montreal had surrendered to General Montgomery; who it was said had likewise taken twelve vessels with a large quantity of provisions, clothing, and a number of Prisoners. A company of our men sent to take possession of the nunnery.

17th. The Canadians were continually coming in to express their satisfaction to the Colonel for having come into Canada. After-noon a deserter from the Garrison surrendered himself a Prisoner to one of our advanced sentinels; but he gave us no particular intelligence. A party of men were sent by the Colonel to Point Levi to bring over some of our people and provisions that had arrived there.

On the 18th nothing material happened. The weather was fine for the season.

19th. Our men left their Quarters; and were marched to Point au Tremble, about seven or eight leagues from Quebec. The part of the Country that they had passed through was well peopled, and cultivated; and most of the Inhabitants were very kind to them. The weather continued good.

20th. Before noon our express arrived from General Montgomery, mentioning that General Carleton had abandoned Montreal; that our People were in possession of it; that they intended to attack the ships lying there with boats, and Row Galleys[128] that carried guns; and that as soon as they were taken he would proceed to join our party with men, artillery etc.

21st. Our People took a soldier of Colonel Maclean's[129] Regiment in Quebec, whom they thought was a spy, a prisoner.

The 22d, an express arrived from Montreal telling the Colonel that the enemy's ships were taken on the preceeding Sabbath; and that General Montgomery was obliged to march to Quebec.

On the 23d, they were informed by another express that the General was on his way to join them; and that clothing was coming down for our Detachment.

24th. Four sail of vessels were seen coming up the River before-noon. Colonel Arnold sent an express to acquaint our Troops that were coming down from Montreal by water there-with.

25th. The Hunter Sloop, a large scow commanded by Capt. Napier; and an armed schooner came up the River, and anchored opposite to our quarters.[130] *A canowe [canoe] was sent up the River to apprise the Troops, coming down in vessels thereof; and an express was sent up by land to inform those of it who were coming that way.*

26th. Nothing singular occurr'd.

27th. The Colonel was inform'd that the Kings Troops had burned Major Caldwell's House, where he held his quarters whilst he was before Quebec. It was very cold.

28th. The Colonel went up to Jacquartiere[131] *to meet the ammunition that was on the way from Montreal.*

The 29th Captain Morgan,[132] *who had been sent down with a Party near Quebec, sent up two prisoners whom he had taken.*

30th. Capt. Duggin[133] *arrived with fifteen barrels of powder, and other stores from Montreal. The King's ships fell down the River.*

Decemr 1st. The General arrived at one afternoon with three armed schooners having troops, artillery, ammunition, provisions & clothing on board. The stores & clothing were given in charge to General Greg (?)for our Detachment. The Detachment was marched to General Montgomery's quarters; he expressed great satisfaction in receiving them & said that they were fine stout and likely fellows.

2d. The small field pieces were ordered to be carried down near to Quebec on sleds & the large cannon on Bateaux. As soon as the cannon were landed, the Bateaux were ordered to go to Point Levi to bring over scaling ladders that were made there.

3d. Our men drew their clothing; each man had a full suit allowed him as a present from the Continental Congress for the extraordinary fatigue they had underwent. The weather was rather cold.

On the 4th, they were ordered to march to St. Foy,[134] a village near six miles distance from Quebec, to canton. They marched accordingly to St Augustine and were elegantly entertained there by the Curate of the parish, who at the same time possessed great regard for them, as well as for the glorious cause wherein they were engaged.

5th. At noon they arrived at St Foy[135]. My company was ordered into the nunnery. It was called the General Hospital[136] too, and was about a mile from the Palace Gate of Quebec.[137]

6th. It was squally & cold.

7th. I had been very ill and was extremely reduced at Pere St. Joses[138] from the 6th of November, & could not join my company until this day. A party of our men took a Sloop with a great quantity of provisions, and Three Hundred Eighty two Dollars of specie on board.

8th. The enemy's Sentinels fired from the Ramparts upon ours. It was fine weather.

9th. We began at night to bombard the Citadel[139]- twenty seven shells were thrown into it; and we began to raise a Battery about half a mile from St Johns Gate[140].

10th. The enemy continued a brisk fire all day on our quarters. A party of our Train of Artillery were sent into St Rocks[141]-- almost under the walls of the Garrison, with five mortars, and two field pieces, covered by eighty men.

11th. Forty two shells were thrown into the City in the night. The enemy returns a few, and some short that did no other damage than killing an old Canadian woman; & they burnt a number of houses in St Johns.[142] A party of our men were employed all night on the Battery. One of our men lost his way in a snow storm, and found himself under the walls of the Citadel, where he was fired at often, and received only one wound in his thigh, with which he got off; & it was not mortal. The weather was sharp squalls with snow & sleet.

12th. We threw forty five shells again in the night. Our Battery was near finished, & the platforms were preparing for it. The enemy endeavored, though unsuccessfully, to annoy our People at work with shot and shells.

13th. Two of our men were apparently wounded in their legs by the enemies shot; the bones were so shattered that it was feared it would be necessary to amputate them.

14th. Five of our Canadians were wounded by another shot that penetrated through our Battery.

15th. We threw twenty four shells; and the enemy kept up a brisk cannonading that did us very little hurt. Our Battery was informed it was to mount six guns, five & twelve pounders, and a twelve inch mortar-. After being briskly served for two hours, they ceased firing by the General's order. A flag of truce was sent [to] General Carleton, but he would not admit it within the Garrison. The gentleman who carried it had some conversation with the King's troops on the ramparts. Afternoon our Battery began again to play on the town. The enemy kept up a brisk fire, though they did not serve their pieces as well as ours were served, as they themselves acknowledged. My company was ordered across Charles's River to the Beau Port side, because the nunnery was now wanted to make an hospital for the sick.[143] I was quartered at one McHenry's, a Presbetarian pastor of Quebec. Two men were killed at our Battery; one gun destroyed & a small mortar dismounted by the enemy's shot. It was now in agitation to storm the lower town.

16th. The enemy cannonaded Colonel Arnold's quarters[144]; he therefore quitted, & took others. We had a man killed by the enemy's grape shot. In the afternoon a Council of War was summoned to confer about storming the town. The majority of the Council was for storming it as soon as they could prepare properly for it, with [illegible] hawl's, spears, etc.

17th. There was a severe snow storm.

18th. We heard Colonel Conlon was coming from Montreal to join our army.

19th. It snowed.

20th. Was very cold. The men drew what muskets they wanted; & were employed in making spears, etc. The smallpox began to break out amongst the men.

21st. We had orders to cause our men to distinguish themselves by wearing a sprig of hemlock in their caps.

22d. The spears & ladders were ready, and everything repined a pace for the important purpose of storming the Town. "The blessings of Heaven attend the enterprise".

The 23d. The officers of our Brigade met [this] afternoon about the subject of the storm. The General frequently visited the men, and said many encouraging things to them, relating to the storm.

24th. The Reverend Mr. Spring,[145] *our Chaplain, preached a sermon in the chapel of the nunnery; it was an elegant little chapel, richly adorned, and had a complete rigged small ship hanging upon it.*

25th. Our Brigade was ordered to meet, and parade at Captain Morgan's quarters. The General attended there, & made a very sensible & spirited speech to them upon the subject of the approaching storm.

26th. A return was made of the men in Colonel Arnold's Detachment who were willing to storm the town; there were only three in my company consisting of sixty three, who dissented from it.

27th. Afternoon all the troops assembled at the place of rendezvous in very high spirits, and were ready to march to the attack, when an order came from the General to send them back to their quarters- because he thought the night too clear and calm for the attack-- though the day had been windy with snow.

28th. The General ordered it to be published "that he had the most sensible pleasure in seeing the laudable disposition with which the troops had moved the preceeding night for the attack. That it was with almost reluctancy he was obliged to suppress their ardour, on account of the clearness of the night; but he must have deem'd himself as in great measure culpable for having been the cause of losing many of those brave men had he led them on to the attack-- whose lives he doubted not would be preserved by only waiting for a more favorable opportunity". He desired that all orders might be made known to the Troops at the calling of the roll; and he hoped that no soldier who was zealous for the success of that Enterprise would absent himself from his quarters at night, as he might perhaps be wanted at a minutes warning.

29th. I had the main guard at St Rocks. A Subaltern & fifteen men went in the afternoon by command of Colonel Arnold to a large distillery near Palace Gate, & brought away the overseer [as] a prisoner, & carried him to Head Quarters. One man was shot through the leg from the Garrison walls. The enemy knocked down one of our guard house chimneys with their shot. We threw thirty shells into the Citadel in fifteen minutes; the enemy returned only a few but they kept up a very heaving cannonading on us.

30th was very windy with snow. When I was ordered off the guard I had orders to be upon the parade at four o'clock the next morning, and all the men were ordered to be there under arms at two o'clock.

31st. The Sergeant Major having neglected to call me in proper time; and [St.] Charles's River[146] *being very difficult to pass across from the highness of* the tide, & badness of the weather; the attack was begun before I could leave my quarters. I was therefore obliged to fall in, in the rear, with my company when I got over the River, instead of being the second company in the front, the post that was assigned me in the attack.

The ATTACK[147] was regulated in the following manner. The General at the head of three Battalions of the New York troops was to march around by Cape Diamond, and to force his way into the Lower Town, by the Pres de Ville[148].

Colonel Arnold was to go round through St. Rocks; to pass Palace Gate[149], and to force his way with his own Brigade through the different barriers into the Lower Town, by the Sault du Matelot[150]. In that manner, the General and the Colonel were to push on through the Lower Town with their different corps until they met.

Colonel Livingston[151] in the meantime with a Detachment chiefly consisting of Canadians, was to make a feint about St. John's Gate; and unless they could burst it open, they were to set fire to it, and burn it with combustibles that were prepared for that purpose.

All of them were to march from their respective places of rendezvous exactly at five in the morning. Accordingly the General advanced at the head of his men to the picquets [pickets]; some of them were cut by the artificers in a moment, and pulled down, the General himself assisting. He then immediately entered through the opening with his Aide de Camp, Captain Cheeseman[152], the Engineer and a few of his men, calling out repeatedly, but in vain, to the rest of his Troops to follow him. Whilst he was advancing with that small party, the enemy fired a volley of grape shot, & small arms that unhappily cut him off together with his Aide de Camp, Captain Cheeseman, the Engineer and some others.

The light in the guard room was by some means knocked out at this time, and there was nothing then to have prevented the Generals Troops from entering, as we afterwards heard that the enemies guard quit their post & ran off. However Colonel Campbell[153] instead of entering with the Troops, ordered a retreat, and carried off our wounded men to their quarters.

Colonel Arnold on the other side sent a Lieutenant & thirty men to march in front as his advance guard. He ordered the Company of Artillery, with a Brass six pounder on a sled, to march out; and the main body to follow them. The advanced party had directions to open to the right & left, as soon as they *came up to a two gun Battery on a wharf where the enemy had a guard, whilst the Artillery fired a few shot at the Battery; and then to rush on with scaling ladders to mount and force the Battery. At the same time it was directed, that Captain Morgan should march round the wharf upon the ice, if it was possible, with a part of the main body, and thereby surround the enemy.*

But the snow being deep; and the road, naturally, extremely bad, the Artillery could only advance very slowly. So slowly did they advance indeed, that they were obliged to leave the gun behind, at last, on the way. To increase the delay, the main body from the darkness of the morning; from a very heavy snow storm beating in their faces; and from the intricacy of the way were led wrong, besides they were harassed with a continual fire from the walls of the Garrison that killed, and wounded many of them.

As it proved impossible for the Artillery to get the gun along, the advanced party were ordered to attack the Battery. Some of them fired in through the port holes, while others with ladders scaled the Barricade[154], and took all the enemies guard prisoners consisting of thirty men. The attack was made with so much activity that the enemy had barely time to fire two guns before they were made prisoners. Not more than two or three men were lost on either side.

When the prisoners were secured, our men immediately advanced to the second Barrier and attempted to force their way through it. But the main body, not having got up in time for the reasons already mentioned, and the General's Troops unfortunately having retreated, the enemy was allowed to turn their sole attention to the Sault au Matelot. [155] So that they who attacked the second Barrier were in a moment surrounded, almost, with a fire from treble their number of the enemy posted behind the Barrier, and in the adjoining houses; and were failed in their attempts.

Unfortunately, I was far behind in the rear with my men, as I before observed; and still more unfortunately for me as I was marching past Palace Gate to join our main body we lost our way from the same cause, that they had lost theirs: and at the same time that a brisk fire was kept up upon us from the ramparts, about two hundred of the enemy sallied out of the Garrison; part of whom took post in the adjacent houses, and galled us with their fire, whilst the rest surrounded us. To add to our misery, our muskets were so wet with snow that not one of them would fire. [Based on] these distressfully circumstances we surrendered ourselves prisoners, upon being promised good quarters. We were immediately disarmed, & marched into the Garrison. When we entered Palace Gate we heard that our men had got possession of the Lower Town;[156]

[Note: Typical of this journal the first word on the next page is shown at the bottom of the current page. On this page, the next word is "That". Unfortunately, there is no next page beginning with "That". It appears that a page is missing from the journal.]

[Now the journal continues]

me and liberty too very heartily, he began to fire very briskly upon us. "I felt vexed at his reply, and tried often very hard to give him his due, but could not get my piece to go off".

January 1ˢᵗ 1776. General Montgomery's body was taken up & brought into the Garrison; he was of good stature, rather slender, yet well limbed; of a graceful, though a manly port; with an easy and polite address. He was both esteemed and loved by the whole army-- who placed in him their entire confidence. His death though honourable, was greatly lamented-- for in him we lost not only an amiable and worthy friend; but a brave and experienced General. Our country suffer'd greatly by that stroke. All our officers, who were not wounded, were put into a large building called the Seminary[157]*, wherein we had good accommodations; and plenty of beds and blankets were sent us by the towns people. Those who were wounded were sent to the Hospital.*

2d. The Governour gave Major Meigs[158] *liberty to go out of the Garrison to our quarters for his own and our baggage. Sixteen of us who had had the small pox agreed to be inoculated. Mr. Bullen, Surgeon of Lizard, was recommended to us as a very skillful physician, and one who was very well acquainted with inoculation. We began to take preparatory medicines from him.*

On the 3d we were inoculated. The Governor made us a present of a hogshead of porter.

The 4ᵗʰ, General Montgomery's body was very decently interr'd. We were allowed to send for four of our men to attend us.

5ᵗʰ. We who had been inoculated were, for the benefit of air, moved into another room. Cooking utensils and fresh meat for soup were sent into us from the Inhabitants. Major Meigs returned with our baggage.

6ᵗʰ. We were visited every day by a Field Officer.

7ᵗʰ. Nothing occurr'd.

8ᵗʰ. The Bishop sent us two hogsheads of port wine, six loaves of sugar, and several pounds of tea in a present, for which we sent him a letter of thanks-- at the same time begged leave to return him the tea, as the majority thought that it would have been imprudent for us to have drank it.

9th. There was a heavy snow, with the wind, from the NE.

10th. We began to prepare a petition to send to the Governor to exchange prisoners; we had no opportunity of writing or sending to our friends. The storm continued.

11th & 12th. The small pox began to appear on us;[159] They who had them in the natural way amongst our people, were extremely ill.

13th. My fever abated much. Nothing material happen'd. 14th.

Mr. Levius[160] formerly a judge of our court in New Hampshire, came to see me, and made me a very kind offer of his service. I rejoiced to find that, contrary to my expectation, I had a friend in the Garrison. Captain Hubbard[161] died of his wound.

15th & 16th. Nothing remarkable occurr'd.

17th. We sent our petition to the Governor by Major Cox the Field Officer of the Day.

18th, 19th, 20th, 21st, 22d and 23d, nothing singular happened.

24th. We were all recovered of our inoculation; I wrote to Mr. Levius for some shirts.

25th. One of our men died of the small pox-- he had them the natural way. I rec'd two shirts and some money from Mr. Levius.

26th. Our people without the Garrison, for some by past nights had burnt houses, woods & vessels at St. Rocks. One of the vessels was loaded with fish belonging to the Town.

27th. A party was sent out of the Garrison to St. Rocks for wood, that was soon obliged to return by reason of our men lying in ambush and firing upon it.

28th. Colonel Hamilton[162] sent us a fine quarter of venison in a present. The 29th was extremely cold.

30th was more moderate. Two of our officers had very bad inflammations in their arms; and another of them was taken ill.

31st. Our people continued to burn St Rocks.

Feb 1st, 2d, 3d, 4th & 5th. Nothing remarkable occurred. The weather was variable. 6th. We were ordered by the Governor to deliver up all of our pens and ink to the Officer of the Guard. 16th. For want of pen and ink I could not keep my journal the nine preceeding days. However nothing material happened unless what follows. I already took notice that we who had been inoculated were indulged with another room for the benefit of air, and the rest of our officers were likewise permitted to visit us; but after the 6th we were not allowed to see them.

On the 14th at nine o'clock at night Colonel MacLean, Major Caldwell, and the other officers of the Guard came into our room and made us remove immediately into the room amongst the rest of our officers. Colonel MacLean said he had particular reasons for removing us so suddenly that we should be acquainted with the next day.

Accordingly on the morning of the 15th he came and told us that one of us had been conversing with one of the Sentinels. Upon an enquiry amongst ourselves we found that Lieutenant Hutchins, one day as he went to the Necessary House, overheard one of the Sentinels say that there were five hundred Yankees at Point Levi; and that he replied, very imprudently, there would be five thousand of them soon.

On the 16th being very unwell I was carried to the Hospital. All our wounded officers were in one room. I heard that our men were falling down with small pox daily in the Prison.[163]

17th. The weather was clear and warm for the season. There was thirty Nuns in the Hospital that attended the sick very carefully; and we were visited daily by Mr. Mabane Surgeon of the Garrison, and his assistants.

18th. I had part of a tooth pulled out that was broke by a pick axe on Winter Hill.

19th. I saw one of my men, he was the first that I had seen of them-- from the time I was taken prisoner. He told me that the rest of my men had had the small pox in the prison and recovered; the poor fellow was without a shirt, which shocked me; I therefore gave him one of the few I had.

20th & 21st. We heard that our People were erecting a Battery at Point Levi. We were accused of talking to the Sentinel. A lamp was ordered to be kept therefore constantly in our room; a pane of glass was fixed in our door, and that was locked, and two Sentinels were placed on the outside of it. The weather was variable.

22d. The Garrison fired a number of guns to annex our men at Point Levi, it was said.

23d, 24th and 25th. Nothing happened. My men wrote to me to beg a little money of me. I sent them ten dollars.

26th. We had leave again to walk in the passage. We esteemed it an indulgence. The officer of the Guard inform'd us that Montreal was retaken by the Canadians; and a Priest told us that the Congress had sent notice to the Commander of our Troops before Quebec, that they could send no more Troops to Canada; and therefore, unless he got possession of the Garrison before the 15th of March, that they had ordered him to retreat to Montreal. The Field Officer of the Day also told us that General Amherst was arrived with 10,000 Troops at New York, and that there was as many more at Halifax[164] waiting only for the Rivers breaking up, to come to Quebec. We likewise heard that Sir John Johnson[165] was at the head of a large body of Scots and savages, against whom General Schuyler[166] had march'd with what Troops were destined for Quebec; but that more Troops were coming to Quebec.

27th & 28th. Nothing material happened.

29th. The Field Officer of the Day inform'd us that two hundred & fifty sleds had been sent from Montreal across the lakes to bring over some of our Troops; and that there were none to bring, but one hundred that they got at Ticonderoga.

March 1st. We were no longer permitted to walk in the passage. A strong partition was made in it with a door, and a pane of glass in that; and the Sentinels were placed without this door to prevent our talking to them: Two Sentinels were likewise placed under our windows, to prevent our getting out at them, & making our escape, we imagined, though we were in the fourth story.

2d, 3d and 4th. Nothing happen'd.

5th. A Canadian came into the Garrison we heard, who said he had been taken prisoner at St Johns and set at liberty after having been carried into New York. He afterwards told us that our Troops at Cambridge had made an attempt to storm Boston, but were repulsed with the loss of 4,000 men who were partly killed & partly drowned by falling through the ice. It was said that General Lee[167] had march'd towards New York with 3,000 men, but that before he reached it he had lost all of them by desertion for want of clothing, except about 300. The Field Officer of the Day informed us that General Carleton had a copy of a letter from General Washington's to Colonel Arnold, where in he told him that he could send him no more men to his assistance, because he could scarcely keep any of his men from deserting at Cambridge for want of clothing. We also heard that 200 men had marched near to Montreal, on their way to Quebec, but that by differing amongst themselves they had killed ten or twelve of each other, and had returned home again.

6th, 7th, 8th, & 9th. We heard of nothing material.

10th. We learned from the Field Officer of the Day that all our People were about to decamp, and to march to Montreal.

11th & 12th. Nothing remarkable came to our knowledge.

13th, 14th, 15th, 16th, 17th, 18th, 19th, 20th, 21st and 22d. We had nothing singular happen'd.

23d, 24th, 25th & 26th. The weather was very cold.

27th. A house wherein our People kept a guard on the Beau Port side was burnt by a shell thrown from the Garrison. Mr. Mabane inform'd Major Meigs, that our officers would soon be removed from the Hospital to the Seminary.

28th, 29th and 30th. Nothing occurred.

31st. We were all removed to the Seminary. There wood being scarce.

April 1. We were inform'd by Major Caldwell, the Field Officer of the Day, that our men had been detected in executing a plan for escaping out of prison, and were therefore all put in irons. I was sorry to hear of their situation.

2d. Our People opened a Battery at Point Levi of four guns. Four of their shot fell into the Seminary garden; a heavy fire of shot & shells was kept up from the Garrison upon it.

On the 3d there was cannonading on both sides.

4th. Several shot were thrown from our Battery at Point Levi through the Seminary. We were granted two more small rooms to lodge in.

5th, 6th, 7th, 8th and 9th. A cannonading was kept up by both the enemy & our People.

10th. We were told by the Officer of the Day that Colonel Arnold was gone up to Montreal; and that General Lee was dying with the gout in his stomach. When he was taken ill, he was on his way to Quebec. There was a firing on both sides.

11th and 12th. The weather was mild; and the cannonading continued.

13th. The Garrison kept up a heavy fire on our People. We were informed by the Officer of the Guard after we were in bed that in case our People without should make an attack on the Garrison, we were not upon any pretense to open our windows, for if we did, the Sentinels had orders to fire in upon us; or if we even opened our windows in the night.

14th & 15th. A smart fire was kept up on both sides; the weather was mild and the Priests began to work in the garden.

16th. *The trace of earth began to appear through the snow; and the Rivers to break up. There was but little firing.*

17th. *The weather was moderate; we were serv'd fresh beef four days in the week.*

18th. *There was a constant fire either of shot or shells from the Garrison chiefly on our Peoples Battery at Point Levi.*

19th. *The weather was warm; but the River was yet full of loose ice.*

20th. *The usual cannonading was kept up.*

21st. *We heard that two of our men who had deserted, and came into the Garrison the preceeding night, said that 300 of our New York Troops had laid down their arms; but that after many entreaties they had been prevailed upon to take them up again.*

22d. *Our People opened a two gun Battery on the Beau Port side, and fired briskly from it, as well as from the one at Point Levi, for some time. The Garrison kept up a very heavy fire upon them both. There was a storm of rain sleet and snow with the wind at NE.*

23d. *We were inform'd by Major Cox, the Field Officer of the Day, that two men arrived the preceeding night from Montreal who said that Colonel Arnold had gone across the lakes with his baggage. A heavy fire particularly from the Garrison was kept up. The River began to clear of ice.*

24th. *We heard that our People had open'd a two gun Battery on the Heights of Abraham. The firing continued & the weather was pleasant.*

25th. *We expected to be sent away soon in a vessel as we began to despair of being retaken. The cannonading was continuous on both sides, but was constant from the Garrison.*

26th. *We were told that our New York Troops had gone home, that they fired upon our own magazine as they went off; and that what remained of Colonel Arnold's Detachment had likewise gone home. There was a very heavy fire kept on both sides; and many shells were thrown from the Garrison. We were told by Major Caldwell that the King's Troops had left Boston, & gone to the southward; that 40,000 Troops were to be sent to America in the summer; that the negroes to the southward were all to be declar'd free by His Majesty's command; and that we might depend on seeing a large number of our People that invested the Garrison drove [illegible] in to keep us company within three weeks.*

28th. *Captain Thayer[168], one of our officers, was detected in attempting* to open a door that led up to the garret of the Seminary by the Officer of the Guard; and was immediately sent on board a vessel where he was put in irons. The weather was pleasant and there was but little firing.

29ᵗʰ. The Sentinels fired upon us for standing at our windows after it was dark.

30ᵗʰ. Colonel MacLean, Major Caldwell, Major Mackenzie, Captain McDougal, Mr. Lanwear the General's Aid de Camp, and the Officer of the Guard[169] with a soldier came into our room, and took away Captain Lockwood[170], and Captain Hanchet[171] without assigning any reason-- nay they scarcely spoke. Soon after Major Caldwell returned again, and inform'd us we were not on any account whatever to leave our apartments after the sun set. The weather was foggy with rain.

May 1ˢᵗ. The Officer of the Guard brought some joiners to fix a strong bolt and a lock on our door. Major MacKenzie, the Field Officer of the Day, informed us that Captain Lockwood and Captain Hanchet had given money, rum, bread and cheese as a bribe to the soldier, whom the other officers and he brought in with them the night before when they took those two gentlemen out, while he was a Sentinel; that he would be shot for having received the things from them; & that they were both put in irons on board of a vessel for having given them to him. The weather was cold & the snow was not yet off the ground. Nothing singular happen'd.

3d. As I went to bed about ten o'clock, I heard one of the Sentinels hail a ship repeatedly but no answer was made. Soon after some person and a ship was arrived, and immediately there was a confused noise, yet I could hear the word, fire, given. I then got up & in a few minutes I discovered a fire that appear'd to be in the Lower Town. The bells began to ring, and I thought I heard a brisk fire of small arms. We concluded then that our People had made a real attack on the Garrison. That imagination of our people being so brave fill'd us with the most joyful satisfaction. At the same time we were apprehensive that it should miscarry as our former one did. Thus between joy and fear we were so agitated that we were in universal tremours; but we soon found that we had only deceived ourselves with false hopes by observing that the fire we thought had been in Lower Town to be only a vessel on fire, and falling down the River with tide. The bells then ceased ringing and all was soon quiet. Nothing material occurred through the day.

4ᵗʰ. The Officer of the Guard told us that the vessel we had seen burning *the night before was a Fire Ship that our People had sent up from the Island of Orleans with an intention to burn the ships that lay in the Cul-de-Sac of the Lower Town; but without succeeding. We were not permitted to speak from our windows to any person. There was cannonading on both sides. The firing continued on the*

5th. About the sun's rising, to our very great mortification, we saw a ship coming up the River; and soon after two more came up. They were all ships of war; the largest was a fifty, the next had sixteen, and the last fourteen guns. At noon Captains Lockwood, Hanchet, and Thayer were brought back to the Seminary. Those gentlemen inform'd us that some of the ships had gone up the River to take some of our ships that were lying at Point au Tremble. We learned that 130 men had landed from the Kings ships, and had gone out with the Troops of the Garrison to attack our People; and we could hear some firing towards the Plains.

7th. Our People decamped with great precipitation from before Quebec at the appearance of Men of War we were told; and that they left behind them most of their cannon, some powder, some baggage, and all their sick; which had filled the people in the Garrison with great spirits.

8th. Two ships came up. We were informed that 55,000 men were coming out to America; 15,000 of whom were to come to Canada. Some of the officers of the Men of War, and of the land officers who came in them were [illegible] us, amongst whom was Major Carleton the Governor's brother. Lieutenant McDougal a commander of one of our schooners who had been taken the previous day at Point au Tremble was brought into the Seminary; there was a considerable quantity of powder on board the schooner, he said; and he told us that our Troops had passed through Point au Tremble before he left it; and added that he expected they would make a stand little above that, where they had two Batterys to prevent ships from getting up the River. We learned too that General Thomas with 300 men had joined General Wooster[172] the day he marched off. It was said that our Men had left fifty of their dead in a house near the town unburied; & that they had been lying in it a long time. The Canadians began to come into the town from the country.

9th. We again heard that the King's Troops had left Boston, and were gone to Halifax.[173] There was thunder with light showers.

10th. We were told that Major Meigs was to be permitted to go home on his parole. We had leave to walk in the passage; and were told that we should have more liberty soon. Three ships arrived with Troops, the 47ᵗʰ Regiment from Halifax.

11ᵗʰ. I wrote to Mr. Livius to intercede for me to get home on parole, along with Major Meigs. He assured me for answer that he would endeavour to obtain it for me, & would supply me with what money I might want. 12ᵗʰ. To our great satisfaction we were permitted to walk in the garden. I received forty dollars from Mr. Levius; but he told me he was afraid that he would not be able to obtain leave for me to go home on my parole.

13ᵗʰ. We walked all day in the garden; and we were informed that the colonies had declared themselves independent, and that no exchange of prisoners would be made until the war ended. A ship came up. 14ᵗʰ. A ship sailed for Halifax. 15ᵗʰ. A ship came up the River. Major Meigs was told by the Governour, who sent for him, that he was to go home in a day or two on his parole. We were all busy writing letters to be sent by him. 16ᵗʰ. Nothing happened.

17ᵗʰ. A ship arriv'd. Mr. Levius came to me before noon and informed me that he had at last with much difficulty obtained leave for me to go home on my parole with Major Meigs, & that we were both to embark that same afternoon. Accordingly the Town Major came for him and me after dinner, and carried us to the Governour. We signed our parole[174], and were then embarked on board of a schooner; and we had been but a short time on board when an invitation came from the officers of the Commodores for us to go on board and spend the evening with them. We went & were extremely well treated by them; and we slept on board of her all night.

18ᵗʰ. We went ashore to breakfast: at nine o'clock in the morning we retuned on board of the schooner[175]; and immediately sailed down the River.

CHAPTER FIVE

PRIVATE JEREMIAH GREENMAN JOURNAL

DESCRIPTION.

The journal of Jeremiah Greenman covers the entire period of the American Revolution from 1775 to 1783. The Quebec expedition makes up only a small portion of the complete journal. It contains just over twenty-one printed pages and covers the period from September 18, 1775, through the end of December 1776, including the time he was held as a prisoner of war in Quebec.

Prior to 1978, Mrs. Edwin R. Loderer of DeKalb, Illinois, who was a direct descendant of Greenman, gave Greenman's journal manuscript to Robert Bray and Paul Bushnell. Bray and Bushnell transcribed the entire manuscript and published it in 1978 as *Diary of a Common Soldier in the American Revolution, 1775-1783, An Annotated Edition of the Military Journal of Jeremiah Greenman.*[176] The transcribers state that the main problem with the Greenman journal is that he was writing only for himself so "what he wrote was a highly uncircumstantial account of his works and days, a kind of written remembrancer…"

In fact the same could be said of most of the journals in this compilation. Most journalists are writing for themselves and one need not accept that those journals are uncircumstantial because of this. A journal is a personal narrative of an important event in the journalist's life which in this case was a military expedition. Much can be, and has been, learned from reading personal accounts of military war experiences. The Quebec expedition would be incomplete and many details unknown without the participant's journals. This journal is particularly valuable due to its length and the details Greenman provides about the march and his imprisonment.

GREENMAN'S PREFACE TO HIS JOURNAL

The following Journal contains the Material Transaction of {events] as they fell under my observations, or came to my Knowledge__ and the Incidents [of] my private Life. T[hose] commence from the thir[teenth] of September, 1775, soon [after] my Entering the Service [of] the United States and were penned entirely for my Own Amusement at the time of writing and as a Memorial of Facts which, I supposed might [offer] me Some Pleasure [in] Recollections. This being the case, if by Accident I should lose them, I request they may [be] conveyed to me, if alive. If I am not, I wish them to be transmitted to my friends, as I don't look upon them as Sufficient Consequence to merit the Public View.

PUBLICATION.

There is only one publication of the Greenman journal which is in the book published by Bray and Bushnell in 1978.

AUTHOR.

Jeremiah Greenman was born in Newport, Rhode Island on May 7, 1758. He enlisted in a Rhode Island company and went to Cambridge after the Lexington Alarm. While there, he enlisted in Captain Samuel Ward's Company for the expedition to Quebec. Greenman was captured in the attack and was held prisoner until September of 1776 when he was released on parole.

After his exchange in 1777, he enlisted as a sergeant in a Rhode Island regiment in the northern campaign of 1777. In 1779, he was promoted to Ensign and in 1781 was promoted again to 1st Lieutenant. In 1782, Greenman was appointed as regimental adjutant for the Rhode Island troops, a position he held until the peace treaty was signed.

In 1784, he moved to Swansea, Massachusetts to open a shop with a fellow officer. He married Mary Eddy in 1784, whose family was involved in the shipyard business, and by 1787 he had joined the Eddy family business. By 1788, he was the captain of his own vessel, and in the 1790's Greenman served as an officer in a revenue cutter on Long Island Sound.

In 1806, Greenman's sailing business failed and he migrated to homestead new lands in Ohio. He settled in Marietta to begin a new life as a farmer. His life in Ohio was not financially rewarding, and in 1818 he applied for a veteran's pension and was placed on the pension rolls until 1821, when he was dropped. Greenman died at his home in Ohio on November 15, 1828, of bilious colic

JOURNAL

SEPTEMBER 1775

M 18. [We] Had orders for to be in readiness for to embark. In the evening went all on board, our fleet consisting of eleven in Number. Our troops consist of 13 hundred; 11 [companies] of musket men, 3 of rifle. We lay in the river on b[oard] of our Shipping.[177]

T 19. Early this morn, weighed anchor with the wind at SE. a fresh gale, our Colours flying, Drums a beating, fifes a playing, the hills and wharfs a Cover [with people] biding their friends a farewell. At Night [it was] foggy. H[ove] too till next morning then set Sail, went into the mouth of Kennebec river[178] *and came to an anchor.*

W 20. This day the rest of the transports came in too.[179]

T 21. This morn [there was] no wind. We was oblig'd for to tow our Ship in [the] morning tide with our boat. We came 15 miles & came to an anchor at george town[180].

F 22. This morn proceeded up the river as far as Coberconta[181] *and there came too.*

S 23. This day pushed to hollowils[182] *where we landed. A Lieut. and 20 men [were] ordered to stay here to see that the flour was baked into bread to proceed up the river with.*

S 24. This morn marched up to fort Western[183] *which was about four miles [where we] encamped, 48 miles up the river. So far this river is navigable with good pilots.*

M 25. Continuing at fort Western. In the afternoon a man belonging to Capt. Goodrich's Company[184], *James Mearn*[185] *being [with] liquor shot Serj't Bishop belonging to Capt. Williams Company*[186]. *He was set upon [the gallows] 10 minutes [and] then was taken down to Cambridge to have another trial.*

W 27. This morn [we spent time] fitting to go on board of our battos [bateaux].[187] *Embarked in my batto [with] 4 barrels [of provisions] & a tent for fort Halifax.*[188] *[We] had to get out and draw our batto over rips [ripples] and rocks in the [place] of rowing. [We were] Up to our arm pits in water and very cold.*

T 28. This morn proceeded on with the battoes. Very swift water indeed and rocky. Came over two pair [of] falls. Got forward 12 miles and encamped in the woods where we made up fires to dry ourselves by.

F 29. This morn proceeded up four miles. Got to fort Halifax where there was a pair of falls 600 rod[s], where we carried our battoes and provisions; then we encamped the other Side of the Carrying place which was nothing but rock and roots and a Swamp.

S 30. This morn set out from fort Halifax. Came 8 miles [in our] boats up over the S[hoals]; in many places up to our arms in water and so swift that we could hardly stand. encamped at the river side in winserlow.[189]

OCTOBER 1775 CANNEBECK {KENNEBEC}

S 1. October ye 1st 1775. This [morn] we proceeded on [through] very bad rips and encamped in the woods in Goshen.[190]

M 2. Set out this morn [and] Got forward __ miles. The water being Strong & being very Swift we w[ere] obliged to get out and [carry] our boats over the rocks to a carrying place called Cowhigens.[191] Camp at [illegible]by the falls where we built up [a] fire as usual.

T 3' Carried our battoes & provisions [about] 100 [rods] & put them in the river again, got forward 5 miles. One of Capt. Hendricks Company[192] killed a young moose weighing 200 weight.

W 4. This morn [we had] smooth water. [In] About 4 miles [we] came [to a place] where I got a breakfast. Then set off [and] came to Norridgewalk[193] and encamped by the carrying place.

T 5. Continuing at Norridgewalk mending our battoes [to make them] fit to carry over ye falls.

F 6. This day carried over Norridgewalk carrying place 1 mile and a quarter over roots & rocks and mud. Here we got some oxen to carry a few of our barrels over the carrying place. After we got all across we pushed on 2 miles & encamped, etc.

S 7. Set out this morn very early. Came 7 miles. Came where [there] was [a] small river [that] led into the main [river]. This branch we took. No inhabitants being here to inquire of, [so] we went up two miles before we found we were wrong. Then the river was so rocky we was oblig'd to turn back. This day [we] left all inhabitants & enter uncultivated country and a barren wilderness. The trees here for the most part [are] Birch, pine & hemlock. There *are places on the river where maple trees grew where the inhabitants made Sugar. Got forward 7 miles today.*

S 8. This morn it began to rain [and] Continuing raining all day and part of the night. This day I went on land through the woods, 8 miles & encamped, etc.

M 9. This morn went with the battos 3 miles. Came to Tintucket or Hell Gate Falls[194]. Carried our battoes and barrels 86 rods over the carrying place. Then proceeded on 4 miles. Very rocky and swift water so that we was obliged to wade and draw [pull] our boats.

T 10. This morn found a place where there was troughs made of birch bark and two old wigwams and a Number of small bowls which we supposed they cooked their maple juice in to make Sugar of. We brought a number of the bowls away with us; this day [we] got forward 12 miles up to the great carrying place[195] & got some of our provisions part way across.

W 11. This day [spent] applying ourselves in making a sort of road through the woods so that we might get our battoes and provisions along. We got some of our baggage across. This day a man was passing [when] a tree that some of the men was cutting fell on him & wounded him so that he died. We buried him there. This carrying place [is] 4 miles [and] 40 rod.

T 12. This day getting over [with] our battoes and provisions to the first pond.

F 13. This day got all across and encamped [on] the west side of the carrying place. Some small spits of snow fell today.

S 14. This morn carried across a pond a half mile over. Then carried our battoes & provisions a half mile and encamped upon low land towards the Second pond.

S 15. Carried half a mile [and] came to the Second pond; crossed the pond which was one mile over, then carried 2 miles [which was] very bad going to the third pond. Crossed the pond which was two miles over [and] came to [a] carrying place 3 miles [and] 3 quarters long. Carried part of the way [and] then encamped upon very high land and made flour cakes, etc.

M 16. This morn carried all across [the pond] which was very bad going; in some places [water] was half a leg deep with mud and mire. Where it wasn't mud and mire it was rocks and hills as steep as a House side almost. We got all across [and] put our battoes into [a] small steam that led into [the] Dead river.[196] This river runs SE and so still you can't perceive which way it runs.

It's black and very deep. [Then] we took to our oars [and] rowed up six miles and encamped.

T 17. We set out this morn very early and came ten miles [and] overtook Capt. Topham's company.[197] *[We] came to a carrying place [and] carried across [and] then encamped. [Our] provisions [were] short.*

W 18. Remaining where we encamped till 12 o'clock [and] then set off [and] came 8 miles, [including] 4 miles [of] very bad rips and rocks. One batto [was] over [turned] and lost. [There was] Rain and some [men] hungry.

T 19. This morn set off [and] came 7 miles. [We] came to a carrying place which was ten rod[s] [and] got forward 17 miles. The water [was] growing swift and the river growing shoaly we put by our oars & took our setting poles again.

F 20. This day we proceeded on [and] came to two carrying places, the first 40 rod[s] [and] the second 60 [rods]; came a few miles [and] came to another a half a mile. We carried the battoes across. A freshet[198] *arose in the night [which] overflowed where we [were] encamped [and] carried away part of a barrel of pork and a barrel of powder. [It was] very cold.*

S 21. This morn I came by land, where I and some more got lost in the woods where we stayed all night. In the morning some battoes come to us [illegible]. We came to one carrying place 20 rod[s] across.

S 22. Proceeded on [for] four or five miles [and came to a carrying place 30 [rods] where we encamped.

M 23. This [morn] the water very swift indeed [and] a number of battoes over [turned] & lost a number of packs. Then [we] came to a carrying [place] which was 30 rod[s] where we held a Council [of War].[199]

T 24. Our provisions growing scant [and] some of our men being sick [we] held a Council. {We] agreed to send the sick and weakly men back & to send a Capt. And 50 men forward to get in to the inhabitants as soon as possible that they might send back provisions, Accordingly the sick was sent back & a Capt. and 50 men sent forward to make the inhabitants as quick as possible. Before this, Colo. Enos[200] *with 3 Companies turned back [and] took with them large Stores of provisions and ammunition which made us shorter than we was before.*

W 25. Set off this morn [and] came one mile and came to a carrying place which was 3 rod[s] across. Came 40 rod[s] and came to another which was 3 quarters [of a] mile long. Came to the first pond on Dead river. Encamped on a hill. Very cold and rain[y]. Some [men] hungry, for our provision[s] is very short.

T 26. This morn set off from the first pond [and] came to the second carrying place, 8 rod[s]. carried into the third pond which [is] 3 quarters of a mile across. The ground [is] covered with Snow and very Cold and our provisions [are] very [low] so that we expect to kill some of our dogs to eat.[201]

F 27. Set out this morn very early from the third pond [and] carried into the fourth which was one mile across. Then into the fifth which was 60 rod[s]. Here the people were cutting up the tents for to make bags to put what small provision[s] they had in. Here it was agreed to leave our battoes and to foot it after being greatly fatigued by carrying over such hills, mountains & Swamps such as men never passed before. We carried two or three battoes over this carrying place to carry the sick down the river Chaudière[202] *in, but could not go down in a batto [the river being] so rapid and [last line missing].*

S 28. Early this morn set out for Chaudière[203] *pond [and] took our provision[s] on our backs and went three miles. Stopped by a small stream running into Chaudière pond where we dealt out 4 or 5 oz. of pork [and] 5 pints of loose flour. Came 5 miles and encamped.*

S 29. This morn set out for the head of Chaudière river. Took provisions on our back which was but a very small quantity. This day we suffered greatly [and] had to wade [illegible] rod[s] & came to another [stream] which was 6 rod[s] across. We was ferried across here and came a few rod[s] and had to wade 20 rod[s] more [and] then pushed on very briskly. Came to an old hut that they said was a guard house but nothing [was] there but the house. Came this day [line missing].

M 30. Set out this morn by daylight. Came 15 [rods] through cedar swamp up to our necks and cold. Got to Chaudière river. This river is very swift water rocky and shoal[y]. [We] overtook Lieut. Shaw['s][204] *[detachment] that went forward with that batto [which] was to carry sick in, but the river [was] so rapid and swift there could no batto go down the river. There was one man lost by the batto [with] a quantity of ammunition and guns, [and] with some money.*

T 31. Set out this morn very early. Left 5 sick men in the woods that was not able to march [and] left two well men with them, but what little provision[s] they had did not last them [very long]. We gave out of our little [provisions and] every man gave some but the men that was left was obliged to leave them (the 5 sick men) to the mercy of wild bea[s]ts. This day as we were passing along the river we saw 3 canoes that went forward with the advance party stove against the rocks. We passed a pair of fall[s]. We had very bad traveling through the woods and Swamps. Our provision[s] being very short, here we killed a dog. I got a small piece of it and some broth that it was boiled [in] with a great deal of trouble. Then lay down [and] took our blankets and slept very hearty for the times.

NOVEMBER 1775

W 1. Set out by day & left the company. Traveled all day very very briskly. At night encamped 5 miles a head of the company. [We are] In a very miserable situation [with] nothing to eat but dogs. Here we killed another [dog] and cooked [it]. I got some of that by good [luck] with the head of a squirrel [and] with a fine parcel of candle wicks boiled up together which made a very fine supper, without salt. Here on this [place] we made a noble feast without bread or salt thinking it was the best that ever I eat & so went to sleep contended [but] not knowing what to [expect?].[205]

T 2. This morn when we arose many of us [were] so weak that we could hardly stand. We staggered about like drunken men. Howsomeever we made shift to get our pack on, them that did not threw them away. We marched off hoping to see some inhabitants by night. I help[ed] to get a pint of water that a partridge was boiled in. About ten o'clock, then I set out strong hoping to find the inhabitants by night but some of them (the men) [were] so weak that a small stick as big as [a] man's thumb would bring them to the ground. In the afternoon when we came in sight of the cattle which the advance party had sent out, it was the joyfullest sight that I ever saw & some could not refrain from crying for joy. The men that came with the cattle told us it was yet 20 miles to the nearest inhabitants. Here we killed a creature and some of the men [were] so hungry [that] before this creature was dressed they had the skin and all entrails, guts and everything that could be eat[en] on the fires a boiling. We had ate meat [before] with strips an inch or two long served out in the room? of bread, but that [meal] was very good. [206]

F 3. This morn [there was] thick raining weather. We set out for to reach the inhabitants it being 20 miles [and] where we was obliged to wade in several small rivers. Some of them up to our middles and very cold. We met some Indians on the march that had some flour cakes & some potatoes, which we bought [off] of them giving a very great price. Then we came in sight of a house, the first I had seen [in] 27 days, where there was beef and bread for us which we cooked very plenty of. Some of the men made their selves sick eating so much. At night [it] snowed but we slept very hardy in the woods.

S 4. Continuing at Sartigan[207] in the Province of Canada. Very cold and snowing. Only one house here & some Indian's wigwam[s].

S 5. This morn march down the river on the frozen ground bare footed and very cold till at last I came to a French house where I [bought?] a pair of seal skin moccasins and had some fine supper made out of cabbage and bread. Here in this house I sleep by the fire.

M 6. Set off this morn. Came up with Colo. Arnold [and us and] the advance party marched off together. The roads very bad; half a leg deep with mud and water. Marched till 2 o'clock at night, marched 17 miles.

T 7 to S 11. This morn set out [and] came a few miles. Came to St Mary's[208] where I continued with Lieut. Shaw. Saturday the 11, [I was] giving out provision[s] to the rear as they came up and so forth.

S 12. Today traveled a few, or twelve miles to Pont Levis[209], [and] took up quarters in [a] French house [about] 1 mile from the river St Lawrence till our troop[s] could get up. Continuing near Headquarters [which was] 4 miles from the city. During the time we stayed this side of the river, we took a midshipman belonging to a ship in the harbor who came ashore with some others to carry some flour away from this side of the river. The river is about 1 mile wide. There layeth in the harbor 1- 28 gun frigate with a sloop of war [and] with some merchant men [vessels]. The men mount spears to storm the city [at] the first word.[210]

M 13. At Point Levis on guard by the river side. The whole guard ordered to turn out to make oar[s] and paddles for to cross the river Saint Lawrence. At night we crossed the river with canoes and boats. Some of the canoes over [turned] crossing the river [but] nothing lost, only a few poles and guns. We all got over [and] landed our men at Wolf's Cove, where Wolfe landed his army.[211] [We] Marched up the bank which was very steep. Came on Abraham's Plains[212] where Wolfe had his battle, where we formed [and] marched back and forth to keep from freezing [while] the officer[s] held a council [to decide] whether to storm the City or not & the most part said not [to] storm. Then we marched about [a] mile to some very good houses which were forsaken by the owner[s]. Major Caldwell's[213] *house for one. He had just gone as we got to the house. Here was a number of teams [of oxen] loaded with potatoes for to carry into the City. We took the teams and dealt out the potatoes to the soldiers, etc.*

T 14. Continuing at [the] French village called Saint Foy[214]. *A guard we had stationed by the river was fired upon by a small ship that lay in the river. About 10 o'clock we was paraded [and] marched up close by the walls of the City [and] gave three cheer[s]. The enemy not being fixed, we stayed there a small spell till they fixed a Cannon, but [we] was obliged to g[o to] a barn to get [cover] bef[ore] they could fire at [us]. Then they fired a few shot among us but did no damage. Then we returned to our Quarters again.*

W 15. This [day was] very pleasant but cold. We were presently alarmed but [it] proved to be a false one. We made an attempt to send a flag into the City but they fired at the flag & would not receive it.

T 16. We took this day a quantity of flour belonging to the enemy & some sheep. They (the enemy) keep a continual fire at our guard[s]. A sergeant of the riflemen had [his] leg shot off and died with the wound.

F 17. Continuing at Saint Foys where we was informed that there were not more than 100 regulars in the City with a number of sailor[s] that came from on board the ship[s], which they [were] compelled to fight. In all, not exceeding 6 hundred und[er] arms. Very cold and blustering weather.

S 18. This day there was a council held where we should storm the City or retreat back till General Montgomery's forces could join us. They (the council) consulted to march 20 miles back to the country. Orders came out at night for every man to be in readiness to march in the morn at 3 o'clock.

S 19. This morn very early [we] marched 20 [miles] up the river to a small town, Point aux Trembles[215]. *Our ammunition being almost expended to [illeg.] with.*

M 20. To T 23. Continuing at Point aux Trembles where we [are] continuing till the 23rd, fitting ourselves for to go to Quebec as [when]ever General Montgomery joined us. News M 20. To T 23. Continuing at Point aux Trembles where we [are] continuing till the 23rd, fitting ourselves for to go to Quebec as [when]ever General Montgomery joined us. News came from General Schuyler that General Montgomery was on the march with 15 hundred men for our assistance.

F 24. This day there was a council held concerning our [food] allowance. We were ordered to have one pound and a quarter of beef & the same of flour. Here we got moccasins made of half tanned leather, which made us comfortable, for we was very bad off for clothes and so forth.

S 25. Continued at Point aux Tremble. 3 ships from Quebec a going up the river and came too against our quarters & lay all night.

S 26. This morn the ships weighed anchor [and] went up 9 miles & one of them got agound and damaged her stern. News came that General Montgomery's cannon was landed. Orders was given for a hundred men to attack (respond) as quick as possible for to meet General Montgomery. [We were] Very cold and poor off for clothing.

M 27. This day the French inhabitants sent to Colo. Arnold for assistance to prevent the Kings troops [from] burning and plundering their houses. A Capt. & two men send down to Saint Foys.

T 28. Continuing at Point aux Trembles. Very cold. [Staying] at a French house where I far[ed] very well for victual[s] etc.

W 29. The ships that went up the other day returned back to Quebec again. A quantity of snow fell. Very cold.

T 30. This day the men that went forward to meet General Montgomery [and] returned back. A Comp[any] of French [volunteers] came with them & a quantity of ammunition.[216]

DECEMBER 1775

F 1. December the 1ˢᵗ 1775. This day 4 vessels came from Montreal with General Montgomery [and] with the York forces who had taken Saint Johns, Chambly & Montreal. In the[se] places they took a quantity of clothing, ammunition & provision[s] with 950 prisoners.

S 2. This day Gen'l Montgomery made a present to most of Colo. Arnold['s] detachment [consisting of] a coat, blanket, vest & so forth. About 8 o'clock at night Josiah Carr died, belonging to our Company.

S 3. This morn very cold. In the afternoon the Company [was at] a funeral. The Chaplin of our division made a prayer over the Corps; then we carried him [Carr] 2 miles & entered a burying yard at Point aux Trembles, where we got [leave] to bury him.[217]

M 4. Set out this morn from Point aux Trembles & marched 15 miles. Came to Saint Ories where I put up in a French house where I [ate] bread & milk &so forth.

T 5. Set out this morning from Saint Ories [and] came to the suburb of Quebec where we pu[t up] at a French house by the river Saint Charles.[218]

W 6 t0 8. Continuing at Saint Charles river. The inhabitants employed in carrying fascines[219] for to build a battery. Very cold.

S 9. A pleasant morn but cold. In the afternoon there was orders given for 440 men to be in readiness. [At] night they was all paraded [and] marched upon the plains where they built a battery with snow and fascines & some earth.

S 10. This day we began the siege on Quebec. Today there was 5 [patriot] mortars set in a town called Saint Roch[220] near Quebec. At night our people sent into the City very plenty of shells. The enemy keep a continual fire all day [which] set a number of houses on fire [and] killed a French woman.

M 11 to the 21. During our time [that] we stayed, we took several prisoners and cannoned and bombarded each other both night & day. During the tran[s] action we heard that two men that was left back with Lieut. MCleelan and [the] other sick [men] retuned. Informed [us] that [the] Capt. [Lieut.] was [buried] at the first French inhabitant and the others died in the w[oo]ds. Continuing fire from both sides [with] a number of men killed & wounded. [We] made another attempt to send a flag into the city but they would not receive it. The small pox [is] very plenty among us. [We are] preparing to storm the city [and] making pike[s] and spears. Nothing very material [happened].

F 22. The enemy set two houses on fire. Very still on both sides. We prepared to storm the city at night but the Gen'l thought it too light so [he] adjourned it.

S 23. The small pox very breaf [prevalent] among our troops.[221] A very brisk cannonading. Our detachment was drawed up and formed a square where Gen'l Montgomery asked us if we were willing to storm the city & the bigger part of them seem willing for to storm the city. The enemy throwed shells into Saint Roch and very plenty (many) killed, and [they] wound[ed] a few. We returned as many [shells] back to [at] them.

W 27. This day being snowy and very stormy, the Gen'l thought best to storm the city at night. We prepared [and] got all in readiness. Turned at 2 o'clock [and] marched to headquarter[s where] we received orders. [We] marched close to the walls of the City [but] the Gen'l thought it too light. We returned to headquarters for the first dark night.

T 28 and 29. Very pleasant. Some of our Company died with the small pox. A very brisk cannonading [from] both sides.

S 30 and S 31. This day it (snow and clouds) began to thicken [so] towards night we got in readiness. Snowed and blowed very plenty. We were order[ed] to be in the greatest readiness for to [storm] the city very hard. At 2 o'clock at night, we turned out; it [was] snowing and blowing very hard. [We] got all in readiness with our ladders, spears and so forth. With hearts undaunted, [we] [began] to scale the walls [and] marched down into Saint Roch, a town near the City, or [and] just under the walls, where we sent off an advance guard of 50 men which soon alarmed the town, at which all bells rang. They (British soldiers) soon turned out where they formed themselves along the ramparts. [They] keep a continual fire on us but we got up to their two gun battery, after losing a great number of men. We soon got into their battery, which was two Nine pounders. We got in [and] took 70 prisoners. Then our men['s] arms being wet, we could not do much. Howsomeever, we tried to force the gate to get into the upper town but all in vain. Gen'l Montgomery being killed, all the [his] men retreated and left us to fight for ourselves. Then they (the British) sent a flag to us to give up. Our Colo. Arnold wounded, Colo. Green took command. Then the officers held a council [and] agreed to give [up]. They marched us into a French Jesuit College after taking away our arms. Here we [were] very much crowded. No room for us to stir, and very cold.[222]

JANUARY 1776

M 1. We were put all into a French Convent where they gave us a gill of rum for a New Years gift & some biscuits. We were allowed by the Gen'l 1 pound of bread and a half a pound of meat, 6 ounces of butter a week, a half a pint of boiled rice in a day. We had a cask of port gave [given] to us be some gentlemen of the town.

T 2. This day the Gen'l sent for all of our names, places of abode and our occupations and [a] list of the old Country men by themselves.[223] *A Flag sent out for our clothes. Most of the prisoners had then sent in to vary our provisions, salt[ed] Meat. But [we] don't get half so much as is allowed by the Gen'l. We live very uncomfortable for we have no room, not [even] enough to lay down to sleep.*

T 9 to S 21. This day to please us we were shut up in a smaller part of the house than before. *Stinking salmon is [the] provision we have. The bigger part of it, though very small, is the same. The bigger part of the old Country men enlisted out [of the patriot army and] into the king's service. The small pox very [prevalent] among us. Our people burned down Saint Roch. We got some of the old boards to burn which we m[ade] up [into] cabins which maketh some [more] room to what [we] had before. Two of our men [were] put in Irons for talking of deserting [because they] got overheard. Hubbard*[224] *died with his wound that was in his heel.*

M 22 to W 31. There was three vessel[s] and a Still house set on fire by our people. The garrison people go into Saint Roch [to] get the remains of the buildings [that were burned] for woods which is very short in Town. 8 of the old Country men ran away. 2 of our men taken that was going to set fire to their shipping. We live very happy & contented though we are in such a dismal hole hoping the first dark night that our people will be in & redeem [rescue] us. Here we continue very lousy making wooden Spoons & [with] one Notion [and] another to apply [to] our very disagreeable time.

FEBRUARY 1776

T 1 to T 5. This day we had another Cask of port gave to us by some gentleman of the town, which was very kind & very acceptable for we wanted something of [a] liquid nature. To revive our Spirits, we had some fresh beef which we made very fine [meal?] of. We are now applying ourselves in [the] picking of oakum for some merchants thinking to get some [as a [present but was very much mistaken. The small pox [is] very bad among us [with] 40 men Sick in prison with it now. Very cold & a very heavy Storm of Ice. There was 3 men [who] perished on Sentry [duty]. Some more of the old Country men that enlisted out ran away. We live very Cold and disagreeable but apply ourselves in all of [the] plays [games] that we can think of.

F 16 to T 29. Very Cold indeed. We get some wheat that is [in] bags below where we go after wood and burn it which maketh very good coffee and selling some of our thing[s], we get some money & so we have once in a while some Coffee. Some more of the old Country men deserted that [had] enlisted [in the British] out of prison and the rest of them was put in prison again. The enemy went out after our Cannon that was on Abraham's Plains but returned without them faster than they went out. There layeth 60 men sick in prison. They were all sent to the hospital where they was used very kindly. There was not more than 4-5 died with the Small pox out of all that went to the hospital.[225]

MARCH 1776

F 1 to T 14. This day we had another Cask of port gave to us. I had a present gave [to] me by Capt. Frost[226] *[consisting] of some Sugar & tea & some money which maketh me very comfortable. We had Codfish 2 days in a [row?]. 1 of the prisoners was put [in] irons for talking with some of the Sentrys. We are pleased with a notion we hear that the enemy is left Boston & 2 thousand men [are] on the march for here. The carpenter ordered us to nail slabs of boards across our windows to keep us from looking out & they are very strict among us.*

F 15 to S 23. Very Cold this night. There was an alarm in the City, at which [time a] large guard was set up by the pr[ison] and field pieces set [up] before the pris[on] door for they was very much afraid of us. Nothing more remarkable the[se] days.

S 24 to T 28. A flag was sent out to our people but did not hear what the business was. The emigrants that is the old Country men that enlisted out of prison were [re]moved from among us & put into some other place, and we are ordered to pack up our things to move. They moved us into a Stone jail,[227] *where it was bombproof & then we went so Many in a room [and] where we gave a list of our names in each room. Where we live [is] some [more] comfortable to what we lived before, but the Stones is very cold indeed. Here we can see our people's Colour & a small breastwork they have left up, etc.*

F 29 to S 31. We being in sight of our people and close to the walls & a guard of old French [men] and boys, we thought it a Shame to be keep in prison by them. So the Sergeant's consulted [together and decided it would] be best to send out a man to our people to inform them & accordin[gly] we sent a man out in the night. If he got clear he was to set a signal on the flagstaff. In the morning we see another flag hoisted below the other. Then most of the prisoner[s]thought [it] best to try to get out then. Our names we gave to the Sergeants [and] we divided ourselves in four parties; 1 to go to the train (artillery) and turn that upon the town; another [party] to Saint John Guard [gate]; another to take the guard of Frenchmen that was over us; another [to] set fire to some houses {near?] the jail. By this time, we were in hopes that our people would come to assist us by [us] sending out one of the Spryest [men] we could get to [go] inform them we were out, but one of the prisoners, taking an axe [and] going into the Lower bombproof [room] where there was a door that we was to go out at, he began to cut the ice to try to get the door open. A boy that was standing Sentry see him [and] he informed the officer of the guard. The officer came in [and] went down the cellar [and] asked what we was cutting the ice from the door for. We told him we did not know. Neither did we know who it was [we said] but they mistrusted that we was agoing to try to get out, but they did not know [it for sure].

APRIL 1776

M 1 to T 30. This day one of the prisoner[s], an old Country man that did not enlist out, told [them] that [he] had carried on [items into the] prison. Then some officers came [and] searched every man's pack and the room to see if they could find some arms or ammunition. They mistrusted that the people of the town [might have] equipped us with arms but they found nothing. Then they put us [in] Irons, some leg bolts & some handcuffs which was very uncomfortable. The officers of the jail or provost master count us twice a day. It is very sickly among us recently. Such provision[s] as they give us, they give us warm biscuits which we think was poisoned for the doctors would cure us just as they pleased. Say or do what you would, they would give us such physique as they thought [appropriate?]. Complain of ever so different an ailment, they would serve us all alike and give one sort of physique, which proved that we was poisoned, but we soon got better. Our people keep a continual fire in the lower town which we are very glad to see, hoping that we shall be redeemed (rescued) very soon, but almost ready to give up fearing they will not come. But we keep up our hearts with a pewter fife that we made out of all the button[s] that we could get off our clothes, which made us very merry. So we passed away the long tedious time.

MAY 1776

W 1 to M 6. The City was alarmed in the night by a Ship that came into the lower part of the town where their shipping lay, but did no damage. They took the Captain off her. This morn about Sunrise 3 Ships came into the [harbor] with a reinforcement with about 1 thousand men at which all the bells in the City rang. They marched out upon Abraham's Plains to give our people battle, but they retreated as fast as possible. {they] left a number of Sick in the hospital with some warlike stores & we see our people retreat, which made us all feel very bad wishing ourselves there to engage them. If they had o[nly] known had bad it was to be a prisoner they never would [have] retreated without giving battle.

T 7 to S 25. The General ordered all the irons to be taken off, thank God. The bigger part of us could take them off without their help. The Gen'l gave the emigrants their Liberty again. A number more of Ships came up the river. A number of troops [have] gone up to Montreal by land. 6 or 8 men brought into prison that was taken who inform us that our people was very unhealthy. There arrived a very great number of Shipping every day. 13 or 14 of our men enlisted out into the Service [of the British]. [As] 1 of our men went out to work they required him to swear allegiance to the king but he would not. Then he was put in Irons & [they] used him very bad & so forth.

S 26 to F 31. Continue in prison. Here we live discontented and quite out of hope of ever being relieved [released] but keep up our hearts all we can. 20 or 30 Sail more of Shipping came up the river with Gen'l Burgoyne & his army, who brought up with him a parcel of Hessians, about 6 or 7 thousand.[228] *A number of the [British] troops marched off for Montreal. The Hessians [were] put on the Provost guard over us, where there is Sentinels, no less than 5, set around the prison. [They] hardly give us liberty to look at the windows. We can't see no Snow but [see] plenty of Ice in our bombproof [cellar]. [We] keep ourselves hearty in playing ball in the yard [elligible].*

JUNE 1776

S 1 to T 4. These [days we] are very Contended hoping we shall go home in a little while. Gen'l Carleton with a number more of officers [and] a parcel of Hessian officer[s] came into prison to see us [and] Inquired if we had fared well. We told him that we had fared well for the station we was in. He asked if we had fared as he promised [and] we told him yes. He then asked if we had behaved as we promised [and] we told him no. We begin to think what was coming. Then he asked if he let us go whether or not we thought we could lay at home & not come [back] there to trouble him. He likewise said that he did not take us as [an] enemy & hoped we [would not take up arms] any more, and that if he could rely on our honours he would send us home. He talked very pretty indeed. We made him [an] answer that we would go home & remain peaceful till we were interrupted. Well, saith he, I will leave [it] to you to think [about it] and so send me an answer tomorrow. Then we began to write [a] petition [with] some one sort & some another. Some thank [him for] his goodness & other[s want to] know upon what terms he would send us home again. This one was written & another [was written and] then there was a disturbance [about] which [one of the choices] should go [in the petition]. We went out into the yard and so we determined it by a vote [to decide] which [answer] should go [to the General].[229]

W 5 to W 12. This morn very pleasant indeed. After the Provost Master[230] *came in, we gave this [petition] as follows to him:*

May it please your Excellency, we the prisoners in his Majesty's jail, return your Excellency our most hearty and unfeigned thanks for your goodness & clemency to us since our imprisonment. Being sensible of your humanity, we return your excellency thanks for your offer made to us yesterday & having a desire to return to our friends & families, [we] again will promise not to take up arms against his majesty, but [will] remain peaceful & quiet in our respective places of abode, & we further assure your Excellency that you may depend on our fidelity. So we remain your Excellency's humble servants.

Signed in behalf of the prisoner[s].

13 or fourteen prisoners were taken out to go fishing. Governor Carleton [has] gone to Montreal. Soldier[s] march off from the garrison every day [and] leave the town almost bare of Soldier. Only a few Hessian[s are here] to keep guard over us. The enemy forces a number of Troops to go out of [to] every parish & so forth.

W 12 to S 16. Very pleasant. We are told every day that we shall be sent on board the transports. A list of all our names was sent foe; Likewise our ages & the province & town where we was born & [our] occupation. Some of the prisoners that went out to work ran [away].

M 17 to S 30. Very raining weather, thundering and lightening. The soldiers in the garrison are cut off their provision[s] a half a pound of bread in [a] week and all the prisoners the Same. We begin to think that we are not [going] to be sent home. We are put off from one day to another and [to] next week, but we keep our hearts up all we can for our situation, for we are very unhealthy by keeping us in such a hole not fit for dogs much more for men. They march off to Montreal every day.

JULY 1776

M 1 to S 21. More ships arrived. Some prisoners put in [our jail who were] taken up to the lake by Indians, who inform us that our people is all gone over the lake & that all the Canadian Indians is joined Burgoyne's army. Capt. Frost came into prison to see me [and] asked if I wanted anything either money or clothes. He would help me to [get] them and would have me sent [them]. He gave me a couple of shirts & a pair of trousers with some Sugar & tea, which I was very glad of for we had nothing but beef & bread & but little of that. Now I live well and my partner, he that was put in Irons, I mean with me. Our hands were put in one handcuff & so we marched together.

M 22 to W 31. This day we are told by the Provost Master that we are to be put on board the transports in a week or ten day[s]. at which we are all very glad. 5 more of the prisoner[s] that went out to work ran away & they have sent a Scout of Indians after them. We hear [that] when the Ships come down that is to convey us, we are to be sent on board. Then again to comfort us we hear that the militia officers of the town, with some others, held a Council concerning our going away & they think [it] is best not to send us home. Then again we hear that we are not agoing today. We hear that some gentlemen of the town that Howe²³¹ is taken. One of our prisoner[s is] taken Craz[y] so that we are obliged to wait with him night & day. The Barrack master & some other officers came into prison today to [tell] us that we were all to be put on board of the transport[s] & all that wanted a Shirt should have one given to them, for some of [them] had no Shirt to put on. The bigger part of us had Shirts gave to us as a present. We were told by the Provost Master that we should have 12 pound[s] of bread in a week & 2 pound[s] of beef, in which killed some of them, after being so Short of provision[s and] then giving us such a plenty. We hear that our officers have their Liberty of the town & so forth.

AUGUST 1776

T 1 to S 3. We hear that all the old Country men that did not enlist out among the emigrants [blank]. Now we are waiting for some more prisoner[s] to come down the river. They let some of us go out into the town by [the] sea stores; them that hath money. Today Capt Frost came into prison to see me to *[tell] me [that] if I wanted any sea stores, to send to [for] him & I should have some, & so forth.*

S 4 to M 5. This day I had sent to me ten pounds of Sugar & two pounds of tea. Now we are in great spirits fixing to go on board the transports. 35 prisoners signed the parole. Our door [is] not locked up. Some of us [are] out of prison which was a very great Liberty.

T 6. This day I had some more money gave [to] me [by] Capt. Frost. All the prisoners signed the parole which we was glad to see. We would [have] signed anything they brought to us if they would carry us home. Here is what we signed.

We whose names are underwritten do solemnly promise unto his Excellency Gen'l Carleton that we will not say or do anything against her person or government but will repair whenever his Excellency Gen'l or any other of his Majesty's Commander[s] shall say or see fit to call [on] for us.

This we all signed.[232]

W 7 t0 S 10. This day we embarked on board the John & Christopher which was a very great change of life after being in prison 7 month[s] in a stone jail. Here we lied in the river Saint Lawrence till 11 [this] day. Here our allowance is meat twice in a week, about two ounces, & a quart of brandy among six men, and three pound[s] of moldy bread & the rest of the day[s] in the week we have about half a point of boiled rice a day.[233]

S 11 to S 18. This day we set sail from Quebec with the wind at NNE. [We] came down the river a little ways [and] came too against the river Saint Charles. In the morn [we] weighed anchor [and] proceed on our passage as fast as we could down the river Saint Lawrence. We have some contrary wind and rainy weather. The river [is] very wide down this way & the land very high indeed. We got into the river Saint Lawrence where we spoke with a brig [commanded by] Capt Rogers from Providence. We left Bonaventure bearing SW by W. The whales [were] very plenty around [our boat}.

M 19 to S 31. Very pleasant. [We] made the Island of Saint Johns where we was detained a day by carrying some letters [and] then we proceeded on our passage. We made [the] Nova Scotia shore [and] spoke with 3 or four vessels. Left Nova Scotia bearing NW. Very stormy weather so that we was obliged to strike our top gallon mast. [it was] very foggy [and] then cleared up. We got out top gallon mast up again. We ar[e] very healthy indeed. Our alternation of weather & climate suits us very well etc. Nothing very [illegible].[234]

SEPTEMBER 1776

S 1 to S 8. Very stormy but not much damage to us [because] we keep below. Nothing very remarkable more than proceding on our passage, which we want to be made soon for we are almost tired out being prisoners so long. No[w] we are in latitude of Rhode Island. One of our transports are run out of sight & they think that the prisoner is carried her into Rhode Island, etc.

M 9 to T 10. This morn [is] pleasant. Sounded [and] got [the] bottom [covered with] black & white land, which we were very glad to see hoping we should now see isn't very soon. At night, sounded again [and] got [the] bottom very much as before. Hauled our course more to the southward and westward.

W 11. This morn [was] very pleasant. Hauled our course up to [the] west [and] gained about 5 or six knots at night. We made the land bearing [as] WNW which we was very glad to see.

T 12. This morn ran in for the land, which we found to be Amboy.[235] We ran in Amboy Bay & came to an anchor till 12 o'clock, then ran up to Staton Island where we came too & [were] very Glad to see that after a long & tedious passage.

F 13 to F 20. This day we see 4 or 5 Ships go up by the town. They keep a constant fire at the Ship but they soon got up the north river out of our sight. There came on board of our Ship, a gentleman [who] told us we need not be concerned for we would be landed in a few days, for whatever Gen'l Carleton had promised, we should be performed. More shipping went up by the town where they keep a very heavy Cannonading on both sides; the Grand battery from New York & another battery from the Jersey side. There came on board the boat [a man that] told us that our people had left New York. Very plenty of shipping gone up towards the town. We see English Colours flying at the town, which we did not like very well. There is orders given out [saying] death for any sailor catched ashore. We hear that a flag has gone to Gen'l Washington to see where we shall be landed. We hear that the enemy is killed & taken great numbers of our people. An officer came on board to get all our names, & told us we should go home in a few day. 2 of our prisoners in the night stole a boat & ran away. Our time seem[s] to be very long staying here on boar[d] of this Ship; almost out of patience.

S 21 to S 22. There came on board an officer [who] told us we should all be landed a Monday at Night. A very great fire broke out in the town and by the look of it burned the bigger part of the town. The river & harbor [are] full of Shipping going up to the town. We hear that there [were] 200 thousand houses burned down in the City.[Obviously a wildly wrong number]. We hear that the man was catched, that set the houses on fire, by the sentry and run through by a bayonet & then the next day he was hung.

M 23 to T 24. This morn we got in readiness to go ashore. We prepared to be landed very soon but were disappointed again. The Steward of the Ship [was] gone ashore by which we could not have any provisions for 24 hours. We are told that the boats that was to land us was taken up in landing the enemy on Red Hook. There comes on board of us, 190 men from other prison Ships. We were to be landed to Elizabeth Town Point. About 12 o'clock we heft up our anchor [and] came to Elizabeth Town where we land one boat. Lord, we lay drinking grog etc. that we got out of the Steward's room. All hands [were] on deck dancing and carousing all night.[236]

W 25. This morn very early [the] remainder of us was landed to the greatest of our joy after being prisoner almost 9 month[s]. Here we was carried to the barracks where we drawed 1 pound of bread & the same of beef. We were ordered by our officers to be in readiness to march in the morn up to headquarters.

T 26. This morn very Cold. Two or three of us went about a mile into the Country where we got a fine breakfast of bread & milk, etc. Then [we] returned to the barracks [and] took our packs, what small ones we had, & came to Newark where we made a small halt [and] then to Seacaucus where we put up. We had come all the way barefooted.

F 27 to M 30. This morn set off from Seacaucus. Very pleasant but very hard without Shoes. [We] Came to Fort Constitution where the Rhode Island Regiments were. He[re we] stopped a little while [and] then crossed the north river [and] came to Fort Washington. We] stayed there till almost night [and] then came to East Chester. Stopped there all Night where we was handsomely entertained. In the morn [we] came to New Rochelle where the paymaster gen'l was [located] but could not get our money till then. We was paid off 9 months pay [and] then I proceeded on [and] came to New Rochelle through Westchester New York. Stopped in Greenwich in Connecticut where I got me a pair of shoes.

CHAPTER SIX

PRIVATE MOSES KIMBALL JOURNAL

DESCRIPTION.

The Moses Kimball journal is a sixteen-page account that was written by a private in Captain Henry Dearborn's Company. The journal came into the possession of Dr. L.C. Walker of Jamestown, Ohio, in 1914. He describes the journal written by Kimball being "in an improvised book made of unruled paper 5" long by 4" wide, sewed by hand without a back or cover." In December of 1928, Walker gave his handwritten transcription of the journal to George E. Simmons, Professor of Agronomy at the University of Maine, who turned Walker's longhand transcription into a typescript.

The provenance of the journal is established by Mary A. Harvey, a great granddaughter of Moses Kimball, who gave the manuscript journal to L.C. Walker. Harvey states that "this diary was written by my great grandfather Kimball, while he was a soldier in the years of 1775-76."

The typescript of the journal by Simmons was obtained by Kenneth Roberts while researching his book, *March to Quebec*, and is located in his papers at the Dartmouth Library. Simmons also gave the Maine Historical Society a copy of his typescript. Walker described his transcription as problematic because of the condition of the original. "A great deal of this is worn by time and is not legible."

Kimball's journal as it appears in this compilation is from Simmons typescript from the Maine Historical Society. The journal is included in this compilation because it is not well known and because it is the only journal which has a List of Carrying Places on the Expedition in one table. Kimball also includes entries from his time in prison in Quebec. It is not certain whether Kimball inserted the table in his journal or whether it was done by Walker.

PUBLICATION

Extracts of the Kimball journal is included by Kenneth Roberts in March to Quebec in the footnotes of James Melvin's journal. The first and only full publication of the journal was in *Voices from a Wilderness Expedition*, pp.161-174.

AUTHOR

There were a surprising number of men named Moses Kimball who served in the Revolutionary War. This made it difficult to identifying the Kimball who wrote this journal. In fact, very little is known of Kimball's personal life. Our Moses Kimball was born in Hampstead, New Hampshire on March 3, 1756. He is shown on a muster roll of Captain Hezekiah Hutchins Company in June of 1775 where his occupation is listed as "blacksmith". His company was part of Colonel Reed's Regiment which participated in the Battle of Bunker Hill.

His name appears on a muster roll of Captain Henry Dearborn's Company on the expedition to Quebec. He was taken prisoner in the assault on Quebec and is on the British Army's list of prisoners. There is no record of Kimball serving in the army after the Quebec experience. According to Kimball family history, he married a woman named Hannah and had three children. He died in Vassalboro, Maine in 1789 at the age of thirty-three.

JOURNAL

List of Carrying Places on Expedition

Carrying Places on Kennebec River

No.	Miles	Rods		Carrying Places on Dead River	
1	0	80	1	0	4
			2	0	8
2	0	45	3	0	4
			4	0	15
3	1	0	5	3/4	0
			6	0	4
4	0	80	7	0	3
			8	0	4
			9	3/4	0
			10	0	8
	Great Carrying Place		11	3/4	0
			12	0	?
1	4	0	13	0	2
			14	0	2
2	3/4	0	15	0	15
3	1/2	0			
				Between Kenebec & Chaudière	
4	1/2	0			
			1	3/4	0
			2	1/2	0
			3	can't read, figures torn out	

Sept

2. *An adjorum --- of the ------ Cambridge to General Arnold*[237]

8 *Winter-hill. In the morning there was some difficulty between me &*
my mess mates. It rose to this degree (that) Lieutenant Emerson put two of us
under guard. In about a quarter of an hour he took us out. I immediately went
to (Remainder of page torn out)

(Top of reverse side of torn page)

------- *I went to Plumb Island. [Illegible]boxes on board of the Eagle*
Schooner [illegible] & these lay on board.

19. *10 o'clock sail'd out of the harbor & stood off on [the side] waiting*
for one of the vessels that got on the rocks in the harbor. The men were put on
board the other vessels & we sailed in the afternoon with a fair wind & steered
for Kenebec River[238] *at night-----*

(bottom half of page is destroyed)

23. *Within 6 miles of Fort Western,*[239] *where we arrived the 23ʳᵈ &*
encamped.

24. *On guard at the Fort at night, James McCormick, being drunken, shot*
Sergeant Bishop belonging to Capt Williams Company. McCormick belonging
to Goodrich.[240]

25. *(McCormick) Was tried by Court Martial & found guilty of murder.*

26. *(McCormick) Was sentenced to be hanged & brought to the gallows*
but was repriv'd till General Washington's pleasure was known.

27. *Got our provisions on board the battows [bateaux]*[241] *& proceed'd up*
the River about 4 miles & stopp'd.

28. *Proceeded up the River and found the water very Shoal in some places,*
which caused a rapid current and about 3 miles of ripples.

30. *Arriv'd at Fort Halifax*[242] *where was the first carrying place & it was*
80 rods. The inhabitants of this place depend much on fishing & hunting.
This day found the water very rapid. The land on this part of the River is
much better than that nearer the sea. This evening we carried our Battows &
provisions over.

October

 1. Proceeded up the river. [There were] Bad ripples & at night [we] lodged in the woods.

 2. Went about 10 miles. The weather very cold & rainy.

 3. We arrived at Skowhigin Falls,[243] *which is 40 rods (a)crossed. Got over our Battows & provisions. The land here is thinly inhabited.*

 4. We arrived at Harrigen_walk[244] *where was formerly an Indian town but now settled by the English. Here we took our leave of houses & settlements, entering the wide wilderness. After two days stay here, [we will face a] carrying place of one mile in length.*

 6. Left Harrigen Walk & went 5 miles, where we encamp'd.

 7. Set out very early & went to [illegible] & encamped & as usual took our bottle to make a drink of grog, but found good creature[s] gone which occasion'd dull looks. The land here is very level & good but the River [is] rapid.

 8. We proceeded up the River & crossed Caratunk[245] *& encamped about 3 miles above the falls. It rained all night. Clear'd up in the morning & was very cold.*

 9. Proceeded up River & arrived at the Great Carrying Place.[246]

 10. Went to the first pond which was 4 miles from the river.[247]

 11. Cross'd the first pond which was 3/4 of a mile wide. At this carrying place near the river, Mr. Carr [Senter] built a log house for the sick.[248]

 13. (No entry for 12th*) We cross'd this carrying place to another pond. This carrying place is 3/4 of a mile wide.*

 14. Cross'd the pond which was 1/2 mile wide & got over the carrying place which is 1 1/2 mile in length. The woods here are chiefly cedar & hemlock.

 16. (No entry for 15th*) Cross'd 3d. pond which is 1 1/2 mile. Same day went over 4*[th] *carrying place, being 4 1/2 in length over a boggy swamp. Found it very difficult getting over our Battows & barrels*[249]*, being obliged to wade knee deep. We launched our Battows into a creek which empties itself into Dead River.*[250] *Here we encamp'd, being all greatly rejoiced at [the] thought of being over [the] worst of our fatigue.*

 17. Set out & went 18 miles up the river. Crossed one carrying place of 4 rods. We encamp'd. Fine land for game but not very good on other accounts. The woods chiefly birch & hemlock.

 18. Set out up the River & overtook Col. Green[251] *& his party about*

25 miles up the Dead River. Here we reciv'd orders to get ourselves in a defensive condition. Here the land appears to be very good but the water [is] unwholesome on account of many sorts of leaves falling into the river.

19. We reciev'd orders to push on & accordingly proceeded about 5 miles. Mr Spring & Mr Burr, [252]*not having a pilot, missed their way & travel'd considerable time before they found their way. It rain'd hard all night.*

20. This day found it tedious being both cold & rainy & our Battows very leaky.[253] *This day cross'd the 10th carrying place.*

21. Nothing remarkable. The land very good.

22. March'd through tedious woods & mountains for the most part, but sometimes (were) on the bank of the River where the water was excessive[ly] rapid. The chief [trees] of the woods is hemlock & fir.

23. About this time, Col. Enos & his party turn'd about & went back.[254]

24. Capt. Hanchet[255] *& 60 men were ordered to march on with the greatest dispatch before the main body. Same day sent back about 40 sick & weak men. In the afternoon continued our march, but slowly.*

25. Continued our march. Very bad traveling.

26. Cross'd the 11th carrying place which brought us to the first pond leading to Chaudière River.[256]

27. Cross'd 2d carrying place which was 3 quarters of a mile. Then cross'd 2d pond. Then cross'd 3d carrying place & 3d pond. Then the 4th carrying place & 4th pond, where we left out Battows & encamp'd.

28. Went 10 miles, wading knee deep a great part of the way, & came to a place over flowing where we stop'd [for] some time, not knowing what to do, & at last were obliged to wade up to our arm pits. The ground giving way [at] every step. We got on a little Island where we were obliged to stay, [with] night coming on. We were all wet & cold. This is Saterday.

29. Cross'd a river & waded 40 rods & came to another which we cross'd, & took a wrong way & went 2 miles & came back again. Then went 2 or 3 miles & came to a bark camp & stop'd that night.

30. Came where the River Chaudiere runs out of the pond. Went 20 miles & camp'd.

31. Went 21 [miles]. Capt. Goodrich's Company kil'd our dog to eat.[257] *Camp'd.*

Wensday, November 1. Travel'd 20 miles & camp'd.

2. *Travel'd 4 miles & met [the group bringing] provisions. [The] Same day arrived at the first French inhabitants & stop'd, which was 14 miles further.*[258]

3. *Went 12 miles further. Snow'd all [day].*

4. *Went 16 miles.*

5. *Went 6 miles & stop'd at a clever old Frenchman's house where they gave us rum & bread & butter, as much as we wanted. There was two pretty girls at the same house. Stayed till the next day.*

6. *Marched 18 miles.*

7. *Marched 8 miles. Stormed all day.*

8. *Marched 5 miles & came in sight of Quebec.*

9. *Took a prisoner named McCinsy who was a midshipman.*[259] *We continued at Point Leavy until the 13th.*

13. *In the evening we crossed the River St. Lawrence & went [to] Major Colwells house*[260] *& there stayed kept guard till the 19th of November.*

19. *We set out from the major's house about 3 oclock in the morning. At night reached [our destination] at Point aux Trembles,*[261] *where we stayed until General Montgomery came down with his army.*

December 3. Set out for Quebec in battows with cannon & came to Wolfe's Cove & there landed.

4. *Stayed at Wolfe's Cove all day.*

5. *Went to a nunery which is in [the] edge of the suburbs of Quebec & there stay'd a few days.*[262] *Then went over the River St. Charles*[263] *to the house of Mr. Henry, a minister, & there stay'd till the storming of Quebec.*

31. *An hour before day, Col. Arnold's party came into St. Rock*[264] *& marched on between the water & the town [at the same time] as General Montgomery*[265] *went by Cape Dimond. After daylight, the enemy sallied out at [the] public gate to that degree we were obliged to surrender. There was 375 [men] taken prisoners.*[266]

January 3, 1776. General Carleton call'd for a list of our names [and] age.[267]

4. *All the old country men*[268] *were picked of[f] & called out.*

5. *They were call'd [out] again to be examined by the General.*

6. *They were call'd out & sent to the Barracks, about 80 in number.*

10. *Wednesday. Norris & Martin went to the hospital. Our living is salt pork, bisket, rice & butter & a sufficient [amount] allowed us. And if we were not cheated in our weight by one Downy who is appointed [as our]*

Master Sergeant to deal out our provisions. For instead of being our friend, [he] proved [to be] our Enemy by defrauding us of our allowance by scanty weight & measure.

21. [We] Were ordered to make a return of all tradesmen amongst us. About this time, two of our company who enlisted in Enemy service escape[d] out of town.

30. About this time, Downy made a complaint [against] 15 men which had agreed to fight their way [out] & make their escape. Two of them were found out & sent to the gaol [jail] in irons.

February 12. I went to the hospital.[269] *I return'd from the hospital. Nothing material happened this month.*

March 1. One of our men was put in irons for abusing the sentry.

2. There was an alarm.

13. We were moved to the old goal [jail]. The same is burn proof.[270]

24. We hear our army have left Canada & gone to the line.

26. We hear they have brought 300 prisoners to town.

28. We hear of a cessation of arms.

30. A ship from England arrived here. Brought intelligence that a French fleet from France had arriv'd at America.

April 1. I myself was put in irons with 200 more [other men].

14. Major McKinzie took Capt Morgan's Company out [of] irons.

17. We had a weeks allowance of fine beef brought in which had been kill'd 3 or 4 months. Of which they boast much.

May 4. About 9 or 10 o'clock at night the town was alarm'd & we saw a fire on the water which proved to be a fire ship sent down by our army, but [it] did no damage.

6. About sunrise, 3 ships came up to town. (They) Brought some troops from Boston who marched [from the ships] at 10 o'clock & drove our people off.

7. Our irons was taken off.

14. A ship set sail for England with a packet.

18. Heard that Major Meigs & Capt Dearborn were gone home.[271]

27. Ten ships arrived with troops on board.[272]

June 1. The Hanoverians arrived & [are] said to be about 4 thousand.

5. The General came in & gave us encouragement of sending us to our own country on condition never to bear arms against the King.

6. [We] Sent the Governor an answer.

10. [We had] A thunder storm with hail stones as large as 2 oz. balls. A young woman was kill'd by the lightening.

(?). [preceding words illegible] have had since the arrival of the first troops, and the butter we had was very ordinary, but as we are prisoners we must be glad of anything we can get. This afternoon [we] heard that we were to be exchanged and were to go from this [place] in three days & cross the Lake.

(?). We hear the militia had voted to keep us here & not let us go home at all. Some time[s] we hear some good [news], sometimes bad [news]. This afternoon [we] heard it contradicted about the militia. We heard again we were certainly [going] to go home & very soon. About this time, one of our company was very near out of his head.

(More Text Not Readable)

28. This day Mr. Murray[273] informed us that we should go home in a week or ten days. Likewise that we should have each of us a shirt.

31. We heard [that] our men ha[ve] taken St. John again.

July 1. We hear the Indians have kill'd numbers of the Americans.

5. One of our plans [illegible] which thing I fear will bring us into trouble.

6. (It) Was found out & told to Prentice [that] there was 2 prisoners brought in.

13. We heard that the Commander had got down here.

14. I had a tooth pulled.

16. There was a trifle of dancing. It seemed like old times. This evening Colonel McClain arrived at town.

19. We heard that we were not to go home but [would] stay where we are.

20. This morning George Conner was taken out for talking saucy [sassy] to the Provost.

21. This morning [we] heard that the Lizard had sail'd for England. [The] Same day [we] heard we were to sail in 7 or 8 days.

[page torn & worn. Hard to decipher.]

[Illegible] for the arrival of General Carleton.[274]

(?) This day had a week's allowance of butter brought in which was the first we [illegible].

22 (?). Last night one of our men made their escape out of goal [jail]. About this time a plan was laid for our escape.

31. Our scheme being found out. One of our men, John Hall, went out & discovered the whole of our plot. Same day they put the Sergeants in irons.

August 1. We heard we were to be delivered to Lord Howe & were not to be exchanged. But [would] lay at his disposal.

5. This afternoon Mr. Prentice & Mr. Murray came in & brought our shirts. [At the] same time they took out 35 of the men. This day is 2 months since the General came & gave us encouragement of sending us home. This afternoon we was to go on board but one of the vessels was not ready so we are to go tomorrow.

6. [We signed] kind [of] a parole of honour to go home this afternoon.[275] *I [have] see[n] Major Bigelow & Capt Goodrich.*[276]

7. This morning we embarked on board of the Mermaid.

8. We drawed brisket & pork, 4lbs. of each to 6 men, & 1 gill of rum to each [man].

9. Draw'd fresh beef & soft bread, 1 lb of each to a man. Rum the same as yesterday.

10. This morning a ship arrived from Bristol named Stranger.

11. This morning there was a gun fired for the sail & 2 ships sail'd about a mile down River. The sun [was] about an hour high. At night, another gun was fired & we weighed anchor. [Went] down the river & came to anchor.

12. Stormy weather. Hoisted sail & sailed 44 leagues & came to anchor.

13. High winds [a]head of us so we could not sail any [today].

14. Pleasant weather & a fair wind. Weighed anchor & sail'd 13 leagues & came to anchor about 12 oclock, the wind & tide (being) against us. [We were] within a league of Choodrough, an island. This day we saw white [illegible]. At 4 oclock weighed anchor again. The wind fair. Came to anchor about 2 oclock at night.

15. This morning about sunrise, weighed anchor & sail'd with a fair wind (until) about 3 oclock. (Went) past the Island of Pik.[277]

16. Continued our sail in the afternoon. Bad wind at night. Stormed & windy all night.

17. [Page worn by age]. Fair weather this morning. Saw the whales spout the water. Our course for several days past has been north & north by east. Today it is east.

18. Today our course is south, the winds easterly. We run about 5 knots an hour.

We passed Gaspa Pint, where [there] is a river [that] comes in from Biscay.[278]

19. This morning our course was east and we were sailing along side of St. Johns Island. About 3 o'clock we saw Capertune & Cape Britten. The banks of St Johns Island in some places is very red. About 4 o'clock we saw a frigate on shore. Our course is south east.[279]

20. This day our course is round about [the] islands. Not getting forward very much.

21. Contrary winds. Poor way ahead.

22. Last night at midnight, Capt [illegible] dropped anchor & lay till the sun rose about an hour high. At night for the barge was gone ashore. After [we] weighed anchor our course was south east & by south.

23. Our course was south east for the biggest part of the day. About the middle of the afternoon, we came to the gut of Canso & our course then was southwest & by south & we got through the gut about 10 o'clock at night.[280]

24. Our course today is south east. At 2 o'clock at night, [the] wind [was] westerly. We tack'd about & went northwest.

25. [Here are a mass of indistinct figures evidently referring to the degree of latitude & longitude].

26. [Top of page torn away]. The sea is very calm. No wind hardly. What there was was west a little. [In the] afternoon, we saw a very [large] number of porpoises.

27. This morning there was a dreadful sea. The wind southeast. Our course southwest & by south. We ran at the rate of 7 knots an hour all day. Th[ough] some of the time we run 7 1/2 [knots] per hour.

28. This morning no wind. We lay tossing about.

29. But little wind in the morning. At noon a good N.E. wind blew our course WSW.

30. Our course the same as yesterday.

31. A very good breeze all day. Steering to the west. This day Lieut. [illegible] caught a dolphin of 7 or 8 lbs.

Sunday, September 1, 1776. This morning the wind shifted into the NWS. Our course is S.W. & by W. At 12 o'clock the Capt. & the mate took an observation & said we were in the latitude of 30 & [a] half.

2. This day our course is S.W. & by S & by W. The wind nice.

3. In the morning for an hour the wind was S, then shifted into the N.W. From 8 to 12 o'clock our course was S. Then tacked & went N. W. The wind

W & by S. This day at 12 o'clock we were in the latitude of 37 & 19. This day I see some flying fish.

4. This morning one of our men caught a small shark. Our course is northerly. We have a head wind. Last night there was flying fish [that] came aboard of us.

5. This morning our course is N west & so continued all day.

6. Our course the same as yesterday. The wind [is] northerly.

7. A calm [sea] all day. At night [we had] a small breeze & [it] arose higher & higher.

8. This morning our course is N.W. The wind in [illegible]. We run at the rate of 6 knots an hour. About 1 o'clock we sprung our main topmast. In the afternoon we had a thunder shower.

9. Continued our course. The wind N.E.

10. Our course [is] westerly. The wind [is] southerly.

11. Our course [was] S.W. until 1 o'clock, then [we] went N.W. This night we made land.

12. This morning we see land all round before us & we saw the light house. About 7 o'clock there came a pilot on board of us. At 9 o'clock [we] came to anchor. At 1 o'clock [we] weighed anchor & sail'd again & went about 5 miles above the narrows where we came to anchor. In this harbor there is 4 or 5 hundred sail of shipping, [the] biggest part of which is transports.

13. Here we lay in the harbor in sight of New York. About 5 o'clock the King's troops lay siege to the town.

14. We lay in the harbor. Nothing of [con]sequence.

15. This morning there was a land engagement between the King's troops & our people & so continued by spells all day. At 3 o'clock [in the] afternoon New York was taken.

16. This night [New] York was set on fire & our men have taken everything out of town that is of any worth.

17. We have no news about having our liberty. Pleasant weather.

18. Pleasant and warm.

19. No news today.

20. Tonight at 11 oclock the Town was set on fire by our men.

21. This afternoon we hear that orders is given out that we shall be landed next Monday at 8 o'clock.

22. Sunday. My disorder increases daily.

23. Those on board of Lord Sandwich came on board the Mermaid. Weighed anchor & went down between Staten Island & the main land.

24. In the morning I was landed at Elizabethtown in New Jersey & stayed there sick until the 20th of October.[281]

19. October. My brother Joseph came to town.

20. Sunday. This morning [we] set out for home where I reach the [illegible].

(Here the record ends)

The above mentioned manuscript came into my hands in the following manner: While traveling through Ohio I met Dr. L.C. Walker of Jamestown, Ohio, who gave me the first information I had concerning the manuscript. He very kindly drew up a copy and forwarded it to me. It reached me shortly after December 20, 1928. This copy was made from the original long hand copy which Dr. Walker sent me. It has been checked by myself and verified by my stenographer.

George E. Simmons
Professor of Agronomy
College of Agriculture
University of Maine

Orono, Maine

July 6, 1934

CHAPTER SEVEN

SERGEANT WILLIAM MCCOY JOURNAL

DESCRIPTION.

In 1776, less than one year after the American assault on Quebec, a printer in Glasgow, Scotland published "A Journal of the March of a Party of Provincials from Carlisle to Boston and from Thence to Quebec." That journal contained the record of the march to Boston and then Quebec made by Captain William Hendricks' Pennsylvania rifle company. The journal covers a longer period of time than most because it begins on July 13, 1775 and ends on December 31, 1775. Based upon the original publishing date of that journal, there is no doubt of its authenticity.

After it came out, several writers concluded that the journal was written by Hendricks himself, and began referring to it as the Hendricks journal, probably because it was a narrative about his company. However, the John Joseph Henry journal states that Sergeant William McCoy gave a "genuine copy of his journal" to Major Murray of the Quebec garrison. Henry was in the Quebec prison with William McCoy of the Hendricks Company, and knew the barracks-master, Major Murray. In 1808, Henry wrote a letter to another expedition alumnus, Francis Nichols, stating that he had been assisted in his own journal writing "by the notes of Gen. Meigs and Wm. McCoy, one of our sergeants." The McCoy "notes" that Henry refers to is the McCoy journal which had been published prior to Henry's journal from 1812. The Meigs' notes would be the journal written by Major Return J. Meigs and published in 1776 in America.

In 1991, Raymond M. Bell and Chauncey E. McCoy published a reprinting of the McCoy journal in which they persuasively made the case for McCoy, not Hendricks, being the author of the journal. Despite the evidence offered by Henry's journal and the Bell and McCoy limited reprinting, the McCoy journal is still most often called the Provincial journal. The arguments supporting McCoy being the real author are provided in *Voices from a Wilderness Expedition* on p. 66.

One of the compelling arguments is that the concluding entries describe the assault on Quebec the night of December 31 and the subsequent defeat of the Americans. Hendricks was killed during the assault and could not have known or written about the events described in the journal about the assault.

Kenneth Roberts did not include this journal is his compilation because he placed it in the same category as the Stocking, Ware, Wild and Tolman journals. He chose to include the Stocking journal as the best representative of that category. A review of the journals revealed that roughly half of the entries from McCoy do have similarities to the other journals in word usage for some phrases or sentences. However, there is no daily entry in the McCoy journals that contains identical or even closely similar language to those found in the other journals that Roberts referenced. Roberts' conclusion in terms of the similarity of the other journals is not supported by the facts.

McCoy's journal is unique because it is one of only three journals from the Pennsylvania rifle companies. The other journals being Private George Morison's, which Roberts includes in his book, and the Pennsylvania Packet journal from this compilation. McCoy's journal is the only one that includes entries describing the route from Pennsylvania to Boston in the summer of 1775. It also has more details of the death of Lieutenant McClellan of Hendricks' Company, who died in the wilderness.

PUBLICATION.

Although the McCoy journal has been in four publications, the only publication that had any notable distinction was in the 1893 Pennsylvania Archives, Series 2, Vol. 15.

AUTHOR.

William McCoy was born about 1747 in eastern Pennsylvania and in 1766 his family moved to Rye Township in Perry County, Pennsylvania.

One source states that prior to the war William taught school in Mifflintown in present Juniata County.

William McCoy enlisted in the Captain William Hendricks Rifle Company in July of 1776 and became a sergeant in that company. He most likely did so because of his friendship with his neighbor, John McClelland, who was also in the company as a lieutenant. McCoy went to Boston with the Hendricks' Company which George Washington assigned to Arnold's expedition in August of 1775. In the assault, Hendricks was killed and McCoy and the rest of his company were captured and held as prisoners in Quebec. According to Henry, McCoy was the "clerk of the kitchen" who gave the prisoners "every advantage our melancholy situation afforded him." Henry also identifies McCoy as one of the organizers of a failed escape plan, which was leaked to the British by one of the Americans. McCoy was released by the British with the other American prisoners and arrived in Elizabethtown, New Jersey on September 24, 1776.

There is no other record of Revolutionary War service by McCoy. After he returned home to Mifflintown, he married a woman named Rachael in the fall of 1777. In 1789, McCoy was appointed by the Provincial Council to be a Justice of the Peace for the Township of Fermanagh in what was then Mifflin County, PA. In 1795, he is listed as one of the signers of a subscription to help fund the completion of a Presbyterian Church in Mifflintown. He was living in Mifflin County in the 1790 Federal Census with five members in his household. William McCoy died in 1797 in Mifflin County leaving his wife and children. He left an impressive legacy of future soldiers. His grandson, Thomas Franklin McCoy, was a Civil War general, and a great grandson, General Frank Ross McCoy, was a well-known soldier and diplomat in the first half of the twentieth century.

JOURNAL

The following authentic Journal, wrote by an Officer of the Party, was sent from a Gentleman in Quebec to his Friend in Glasgow, who put it into the hands of the Printers. They have subjoined an Account of the Engagement at Quebec, which was wrote by the same Gentleman who transmitted the Journal.

(THE JOURNAL of Captain William Hendricks, and Captain John Chambers, of the Rifle Men, from Carlisle in Pennsylvania to Boston in Massachusetts, and from thence to Quebec, begun July 13th, and ending December 31st, 1775.)

July 13. Marched from Carlisle, the county town of Cumberland, with my company of 90 men, John McClellan, Francis Nichols, and Matthew Irvine, [were] my lieutenants. First day came to John Harris's ferry on Susquehanna River, two miles wide, and there we encamped. 18 miles.

July 14. Marched to Hummelstown, 8 miles.

July 15. To Lebanon. 17 miles.

July 16. To the sign of the King of Prussia. 18 miles.

July 17. To Riding [Reading, PA.], county town of Berks. 14 miles.

Stayed at Riding until the 22d. Here we met Capts. Paterson, Smith, Lowden, and Noggle, with their companies, destined for Cambridge.

July 22. To Swan's Tavern [Kurtztown, PA.]. 18 miles

July 23. To Allan's town [Allentown]. 18 miles

July 24. To Bethlem [Bethlehem], over the rivers Jordan and great Lehay, to Easton. 18 miles. Note: Bethlem is a small town pleasantly situated on the banks of the Lehay. Here are beautiful gardens, with all kinds of fruit and flowers, and also an elegant nunnery.

July 25. Crossed Delaware river into Jerseys, and to Oxford Meeting-house. 13 miles

July 26. To the Log gaol [jail], where we tarried and feathered one of the ministerial tools, who refused to comply with the resolves of our Continental Congress.

July 27. To Sussex Court house. 10 miles.

July 28. To Dr. Hinksman's. 23 miles.

July 29. To Brewster's Tavern. 22 miles.

July 30. To New Windsor, on North or Hudson's river. 11 miles.

July 31. Rested at New Windsor, to get our linens washed, and ourselves recruited, being weary, marching in exceeding hot weather.

August 1. Proceeded on our march to Tarkin's, 27 miles.

August 2. To Baker's Tavern. 25 miles.

August 3. Thro' Litchfield, a small town in Connecticut government, where Capt. Price, from Maryland, came up with us, and brought with him another ministerial tool, whom he had caught on his march. Here they tarr'd and feather'd him; and, after his making acknowledgments, was drummed out of town. We then marched on to [illegible] Tavern, 29 miles.

August 4. Arrived at Hartford, the chief town in Connecticut government. This town is pleasantly situated on Connecticut river. In this place are seven very elegent Presbyterian parish churches. 22 miles.

August 5. Crossed the river, about 80 perches wide, and marched through Farmington

to Tunis, 29 miles.

August 6. To Mr. Thomson's Meeting-house. 28 miles.

August 7. To Mindon, a small village. 21 miles.

August 8. To Mr. Ellis's Tavern. 23 miles.

August 9. To headquarters at Cambridge, four miles from Boston. Encamped at Cambridge until the 11th of September, and met with 11 companies of musqueteers, which, with our two companies from Carlisle, made 13, amounting to 1000 men, under the command of Colonel William Thomson of Carlisle. During our stay here, nothing very material happened until the:

3d of September, that 1000 of the American troops went from Prospect-hill, to raise a battery on Plowed-hill, about a quarter of a mile from the enemy on Bunker's-hill; during the time that our men were at work, the enemy kept a constant fire from their cannon on Bunker's-hill, and from a floating battery which lay contiguous to us in the bay, which killed 2 or 3 of our people, and wounded a few more; but as soon as our people got some of their cannon mounted, they sunk the floating battery, killed several of the enemy, and obliged them on Bunker's-hill to keep close within their entrenchments. This day was wounded Mr. William Simpson, a young gentleman volunteer with Capt. Smith, from Lancaster county (Pennsylvania). He was wounded in the foot, had his leg cut off, and died soon after. During these transactions, we were informed General Washington had received letters from gentlemen in Quebec, inviting him to send some troops thither, concluding it would be for the safety of the colonies.

Accordingly General Washington ordered 11 companies of musket-men, with three rifle-men [companies], to march for Canada. The rifle captains cast lots who should go, and it fell to Capts. Hendricks and Smith of Pennsylvania, and Capt. Morgan of Maryland [Virginia], who, together with 11 companies of musket-men, under the command of Colonel Benedict Arnold, began their march for Canada; the whole detachment amounting to 1000 men.

September 11. Marched to Mr. Neal's Tavern, 13 miles.

September 12. To Mr. Bunkham's Meeting-house. 15 miles.

September 13. Arrived at Newberry[282], a sea-port town, 45 miles N. E. Of Boston, and there encamped until the 18th, when we embarked on board 11 sail of sloops and schooners, which lay ready to receive us.[283] Lay on board all night in the harbor.

September 19. In the morning we weighed anchor and steered our course for Kinnebec river, 36 leagues N. E. of Newberry.[284]

September 20. Arrived at the mouth of the river in the morning, after a good passage of 23 hours. Fair wind, round sea. Most of our people were seasick. 125 miles

September 21. Sailed up the river for Fort Western, where we arrived the 23d, 45 miles[285]

September 25. Embarked on board 200 batteaus ready to receive us, and rowed up to Fort Halifax. 18 miles[286]

September 27. Pushed against the stream to Taconic falls.[287] Here we carried our boats, provisions, etc., forty perches or so, and pushed up farther, 3 miles .

September 28. Pushed up eight miles, the water full of rocks and shoals. The men got into the water to haul the boats over; the bottom so uneven, that the men were sometimes up to the chin in water. 8 miles

September 29. Pushing against the stream to the second Carrying Place, Cohigin falls.[288] 10 miles

September 30. Carried boats, etc., over 60 perches and pushed up the stream, 5 miles

October 1. Pushed and dragged up over rocks and shoals, where we, from the unevenness of the bottom, sometimes plunged over [our] head. We got to the third Carrying Place, Norridge Walk falls.[289] 7 miles

October 2. Carried over boats, etc., and encamped, and entered a wild barren wilderness, birch, pine, hemlock. Some parts of the river side good bottom, with sugar trees. 1-1/4 miles

October 3. Pushing and dragging. Today killed a moose-deer. 11 miles

October 4. Pushed and dragged to Tentucket falls [Hellgate or Devil's Falls].[290] *Carried 40 perches, and encamped. 8 miles*

October 5, 6, 7. We poled and dragged against a shallow stream, and encamped at the place where we leave Kinnebec. [In] Three days made 20 miles.[291]

October 8. Lay in our tents on account of a heavy rain.

October 9, 10, 11. [We] Carried boats, etc. three miles and a quarter over a high hill, [a] very bad way, to the first pond in the Carrying Place, and made one mile and a half more, and encamped.[292]

October 12, 13. Carried three quarters of a mile to a second pond, a mile over; then two miles land to the third pond, two miles over, and encamped. 5 miles.

October 14, 15. Carried three miles and a quarter to Dead River, a mile of this way [was] very swampy. We were up to the knees in mud. Then up the river's side a mile more.[293]

October 16. The water now being deep and dead, we plied our oars, and rowed. This river comes from the N. W. running S. E. four perches wide. Here the water very black. 10 miles.

October 17. After having carried over a short Carrying Place, [we] rowed, 16 miles

October 18. Rowed up 20 miles, and carried over a short Carrying Place. 20 miles

October 19. This day we made 4 Carrying Places and on our way, 5 miles

October 20, 21, 22. Encamped on account of the heavy rain.

October 23. The water now being shallow, we threw our oars aside, and took to our poles. We pushed up, 10 miles.

October 24. [Because] Our provisions now growing very scant, and some of our men sick, the several captains concluded to send the sick back, and a captain with 50 men forward, to reach the inhabitants as soon as possible, in order to send us supplies of provisions before we should run out. Accordingly the sick were sent back, and Capt. Hanchet, with 50 men, [was sent] forward. Sometime before this, Colonel Innes [Enos}, with three companies of musket-men, turned back, being discouraged by the many difficulties they met with; and our third lieutenant, Mr. Irvine, being sick, was left at the first pond, in care of a corporal and three men. This day several of our boats were overset, and much baggage, provisions, and ammunition, were lost, with some few guns. We got forward this day, 9 miles.[294]

October 25. Snowed all last night, and very cold. Pushed up this day, and crossed two Carrying Places, 8 miles.

October 26. This day pushed up through four ponds, and carried over two Carrying Places, one a mile over, the ground covered with snow, 7 miles.

October 27. This day crossed a pond half a mile over, carried 15 perches to another pond, two miles over, to the greatest Carrying Place. Here it was agreed, by the several companies, to leave all the boats, except a few to carry the sick down Chaudiere[295] *after having carried them near 20 miles over mountains and rocks, and through such swamps as were never passed by man before. Our shoulders were so bruised by them that we could not suffer anything to touch them. Our company carried but one boat over, which was to take our lieutenant down the Chaudiere. The carriage here [was] to a small stream leading to Chaudiere pond, four miles and a half. Here we encamped, 7 miles.*[296]

October 28. We dealt out our flour, (meat we had none) four pints per man. Here we received a letter from Colonel Arnold, who had gone two days before, letting us know we were within four days march of the inhabitants, and might expect to meet provisions in three days time. [Also]That General Schuyler had gained an advantage over the ministerial troops near St. John's, by killing and taking a number of them. This news put us in high spirits; but it proved hurtful to many of us; for we, supposing we were much nearer the inhabitants than we really were, ate up our bread more lavishly than otherwise we would have done.

October 29. Set out thro' the woods for the head of Chaudiere river, and marched fourteen miles today, through swamps, in many places up to our knees, and over trees; that lay on the ground, covering it for several perches together, 14 miles.[297]

October 30. This day went astray over mountains and through swamps, which could scarcely be passed by wild beasts. Waded a small river up to our [waists], then marched on until night in our wet clothes. At night we found ourselves within five miles of the place we started from. We marched fifteen miles in vain.

October 31. This morning set off on the path our advanced party had taken before, in better spirits than for many days past. In the evening came up with Mr. McClellan, our first lieutenant, who had come down the Chaudiere, in a batteau, with four of our men to row the boat. They had been overset in the river, narrowly escaping being drowned; they lost clothes, blankets, and ammunition. Capts. Smith and Morgan were also cast away in the river. Capt. Smith lost his chest and clothes, with his officers' clothes, and a considerable sum of money. Capt. Morgan also lost his clothes and cash; one of his men was drowned. They then all took to the land and made the best of their way towards the inhabitants. Mr. McClellan being far spent, and unable to march, was left in care of two of our company; he was greatly beloved by the whole detachment. Here our Captain, and some others of our company divided their small moiety of bread and flour with him, parting in great tenderness, never expecting to see him more; we then marched on till night, in a very deplorable condition, several of the company being out of provisions. We marched today, 25 miles.[298]

November 1, This morning many of the company falling behind, being weary and faint for want of provisions, Capt. Hendricks thought it best to make forward as fast as possible to the inhabitants, with what men were with him. Our case being desperate, and every man, willing to save his life, if possible, marched on over mountains, and through swamps, enough to weary and discourage the stoutest traveler. On our way, passed some of the musket-men eating two dogs, which they had roasted skins, guts, and all, not having eat[en] anything for two, some three, days before. I myself saw one of them offer a dollar, to one of our company, for a bit of cake not above two ounces. At night, we encamped in a very deplorable condition; some of us had not eaten for 24 hours. We made today, 20 miles.[299]

November 2. This morning, when we arose, many of us were so weak that we could scarce stand; I myself staggered about like a drunken man. We got our packs on our backs, and marched off, hoping to see the inhabitants this day: A small stick, lying across the way, was sufficient to bring the stoutest of us to the ground. In the evening, we saw some cattle coming up the river, the most joyful sight that we had ever seen. When we came to them, the men who drove them told us, we were then 20 miles from the nearest inhabitants; and that Colonel Arnold had got in two days before, and immediately sent off these cattle for our relief. Accordingly some went to work, and, in a short time, had one of the beasts killed and dressed. This night we fared sumptuously. We marched this day, 20 miles.[300]

November 3. This day marched 20 miles, wading several small rivers, some of them up to our waists, the water exceeding cold. In the evening came in sight of a house, the first we had seen for four weeks. Here we encamped all night, and got plenty of good beef and potatoes, little or no bread. 20 miles.

November 4. Snow in the night. Marched down the river, which was thickly settled. 10 miles

November 5. Continued our march down the river, the people kind and hospitable, provisions plenty, at a high price; we paid 1 sh[illing] Sterl. per quart of milk, and 1 sh[illing] for a small loaf of bread, about 3 lb. Today we came, 12 miles.

November 6. Came up with Col. Arnold and the advanced party. [We] halted till 2 o'clock, then marched till 12 at night. Most of the way half leg deep in mud and water, 17 miles.

November 7. Marched this morning 3 miles, halted till evening, when a Lieut. with 20 men, was ordered forward to see if the way was clear. Accordingly they marched till near 2 o'clock in the morning, then halted in sight of Quebec, the river St. Lawrence being between us and the city, 9 miles. In all 979 miles.

November 8. Quartered along the river's side [Point Levi] until our men, which were behind, should come up. Remained here until the 13th, when most of the men who were behind alive came up, [and] who informed us that several of the musket-men had perished of hunger in the woods, and also some rifle-men, among whom was John Taylor of Capt. Hendrick's company. During our stay here, Capt. Morgan took a midshipman, belonging to a frigate in the harbor, who came ashore, with some men in a boat, to carry away flour from a mill on our side the river. A frigate of 20 guns, some few merchant-men, and small craft, [were] in the harbor.[301]

November 13. Crossed the river, this night, in long boats and canoes. Some clothes and guns were lost. Got all safe over in the morning to a place called Wolf's cove.[302]

November 14. This morning were fired upon by the frigate, but received no damage. Took up our quarters in some good houses near the town, which were deserted by the owners. Took several prisoners, who informed us that there was not more than 100 regular soldiers in the town, besides a number of sailors, and other new recruits, amounting, in the whole, to between 3 and 400 men under arms. The first day we came over the river, we passed close by the city walls, and gave three cheers, then marched off, without being molested by them in the town. They fired some cannon, but did no execution.

November 21. Marched up the river to Point au Tremble, 20 miles; our ammunition being insufficient to attack the town with. Here we were joined by Gen. Montgomery, with the New York troops, who had taken St. John's, Fort Chamblee and Montreal, where they found considerable stores of ammunition, provisions, and clothing, with a great number of cannon, and took near 700 prisoners. Here the two men, who had been left with Mr. McClellan upon Chaudière, came to us and informed us that they had buried him at the first inhabited house they came to, after he had been brought down by two Indians hired by Capt. Smith for that purpose. Continued at Point au Tremble till the 5th of December, when we marched back to Quebec, and laid siege to the town. We continued the siege till the 30th of December, during which time some were killed on both sides.[303]

The evening of the 30th prepared to attack the city. Gen. Montgomery, with the New York forces on one side, and Col. Arnold, with his detachment from Boston, on the other side. Accordingly, about 5 o'clock in the morning of the 31st begun the attack; but the snow being so deep, where the General made the attack, they could not reach the wall; they retreated back to their quarters. Col. Arnold's party carried on the attack, but he being wounded in the beginning of the affair, went back. Captain Morgan then took the lead, who with Capt. Hendricks, and four or five other companies, with some of their men, got over the walls, drove the enemy from their cannon, and got a considerable way into the town, when at length, they being surrounded on all sides, and over powered by numbers, we were obliged to surrender [as] prisoners of war, being assured of good quarters.[304]

The End of the JOURNAL.

CHAPTER EIGHT

MATTHIAS OGDEN JOURNAL

DESCRIPTION.

The original manuscript journal written by Matthias Ogden is located in the Lloyd W. Smith Archival Collection in the Morristown National Historical Park. It was originally in the Collections of the Washington Association of New Jersey at Morristown, but was donated to Morristown National Historical Park sometime after 1928 when it was first published by the New Jersey Historical Society. The Morristown National Historical Park has provided me with a copy of the Ogden journal manuscript on microfilm. The journal begins on October 27, 1775 and ends abruptly on November 15, 1775.

The authenticity of the Ogden journal is confirmed by various entries in the journal which are verified by other contemporary documents and journals as explained below. I first encountered the argument for the authorship of the journal attributed to Matthias Ogden by Marie Blades' in her pamphlet published by the Morris County Historical Society in 1980.[305] Blades makes the beginning of the case that the journal she found in her local library was the journal of a volunteer on the expedition named Matthias Ogden. Unfortunately Blades was not aware that Ogden's journal had already been identified and published in 1928 in the New Jersey Historical Society Proceedings.

The Ogden journal has an entry for November 14 explaining that Arnold wrote a letter to the British Commander demanding the surrender of the city and sent it to the walls of Quebec by a man and a drummer. The journal states that "I was the person appointed for going in with the flag." The British responded to the flag with a cannon ball and Ogden says that he and his drummer "retreated in quick time till under the cover of the hill."

This is a clear statement of an action by the journalist and would confirm Ogden being the journalist if it was verified by others. Based on my research, I have discovered the following two journals that mention Ogden by name as being the one who went in with the flag on the 14th.

- Senter's Historical Society of Pennsylvania journal as found in Roberts has an entry for Nov. 14: "Attempted to send a flag of truce by Maj. Ogden…"
- Henry Dearborn's original journal entry for Nov. 14 states" 'Capt. Ogden was sent with a flag of truce to demand the town and citadel… but they fired upon him."

Dearborn's Massachusetts Historical Society journal, Meig's journal and Arnold's letter to British Lieut. Gov. Cramahe on Nov. 15, all of which are found in Robert's book, mention that a flag of truce was sent out on Nov. 14 but was fired up before it reached the wall. None of these journals mention the name of the officer who went out with the flag but do confirm that a flag was sent out.

Another entry in Ogden's journal for November 14 is a description of his being selected by Arnold "to set the out-sentries next [to] the town. I accordingly did, after which, on hearing the ship firing at our guard that was placed at Wolfe's Cove over the canoes, on my return I observed the guard turning out." This assignment was referred to by John Joseph Henry in his journal, included in Roberts' compilation, as follows: "a Mr. Ogden, a cadet from Jersey, a large and handsome young man in favor with Arnold had been authorized by Arnold to place the sentinels that day."

The above references are sufficient evidence to confirm that Ogden is the author of the journal. The title of the journal in Morristown National Historical Park is "Journal of Gen. Matthias Ogden while serving as a volunteer in Arnold's Campaign against Quebec."

As Blades points out, Senter's journal indicates that during the assault on Quebec, "Before the Colonel was done with, Major Ogden came in wounded through the left shoulder, which proved only a flesh wound." Colonel Benedict Arnold confirms this fact in his letter to General Wooster in Montreal on December 31st after informing him that Montgomery had been killed also informs him that he (Arnold) was wounded and carried off the field to the hospital. He further informs Wooster, "The loss of my detachment, before I left it, was about two hundred men, killed and wounded. Among the latter is Major Ogden…" John Pierce in his journal confirms that both Arnold and Ogden were wounded in the assault. "Col Arnold is very bad with his wound, Majr Ogden is some better…"

John Joseph Henry's journal makes the claim that Ogden was one of the men who supported Arnold when he left the field to go to the hospital after he was shot in the leg. No other account mentions the presence of Ogden at that time, and if the wounding of Ogden is accurate, one wonders how much support he could have offered to Arnold who did have a serious wound. It seems more likely that Ogden had followed Arnold to the hospital.

The journal as published by the New Jersey Historical Society suggests that first part of Ogden's journal was likely lost because the journal they have begins on October 27, 1775, which is more than a month into the expedition. The introduction states: "It is evident that what was written was done often under circumstances of haste, and we have occasionally supplied words where necessary and corrected misspellings."

Ogden's journal is well written and he is able to describe his experiences in clear language. His entries contain just enough detail to give the reader an understanding of how difficult the journey was and how much the men suffered as they made their way through the wilderness. Although Ogden's account covers a limited period of time, it is easily one of best journals written about the expedition. It deserves more recognition than it has earned to date.

Ogden's journal includes the only detailed description of the expedition's crossing the St. Lawrence River to Wolfe's Cove. Ogden makes it clear that the crossing was more difficult than any of the other journals portray. Ogden's account adds a further dimension to this important event.

Although published in 1928, Ogden's journal has not attracted any significant attention and is largely unknown. One reason may be that Ogden was a volunteer on the expedition and some might have assumed that his experiences were not significant. His friendship with Aaron Burr may also be a factor due to Burr's negative reputation as the killer of Alexander Hamilton in their famous duel. His friendship with Benedict Arnold may also be a factor after Arnold, due to his changing sides, became the negative representation of the war. Whatever the reason it is clear that Colonel Benedict Arnold had high respect for Matthias Ogden for his efforts on the expedition. Due in some part to Arnold's favorable impression, Ogden was given a larger role during the expedition and the assault than his initial volunteer status would indicate.

PUBLICATION.

The only significant previous publication was in the 1928 Proceedings of the New Jersey Historical Society, Vol. XIII, No. I.

AUTHOR.

Matthias Ogden was born in Elizabeth, New Jersey on October 12, 1754. He attended the College of New Jersey in Princeton where one of his classmates was Aaron Burr. In the late summer of 1775, Ogden and Burr joined the Arnold expedition together as gentlemen volunteers. Ogden was wounded in the shoulder in the assault on Quebec and joined Arnold in the hospital. After the battle, Arnold wrote a letter to Washington offering high praise for volunteers Ogden, Burr and Eleazer Oswald, all of whom he said "behaved extremely well."

In March 1776, Ogden was commissioned as a lieutenant colonel in the First Regiment of the New Jersey Continental Line and was promoted to full colonel on January 1, 1777. He served at Fort Ticonderoga in 1777 and was in the Battle of Monmouth. Ogden was captured by the British at a skirmish in Elizabethtown, New Jersey, in November of 1780 but was exchanged after being held in New York for a few months.

In 1783, Ogden was granted a leave from his military duties by Congress in order to secure a business relationship with the French government. Ogden traveled to France to negotiate an agreement with the French and was awarded with a special honor by the French King. While he was in France, Congress commissioned him as a Brigadier General by brevet in September 1783. He returned from France on October 31, 1783 to personally deliver the news of the signing of the Treaty of Paris ending the war.

After the war, Ogden served in the State of New Jersey Legislative Council and made his living operating one of the mints making a new state coin for New Jersey. In the 1789 Presidential election, he served as an elector for New Jersey. Ogden died of Yellow fever in Elizabethtown on March 31, 1791, at the age of thirty-six. His early death could have prevented Ogden from becoming even more famous than he was at the time of his death.

JOURNAL

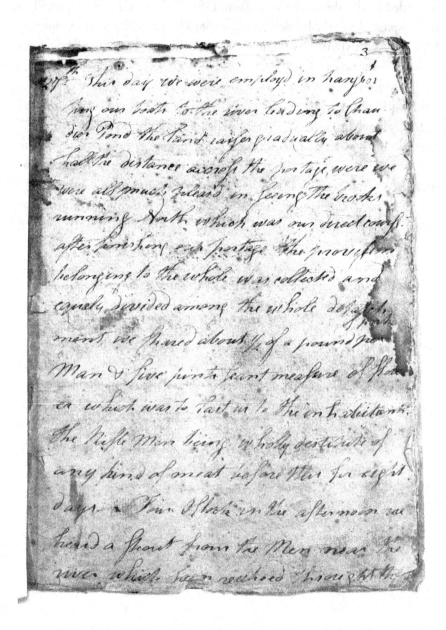

In the Fall of 1775, Colonel (afterward, Brigadier-General) Benedict Arnold, under instructions from General Washington, with a detachment of about 1,100 men drawn from the army about Boston, headed an

Expedition against Quebec. Major Matthias Ogden (as he then was; later a Colonel and still later Brigadier-General) was one of the officers who went with it. He was the son of Robert and Phebe (Hetfield) Ogden, and was born at Elizabethtown, New Jersey, Oct. 22, 1754. Gov. Aaron Ogden was his brother. Matthew died at the age of 36 years, and is buried in the First Presbyterian graveyard, in Elizabeth, New Jersey. The journal kept by him, as published below, is prefaced by a note by some later writer, which says:

"This Expedition was in two Battalions, one commanded by Lieut-Col. Christopher Green, the other by Lieut-Col. Roger Enos. The latter, on October 25, turned back with his division of about five hundred men, abandoning their comrades, who were in advance. The Expedition left Cambridge, Mass., September 14, and marched to Newburyport. From thence the men were transported to the mouth of the Kennebec by water. They proceeded up the Kennebec and over the carrying places to the Dead river; up the Dead river to the Height-of-Land, where they carried their boats over to Lake Ammeguntic, the head of Chaudiere river. This journal begins at this carrying-place.

"Down the Chaudiere river the Expedition proceeded to the St. Lawrence, which was reached on November 8th. Arnold crossed the river and ascended to the Heights of Abraham, but his force was too feeble to make an attack. The journal ends with an account of his flag of truce.

"On December 1, Gen. Montgomery arrived with reinforcements and, on the night of December 30, the unfortunate assault was made. Ogden was with Arnold's party in its attack through St. Roc and was wounded in the shoulder. The same day Arnold sent an express to Gen. Washington, in which he said, after giving an account of his part in the engagement: 'The loss of my detachment, before I left it, was about twenty men killed and wounded; among the latter is Major Ogden, who, with Captain Oswald, Captain Burr and the other volunteers, behaved extremely well. "On his return to the main army Ogden was commissioned Colonel of the First Regiment in the New Jersey Line and served as such until near the close of the War, when he was promoted Brigadier-General, vice Maxwell, resigned.'"

THE JOURNAL STARTS AT THIS POINT

Oct. 27ᵗʰ. This day we were employed in transporting our boats to the river leading to Chaudier Pond.[306] *The land raises gradually about half the distance across the portage, where we were all much pleased in seeing the brooks running north, which was our direct course. After finishing our portage the provision belonging to the whole was collected and equally divided among the whole detachment. We shared about ½ of a pound of pork per man and five pints, scant measure, of flour, which was to last us to [reaching] the inhabitants. The Rifle men were wholly destitute of any kind of meat before this for eight days. At four o'clock in the afternoon we heard a shout from the men near the river, which soon reached throughout the Camp. We received a letter from Col. Arnold*[307] *informing us of the return of the two Indians, from whom he received an answer to his letter to Quebec, informing him that the inhabitants were much rejoiced at our near approach, would assist in repulsing the King's Troops there and forever go hand in hand with us.*

Our men were much rejoiced and their spirits animated at this good news, for never were men more fatigued. At any time, nor ever, could men bear up under it better than they. Surely no person, unless he was present, could form any idea of the hardships surmounted.

In Col. Arnold's letter he directed us to take a northeast course from the height of land,[308] *which would bring us to Chaudier river*[309] *beyond the pond. At this they returned (all but those belonging to the boats) to the hill, where they encamped. The remainder belonging to the boats, about 10 in number, had orders to set off by daylight and wait the arrival of the landmen at the entrance of Chaudier. Col. Arnold informs us likewise that in six days he will meet us with provisions.*

28ᵗʰ. In the morning, being disappointed in my boat that was taken back by the express sent by Col. Arnold, Col. Green[310] *sent word that I might send back the boat's crew belonging to the Company and take her for myself. Accordingly, by sun-up I set off with Messrs. Burr and Melcher with a Lieut. belonging to Capt. Thayre.*[311] *We followed a small stream, which in about 10 miles led us to Amegunti Lake, or Chaudier pond. We then steered northeast and overtook Capts. Morgan and Smith*[312] *at an Indian hut by the side of the lake. We kept our course till we were stopped at the upper end of the lake, [which is] about 16 miles in length.*

We found we had passed the mouth of the river. We, however, encamped. The sight of our smoke led up Capts. Morgan and Smith's boat, with one belonging to Capt. Ward.[313] *Being late, they all encamped with us.*

29th. After rowing about three miles back we made the mouth of the river. We put in and ran down the river with amazing swiftness from the rapidity of the current, about 10 miles, where we found one of Capt. Smith's boats dashed on the rocks with all her lading lost. We stopped and agreed to join with him and set off immediately for the inhabitants. We set off on foot at 2 o'clock, seven in number. After travelling two miles we came up with an officer belonging to Capt. Goodrich, who informed us that his boat split against the rocks, and he had lost four days' provision per man belonging to the Company, with every other thing in her. We travelled on, steering northeast.[314]

In about an hour after, Capt. Goodrich passed us with his men, who had been out of provision two days. We encamped by sunset beside a brook, we judged 18 miles from the river's mouth.

This day was somewhat solitary. We were separated from the main body and almost destitute of provision of any kind. What little we had we were obliged to share with Capt. Smith and his two men with him; we were likewise destitute of a guide or path, and how far from the inhabitants we knew not.

30th. After travelling a short distance we came on Capt. Goodrich's track, which soon led us to where he encamped the evening before. We here found a part of two quarters of dog they had killed and hung up for the remainder of his Company that was behind;[315] *the other they had eaten and taken with them. One of our Company, rejoiced to find the prize, immediately cut a part of it, roasted it on the coals and ate it very greedily. About an hour after we fell in with the rest of the Company which had passed another way. We found them much dejected and spent with fatigue and hunger. We informed them of the meat, at which they sent two men for it immediately.*

We then travelled on in a very bad road, sometimes over shoes in mire, sometimes climbing on all fours, and at others scarcely able to see for the thickness of the bramble and small fir shrubs. At 3 o'clock we hailed Capt. Derbon[316] *and one more going down stream in a birch canoe. They informed us that Capt. Morgan had his boat split upon a rock, the most of his effects lost, and one man drowned; that he saw where Col. Arnold's boat was stove; what his loss was he knew not. After travelling about 20 miles with our packs on our backs, we encamped by sunset much fatigued and very hungry.*[317]

Nov. 1ˢᵗ. By daylight in the morning began our march. In about two hours we came up with the wreck of a birch canoe that was foundered on a rock, which we supposed to be Capt. Derbon's. We marched very steadily in the track of some few that had gone on before, leading along the river. About 2 o'clock we came up with a man belonging to Capt. Goodrich. Being asked why he lay there he replied he had eaten nothing for three days and that he was far spent; he had not strength to proceed. Here I would have parted with anything in my possession to give him relief, but my very small pittance of provision, and notwithstanding I knew not how long before I should see any more, I could not part with him until I gave him the full half of my pork, which was scarcely two ounces. Capt. Smith gave him half his bread, not amounting to that weight. He immediately ate it and said he felt greatly refreshed, so that he came on with us.

We continued our march till sunset, when encamped; we judged 22 miles from our last encampment. One of our Company had a small bit of chocolate, which we boiled and divided out equally by spoonfuls. This day to me was very [hard], my boots being worn out entirely. Some days before I made a cover for them of the bag our flour was in, but being worn out it likewise occasioned my feet to be very sore.

2ⁿᵈ. As soon as the day dawned we began our march. After travelling about 8 miles we were blessed with the finest sight my eyes ever beheld; no sensation could be equal to it. Scarce one of us but with tears of joy expressed the gratitude of his heart at seeing five horned cattle and two birch canoes loaded with mutton and flour brought forward by French men.³¹⁸ They appeared glad to see us and welcomed us to Canada. After taking off the meat and flour enough to satisfy our hunger, we hastened them on to the main body of the detachment.

After broiling some of the meat we set off and marched about 10 miles. We again received new life from the sight of a house. When we came up with it we found it to be an Indian's, with several more about it. They were very officious in ferrying us across the river and seemed fond of seeing us. The next house was a Frenchman's, where the Colonel had placed an officer with bread, butter and potatoes to serve the men as they came up. Nothing to me ever tasted half so sweet.

After eating sparingly I took passage in a birch canoe and came down five miles to St. Francisway, where I found Col. Arnold. He informed me he had been as far as Sartigan³¹⁹; was very kindly received by a great number of the inhabitants, who told him they imagined he was sent from heaven to restore them liberty and rang the parish bell on the occasion.

3*rd*. In the morning a number of Indians belonging to different tribes, by Col. Arnold's desire collected themselves and desired to be informed of the nature of the quarrel between the King and his children. After it being made known to them they very willingly agreed to go with us and fight anybody who should molest us, but they would not agree to go with us in any garrison, and they must have bread not only for themselves but their children. Col. Arnold agreed to give as many of them as were fit to go to war eight dollars per month. Thirty-two of them enlisted and received two dollars per man advance.

Toward evening [met] Col. Green, with some officers of his division, much worn and wasted with the excessive hard marching and want of provision. Col. Arnold proceeded forward six leagues to meet his express sent forward to Quebec.

4*th*. Last evening fell a slight of snow about two inches deep. At 9 o'clock Col. Green and myself took a boat belonging to a Frenchman, who agreed to transport us six leagues down the river for three dollars. We stopped at one of the inhabitants, who treated us very civilly indeed, and seemed much pleased. The old woman sung the "Lexington March" for us in taste. The whole of these six leagues is along the river; is very beautiful; the river very mild and the banks lined with inhabitants. We passed the chapel of St. Mary, situated on a pleasant part of the river in the parish of St. Joseph.

5*th*. We fell down the river two leagues to the parish of St. Mary[320]. Here we were met by several of the inhabitants, some of whom informed us that Carleton had taken our express and confined him; that he and twenty of the inhabitants were under sentence of death and would be executed in two days' time unless we got in to assist them. Others informed us Carleton was taken prisoner and that a number of the citizens were shipping what cannon they could and destroying the rest. How matters stand we are not able to judge. This, however, we are assured of, that we have had not the least certain intelligence from Quebec since our setting out; that the Indian's express had betrayed us and given up our letters; and that our second and third express were detained in Quebec. However, at all events we are determined to go forward. We were kindly received in the parish of St. Mary, especially by the priest, who appeared to be subtle, artful and much of a gentleman.

6*th*. Ordered that the men should proceed on as far as the village of St.

Andrew, six leagues from this place. This morning the Colonel, on hearing that the enemy had destroyed all the boats on the river St. Lawrence, purchased a number for transporting the men across the river. On our way to St. Andrew we were met by two Frenchmen, well mounted. They informed us they had heard of our coming and were determined to be assured of it, even if they went to Chaudier pond. We asked them many questions relative to Quebec. They informed us that there were a number of the French citizens under arms, but that they were determined to lay them down as soon as our army appeared. They likewise informed us that there were several small frigates at Quebec.

At sunset we were near three leagues from St. Andrew. The depth of the road made it very heavy travelling, and, what was still worse, a light snow, about two or three inches deep, which, together with the mud, took us half leg deep. By 9 o'clock we got through the swamp and came up with two or three small huts one league from St. Andrew. Here we stopped, wet and cold; the houses not large enough to contain near all the men, and many were obliged to lay down in the barns and stables.

7th. In the morning we marched in a heavy snow storm and reached St. Auree at 9 o'clock, where, from the best information we could obtain, we concluded the two Frenchmen we had seen yesterday were spies. We remained here waiting for the rear to come forward, which we supposed were at least two days' march behind. Toward evening the storm abated and we received a messenger from Point Levi,[321] informing us that there was a quantity of flour and wheat stored in a mill; that it was guarded by a few of the inhabitants, who expected a party over from Quebec that threatened to burn the mill unless they would give it up. He informed us that on Sunday a 26-gunship has arrived in the harbour, but that he knew not how many came in her, nor could he give us any account of the number of the enemy in Quebec, but there were several sloops of war and cutters lying in the harbour. The Colonel ordered a reconnoitering party, consisting of a subaltern and thirty men to proceed to Point Levi this evening and send back all the intelligence they could get, and inform the inhabitants that he would be there himself in the morning with what men there were forward.

Our situation now seemed somewhat ticklish. As yet we had no certain intelligence of the strength of the enemy at Quebec, nor had we heard a word from General Schuyler[322] or his army; our whole number not exceeding 600 and they not all effective; the most of us naked and barefoot and very illy provided with ammunition; the winter approaching in hasty strides and we had no quarters we could call our own, nor any possibility of retreating but by fighting our way to Gen Schuyler, with a handful of men, through all Carleton's army. We determined, however, to make a bold push for Quebec at all events.

8th. About one o'clock we were awakened by the sentinel, who informed us there were two Indians who came express from General Montgomery. This gave us new life and spirit. In the morning we were ordered to march to Point Levi and Col. Green was sent back to bring up the rear as soon as possible with the canoes, as the Frenchmen informed us all on the river St. Lawrence were destroyed to prevent our crossing.

We reached Point Levi at 12 o'clock, three leagues from St. Auree. Here we had a full view of the harbour and a part of the town. We found one frigate of 26 guns, which had arrived the last Sunday and one sloop of war of 16 guns, called The Hunter,[323] besides several armed cutters.

Mr. Halstead, an American gentleman, who had taken his family to the Island of Orleans, not daring to be seen in Quebec, hearing of our coming, met us at Point Levi. He informed us that the frigate was from London, but the account she brought was not known but by the King's party, [which was] that a transport arrived yesterday from St. John's, at Newfoundland; she brought 150 recruits; that the frigate yesterday landed 50 marines; these, with about 100 Tories and 200 Canadians, were all within the walls in the upper town, and were exclusive of the militia, of which there were 11 Companies; that they had taken under pay three small vessels belonging to the merchants in the town, with all the sailors they could press out, of which he supposed they had sent 150 in the town. Mr. Halstead imagined the Canadians (all except the 100 Tories) would lay down their arms. He informed us that our Indian express had given our letters to the enemy, who immediately sent Mr. Mercier[324], the unhappy gentleman to whom the letter was directed on board the frigate, without acquainting him with the reason of his being confined.

Our Colonel dispatched the two Indians back to General Montgomery, acquainting him with our situation and desiring him to send us a reinforcement as soon as possible.

9th. We found this morning that the enemy had posted many sentinels along shore as far as the Hunter, which had fallen up the river with the tide about 1½ miles; we imagined to prevent our crossing the river. Two of our Companies came up about noon.

About one o'clock the ball was opened between us and the enemy. A barge, belonging to the Hunter, landed at a mill; was discovered by some of our men, who crept up expecting the whole boat's crew would land, but [only] one of them went on shore. The remainder in the boat discovered our men on the bank and alarmed the one on shore, at which they fired on the boat, then returned and left their fellow on shore to shift for himself. He took to the water. Our men fired several shots at him and the boat, which were answered by several shots both from the frigate and boat, but fortunately missed him. Two or three of the men jumped in and followed him, with one of our Indians, who came up first and brought him in. We found him to be a brother of Capt. W. Kinsey, a lad of about 18, who was a midshipman on board the Hunter. He appeared very willing to satisfy us in answering questions asked him. He informed us that they had certain intelligence that St. Johns had surrendered and General Carleton was at Montreal with the remainder of his force, except what was at Quebec. He could not tell us the number of men in the town, nor the number on board any of the vessels except the one he belonged to, which had 100, but he thought the frigate had 280; she was called the Lizard[325] *and arrived on Sunday, the 5th, from London, and brought no other information that he knew of, but that the Ministry were determined to carry their point and subdue the Americans, for which purpose 20,000 Hanoverians were already embarked for America. He said, likewise, there were five Regiments on their way from Boston to Quebec. These ill-grounded and false reports we easily perceived was an artifice made use of by the principal officers to encourage the inferior ones and privates.*[326]

10th. Toward evening Major Miggs [Meigs][327] *came up. He informed us 17 canoes would be up tomorrow with the rear of the detachment. A party with a French guide were sent to the parish of St. Nicola to bring down in the evening a number of canoes belonging to the inhabitants. The frigate fired several shots at the mill and our guard but without the least damage to either. Our sentries observed three boats loaded with men go on board the Hunter - we imagined either for fear of being boarded by us in the night or else to make an excursion to the mill. The Colonel ordered the guard to be doubled for fear of the latter.*

11th. & 12th. Lay at Point Levi, making preparation for scaling the walls and waiting the arrival of the rear [division] with the canoes.

13ᵗʰ. In the morning a French inhabitant came in and informed us that one Indian, who carried the letters to General Montgomery, was taken by three men in war boats which happened to be coming from Montreal; the other made his escape and proceeded on his journey. (Lucky for us). The Indians, for fear of being taken, were informed of the contents.

This intelligence was confirmed directly after by an express from Col. Easton, commander of our troops at Sorrel, informing us of the reduction of St. Johns, etc., and desiring an account of our present situation that he might remit it as soon as possible to General Montgomery, then lying before Montreal.

The Captains of each Company were ordered to be in readiness with their men to cross the river St. Lawrence. A council was held and left to the Colonel's pleasure whether we should storm the town immediately after landing or not. It was his opinion we ought to do it immediately. Accordingly the scaling ladders and pikes were carried to our place of landing. The Hunter, being in the place where we intended crossing, to wit, Scillery, we fixed on Wolfe's cove, about halfway between the Hunter and the Lizard," not doubting but, as the cause was superior to his [Wolfe's], we might at least expect as good success.³²⁸

At eight in the evening the first load for the canoes embarked. After we had crossed two-thirds of the river, we heard the Hunter's boat rowing under the shore. The Colonel, whose boat I was in, gave orders for [us] to lay upon our paddles and let her pass, which she did, without noticing us. After we had landed and sent off the boats we amounted to but 27, out of which we dispatched six on each wing as a flank guard, and drew the remainder up in a body ready for keeping the ground we had taken against any number that might have disputed it with us. The scarcity of canoes made it very tedious getting over the men. We, however, executed it by 2 o'clock without any other damage than the loss of the guns and baggage belonging to one boat, which foundered in the middle of the river. The men were all saved by towing them after the others.³²⁹

After a second freight being landed, a party of sixteen was ordered to take possession of a house near the road leading up the bank from the cove in which we expected they had a guard, but we found it destitute of any inhabitants.

After the most of our men were landed, we perceived a boat rowing from one ship to the other, which, for the advantage of keeping out of the current, stood close along shore. Six or eight of us crept out on a point and lay undiscovered till she came opposite; we then rose and ordered her to bring to.

121

They answered "yes," but turned her head off, upon which we fired on her, but she rowed off. We heard the shrieks of the wounded a long time.

It was near the morning before the last of our men [got] over and not a single ladder. After we were landed the subaltern belonging to the guard on the side reported that he had taken up a man, who called himself a deserter from Quebec and informed us Colonel McLean's[330] new-raised Regiment landed the day before. We formed ourselves on the Plains of Abraham[331] and marched up to Major Caldwell's house.[332] We found nothing in the house but a few servants, who had been left to take care of the house. We took possession of it, together with two or three horses we found in the stables.

14th. In the morning early I walked round with Major Bigelow[333] and Mr. Halstead to view the walls of the town. By the time I returned the guard was going out; the Colonel ordered me, as I had seen the ground, to set the out-sentries next the town. I accordingly did, after which, on hearing the ship firing at our guard that was placed at Wolfe's cove over the canoes, on my return I observed the guard turning out. I ran as fast as possible to know the reason and found the enemy was sallying out, and gave the alarm. We marched up briskly near the walls. The enemy had retreated with one of our sentries they had surrounded and taken, which was all their errand.

We drew up on the Plain hoping they might come out and give us battle, which at that time they did not choose. We gave them three huzzas, which was answered by an eighteen-pounder from the town. It was followed by a shower from different parts of the town until we were covered by the hill in our retreat. What was very surprising, we had not a man touched notwithstanding we were so very near and there was not a countenance scarcely among the whole that appeared concerned.

Mr. Glenney, a gentleman who came to us (and had left the town this morning) confirmed the information of Col. McLean's arrival, with 200 of his Regiment and about 80 of the Eighth. As the number of the enemy now exceeded, beside the shipping, we lost all hopes of taking the town by storm. We were without one piece of cannon and scarcely ammunition to serve us one-half hour in battle. In this situation we could expect nothing more than to stand on the defensive until we received reinforcements from our army above.

Colonel Arnold dispatched an express to Montgomery, acquainting him with our circumstances and requesting an immediate reinforcement.

Toward evening the Colonel wrote a letter to the Commander-in-Chief in *the town, demanding a surrender of the place and letting them know what they might expect should they put him to the expense of taking the town by storm. I was the person appointed for going in with the flag. According to custom I took a drummer with me, who, as soon as had risen the hill, beat a parley, and I at the same time raised my flag and marched on, waving it in the air, until I was within four rods of St. Johns' Gate, when I was saluted with a eighteen-pound shot from the wall. It struck very near and spattered us with the earth it threw up. I at first thought it had killed the drummer, but he had only fallen with the fright. We did not wait for a second, but retreated in quick time till under cover of the hill. We could not account for this usage, unless we either came out of season (for the evening gun was fired just before), or else they did not intend to treat us any other way than as rebels and not give us quarter.[334] We stopped several persons going and coming from the town, some of whom informed us we had killed three of the boat's crew and wounded a fourth dangerously.*

This day the enemy burned two block houses, which stood near the wall, with several of the houses of the inhabitants without the walls. Here a shocking scene presented itself; several houses in flames and the inhabitants obliged to fly they knew not whither, and we unable to assist them without running in the mouths of their cannon.

15th. To be assured whether the reason for their not receiving our flag was its being out of season or for other reasons, the Colonel desired I would try them once more, but my drummer could not be persuaded to go with me. I took another in his place and showed ourselves a second time. After beating the parley I ordered the drummer to stop, whilst I advanced slowly toward them waving my flag. They soon gave me the old salute; the ball passed just over me in a very straight direction. I left them the ground and returned. The drummer told me he saw them load the cannon and then bring the match; that he called to me several times and thought I heard him. The reason of my not seeing it was that I looked at the place that it came from before, but this came from a different part of the wall. The reason of their firing there was because the cannon was smaller and, of consequence, a ball might be thrown with greater exactness. The Colonel, whilst I was gone, was informed by a Canadian who had just left the town that one man they had taken was thrown in... [Here this interesting journal suddenly stops]

CHAPTER NINE

CAPTAIN ELEAZER OSWALD JOURNAL

ELEAZER OSWALD,
Lieut. Colonel of the Revolutionary War.
Nat 1755 – Ob 1795

From a print in the collection of C K Hildeburn Esq

DESCRIPTION.

Eleazer Oswald was a volunteer on the expedition. Since he was a close New Haven friend of Benedict Arnold and had served with him at Fort Ticonderoga, Arnold assigned him to be his aide and secretary. In that position he wrote journal entries starting on September 15th and ending on October 13th. His entries are similar to the ones in Benedict Arnold's account of the expedition during the same time period, but he does have different entries for a few comparable days. Justin Smith suggests that it could be "the copy of my journal" that Arnold sent to George Washington on October 13 1775. Based on the ending date of Oswald's journal being October 13, that claim makes perfect sense, although no copy of this journal, or any other journal from Arnold, was found in Washington's papers.

Oswald's journal is written as though Arnold himself wrote it. The closeness of the two men at that point in time and Oswald's position as Arnold's Secretary allowed Oswald to write it as if it was authored by Arnold. In effect, he acted as Arnold's spokesman. Oswald's account is not credibly the missing first pages of Arnold's journal as suggested by John Codman because it covers a longer period of time. Arnold's journal as it appears in Roberts starts on September 27 and ends on October 30. Roberts also includes entries from Oswald's journal for Sept. 15 through Sept. 27, but not the entire Oswald journal.

Oswald's journal first appeared in Peter Force's American Archives titled "A Journal of an Intended Tour from Cambridge to Quebec, via Kennebeck, with a detachment of two Regiments of Musketeers and three Companies of Riflers, consisting of eleven hundred men, commanded by Benedict Arnold." Force's copy shows it as being signed by Eleazer Oswald as Sec'y Pro Tem. There is a handwritten copy of Oswald's journal in the Charles E. Banks Papers in the Massachusetts Historical Society, in the handwriting of Banks. The Banks copy has the same title as the journal in American Archives and identical entries but it does not identify Oswald as the author. The original Oswald journal is located in Continental Army Papers. Ltrs. From General Officers, 1776-1789, Vol. I, p. 28. NARA M247, National Archives and Records Administration.

PUBLICATION.

1st and Only Previous Publication. Peter Force. American Archives, Ser. 4, Vol. III. Washington, D.C.

AUTHOR.

Eleazer Oswald was born in Falmouth, England, in 1750 and came to America in 1770 after his father disappeared. He landed in New York where he became an apprentice to the printer, John Holt, the publisher of *The New York Journal*. He married Holt's daughter, Elizabeth, in December of 1771.

Oswald moved to New Haven, Connecticut, after his marriage, and continued in the printing business. In March of 1775, Oswald joined with Benedict Arnold and others to form a military company known as the Second Company Governor's Foot Guard. After the Lexington Alarm, Arnold marched his company, including Oswald, to Boston. He was Arnold's aide at Fort Ticonderoga and served as the Captain of Marines on the schooner *Liberty* in the raid on St. John's in May, 1775. Arnold appointed Oswald as his volunteer aide-de-camp and military secretary, with the brevet rank of Captain, in the expedition to Quebec.

Oswald was the leader of the "Forlorn Hope" in the assault on the barricades in the battle of Quebec. The forlorn hope carried the day at the first barricade using bayonets and captured the Captain of the Guard. Oswald was taken prisoner in the assault and was exchanged in January of 1777. After being exchanged, he was promoted to Lieutenant Colonel in the 2nd Artillery Company, commanded by Colonel John Lamb. Oswald served with Lamb's company in opposing the British raid on Danbury and at the Battle of Monmouth.

In 1778, Oswald got into a dispute with Congress over his seniority. Arnold wrote a glowing letter in support of Oswald but a satisfactory resolution of the dispute could not be achieved and Oswald resigned his commission on October 28, 1778. His resignation letter to Washington stated that he "could not possibly remain in camp and subject myself to the Commands of a junior Officer." He goes on to say that he must resign because "nothing but Injustice, by depriving me of my right, and transferring it to another, determines me to leave the Army."

After he left the army, Oswald returned to his previous occupation of printer, first in Baltimore and then with his own newspaper, *The Independent Gazetteer*. In the period after the war, Oswald's newspaper continually attacked Alexander Hamilton's proposed financial policies and ultimately Oswald challenged Hamilton to a duel, but the matter was resolved and no duel was fought. Oswald was an avid anti-federalist and strongly opposed the adoption of the new Constitution. His newspaper published twenty-four essays written by anti-federalist leader Samuel Bryan. Some historians consider this one of the leading arguments against ratifying the Constitution.

In 1788, Oswald was charged with contempt of court by Pennsylvania Supreme Court Justice Thomas McKean for his writings on the Constitution calling Oswald a "seditious turbulent man." In a highly publicized case, Oswald was convicted of the McKeon charges and sentenced to a fine of ten pounds and one month in jail. Later Oswald was involved with the unsuccessful attempt to get the Pennsylvania legislature to impeach Chief Justice McKeon.

In 1793, Oswald gave up his printing business and went to France where he was commissioned as a colonel of artillery and regimental commander in the French Republican Army. He was subsequently commissioned to go to Ireland to assist the Irish revolutionists in that country. When he returned to France he had problems with the French Republican government over his mission in Ireland and the back pay he claimed was owed. His disgust for the French Republicans caused him to return to the United States, where he died of yellow fever on December 2, 1795. Oswald is one of the forgotten heroes of the Arnold expedition and his efforts that contributed to the passage of the Bill of Rights are largely forgotten.

JOURNAL

j_OswaldJournal_DONE

A Journal of an intended Tour from Cambridge to Quebec via Kennebec, with a detachment of two Regiments of Musketeers & three companies of Rifles, consisting of about 1100 effective men, commanded by Benedict Arnold.

Having received orders from his Excellency General Washington to march with the above detachment, I set out on Friday morning, the 15ᵗʰ of September, from Cambridge, dined at Salem, where I procured two hundred pounds of ginger, & engaged a teamster to transport that & 270 blankets, received from the Committee of Safety, by order of Major Mifflin, Quartermaster General, to Newburyport, where I arrived at 10 o'clock the same evening.

Saturday, 16. This evening the whole detachment arrived; dispatched three boats to Kennebec, Isle-of-Shoals, and along shore, to look out for Men of War & cruisers, with orders to give us the earliest intelligence, if they discovered any on the coast; and procured a quantity of small stores, etc, N.B. Contrary Winds.

Sunday, 17. Head winds & thick weather; made preparation to embark.

Monday, 18. The whole detachment embarked; one of the boats just returned, & informs us the coast is quite clear.

Tuesday, 19. Weighed anchor at 7 o'clock, A.M., & at noon all transports, being 11 in number, got safe out of the harbor, except the Schooner Swallow, which ran on the rocks, & could not be got off this tide; took all men from on board her, except twelve, including Captain Scott, whom I ordered to follow us, as fast as possible. As soon as our fleet passed the bar, ordered the Captain of each vessel to be furnished with a copy of the following signals, which are to be hoisted on board the Schooner Broadbay, Captain James Clarkson, who is to lead the van:[335]

1. *Signal for speaking with the whole fleet: ensign at main-topmast head.*
2. *Signal for chasing a sail: ensign at fore-topmast head.*
3. *Signal for heaving to: lantern at mast head, & two guns, if head on shore; & three guns, if offshore.*
4. *Signal for making sail in the night: lantern at mast head, & four guns, In the day, for making sail: jack at fore-topmast head.*

5. *Signal for dispersing, & every vessel making the nearest harbor: ensign at main peak.*

6. *Signal for boarding any vessel: jack at main-topmast head, and the whole fleet to draw up in a line, as near as possible. N.B. No guns to be fired without orders.*

This being done, bore away for Kennebec, wind W.S.W., about 4 o'clock, P.M., brought to and spoke with two fishing schooners, who could give us no intelligence; The weather came on thick and foggy; continued a N.N.E. course till 12 o'clock at night, when we hove to, with head off shore, off Wood Island, and at 2 o'clock made the signal for heaving to, with head on shore.

Wednesday, 20. Made sail again early in the morning; weather still continues very thick & foggy, attended with rain, and at 9 o'clock, A.M., arrived safe in the mouth of Arowsick, with all our fleet, except three, without the least molestation from the enemy, anchored about six hours at Eels Eddy, sent on shore for some refreshment, as many of the people were extremely sea sick on the passage; Weighed anchor & proceeded up the river as far as Georgetown,[336] *where we lay all night, when one of our fleet, viz: Captain [illegible] overtook us.*

Thursday, 21. Weighed anchor at 5 A.M., after sailing a few miles, discovered the other two of our fleet coming through Sheepscut Creek, they having run past the mouth of Arowsick the day before; Left the transports in the river, wind & tide unfavourable, & proceeded as far as Gardinerstown.[337]

Friday, 22. This morning arrived three of the transports; were employed the whole day in forwarding the men, provisions, bateaux, etc., to Fort Western; engaged two caulkers, some guides, and assistants; At 4 P.M., arrived the Schooner Swallow, which run on the rocks off Newbury; she brings intelligence that the Houghton, Captain Somersby, with 120 men, and the Eagle, Captain Maby, with 84 men, were aground fifteen miles down the river; Engaged the Swallow, & a number of men, to go to their relief.[338]

Saturday, 23. Embarked the men, & sent them on to Fort Western, with their batteaus laden with provisions; All the vessels weighed anchor, and stood up the river, and anchored above 5 miles short of Fort Western, the water not permitting them to go higher; At 6 P.M., arrived at Howard's, at Fort Western.

Sunday, 24. Dispatched Lieutenant Steel, with six men, in two birch canoes, to *Chaudiere Pond*, to reconnoiter, & to get all the intelligence he possibly can from the Indians, who I am informed, are hunting there; and also Lieutenant *Church* and seven men, with a surveyor & pilot, to take the exact courses & distances to the *Dead River*.[339]

Monday, 25. Dispatched the three companies of Riflers, with 45 days' provisions, under command of Captain *Morgan*, as an advanced party, with orders to proceed to the great carrying place, & to cut a road over to the *Dead River*; About 3 o'clock, P.M., Lieutenant *Gray* arrived, with a number of manifestoes & a letter from Colonel *Reed*.[340]

Tuesday, 26. The Second Division, consisting of three Companies, viz: *Hubbard's, Topham's* and *Thayer's*, under command of Colonel *Greene*, embarked; *James McCormick*, a private in Captain *Goodrich's* Company, tried by a Court-Martial for the murder of *Reuben Bishop*, a Sergeant in Captain *Williams's* Company, and received sentence of death, but respited till his Excellency General *Washington's* pleasure be known, & ordered to Head-Quarters; a number of our men employed in bringing up provisions, etc.; wrote his Excellency General *Washington*, & dispatched back five of the transports.

Wednesday, 27. The Third Division, consisting of four Companies, viz: *Hanchett's, Ward's, Dearborn's* and *Goodrich's*, under command of Major *Meigs*, embarked; sent down a number of boats to bring up all the flour from below, & sent to the Commissary to forward on all the batteaus, etc.

Thursday, 28. Part of the fourth & last Division, *McCobb's* and *Scott's* Companies, embarked; Captain *William's* Company being left for batteaus, oars, paddles, etc.; Sent for Colonel *Enos* and the Commissary to come up from *Coburn's* with all the men & batteaus; Ordered the sick & criminal on board the *Broadbay*, Captain *Clarkston*, with stores, etc.

Friday, 29. Set out in a birch canoe, about noon; left Colonel *Enos*, with Captain *William's* Company, to bring up the rear, with the provisions behind; Our canoe proves very leaky; stopped at *Vassalborough*,[341] eight miles above *Fort Western*, & changed her for another, and having gone about 12 miles, lodged six miles short of *Fort Halifax*.

Saturday, 30. At 6 o'clock, A.M., crossed the *Six Mile Falls*, & at 10 arrived at *Fort Halifax*, where I found Captain *Dearborn's* & *Goodrich's* Companies first passing the carrying place, which is about 60 rods over; course of the river from *Fort Western* to *Fort Halifax*, N.N.E.; distance 18 miles; At 2 P.M., dined at *Crosier's*, & hired him, with his team, to carry our baggage *over land about 5 miles, to avoid the ripples and quick water above the falls, which are very dangerous & difficult to pass; At 5 P.M., left the landing place, & proceeded up the river about two miles, when we overtook Major Meigs and party, with whom we encamped [in the woods]; whole distance this day 13 miles, course N.*[342]

Sunday, October 1. Left our encampment early in the morning; At 10 A.M., passed the seven & fifteen mile streams; dined at one Western's; At 4 P.M., reached Scowhegan Falls, where we overtook Hubbard's & Thayer's Companies; after crossing the carrying place, which is about 100 rods, launched our batteau again, and proceeded up the river about five miles; and at 8 P.M., encamped at the widow Warren's; distance seventeen miles; course to Scowhegan Falls, about N.; from falls to where we lodged, S.W.; water quiet part of the way; quick [water] and small falls.[343]

Monday, 2. After going a mile. overtook Colonel Greene, Major Bigelow, Captain Topham, & Company; about 8 A.M., passed the Bombazee Falls, & at 10 arrived at Norridgewock Falls, six miles & a half from the widow Warren's; great part of the way swift water & rapids; The land from Fort Western to this place appears, in general, very good & fertile, but is thinly inhabited; Here we leave the English settlements, no inhabitants being above the falls, which, by the best estimation, are 50 miles from Fort Western; Here I overtook Captain Morgan, with his Division, who had just got their baggage over the Carrying Place, which is one mile; course N.W.[344]

Tuesday, 3. The Riflers proceed for the great carrying place; Topham's, Thayer's & Hubbard's Companies employed in getting over their baggage, & examining their bread, great part of which is damaged by the boat's leaking, & the difficulty of passing the rapids, which is impossible for people unacquainted to get up the boats without shipping water; Here are some small vestiges of an Indian Town, destroyed by the English about 50 years since, namely, the foundation of an old church & altar, the monument over St. Francis, the founder of the church, etc.; the whole tribe, we are told, are extinct, except two or three.

Wednesday, 4. Carpenters employed in repairing batteaus, & the several Companies [employed] in carrying over their provisions, some of which prove unfit for use; Colonel Greene's division proceeded forward; Major Meig's division arrived with Colburn.[345]

Thursday, 5. Companies employed as the preceeding day.

Friday, 6. Major Meigs, with his Division, went forward; Colonel Enos, with the Rear Division, arrived.

Saturday, 7. The last Division employed in examining their bread, part of which is wet & unfit for use, & carrying their baggage & provisions over the portage.[346]

Sunday, 8. We have not been able to get our baggage, etc., over the portage until this morning, though we have had constantly two sleds going with oxen, owing to the height of the hill & the bad road; A storm of rain prevents our proceeding this day.

Monday, 9. Struck our tent, carried our baggage over the portage, embarked & proceeded up about three miles, a N.N.E. course; here the river makes a remarkable turn to the E.N.E., about three-quarters of a mile, then turns W. and N. about three-quarters of a mile more, and then returns to its proper course again; we crossed the elbow over land, being about 30 rods, which saves more than a mile of rapid water; At 12 o'clock passed the seven mile stream; at 3 P.M., dined on one of the islands, & at five encamped with Captain McCobb, on another island, within two miles of Caratunker, or Devil's Falls; whole distance this day, 16 miles; course N.N.E. easterly, the water very rapid; the land, from the mouth of the river to Caratunker Falls, appears level, & in general fertile, & tolerably well wooded, with some oak, elm, ash, beech, maple, pine hemlock, etc.

Tuesday, 10. At 9 o'clock, A.M., arrived at Caratunker Falls; The fall of water, 15 feet; the portage near 50 rods over; we proceeded up the river, about 5 miles, against a very rapid stream, course N.; here the mountains begin to appear on each side of the river, high and level on the tops, & appear well wooded; the river, from Norridgewock to the great carrying place is very irregular in width, but in general about 400 yards, & full of small islands, which appear very fertile land; we ascended the river this day about 12 miles; in general very rapid & shallow water; encamped late in the evening, much fatigued.[347]

Wednesday, 11. We embarked early this morning, & proceeded up the river; the stream very rapid indeed; About 10 A.M., arrived at the great carrying place, which is very remarkable [having] a large brook emptying itself into the river above, which comes from the first lake; when abreast of the carrying place, in the river, you will observe, at about 400 yards above you, a large mountain, in shape of a Sugar Loaf, at the foot of which the river turns off to the eastward; this mountain, when you are at the carrying place, seems to rise out of the middle of the river.[348] *Here I overtook Captain Morgan and his division, and Col. Greene, with his division; part of each had proceeded as far as the second lake; Major Meigs arrived just before me; met Lieutenant Church, who had been at the Dead River, on a survey, & reports as follows:*

From Kennebeck, over the portage, to the first pond or lake; course W., 27 degrees N.; distance 3/4 of a mile, rising ground; bad road, but capable of being made good; over the first pond, ½ mile, which pond is 1/4 of a mile long; Here our people caught a prodigious number of very fine salmon-trout, nothing being more common than a man's taking eight or ten dozen in one hour's time, which generally weigh half a pound apiece; the second portage is W., six degrees N. half a mile & 20 rods; very level, but rough road; the second pond is in length, from north to south, 2 ½ miles, and half a mile wide; the third carry place is one mile and a quarter and forty rods; the road very bad; course W., ten degrees N.; the third pond is in length, from north to south, 3 miles, and 2 miles wide; course over it, W. by N.; the fourth or last portage is W., 20 degrees N.; distance 2 ¾, and 60 rods; the first part of the road tolerably good; the last mile a savanna, wet and miry, about 6 or 8 inches deep.

Thursday, 12. Lieutenant Steel returned from Chaudiere Pond, & says he discovered no Indians; that the Dead River, from the last carry place, he judges to be 80 miles, most part of the way a fine, deep river; the current hardly perceptible; some fine falls, and short carrying places, & rapid water; the carrying place from Dead River to Chaudiere Pond, about four miles; very good & even ground, most part of the way, and plenty of moose & other game on the river; This day employed Captain Goodrich's Company in building a log house on the second portage, to accommodate the sick, eight or ten in number, who we are obliged to leave behind; also a party on the east side of the first portage to build a small log house for men & provisions; Ordered Lieutenants Steel & Church, with 20 axe-men and a surveyor, to Chaudiere Pond, to clear the portages & take a survey of the country; Lieutenant Steel to go down Chaudiere, near the inhabitants, & examine the falls, portages, etc., and return to the pond as soon as possible.[349]

Our men are much fatigued in carrying over their batteaus, provisions, etc., the road being extremely bad; However, their spirit & industry seems to overcome every obstacle, & they appear very cheerful. We have had remarkable fine weather since we left Cambridge, & only one death has happened, & very few accidents by water, which is the most remarkable, as there seldom passes a season without some people being drowned in the Kennebec, which is very difficult & dangerous to ascend.

Friday, 13. This morning dispatched one Eneas and another Indian with letters to some gentlemen in Quebec, & to General Schuyler, sent a white man with them, who is to proceed as far as Sartigan, & after discovering the settlements of the inhabitants, & procuring all the intelligence he can, is to return to us at Chaudiere Pond, where we expect to meet him in about 7 or 8 days; Two divisions have this day reached the Dead River.

Signed:
Eleazer Oswald, Sec'y pro tem.

CHAPTER TEN

PENNSYLVANIA PACKET JOURNAL

<u>DESCRIPTION.</u>

Robert Stevens from Maine, a friend and colleague, discovered the existence of this journal in early 2018. Informed this author that he had found this unknown expedition journal in the *Pennsylvania Packet* newspaper. I was astonished that an expedition journal was published in a newspaper after the march and it has never been referenced. The journal was serialized in the newspaper on March 15, 18, 20, 23 and 27, 1779. It is remarkable that despite the journal being printed in a newspaper four years after the events described, it has remained unknown for almost 240 years.

No clear identity of the author is offered in the *Pennsylvania Packet*. However, based on text analysis, it seems likely that it was written by a volunteer from Pennsylvania who was not formally enlisted in a specific company. If that is the case, there are two possible authors, Dr. Joseph Coates, a surgeon from Pennsylvania, and Matthew Duncan, a volunteer from Pennsylvania. Both were associated with the two Pennsylvania rifle companies. However, based on the information contained in the journal, there is no way to ascertain which man wrote the journal.

The possible identity of the two possible authors is based on analyzing the text of the journal resulting in the following observations.

1. The author was attached to a rifle company because he uses the word "we" in reference to the 1st Division, which was composed of the three companies of riflemen that were on the expedition. He uses that reference more than once. That usage indicates that the author was attached to one of the rifle companies.

2. It is reasonable to assume the author is a Pennsylvanian since he provided his journal to the Pennsylvania Packet. Two of the three rifle companies were from Pennsylvania and the other one was Daniel Morgan's Company from Virginia. Why would a man

from Virginia offer his journal to a Pennsylvania paper when there were newspapers in Virginia at that time period?

3. Based on the use of words in the text and the descriptions used, it seems clear that the writer was educated. Therefore, it is likely that the author was what some have referred to as a gentleman volunteer. I accept that it is possible that the journal submitted to the Packet could have been edited and that the writing reflects the Packet and not the author. However, since no mention is made that the journal was edited, I am working on the assumption that the writing style is the author's.

4. The author does not identify himself with a particular rifle company so my conclusion is that he was probably a volunteer, and not an officer, in one of the Pennsylvania companies.

5. In the 3rd paragraph of the journal, the author refers to "several young gentlemen, who were…" Since he did not use the word "officers", I take that to refer to volunteers rather than appointed officers or non-commissioned officers. The fact that he even mentions those "gentlemen" indicates that he had a high regard for the volunteers because he was one himself.

6. Dr. Coates is included as a possible author because the entries for Oct 10th and Oct 23rd suggest a familiarity with medical conditions that is not present in the other expedition journals other than the one by Dr. Senter, the lead expedition doctor.

PUBLICATION.

The only previously published text of this journal was in the 1779 Pennsylvania Packet.

AUTHOR.

No biography as author is unknown

JOURNAL

To the Printer of the PENNSYLVANIA PACKET
SIR,

    As I flatter myself an account of Gen. Arnold's march from Cambridge to Quebec will be acceptable to the public, I have endeavoured to collect the particulars from my journal, and can only regret that my abilities and want of leisure will barely do it justice. The facts are indisputable, and I beg you will give it a place in your paper.

    On the commencement of hostilities between the parent state and her colonies in the year 1775, every man deemed it a duty incumbent on him to quit the sweets of domestic life, and turn out to resist, as far as in him lay, the strides of cruel, lawless oppression.

    In the course of a few weeks a large army was collected at Cambridge, which was hourly increasing by the great number of volunteers from the remotest provinces. A force being thus at once established sufficiently powerful to check the King's forces and blockade them in Boston, a second was immediately assembled under the command of Gen. Schuyler[350], who was ordered to proceed into Canada by the way of Ticonderoga, and to act offensively by reducing St. John's and other British garrisons, thereby endeavouring to bring to a constitutional accommodation those who had been the aggressors. As it was more than probable that the appearance of these forces would draw the troops from the garrison at Quebec, to the relief of the posts in the upper part of the province, an expedition was proposed against the capital of Canada by the way of the Kennebunk river[351], and the command given to Col. B. Arnold[352], a gentleman who had remarkably distinguished himself in the reduction of Ticonderoga, and whose prudence, courage, and other military abilities in several important transactions, justly entitled him to the command of this arduous undertaking. Preparations for this enterprize were conducted with the greatest secrecy, as the success of the expedition depended much upon a surprise.

    In the month of September 1775, a detachment, consisting entirely of volunteers from the New England troops[353], with one company of riflemen from Virginia[354], and two from Pennsylvania[355], the whole consisting of about one thousand and fifty, were ordered to hold themselves in readiness to march at the shortest notice. To these may be added several young gentlemen[356], who were anxious to distinguish themselves as volunteers to a cause, where they deemed it meritorious to sacrifice ease, affluence, health, nay life itself.

On Monday September the eleventh, the first division consisting of the riflemen, filed off towards Newburyport[357], which was appointed the place of general rendezvous, where we arrived the thirteenth, the distance being about forty miles. Here we were entertained with the greatest politeness and hospitality, and spent our time very agreeably; different companies of the detachment continued to come in till the sixteenth, when we were complete. We were now busy in preparing for our voyage to Kennebunk; for which purpose eleven schooners and sloops[358] were provided.

The eighteenth we were ordered to embark, which took up our time [in the] chief part of the day; and at nine o'clock, A.M. of the nineteenth, the wind being fair, we weighed anchor, and stood out to sea. During the course of the day, we hailed and spoke with several vessels, without meeting any that were armed to oppose us. Towards evening the weather became very foggy; we continued our course till ten at night, when the signal was given to lay too.

The twenty-second [should be the twentieth] at day break we set sail, none of the fleet being in view. A high gale rendered the sea very rough, which produced a droll scene among the soldiers, few of whom had ever been at sea before. After some time six sail joined us, and at nine A.M. we made the mouth of Kennebunk[359] and entered it. Here we dropped anchor; and at three P.M. one of our schooners joined us, at which time we proceeded up the river.

The twenty-first of September, 1775, as some of our fleet were still missing, we were very uneasy about them, and Col. Arnold ordered a barge to cruise for them; we pursued our course up the river, and in the evening to our great joy descried our companions, who had been beaten off the mouth of the river, The channel being very intricate, we dropped anchor at dark.

The twenty-second we continued our voyage, and at noon arrived at Cabassy Conty[360], (Indian Sturgeon Land) where we went on shore to view the batteaus which were built for us at this place, consisting of two hundred and forty[361], and in which we were to proceed. A number of men were draughted from each vessel to conduct the boats to the river, and the vessels were ordered to Fort Western[362], where we arrived in the evening. As the tide flows only three or four miles above Fort Western, we were busy on the twenty-third all day in unloading the vessels, and making preparations for pursuing our route, And as there are a number of carrying places in this river, the colonel thought *proper that we should march in four divisions*[363]*, by which means we should not obstruct each other; and by leaving Fort Western on different days, the first division would get over any carrying place by the time the second had reached; and so on with the third and fourth. This evening a soldier*[364] *shot one of his companions, who expired a few hours after; he was tried by court-martial, found guilty of murder, and sent to Cambridge under a guard. As each division encountered the same fatigue etc. the whole may be included in the particular account of any one of them.*

On the twenty-fourth the first division, consisting of the three companies of riflemen, received orders to march, but it being late before we were in readiness, we proceeded only three miles. The season was now advancing when we might expect bad weather; and though the middle of the day was pleasant, the mornings and evenings were uncomfortably cool.

On the 26th we reached Fort Halifax[365]*, having been two days going twenty miles, owing to the difficulty of setting the batteaus against the stream (which in many places is very rapid) and few of the men were expert boatmen. This Fort is situated on a point of land bounded by the Kennebunk and Sebesticocke*[366] *rivers, there is a block house near it. It was originally intended as a security against the Indians, but is at present capable of little or no resistance.*

On the 27th we proceeded to Ticonick Falls[367]*, which are about two hundred yards above the Fort- This was our first carrying place, the distance being about four hundred yards. Here we had an idea of the fatigue we were to undergo, being obliged to unload the boats and carry them on our shoulders, as well as our provisions, baggage, etc., the officers bearing no inconsiderable share of the duty. Though we used the utmost diligence, it delayed us so long that we could proceed only five miles further, the water being very rapid near the Falls; and we encamped in a thick wood, the rain pouring down in abundance.*

On the 28th we crossed the river, as there was no path on the side we were encamped, and marched fifteen miles, for no person was permitted to go into a boat except two in each, who were relieved every morning as it was very severe duty.

The 29th we started very early and reached Scowheggin Falls[368]*, our second carrying place, the distance much the same as the former. The stream for a considerable way below the Falls was exceedingly swift, that it was with the greatest difficulty and labor that the men could get the batteaus up, and the ground over which we were to carry being very uneven, rendered it near dark* *before we finished. We encamped near the Falls, and this evening it snowed a little.*

The 30th of September we marched early in the morning, and after encountering a number of obstacles, we reached Norridgewalk[369], which is the last settlement up the river, and is near a hundred miles from the mouth of it. The country does not appear to be settled except on the river side and the inhabitants depend chiefly upon fish and lumber for their subsistence. Their salmon are fine and in great plenty. The country abounds with a number of animals, among which the moose (large species of deer) may deservedly be preferred. Their inhabitants, some few excepted, are in general ordinary. They raise little or no grain, except Indian corn and rye, which, with potatoes, they use for bread. At this place we took leave of the inhabitants, as we did not expect to see anything civilized for a considerable time, and encamped two miles beyond the settlement near a fall, over which we are to carry tomorrow- this being the third place.

October 1st. The distance being one mile and an half to carry, and the road stony and hilly, made it very fatiguing, and we did not accomplish it till the 2nd about noon, at which time Col. Arnold joined us, and gave us orders to continue up the river, which we did, and encamped in a thick wood of hemlock; it rained very hard all night. Early in the morning we proceeded, and lost ourselves after marching a few miles, having been deceived by a branch of the river. The Colonel sent us a pilot and we proceeded, though on account of hills, islands, fallen trees, reeds, etc., we could scarcely get along, and were obliged to ford a branch of the river. As we considered ourselves in a savage county, and did not know the moment we might be attacked, we for the first time fixed a regular guard. A party of men who had been sent out to hunt returned with a moose, which was very acceptable to us; we likewise caught a number of trout which abound in this river.

The 4th we marched to, and carried our boats, etc. over the Caratencks or Devils Falls[370] - This our fourth carrying place, and though the distance was short, it is much worse than either of the preceding ones, being very rocky and high, so that a misstep or slip might be productive of bad consequences.

The 5th. We proceeded ten miles, to perform which required no small exertion, as we marched chiefly through a swamp. The islands in this river are numerous though small. We observed no traces of an human being, except a note left by our advanced guard, letting us know they were well.

The 6th, This day's march about the same distance as yesterday, having the same impediments to obstruct us both by land and water, the latter so bad that several boats did not get up till very late. We received positive orders the 7th, at day break to strike our tents and proceed to the great carrying place[371], where we arrived about nine o'clock, and found part of advanced guard, who had been prevented by sickness from going on further. As soon as the men were refreshed they were ordered to cut the road, the distance of the carrying place was three miles and a half, through a thick wood, hilly and rocky. We cleared about a mile today, and the hunting party killed a second moose. It rained very hard in the night, and continued the 8th, which retarded the progress of the men who were still at work upon the road.

The 9th. A very fine morning- and we this day finished the road, while others were unpacking the pork, as we concluded to leave the barrels behind us. A considerable quantity of provision having been by this time consumed, a less number of boats were necessary, we accordingly condemned a number, they having been made slight at first, and were rendered unfit for service from the injuries they had sustained at the different carrying places, etc.[372] This evening we were ordered to pack our baggage in as small a compass as possible, so that it might be carried with more convenience should we be obliged to retreat either from an attack or any other cause.

The 10th. We began to carry very early in the morning, and it was late in the evening before we completed it. Notwithstanding we labored almost without intermission, and we encamped on the edge of a lake, in a swamp so thickly timbered that we could not stretch our tents to their common size. Here we regaled ourselves upon excellent trout, which were in the greatest plenty, one gentleman in particular having caught eleven dozen in an hour or two, and not a fish of any other kind. The first division of the musket men encamped this evening on the spot we left this morning. Our men, from being constantly exposed to wet swamps while they marched, or almost incessant wading while on fatigue with the boats, together with their diet (salt pork and bread) began to complain. Many of them were affected with glandular obstructions, every symptom of which became more violent on their being exposed to wetting even their feet, a thing almost impossible to avoid; others were afflicted with chronic rheumatisms and diarrhea, and a few with dysenteries, so it began to be somewhat difficult to furnish the number of men requisite for the boats. Col. Arnold, during our march to this place, was indefatigable, at different times in the front, center and rear, animating the troops as much by his presence and example, as by the prudent dispositions that he made. Every one saw the propriety of his orders, all paid an implicit obedience to him. No murmuring or discontent was heard, while on the other hand each person exerted himself for the common good of the whole. At this place the Colonel informed us a magazine of provisions was to be laid in, that in case of a retreat we should be enabled to subsist till we regained the New England settlement. The policy was good, for not a few were sensible that our stock was daily diminishing, and that we might have obstacles to encounter, which would oblige us to return or perish for want of necessities. We saw the difficulty of conveying provisions so far, but as we were anxious to have it done we flattered ourselves with the gleam of hope the Colonel inspired us with.

The 11*th*. The batteaus crossed the first lake, which is not more than three quarters of a mile wide, and the troops marched on the edge of the lake, which is very mountainous and rocky. Having reached our boats, we encountered a carrying place of half a mile to a second lake, and after the road was cut, tolerably good; this, however, kept us busy until evening, at which time we encamped on the side of the second lake, enjoying as before very fine trout.[373]

At this place Col. Arnold laid out a block-house[374], which he ordered to be built immediately for the accommodation of the sick, whom he ordered to be left here.

The 12*th*. The first division was ordered to proceed, which we did after taking an affecting leave of those whose indispositions rendered it impossible for them to go on. We crossed the second lake, and carried our boats, baggage, etc. one mile and an half through a level rich bottom, and encamped pretty late in the evening on the edge of a third lake. Lieut. Col. Steel[375], who had been sent with a party as a scout to the Chaudiere River[376], returned, and informed us that he had seen no person. He received orders to proceed there again. This evening it snowed considerably.

The thirteenth of October, 1775, a very stormy morning, it hailed and snowed violently. About ten o'clock, we crossed the lake, which is two miles and an half over, and as the wind was high, and our boats small and heavy laden, it was somewhat dangerous tho' we were fortunate enough to get over without any accident. The carrying place from this lake to the Dead River[377] is two miles and three quarters; fatigue by this time, had become familiar to us, and both officers and men exerted themselves so much, that we carried everything to the

West Meadow, over which we began to carry very early on the fourteenth. 'Tis a low barren swamp; in many places we were obliged to lay bridges, the soil being so spongy, that upon breaking through the superficies, there was danger of sinking two or three feet deep. In the evening we pitched our tents upon the banks of the Dead River, which is said to be the Kennebunk continued; but by crossing where we did, we avoided a route of 180 miles, exclusive of a rocky carrying place 18 miles long. We had been a week going twelve miles, though we used the utmost diligence; but we flattered ourselves that the worst was past, and that the river, as well as the country, would be more favorable to us. At this place each mess (consisting of six or seven) received their allowance of pork, and their future subsistence depended upon the care they took of it.

Our boats were so much shattered, that we obliged to halt, and we were busied in caulking and otherwise repairing them till the sixteenth; when we decamped and proceeded about ten miles to a carrying place, which was so short we soon got over it, and went a mile further having marched all day thro' a thick cedar swamp. This evening a soldier was killed by a tree falling on him. The pheasants were numerous, but we were not permitted to kill them, our stock of ammunition not adequate and Colonel Arnold passed us this evening; and finding that the flour began to grow short, ordered that one [illegible] be issued to each man per day instead of a pint, and to halt.

The seventeenth at day we marched; about eleven miles were performed with ease. About three o'clock we passed a deserted wigwam belonging to Vattances[378], an Indian Chief, whose savage cruelty rendered him very odious to the inhabitants on the frontier; soon after we overtook the Colonel from whom we received some fresh orders, and continued through a watery swamp; and the river not being rapid, the batteaus easily kept up with us. The whole day's march computed to be at least twenty miles. Our allowance of provisions was thought by no means sufficient but our situation was without remedy.

The eighteenth. It froze very hard last night and was exceedingly cold in the morning. After marching [illegible] miles we came to a ripple where the water was so rapid that the men were obliged to wade and drag the boats seventy yards, which having crossed, we proceeded then thirteen miles. This day's marching was in general ok; the country being mountainous and swampy. We encamped in the evening among some deserted wigwams at the feet of a fall, over which we are to cross in the morning.

The nineteenth we started early. The morning was cloudy, and it began to rain; we carried everything as usual two hundred yards, and proceeded; at three quarters of a mile distance, we reached the second carrying place, which was longer, very rocky and dangerous. Half a mile farther we arrived at the third, which was four hundred yards, and at a small distance a fourth, which was exactly four thousand three hundred and twelve yards, and very bad carrying. During this time it rained very heavily and as there was the appearance of its clearing up, we did not proceed further before we encamped in a dreary wilderness of hemlock, fir-trees, etc. for during our long march, we had seen no oak or hickory, but constant ever, in some places intermixed with birch and maple. Our situation was very uncomfortable, as every part of our baggage was wet, and it rained so hard that we could not easily dry it.

The twentieth. It rained all last night, and this morning was ushered in by its continuance in so violent a manner that we dropped all thoughts of proceeding any further this day.[379] After 10 A.M. we were tantalized with a prospect of its clearing up, but were soon convinced of the mistake, and this evening it bids as fair for continuing as last night. From our present scanty allowance of food, we began to think of reducing it. As for the pork [it was before observed] each mess had their share entirely at their own disposal, and they would fare better or worse according to their present economy. The prospect was very gloomy, advancing further into a savage, perhaps an enemy's country, with but a few days provisions, even at the rate we lived. The men suffering from constant fatigue, want of provisions, clothing, etc.

Saturday, the twenty-first. The morning, such as we expected, and it continued raining all day. The river races very fast, and tho' the bank on which we were encamped was four or five feet above its surface, it was by evening nearly on a level. Col. Arnold passed us about [illegible] P.M. he had come ten miles through the rain, and the effect his presence had upon us can only be known by men in our situation. And while we admired his [illegible], his sufferings and attention, we forgot what we ourselves endured. He proceeded two or three miles beyond us and encamped.

The twenty-second, we were roused before day by the river's rising so much as to lay our camp under water and produced a scene truly shocking. As soon as we could see, we packed up our baggage, in order to hunt a more favorable spot. The river became very rapid, and instead of being dead, might with propriety be termed the liveliest. In an hour or two it cleared up; and we were blessed with the sight of the sun. We proceeded, the batteaus moving very slowly, and as *the country was much overflown [with water], those who marched were obliged to make short circuits, and were lost a considerable time by taking the wrong branch of the river, and to our great joy discovered the boats near dark. The batteaus passed two carrying places this day, which on account of the depth of the water from the late heavy rain, were navigable. Colonel Arnold returned to the other divisions; he had likewise been overflown and obliged in the night to remove to an adjoining hill.*[380]

The twenty-third, we decamped early, after proceeding one mile we came to a carrying place, the current for some distance below it was more rapid than any we had been met with, and though we exerted ourselves as much as was possible for men to do, several boats were overturned and everything in them lost. It is easier to conceive than to describe the sensations of men, who were in an instant deprived of the small remains of their provisions (pork), baggage, etc. Many had not even a kettle to boil their [illegible] in, which mixed with water and known among us by the name of [illegible], was to constitute their future diet, and were obliged either to borrow of some other mess, or bake in the ashes. Horror and despair were painted in their countenances; they were dejected and appeared to be worn out, not having enough to support nature, much less to go through such fatigue.[381] *We encamped near the carrying place, and in the evening Col. Arnold with some officers of the second and third divisions joined us.*

The twenty-fourth. At a council[382] *held last night it was determined to proceed at all events, and that an officer and six men be draughted from each company and proceed with all possible expedition to the Chaudiere river, and the messenger that the Colonel had dispatched some time before to Sartigan [the first Canadian settlement] should return with a favorable answer, they were to proceed to the inhabitants and procure provisions, etc. It was likewise determined that all the sick should return with a few healthy men to escort them, and the whole was put into execution early this morning, and we marched on about ten miles; we would have gone further on account of our low ebb which our provisions were reduced, but the stream was so rapid that the boats could not keep pace with us. We halted at the foot of a fall over which we carry in the morning. Col. Arnold continued on to Chaudiere.*

The twenty-fifth. The ground this morning as covered with snow, which continued falling plentifully. The carrying place was fifty-five yards; we proceeded, and at a mile's distance we came to a second fall forming a beautiful semicircle, not more than seven or eight yards to carry; we marched about six miles further to a third carrying place half a mile long, at a short distance from which the batteaus entered a lake, and passed from that into, and crossed a second one, while those who marched being generally on a ridge of mountains, felt the keen north wind very sensibly. We lost ourselves in the woods, and did not reach the batteaus till late in the evening.

The twenty-sixth. Last night was very cold and sleety, which continued this morning; we started very early, and during our march passed an Indian storehouse and several wigwams; the boats crossed two lakes, one of them pretty large, and arrived at a carrying place sixty-five yards long, where we took leave of the Dead River, and were all very sincere in our wishes that we might never see it again. The batteaus then proceeded over a third lake, from whence we had a carrying place of one mile, and encamped near the edge of a fourth lake, where we found a note left by Colonel Arnold, informing us that we were eight miles from Amaguntic Lake.[383] These ponds or lakes are surrounded by high mountains, upon which we marched. The distance [was] about sixteen miles. The woods tolerably clear, but very fatiguing in going down one mountain and climbing another.

The twenty-seventh. We decamped very early, and the batteaus crossed the lake to a carrying place of three hundred and eighty-eight yards to a second lake, which having crossed we came to a carrying place two hundred and forty-two yards; this led to a third lake, and having crossed it, we came to an exceedingly high mountain, called the Height of Land;[384] over it we were obliged to carry, the distance at least four miles.

By this time the three first divisions of the detachment had got into one body, and it was determined that each company should carry one boat over the mountain for the accommodation of the sick, which alone with our baggage, was very fatiguing, as hilapee did not add much to our strength; those who were able to march were to carry their baggage and provision, and proceed as fast as their strength would admit. We encamped that evening on the banks of French River, seven miles from Chaudiere Lake, upon a barren heath. Colonel Arnold had proceeded on, and it may not be amiss to add, that he fared as we did, or rather worse, as he distributed part of the little he had to such as were in want. We this evening heard that, Lieutenant Colonel Enos[385], who commanded the rear division, had held a consultation in the same place where Colonel Arnold had called a council on the twenty-fourth, and determined to return, as they concluded they would inevitably perish should they proceed.

The author of this journal does not mean to reflect upon Colonel Enos and the Gentlemen who composed his division, as he makes no doubt of their having given satisfactory reasons for their conduct.

The twenty-eighth. It was determined that an equal distribution of the flour be made, which was accordingly done, and each man received four pints, which in our half-starved condition was little more than sufficient for one day; but we were sensible it must be managed with the greatest care, as no one could expect to be relieved by his companion out of so small a stock. We immediately baked it in ashes, after which we made knapsacks of our tents, and packed up such of our baggage as each thought he was able to carry; everything else was left behind. In the afternoon we received a letter from Colonel Arnold, the purpose of which was, that his express had returned with the good news of the French inhabitants waiting our arrival with pleasure. It produced an instantaneous effect. Our difficulties seem to vanish, and after mutually expressing the infinite obligations we lay under to our commander, for his vigilance and unequaled perseverance to alleviate our sufferings though surrounded by innumerable obstacles, we honored his letter with three huzzas, and immediately began our march.

The twenty-ninth. As soon as we could see we proceeded, and were some hours in going through a thick swamp; after which we continued on about fourteen miles further, where we slept in huts that we made with branches of hemlock, which, with a good fire, were very comfortable.

The thirtieth. Last night it snowed. As soon as the dawn appeared we were on our way, and after marching a few miles lost ourselves. About eleven o'clock we came to a river, near which for many miles the country was barren, so that we were under a necessity of wading it, there being no timber with which we might lay a bridge over it. Having found a ford, though nearly our depths, we crossed it. The water was excessively cold. We proceeded and about four P.M. we reached the Chaudiere Lake, which convinced us to our great joy that we were once more right, though we had made a very unnecessary circuit through a country as badly calculated for marching as can be conceived. We halted near the lake on a very level rich piece of ground, covered with fine poplar, birch, etc.

The thirty-first. As our little flock was near exhausted, we marched before day, the good ground did not continue far, before we entered a thick cedar swamp. At nine o'clock we reached the head of Chaudiere River, and five miles below it we overtook Lieutenant McClayland who lay very ill, and we learnt that two of the boats had been sunk near this place, and that one man was drowned. In the Chaudiere there are many ripples and carrying places, so that all of the boats that were taken over the height of land, only one or two ever reached the settlement. We took leave of the Lieut., who died some little time after, and computed the days march to be twenty-five miles; many of the men by this time consumed their little all, and hides, candles, etc. were devoured with avidity.[386]

November the first. From our calculation we supposed it to be about twenty-five miles to Sartigan[387]. *Every man at this time exerted himself, and according to his strength he was in the front or rear. The officers and men were mingled together. This day two dogs, who had followed us, were eat; and even the intestines did not escape.*[388] *At dusk there was no sign of any settlement, though we computed we had marched at least thirty miles, great part of which we ran.*

The second we began our march very early, anxious to find some place where we might satisfy our appetites, and expecting at every turn of the river that we should see Sartigan, few of us having tasted a morsel since the morning before. About twelve A.M. to our inexpressible joy, we beheld some Canadians driving five cows and two horses, which Colonel Arnold had purchased and sent; they had likewise some flour in canoes, and a few sheep, for the sick. There were about a hundred of us in this first party, and one of the cattle was immediately killed; sentinels were placed over it, while the butchers were preparing it, to restrain the men, who sufficiently expressed their impatience by their countenances. The rest of the cattle were drove on; without them numbers must have perished; and we could not help thinking they might be too late for some who were far in the rear, being disabled from marching by the rheumatism or some other disease. Having feasted sumptuously, we proceeded about five miles; from whence to Sartigan was exactly twenty.[389]

The third. We set off very early, not expecting to meet with any refreshment till we reached the settlement. After marching about fourteen miles, we passed a very high fall, much more than any we had hitherto seen. Soon after, we were obliged to ford a large branch of the river, and as it snowed through the whole day, the water was so cold, that we were almost perished before we reached Sartigan, which, however, we last accomplished, after a march of thirty-two days through a wilderness. Here we found plenty of provisions stored for us, and the Canadians striving who should be kindest. Some did not arrive for two or three days, and a few perished.

Thus have I endeavored to describe General Arnold's march. I may probably, at some future day, continue it to Quebec, which is thirty leagues from Sartigan. In the mean time, I am,

Yours, etc.

Errata in last Tuesday's account of General Arnold's march. In the second paragraph, for "Vattances" read "Nattanus". In the third paragraph, for "exactly four thousand three hundred and twelve yards," read "exactly four hundred and thirty-two yards."

CHAPTER ELEVEN

PRIVATE WILLIAM PIERCE JOURNAL

<u>DESCRIPTION.</u>

While researching *Voices from a Wilderness Expedition*, I uncovered this journal located in Volume XII of a little known history journal, *The American Antiquarian and Oriental Journal,* published in 1900.[390] This journal, by a then unknown author, was not known to previous historians of the Arnold expedition. The reason it may have remained unknown is because of the limited circulation of the source magazine.

The provenance of the journal has extensive links involving four people. The earliest owner of the journal was a Mrs. Collins who lived in Collins Landing in the State of Washington. Stephen Burke shows that the Collins family was originally located near Hadley, Massachusetts, where the Pierce family lived. The geographical connection between the two families seems to verify a reason the journal was in the possession of Mrs. Collins. She gave the journal to Robert S. Stubbs, who was Chaplain and Superintendent of the Seaman's Bethel in Portland and then in Tacoma, Washington. Stubbs subsequently gave the journal to the Washington State Historical Society. One of the board members of the Society, James Wickersham, was a lawyer and later a Probate Judge in Tacoma. He also had serious interest in history and was described as a "statesman, author, historian and scholar." In 1891, he and a group of interested people formed a state historical society in Washington which later became the Washington State Historical Society.

Wickersham had started writing articles for *The American Antiquarian and Historical Journal,* which was the brainchild of Rev. Stephen D. Peet, Ph.D. Peet was a graduate of Beloit College in Washington as well as Yale Divinity School. Peet started his journal in 1878 and was its primary manager until he retired in 1910. At some point Wickersham showed the original Pierce journal to Peet so that it could be published in his historical journal. It is unclear whether Wickersham or Peet transcribed the journal, which was described as "a little old brown book." In the introduction to the journal, Peet described it as "eleven pages of this diary are in very small script with the details of the memorable journey from Boston to Quebec of 1,200 men of a Boston army contingent, and of the terrible march through the wilderness of the Kennebec River, Maine."

After *Voices* was published, Stephen Burk contacted this author about an ancestor who was on the expedition. Based on our correspondence, Burke decided to research the author of the Anonymous journal originally published in the Peet publication and identified in *Voices*. Burk was able to identify the author of that journal as William Pierce of Hadley, Massachusetts. Pierce was a private in Captain Hubbard's Company. An article was then published in *Early American Review* in 2013 spelling out the reasons for concluding that William Pierce was the author.[391] This identification happened 130 years after the journal was donated to the Washington State Historical Society by Mrs. Collins and 237 years after the assault on Quebec.

William Pierce and has brother David were both in the Hubbard Company on the expedition. The journal of John Pierce, the expedition surveyor, found in Roberts' book, has an entry on Dec. 30 stating that his friend and namesake David Pierce died while on the expedition. This Pierce journal has an entry for Dec 28 stating "my brother died after 39 days illness with fever and flux." In his *History of Hadley*, Sylvester Judd listed the two brothers as being on the expedition and said that David "went with Arnold to Canada and there d. unm[arried], Dec. 28, 1775." It is clear that David Pierce is the brother referred to in the journal. The pension application of Samuel Cook states that he and William Pierce were the only members of Hubbard's Company not taken prisoners at Quebec.

PUBLICATION.

The only publication of Pierce's journal was *The American Antiquarian and Oriental Journal*, Vol. XXII, January-December, 1900, pp. 224-228.

AUTHOR.

Unfortunately, there is very little information on the life of William Pierce. A son of Josiah Pierce, a graduate of Harvard College and a school teacher, Pierce was born in Hadley, Massachusetts on June 21, 1752. He and his brother David joined Captain Eliakim Smith's Company, which marched to Boston on April 20, 1775, "in response to the alarm of April 19, 1775." In his journal, William states that after volunteering for the Quebec expedition, "We formed our fellows into companies, myself and diverse others from Capt. Smith's company formed ourselves under the command of Captain James [Jonas} Hubbard of Wooster [Worchester]." Among the "diverse others" was his brother David.

William fortunately escaped being taken prisoner at the assault on Quebec and on January 3, 1776, he and Samuel Cook left Quebec for Montreal because their enlistments were up. At Montreal, they enlisted for an additional three and a half months but became separated when Cook contracted small pox. By the summer of 1776, both Pierce and Cook met up again in Hadley.

William Pierce never married and died in Hadley on January 11, 1832 at the age of 79. His grave stone is in the Old Hadley Cemetery. There is no record of him serving in the Revolutionary War after he returned home in 1776.

JOURNAL

FROM BOSTON TO QUEBEC

Cambrig, Sept 13, 1775-

Sixth instant orders came from his excellency General Washington for 1300 men of the army (stationed around Boston) to march to Quebec. We formed our fellows into companies, myself and divers others from Captain Smith's company formed ourselves under the command of Captain James Hubbard[392] *of Wooster.*

Tenth instant we marched from Dorchester to Cambrg and lay there till the Thursday following.

13th instant. We marched through Mistie and [reached] Malden, 7 miles.

Fourteenth instant marched through Lyn and lay at Danvers, 10 miles.

Friday, 15th instant we marched through Salem, Beverly, Wenham, Ipswich and lay at Rowley, 18 miles.

Saturday, 16th, we marched through Newbury and lay at Newburyport,[393] *8 miles.*

The Tuesday following we got sale [sail] at Newburyport for the Canabeck[394] *river and landed there the next morning, which is Wednesday, the 20th inst., and lay there until towards night, and then hoist sale [sail] and come within three miles of Fort Weston*[395]*, but could not get any farther with our schooner for want of water.*

Then we quit our schooner and come by land, which was three miles, and arrived here on the 23rd instant on Saturday in the afternoon, which fort is fifty miles from the mouth of the river.

The night following one of Captain Goodrich's men most foully murdered one of Captain Williams' men by firing a ball through his body, by which wound he dyed [died] the next day. On Monday the murderer was sentenced to be hanged.[396]

On Monday the 25th instant we got up the river about one mile and campt down that night.

On Wednesday the 27th instant we arrived at Fort Halifax[397]*, 17 miles from Fort Weston.*

Thursday morning, 28th instant, we carried our battoes[398] *by the falls,* about one-quarter of a mile; then we had five miles to go to get to the head of the falls. The same day with much difficulty we got two miles and a half.

Friday morning the 29th we got off again and got up the head of the falls and about three miles farther.

On Saturday morning the 30th instant we put forward and got within a half mile of the falls, which is the second crossing place upon this river, about seven miles farther.

On Sabbath day, the 1st of October, we come up to the falls and crossed by our battoes, and

[upon] landing [we] mended our battoes. The crossing place is about 30 rods and very wearysome we found it to be to get this far up the river by falls and swift water.

Monday, 2d October instant, we got off from the swift water and falls and come to the upper part of the great falls of Norridgewalk^399, 32 miles from Fort Halifax.

Wednesday the 4th instant, we carried our battoes by the falls, which is one mile. The last house upon the river is one-half mile below the falls, and we have the woods to go through without any settlements. We got off that night and come ahead about two miles.

Thursday the 5th instant, we come up the river about 11 miles;

on Friday, 6th instant, [we went] five miles and met with falls, where we had to carry our battoes and

loading about twelve miles, but without much difficulty, and passed in above the falls and come three miles.

Saturday, 7th instant, we came six miles.

Sabbath day, 8th inst., we lay still and kept ourselves as sly as we could in the woods.

On Monday, the 9th inst., we arrived at the great carrying place^400, five miles, which is twenty-two miles from the upper fall at Norridgewalk.

Thursday, the 10th inst., we quit this river and began to carry towards Ded river.^401 This day compleat's just one solar month from the day we left the mouth of the river, and fourteen days since we left our schooner. Those seventeen days we had hard times, for we found it to be a hard piece of work to get up this river, which we found very rocky, uneven, swift water and falls also. We are now 132 miles from the mouth of the river. The general run of the river is *from northeast to southwest, and we have twelve miles to carry to get to Ded river, except three ponds, which is four miles of the distance to go by water.*

Wednesday, the 11ᵗʰ inst., we got over to the first pond, which is three and a quarter miles.[402]

Thursday, the 12ᵗʰ inst., we got over the second pond, where we had one and three-quarter miles.

Friday, 13ᵗʰ inst., we came to the third pond. Then we had to carrying our loading two miles and a quarter and forty rods.

Saturday, 14ᵗʰ inst., we carried from the third pond to De[a]d river, two miles and three-quarters and forty rods. We put into Ded river by the Blue hills, so called- and extremely high mountain it is.

Sabbath day, 15ᵗʰ inst., we put in and come up De[a]d river about four miles.

Monday we came three miles and met with falls. Then we had to carry our battoes about six rods. We come about sixteen miles that day. The point we steered in coming from the Canabeck river to the Ded river is about west.

Tuesday, 17ᵗʰ, we had orders for thirty-two of our company to go back to the carrying place to help the hindermost of the company. The men were taken from Captain Shaver's[403] *and Captain Joppin's*[404] *companies.*

Saturday, 21ˢᵗ inst., we got back again.

Sabbath day, 22d inst., we got off up the river once more after so much hindrance for naught, which was the means of such times as I never saw before, for we were obliged to live upon very short allowance.

Friday, 27ᵗʰ inst., we arrived at the head of De[a]d river, about fifty miles from the great carrying place.

Saturday, 28ᵗʰ inst., we left Ded river and put into Chaudere,[405] *which is four and a half miles.*

Sabbath day, 29ᵗʰ inst., we swung our packs with what little food we had and marched to the head of Chaudere river, and we arrived there on Tuesday, 31ˢᵗ, inst. Then we marched down the river as fast as we could to the inhabitants as quick as possible, for we are to suffer very much with hunger, some of us being out of provisions already, and others not having enough for one meal. Some had nothing to eat for three days and eat dog at last.

We marched on with hungry bellies until Thursday Nov 2d, and there met some cattle, Colonel Arnold having gone forward and sent them out by some Frenchmen, which was a very pleasant sight to us.[406]

Friday, 3d inst., we came to the in habitants, 90 miles from Ded river, 200 miles between inhabitants. Then we had 90 miles to march to Quebec.

AT THE ST. LAWRENCE RIVER

On Thursday, 9ʰ inst., we come to the river St. Laurence,[407] over against the city. We was two months upon the march from Boston to Quebec.

On the night of Monday, the 13ʰ inst., we come over the St. Laurence and landed at the place called Wolf's cave [cove][408]; and marched across Abram's planes [plains][409] and found some houses about one and a half miles from the city and there quartered for a few days.

Saturday, 18ʰ inst., about 4 o'clock in the morning, we left our quarters and fled away towards Montreal, 25 miles, because we found it not safe to stay there for want of amminition [ammunition], for we had lost the greater part of it on our journey, our numbers being small to theirs withal. For about one-half of the way we were turned back upon the march, because our provisions was forgot. So we thought best to flee, seeing our men so few and aminition so short, for we had certain news from a prisoner that they were coming out upon us; and we stayed at a place called Point of Tremble[410], waiting for General Montgomery[411] to come down from Montreal to assist with men and aminition.

Friday, Dec 1ˢᵗ, he [General Montgomery] came with artillery, arms, aminition and a part of his army—more came afterwards—and clothing for our army, who came almost naked in this cold country. Some of us lost our clothes in the rivers, some wore them out, and some were so weak by reason of hunger that they could not carry them and so left them in the woods, and several died in the woods by reason of the cold and hunger, and some actually starved to death.

Monday, 4ʰ December, the army marched back to Quebec again from Point of Tremble, all but the tenders [nurses] of our company. My brother was sick and I stayed to tend him.

Twenty-eighth December, about 2 o'clock, my brother died after 39 days illness with fever and flux. He seemed to be getting better and went out doors, and I think he took [a] cold. Sabbath day, 17ʰ December, he was taken worse until he died at Point of Tremble, 24 miles to the south of Quebec. Friday, after the funeral, I came down to the army.

THE ATTACK ON QUEBEC[412]

On Sabbath day morning, 31ˢᵗ inst., about 3 o'clock our army made an attempt to take Quebec. Arnold's men went to the lower town and got over the walls, and Montgomery's men went to the upper town and some of them over the walls.

Then the general [Montgomery] was killed and the men retreated immediately. Then the enemy came upon our men in the lower town about 9 o'clock in the morning. They made no attempt to escape until it was too late, for they thought the other party was in the upper town. Captain Hendrake[413] was killed, Captain Goodrich is wounded, Colonel Arnold[414] was wounded, but made his escape. About four hundred in all was killed and taken, chiefly taken, not very many killed.

Jan. 3d, on Wednesday, we left the army and got off for Montreal. Saturday, 6ᵗʰ inst., we got to Three rivers,[415] 90 miles from Quebec. On Monday morning, 9ᵗʰ of January, we arrived at Montreal.

CHAPTER TWELVE

PRIVATE WILLIAM PRESTON JOURNAL

DESCRIPTION.

In 2008 William Preston's journal was discovered in the library of the New Hampshire Historical Society (NHHS) by Mari Preston Berry, one of his descendants. The journal was located in the *Papers of Charles H. Herbert* that were donated to NHHS after his death, presumably by one of his descendants. The Historical Society has no record of the date and by whom it was donated. As it turns out, Herbert was a nephew of William Preston through his second wife, Mary Herbert of Concord, New Hampshire.

The Preston journal was located by Charles Herbert through Preston's daughter, Hannah Herbert Preston Webster, who inherited it from her mother, Mary Herbert Preston. Herbert visited his cousin Hannah in 1857 and obtained from her various Preston family historical documents, including the journal by William Preston, which he copied. Herbert described the original manuscript journal as a "dilapidated little square manuscript rescued from fire and wrongly sewed." Herbert said he "made such a copy... as I could decipher at Elgin, Ill., at the residence of Maj P's daughter, my cousin, Mrs. Hazen Webster." His copy was probably then transcribed again into a handwritten document composed of thirteen pages, which was donated to the New Hampshire Historical Society.

The discoverer of this journal for the purposes of this book was Robert Stevens of Maine. Rob found out about the Preston journal doing a search on Amazon.com. He found a history of the Arnold expedition of which he had no prior knowledge. One of the reviewers of that book, Annette Lamb, was a descendant of Preston's who indicated in her comments that she had a copy of her ancestor's journal. Being curious, Rob emailed her and subsequently obtained the information about the Preston journal in NHHS which had been discovered by her relative, Mari Preston Berry. Annette Lamb graciously provided him with all the available information she had on Preston and his journal and she subsequently provided the same to me.

A copy of Herbert's hand-written transcription of the journal was obtained by this author from Paul Friday, Reference Librarian of the New Hampshire Historical Society, and transcribed into a typewritten document which is presented in this book. This journal would not have been identified without the interest in the Arnold expedition by Robert Stevens and his pursuit of a comment by a reviewer. It is a previously unknown journal and deserves recognition for its contribution to the history of the march by an enlisted man.

William Preston's second wife, Mary, obtained a pension for her husband's service. Her pension application makes no mention of her husband's journal. However, it does contain a one page document written by William Preston outlining his record of service during the Revolutionary War. The pension application does contain various statements from people who knew Mrs. Preston in Ogdensburg, New York and Elgin, Illinois. It is clear that she put together a lengthy submission so one wonders why she did not use her husband's journal to verify his service.

PUBLICATION.

There are no previous printings of the Preston Journal.

AUTHOR.

William Preston was born in Chester, New Hampshire on July 6, 1754, the son of William and Hannah Preston. In early May of 1775, Preston enlisted as a private in Captain Joshua Abbot's Company and marched with his unit to Charlestown, Massachusetts in response to the Lexington Alarm. He fought in the Battle of Bunker Hill. In early September, Preston enlisted in Captain Henry Dearborn's Company for the expedition to Quebec.

He was taken prisoner at the assault on Quebec on December 31, 1775, and remained in captivity until the release of the prisoners on parole by General Guy Carleton in August of 1776. William returned to his home in Rumney, New Hampshire, and was exchanged after the Battle of Trenton. In early 1777, he enlisted for three years in Captain Benjamin Stone's Company, 3rd New Hampshire Regiment, with the rank of sergeant. Preston served in the Battles of Saratoga in the fall of 1777, where he was captured again by the British. However, he quickly escaped and returned to his company prior to the surrender of British General John Burgoyne.

Preston fought in the Monmouth Battle in 1778 and was a participant in Sullivan's Indian expedition in 1779. He was discharged from the army by Brigadier General Enoch Poor on January 21, 1780, at Danbury, Connecticut. After the war in served in the New Hampshire militia, and from 1800 to 1802 he was a Major in the 1st Battalion, 14th New Hampshire Regiment.

William Preston was married to Elizabeth Clark and Mary Herbert, and had a total of fourteen children. He was active in Rumney politics serving as a Selectman and a representative to the General Court. He died at Rumney, New Hampshire on January 17, 1842 at the age of 88.

JOURNAL

The expedition started from the camp before Boston, Sept. 13, 1775.

Sept. 21. Six miles from Fort Western.[416]

22. Arrived at Fort Western and encampt by the fort. One James McCormick of Capt. Goodrich's Comp[any], being drunken, shot Sargent Bishop of Capt. Williams Company.[417]

25. McCormick was tried by a Co[u]rt Martial & found guilty.

26. McCormick was sentenced to be hanged & brought to the gallows & Reprieved til' General Washington's Pleasure should be known.[418]

27. Got our provisions into the battows [bateaux] & Proceded up the river about 9 miles. We had 45 days of Provision with us consisting of Salt Pork, bisquit, Salt Cod, some peas & flower [flour].[419]

28. Proceed up the river & found the water shoal in some Places & all the way there was six to a battow, three going by land & 3 by water, taking turns.

30. Arrived at Fort Halifax where was the first carrying-place. The fort was on the East Side of the river opposite of the carrying place.[420] *Here the water was very riply. This evening we carried our battows over & the provision.*

October the 1, 1775. Proceed up the river and encampt in the woods.

2. Went about ten miles. Cold & rainy weather.

3. We arrived at Skowhegan Falls.[421] *Got over our Provision & battows. The carrying place was about 40 rods long. Here is a mill a building. Had a very steep bank to carry up. Few inhabitants. We left a barrel of bisquit here which was spoiled.*

4. Norridgewalk[422] *is formerly an Indian town but now settled by the English. Here is the last inhabitants around this place. Stayed here two days. Here is a carrying Place one mile long. We had oxen to help our things over. Here our battows being leaky, we caulked them & mended them.*

5. Here we had fresh beef.

6. Left Norrigwalk & went about 5 miles & encamp from the battows.

7. Got out early. Went about 12 miles & encamp. Rained all night. Lieut. Andrews encamp at the falls carrying place.

9. Proceed up the river & arrived at the great carrying Place.[423] *Here we had an ox killed. One of the inhabitants of Canada brought two barrels of Rum & a little Tabaco. Here is a log house built for the sick.* [424] *One of [the] men was killed by the falling of a tree.*

10. Here we were assembled & Mr. Spring, our Chaplain, went to prayer. We went to the first Pond, which was 4 miles from the river. Cross[ed] the Pond which was about ¾ of a mile wide where we crossed it.[425]

13. We crossed the carrying place from the pond to another, which is about a mile.

14. Crossed the pond about 2 miles over & got over the carrying place about 2 miles in length. The woods here chiefly Cedar & hemlock.

16-31. [no dates delineated]. Crossed the 3d Pond, about 12 miles. Went over the 4ᵗʰ carrying Place, being 4 miles in length. Part of the way over [was] a boggy swamp overgrown with moss & bushes, which all seemed half withered. Found it difficult getting over our battows & barrels. [We were] sinking knee deep in mud & moss.

We launched our battows into a small creek which enters Dead River, so called because the water was very still, & found it otherwise. Here [we were] about 30 or 40 miles up [from the Kennebec River].

Set out & went 13 miles up the Dead River.[426] *Crossed one carrying place of 4 rods & encamp on fine land for game but not good in other accounts. The wood being chiefly birch & hemlock.*

Proceed up the river & overtook Col Green[427] *& his party about 20 miles up the river. We had orders to put ourselves into a defensive state. We made a great number of cartridges & every man's powder horn filled. Our cartridges were spoiled. One kilt.*

We had orders to march. Went 5 miles this day.. Found it tedious & cold. It rained & our battow was leaky & indeed they were all [leaky].[428]

Nov 1ˢᵗ Travelled 12 miles.

2. Travelled 4 miles. Met provisions & the same day French inhabitants. A cow killed.

3. Went 12 miles.

4. Went 16 miles. We had warm houses to be in which was a great thing for us having lain on the ground for four or five nights.

5. Sunday reached [Sartigan].[429] *Col.[Arnold} & other men went forward & made ready provisions for us. What little money we had we laid out for bread & other articles, but they were so Extravagant in their prices that our money went but a little way. Today Flood, a rifleman, was whipt 20 lashes for stealing Capt. Dearborn's pocketbook.*

6. Marched 18 miles. Here was 12 miles of woods.

7. Marched 8 miles. Snowed all day.

8. Marched 8 m[iles] & came to Point Levi[430] on the river St. Lawrence opposite of Quebec.

9. Took a prisoner here. We stayed until the 13th making scaling Ladders & collecting canoes to cross the river.

12. Sunday. Nothing remarkable except we had very cold weather to keep guard.

13. We cross the river St. Lawrence above Point Levi & landed at the cove[431] where Gen. Wolf did in the year 1759 & held a counsel whether to make an attempt on the town or not. But for several reasons it was omitted for the present. Went to Major Caldwells House, about a mile from the City, where we stayed till the 19th.

14. One of our men taken being on Sentry. The town was alarmed. We expect[ed] they were coming to give us battle. The whole detachment turned out to meet them & marched within gunshot of the City walls. But saw no opposition, but when we turned to go back they Fired several cannon shots at us without doing any damage.

19. Sunday morning about 4 o'clock [we] set out on our march to Point [aux Trembles], about 25 miles from Quebec, where we continued till General Montgomery came with his army.[432] We kept guard at a river called [illegible], 8 miles from Quebec, & on a bridge further up the country [with] about twenty soldiers.

20. Sunday. Lieut. Hutchins [plus] 60 other men with myself went to meet the gunpowder & other stores & help to bring them down.

December 3. Sunday in the afternoon some of the cannon was put into the battow & brought down the river & Launched at Wolf's Cove. It snowed & the wind blew so hard that the battow was in some danger.

5 thru 24. The Detachment marched to Quebec to a nunnery within gunshot of the walls, where we stayed 8 or 9 days, but the Place being wanted for a Hospital we moved our quarters over the river St. Charles to the house of Mr. Henery, a minister.[433] We were now very busy making scaling Ladders & erecting a battery within half mile of the walls, where several men were killed because the battery was not strong. Being built with Snow & Ice.

25. The General [Montgomery] desired that we would give our opinions whether we would turn out to scale the walls of Quebec or not. We thought we had better [do it] than to [continue to] block up the city. [It] being very cold standing on the ground, we scarce could keep from freezing.

26. We turned out to scale the walls but the General ordered us back, thinking it not Dark enough. The Enemy fired busily.

29. [Same as the 26th.]

30. [Same as the 26th.]

31. Sunday [at] 4 o'clock in the morning we mustered in order to scale the walls. Twas dark & stormy. Our guns [were] in poor order [as] we had not timely notice. Being belated, [our company] fell in the rear, but made all possible haste & met Col. Arnold wounded. We marched on & the Enemy fired briskly behind us & took us. Being obliged to surrender. There was 375 in all that was taken prisoners. We was put into the [building] where [there] was Friars. One of which was very kind. Bringing wine for the sick & many other things.[434]

January 1, 1776. Now a prisoner in Quebec. WE had each man a blanket & a straw between two of us.

3. General Carleton ordered us to give a list of our names, age & what Regiment we belong to [& where we were born].[435]

4. All the old country men[436] were Picked off & called into another Room & after some talk they came back.

5. They were called for again & Examined by the General & were obliged to [en]list & fight against us til the 31st of May. About 80 or 90 in number, the old country men were taken out.

9. Some four men were taken with the Small Pox. [437]We expected it, A general disorder [among the men] having eat chiefly Salt Pork, bisque, rice & butter. Sufficient of allowance if not cheated by our men.

10. Some suspected Dewey who acts as Quarter Master Sergent & dealt out our Provisions to be our Enemy.

14. Sunday.

15. The time seems long having no employment.

16-17. Several [men] gone to the Hospital having the small Pox. Some clothes were sent in to some of the company

20. Dewey made complaints of 15 [men] who agreed to run away & two were put in irons & sent to the goal [jail].

21. We were ordered to make a Return of all the tradesmen amongst us.

Two of our men in our company made their escape, who [had] [en]listed in the Enemy's service.

24. Last night our army burnt four of their vessels.

February 16. [One] of our men put in irons for calling one of the emigrants a Tory. All the Emigrants were put in Prison again because some of them Deserted last night.

24. Various reports concerning us. Some say that we shall be sent to England & sold for slaves, or some say Guinea, or some other India Island & some say that we shall be hanged & some say that we shall be sent to Boston to be Exchanged. But we expected to be relieved by our men taking the town.[438]

March 1, 1776. One of our men put in irons for answering one of the Sentry who abused him.

9. The town was alarmed.

13. Today we were moved from this place to the goal [jail] near St. John's gate which was burn proof & [we] had the liberty of the yard, about a quarter of an acre.[439]

26. Last night Martin escaped out of goal & got away clear. About this time there was a Plan laid for our escape & to regain our Liberty by seizing the guards & turning the cannon against the town.

31. Our scheme was found out. Being Sunday. The Sentrys hearing one of our men make a noise in the cellar in the night & they came in the morning & searched, the cellar door being loose, & found that we had an intent to get out.

April 1. One of our men, John Hall, went out & discovered the whole plot & we were put in irons, two & two. This morning before Day the guard turned out & fired their guns off before the goal for some time. Then the alarm bells Rung & the cannon on the walls was fired as we supposed to Draw out our men to the walls to cut them off with grape shot.

2-3. Fired briskly on both sides. Our men [were] erecting a battery at Point Levi.

7. Much firing on both sides.

14. Major McKinsay took Capt. Morgan's Company out of irons.[440]

15. This day the New York [regiment] was out of their enlistment & wanted to go home, which made no small disturbance, but were compelled to stay.

16-17. We had a weeks advance of fresh beef, which was killed 3 or 4 months before. They thought it more than we deserved.

18. The cannon continued firing on both sides.

25. Our army crossed the river from Point Levi.

28, Some of our officers tried to make their Escape but [were] found out & put in irons.

May 3. Heard cannon up the river.

4. 9 or 10 o'clock at night the town was alarmed & set a fire on the water which proved to be a fire ship sent by our men but did no harm to the Enemy.

6. Monday about sunrise the town was alarmed & three ships were up the river. Some troops landed & [at] one o'clock marched out. Our army Retreated leaving some few sick men behind which were brought into town.

7. Major Carleton came into [the] goal & ordered our irons off.

9. Six prisoners brought into the goal.

10. Two riflemen went out. We know not on what terms. Two others taken amongst the bushes by one Frenchman.

June 30. We hear that a French fleet is come to Philadelphia on our behalf.

July 1. We hear that the Indians have scalpt a good many of our men.

4. Two prisoners brought in that was taken by the Indians.

5. One of our men took out one of the grates & was mistrusted of breaking out.

6. Today is my birthday. [It] was [the] twentieth year of my age. We saw 3 ships coming up. We informed Mr. Prentice of the man who pulled out the grate, so that we hope it will have no ill effect.

7. Sunday. The man who took out the grate fought with the man who informed [about] the evil which he did, & Castle informed Mr. Prentis of the same. We heard that the General had information of our other attempts to break out [of] goal.

8. We hear that Col. McLain is taken or killed & that we are to go home soon. We hear that Col. McLain is killed.[441]

11. [We hear that] 2 thousand men [are] crossing the Lake. We hear that there is a French fleet coming here & that the German troops are going home.

12. We hear that we are to sail to New York within 10 days.

13. Fair & warm;

14. Sunday.

15. We hear that the Governor[442] *is expected in ten days in town & that we shall know whether we shall go soon or not.*

17. We have bread instead of butter today.

18. We hear that Col. McLain is come down & that the general was expected every minute.

19. The weather is so cold that the Canadians expect but a bad Crop of corn. It is so cold that the French wear a great coat & mittens.

20. Conner, one of the last prisoners that came into the goal, was taken out & put into the new goal & we suppose he is put in irons for talking Impertinence .

21. We hear from our officers that we are to go home soon & we hear that the French, Spaniards & Prussians are at war with Great Britain & that there is a Large Fleet in the Gulf of the river St. Lawrence.

22. This afternoon the Governor arrived to Quebec, which gives us hope for relief. Expecting he will release us by setting us at liberty or Exchanging us, for he was a gentleman & beloved by everybody that knew him for his honour & up-rightness of Conduct. At his arrival [he] was saluted with 15 guns.

26. We hear that the governor has sent [a message] to let our officers know that within 3 days they shall know when they shall go home. We saw 2 ships coming up.

28. Today Mr. Murray, the barracks Major, came in & told us that we shall go away from this[place] within a week or ten days at most, the outside. Now we begin to believe that we shall go soon. We have heard so many stories about going home that we can scarce believe anything we hear.[443]

31 We hear that our men have taken St. Johns & the dutch general is killed & English Cols. We her that we are not to go home till the prisoners was come down that was taken at St. Johns.

Aug 1. Rainy morning.

2. Fair weather. The news today is that our Army have wounded the German General mortally & taken 500 wounded prisoners at Lake Champlain. We have it confirmed that we are to go on board the vessel on Sunday next.

3. Fair weather. [We] hear that our sick men at the Hospital are to go on board this evening. We expect to go tomorrow morning.

4. We expected to go on board this morning . The prisoners that was out to work lie waiting all day. Expecting to go on board. About 5 o'clock Mr Prentis and Mr Henry come in & brought in our shirts. Every man had a shirt & 35 men signed & went on board.

6. They did not lock us up last night. This afternoon we was to go on board, but one of the vessels was not ready so we are to go tomorrow. This day

we signed a parole of honor to go home. This afternoon I see Martin, [Major Timothy] Bigelow & Capt. Goodrich.[444]

9. Today at 9 o'clock we were took out of goal & put on board the Mermaid with [illegible] who I had not seen for 7 months.

10. Today we hoisted sails & [then went] for six or seven miles out of the sight of Quebec.

11. Set sail about 7 o'clock & sailed till midnight & then dropped anchor.

12. Stormy weather in the morning. About 6 o'clock we sailed with the tide 4 Leagues & came to anchor, for the wind was strong against us. Stopt within one League of the end of the Isle of Orleans.[445]

13. We lay at anchor all day.

14. Pleasant weather. Today at six o'clock we sailed with the wind & did thirty leagues & came to anchor about one league off the Island called Coudres. Before noon this day we saw white porpoises. At 4 o'clock weighed anchor. The wind fair. Came to anchor again about 2 o'clock at night.

15. This morning about sunrise weighed anchor & sailed with a fair wind. About 3 o'clock pass the Isle of Pic.[446]

16. Continued our sail. At night [it] stormed.

17. This morning [it] cleared up & was fair weather. This day we see several whales. We past[ed] by Point Gaspe. It is said that we are quite out of the mouth of the river [St Lawrence]. A favorable wind attends us now.[447]

18. A modest breeze of air this morning & we got quite out of the sight of land.

19. This morning we came against the middle of St Johns Island, so nigh that we saw several houses. The said island is called 60 miles long. At one o'clock [this] afternoon we spied Cape Breton Island & we passed through between St Johns Island & Cape Breton.[448]

20. This morning at 2 o'clock the frigate fired a gun for us to lay to & at 6 o'clock they cast anchor. But lay not many minutes before we sail again for now the wind begins to blow some

21. It is supposed that we came ten leagues since yesterday morning till tonight. The wind being low and contrary & the islands so many that we made but a poor way a passing, & now between the mainland & the sea board is islands.

22. Last night at midnight we dropped anchor & sent a barge to shore. The Island called Government Island lies to the South of us & the Island called [Port Dauphin] lies to the North. Tonight about sundown the Commander

171

gave orders to the rest of the ships to be in readiness & [we] follow[ed] her hoisted sail with a good wind briskly all night.

23. A good side wind now blowing between Cape [Nova Scotia] & Cape Breton & at night steering southeast. [At] 12 oclock, just through the Gut of Canso.[449]

24. Today a high side wind. Now out of sight of land.

25. Sunday. In some more calm. So much headwind that we can get along but slow.

26. No wind & we don't get along none hardly. This morn saw a shark about 12 feet long. His fins 3 feet long [and] a head like a pickerel. About 1 o'clock we [we] had a fair wind.

27. Very rainy this morn. The waves very high.

28. Today we had no wind at all but lay tossing on the sea.

29. We are now in the latitude of 36 & 42. But little wind. We go at the rate of 4 mile an hour. At noon the wind blows well at the [illegible].

30. We go 5 knots a hour brisk. All day steering to the [illegible].

Sept ye 1, 1776. On board ye Mermaid. Sunday. We now steer slow being obliged by a high wind which is contrary for our voyage.

2. We steer the same course in the same wind.

3. Today at 12 [o'clock] we made it back & steered northwest. We are now in the Latitude 37 degrees. About 4 o'clock the wind shifted to the southwest & held there all day.

4. Last night it acted a good deal squally. This morning a flying fish flew into the ship & we catched it & a shark last night.

6. Last night was squally & the wind shifted to northwest & soon got in the North & the wind was very high. We [are] steering about right for Philadelphia being about west. The seas are high.

7. Last night the wind went down. Today moved but a little or none.

8. But last night the wind blew a pleasant gale to the northeast [at] 8 or 9 knot breeze. Sunday. Towards night came a heavy thunder shower.

9. A spanking breeze made every one looking for Land & steering towards New York.

10. Pleasant wind [and we] go 3 knots an hour. At night the frigate steered to the south till morning.

11. Then back to the northwest. Expecting to see Land tonight but was disappointed.

CHAPTER THIRTEEN

DOCTOR ISAAC SENTER'S SECOND JOURNAL

DESCRIPTION.

There are two Senter journals that are very different but both have authenticity and provenance. The only known Senter journal up to the publication of *Voices* was the journal located in the Historical Society of Pennsylvania (HSP) and included in Roberts' book. For some reason no one had discovered the journal attributed to Senter in the Rhode Island Historical Society (RIHS). A copy of the RIHS journal was provided to this author by their library and it was transcribed and included in *Voices*.

The RIHS journal was discovered by the daughter of former Rhode Island Governor John Brown Francis "among some old papers of her father's." When she realized what it was, she sent the manuscript to Isaac Senter's granddaughter, Mrs. Crawford Allen. Mrs. Allen presented the manuscript to the Rhode Island Historical Society on April 30, 1878.

The manuscript that was discovered by Francis's daughter was slipped into a copy of the HSP journal so for a time it was thought that it was the "missing" HSP journal. However, even a cursory examination of the two journals reveals that they are entirely different. So different that is difficult to reconcile that they were written by the same person. When the discovered journal included in this compilation was given to Senter's granddaughter and then was compared to the HSP journal it was obvious that they were two different journals.

There are two notations in the RIHS manuscript that demonstrate a connection to Isaac Senter.

The first is a note written to Senter by the estate of the Reverend James Manning, President of Brown University. The note is dated July 28, 1791, and is addressed to Senter. Senter signed Manning's note on the bottom with the words, "Errors Excepted." Since Senter was alive in 1791, the note and the signature by Senter established a clear link. The words used by Senter could only apply to a written document.

The second notation is a signature of John R. Bartlett on the back page of the manuscript. Bartlett was Secretary of State of Rhode Island from 1855 to 1872. In addition to being active in Rhode Island politics, Bartlett was also a former bookseller in NYC and a member of several historical and scientific societies. From 1854 until his death in 1886, he was the librarian of the John Carter Brown Library. Bartlett's credibility as a historian and book expert is beyond question so his signature on the manuscript is solid evidence for its authenticity.

The existence of the two journals caused some confusion and arguments favoring one over the other. Both Justin Smith and Kenneth Roberts made arguments that the HSP journal was the correct Senter journal and the one that should be used. Because of its three introductory pages, this

RIHS manuscript by Senter was written after the assault and it can be argued that it was used by him as a guide for writing the more detailed and descriptive HSP journal. H.M. Chapin, the librarian of RIHS, supports this conclusion in a letter he wrote to William Abbatt in 1915. Chapin argues that the RIHS manuscript journal is "the original notes which Dr. Senter made during the expedition, or possibly a first draft from those notes, which he may have made upon his return home, and that the (HSP) Ms. is probably his second draft, based either on our Ms. or upon his notes written at a later period." Based on the above information, Chapin's explanation seems more compelling than the arguments advanced by Smith and Roberts.

PUBLICATION.

The only previous publication of the Senter original journal was in *Voices from a Wilderness Expedition*, pp. 150-159.

AUTHOR.

Isaac Senter was born in Londonderry, New Hampshire, in 1752 and moved to Rhode Island with his family when he was a young boy. He studied to be a physician under Dr. Thomas Moffat, a physician in Newport. When the Revolutionary War broke out, he marched to Boston as a physician with the Rhode Island troops under the command of Colonel John Church.

Senter was appointed as the physician and surgeon to the Arnold expedition in September of 1775 in Cambridge and marched with the expedition to Quebec, recording his experiences in two different journals. After the attack on Quebec, he treated the wounded men, including Arnold, in the General Hospital near Quebec. He returned home with the American forces in June of 1776 and settled in Cranston, Rhode Island, to practice medicine.

In 1776, Senter was appointed Surgeon-General of Rhode Island, and served as the Cranston representative to the Rhode Island General Assembly from 1778 to 1780. Senter moved from Cranston to Newport in 1780, and lived there, practicing medicine, for the rest of his life. He received an honorary medical degree from Brown University as well as Harvard and Yale because of his articles in various medical journals. He was a member of the Massachusetts Historical Society and the American Philosophical Society. He was the Director of the Rhode Island Military Hospital from 1794 to 1799.

Senter was a close friend of General Nathaniel Greene and actively treated that family for a number of years until they moved to South Carolina. Isaac Senter died in Newport on December 20, 1799, at the age of 45, leaving his widow and six children. At his death he left an extensive and valuable medical library which was donated to the Rhode Island Medical Society in 1881.

ISAAC SENTER JOURNAL

RHODE ISLAND HISTORICAL SOCIETY

To such a pitch of initiation had the contest arrived between Great Britain & the United Colonies early in the year of 1775, that it was thought necessary by the latter to take the most advantageous & effectual measures to secure our frontiers, bordering on the Lakes of Canada, from the hostile invasions of the English & their savage allies, the northern Indians. Consequently the Garrisons of Ticonderoga & Crown Point, the gates & sluces through which these incursions were to have been made, were of too much importance in the eyes of the Americans, not to attract their early attention. Already has the British Governor Carleton, commander of that colony, been authorized by a Commission as new as it was extraordinary, & [to] arm the French Canadians & march them out of that Colony for the express purpose of subjugating the Anglo Americans, & if he found it necessary in the completion of his work to capitally punish all those in any Colony whom he should deem rebelious opposers of his measures. Altho the Canadians in general were not favorably disposed to comply with this despotic request, still it was too evident to the United Colonies that the arrival of the British forces in that country in the course of the lesson would enable him to, by compelling the Canadians by arms, carry out his plans into effectual operation.

At the same time, it was well known that he had already embodied a considerable number of the different tribes of savages into his service, who only waited for an opportunity to lust the blood of the intended victims of the ministerial wrath, to assemble with a rapid association & diabolical sympathy all the rest of these infernals from affiliation by their [illegible] & passions in [illegible] & laughter. When with many more aggravating circumstances as well as [illegible] hostilities under General Gage in New England too numerous to mention were sufficient to authorize any effective measures on our part. Indeed, to have waited to be attacked by such a barberous combination as ever forming in Canada & threatening our frontier settlements bordering on that country would have been little short of self murder.

Thus the Americans felt & thus they reason'd, which the timid patriots & ministerial advocates unitedly represented offensive measures at this period especially in Canada as entirely unjustifiable upon the principles of reconciliation, which was the vain hope & the expectation of no small & influential part of this country. To seize the present opportunity & forestalling the designs of the enemy & to pierce him deep in the most vulnerable part was a conduct worthy of exasperated freemen.

To this end Cols Allen, Arnold & Warner, with a few more decided & patriotic characters, hastily collected a number of provincials for the occasion by a rapid march from Vermont & threw themselves successively into Ticonderoga, Crown Point & St. Johns, bring[ing] off from the latter all the cannon & prisoners which they could & garrisoned the others. This coup de main so favorable to the Americans in the infancy of their struggle, besides the prisoners & military stores achieved, paved the way for a more solid impression of American arms.

This was undertaken authoritatively by Genl Schuyler[450] as chief, but for want of health carried on by the amicable, the brave, entripid Montgomery,[451] who united in character all the accomplishments of the soldier & gentleman. Had this armament followed up the first strike on the lakes early in the summer, that country in all probability would have long ere this constituted one of the United States.

While the American army were successful progressing in Upper Canada under the direction of these two generals, a plan was found for penetrating into lower Canada through the Province of Maine directed against Quebec, its capitol. Through this unexplored wilderness, the British could form no conception of an attack from their antagonists, consequently Carleton had left it defenseless in order to meet Montgomery in the vicinity of Montreal.

Colo. Arnold[452] who had shown no common spirit of enterprize as well as attachment to the cause of his country, was the first to solicit the conducting of this extraordinary & hazardous undertaking.

It was accordingly given him an armament selected for 1100, including officers, from the Americans camped at Cambridge, who march from thence on the 13th of Sept 1775, and arrived on the 15th at Newburyport,[453] which on the 20th sail'd with 11 transports for the mouth of the River Kenebec[454] where they arr'd the next day.

From this to the 23d, the transports were employ'd in ascending the stream to within a few miles of Fort Western[455] to the head of the navigable water on the River. There were mostly finished a number of Batteaux[456] hastily constructed with green soft pine to the number of nearly 200, which *were intend'd to convey up the Kenebec all the provisions, military stores etc. belonging to the army.*

From this to the 25ᵗʰ the troops were employed in unloading the transports and in adjusting the Batteaux, & carrying all the effects belonging to the army up the falls at this Fort.

During this time, the army had been arranged into three Divisions. A part of each Division to [take] the charge of the boats with all the stores etc., while the others were destined to march on the east bank of the Kenebec, in such progressive [illegible] with the batteaux as for each Division to every night encamp at the same stage.

Capt. Morgan⁴⁵⁷ with the three rifle companies constituted the first Division, Lieut. Col. Greene⁴⁵⁸ the 2d, & Lt. Col Enos⁴⁵⁹ the third. Two of the guides & pioneers who had been hunters in this wilderness were also engaged in the front Division to assist in discovering the least difficult passages in the woods, as well as to help clear the way in the various carrying places.

Our provisions consisted of 1ˢᵗ, salt pork; 2d, flower; 3d, barrel's beef; 4ᵗʰ, barrel's dry bread; 5ᵗʰ, salt cod fish; & 6ᵗʰ, barrel's pease [peas];

And having no artillery, our military effects were inconsiderable in point of hefts. We had only fuzens & side arms with kegs of powder & ball & flints. These, with a tent to each Battalion, a few boxes of candles, soap & hospital stores, constituted then nearly all the effects to be transported by water.

The batteaux were furnished with each a setting pole, oars, & pointer at the head. Thus arrang'd & equip't, we left Ft. Western, where the officers had been very entertain'd at Mrs Howard, a polite, hospitable & excellent family, in the following order: 1. Morgans Div. five in the a.m. of the 25ᵗʰ. 2d. Green's on the 26ᵗʰ, & 3d. Enos's on the following day.

From this to the 30ᵗʰ, we were employ'd in ascending the River to Fort Halifax⁴⁶⁰, a distance of only 18 miles. We soon experienced how illy adapted these large & heavy boats were to force against a stream, the current of which, in this stage, mostly ran much short of three knots an hour & in many places much more. In this, much skill as well as strength was requir'd. In the former we generally [lacked] for very few of the men had ever been acquainted with [this] kind of savage navigation. The first Division had propos'd this carrying plan before the last arriv'd. This is a large water fall & the last stands on a point of land made by the confluence of the Kenebec & Sabasticook Rivers. The Indian name of these falls is Tucconnic⁴⁶¹. Here was our first carrying place

179

by which we were exercised in a way little to be envied by any short of gall[e]y slaves. The rear Division did not all pass this [way] till the 2d of Oct.

From this to the 5th the two last Divisions were almost incessantly employ'd in forcing up this rugg'd stream, & before our arrival there, several of the batteaux were become so leaky that it was the work of one hand to bale one of them, Between Fort Halifax & Norrigwok[462], we passed two water falls, the first was call Wassarun, & the second Scunkhegan.[463]

At Norrigwalk, many of our batteaux being joined in such a shatter'd state that the Company of artificers we employ'd [had] to repair them.[464] We now had arriv'd to the extreme settlement on this River & where there were but a few families who had but lately plac'd themselves at this frontier.

We now began to discover that courage & bodily prowess were the only requisites for conducting such an enterprize as this successfully. The water which had been taken in to the boats, as well through the leaks as over their sides, had so [ruined] the floating salt fish that we could not longer reckon on that article for support. The casks of biscuit & dry pease [peas] by the same means began to soak & burst & to finish the climax, our salt beef which was put up in hot weather was sufficiently ripon'd [ripened] for the most improved modern epicures. In fine we had little else now to depend on to keep body & soul in [illegible], just the solid junks of salt past[e] & flower [flour]. The fact [is that] we had been able to purchase fresh meat, by the generous inhabitants through which we passed, to [satisfy] all our wants, but this could last no longer than [the time] which [we were] in this stage.[465]

The forward Division of Riflemen, who were better acquainted as well with the disadvantages of a life in the wood as well as this kind of inland navigation than the New England troops who made up the two rear ones, did not experience such a deduction in the proportion of their provisions. They however [also] soon became pinch'd in this respect, but derived some assistance from being in the front of the whole, and excellent marksmen. Not long after we arrived at this stage it began to rain & this added not a little to the injury of the provisions as we possessed no covering for it.

It was during our tarry here that Col. Arnold laid the foundation which finally blasted all our reward.

Measures were not only taken by the Lt. Govr [for] defense [of] the city against a surprise by all those who were in the place, but [he also] directly destroyed all the boats, canoes etc. on the

> *south side of the Rivr St. Lawrence for 30 miles up & down the Rivr.*

I now resume my narrative.

9th. The last Division greet Norrigwalk & in the course of the day passed a small rivr 7 miles from hence call'd the Seven Mile Stream & encamp'd three miles above.

10th. As soon as the light would favor us we were moving & in the course of three miles we came to a fall[s], call'd by the Hunters Caratunuc⁴⁶⁶. The carrying place by this fall was about 40 rod & we encamped a mile only in advance. The water for this day [was] unusually rapid. The land & timber however was superior to what we had before seen on this stream.

11th. The water still continued so rapid that our oars were of little service the most of the day, & the only way we had left us to advance with the bateaux was by seizing the inclining bushes which grew on the banks of the River & by that means haul our boats forward. The distance which we advanced daily is not easily ascertained. We encamped on the June grass which grows on the sides of the Rivr here with great frequency.

12th. This day we expected to reach to the Great Carrying Place⁴⁶⁷ & we accordingly arriv'd there at past 4 o'clock p.m., where we found a very considerable part of the army busily engaged in transporting boats on thin bark directly into the wilderness, leaving the Kenebec on the right & proceeding by a west course. There the Rivr, which we were now leaving, appeared to come from a point east of north & as far as we could discover was one continuous impossible rapid. The rifle companies, with the pioneers, had pushed their way through the woods in Quest of a [illegible] which we were told was within 4 miles of the River. Little had been done by them to alter the face of nature in rendering the obstacles less difficult. This was a stage of extreme fatigue. Not less than 7 or 8 times were each boats crew obliged to pass [back and forth] before the last article was carried over. High hills, miry morasses & almost impenetrable woods were continually opposing us. Our bateaux in gen'l weighed not less than 400 lbs, which, with the provisions, we made not less than 800 weight on average, to be transported by 5 or 6 hands over each carrying place. This encumbrance however was easily diminishing as scarcely a day passed without several of the boats being stove to pieces & all or part of their loading lost.

It was not till the 15th before the army crossed this laborious passage. Added to our other difficulties, the number of our sick & infirm were daily increasing & so bad were several of them, that they were obliged to be transported by hand in the same way over all the carrying places. We had for several days been entirely in solid provisions, which create a constant thirst, & to allay which we got nothing but water more or less [illegible]. The first pond which we came to was entirely surrounded by a filthy [illegible] & the water was as yellow as a mixture of saffron & water. This, partly from its [illegible] quality & perhaps from the quantity we were obliged to use, brought on a vomiting & diaherrea which harassed many of the men.

From the 15th to the 16th we were employed in crossing the first pond, & it was not till the 18th the army got across the 3d pond. Two of these ponds consist of waters which were pernicious to the soldiery. The salt provisions with which they were now exclusively [illegible], call'd for the frequent use of drink & we were entirely dependent upon such water as nature afforded us to supply our wants. Their water was not only yellow but very bitter, which brought on either vomiting or diaherrea, or both, to a very considerable part of the army. The 3d pond was less injurious. At this pond we supposed ourselves only 12 miles from the Kennebec.

There follows two different narrations.

1st. This day we met Majr Bigelow[468] with [Capt] Hanchet[469] of the 2nd Division of the Army returning in pursuit of provisions, who informed us that they could proceed no further without. We now ascended a mountain. Our woods beyond which we expected to find a small water stream which would conduct us to what was call'd the Dead River[470], & after traversing this height for about 27 miles, where we began to descend in to a hideous spruce & cedar swamp, in which we labored for another mile & a half.

2nd. This day we met Majr Bigelow & 27 men who were returning from the 2d Division in search of Provisions, & inform'd [us] that the men forward would advance no further without. From a S.W. course which we had follow'd since leaving the Kennebec, we now varied it nearly N.W. & ascended a mountainous & [illegible], and then descended in to a spruce & cedar swamp so deep & almost impenetrable brush for a mile & a half more till we came to a stream of slow water serpentine course apparently coming from S.W. part of the high wood we had just crossed. This was mostly about 12 feet wide and frequently as many deep. There are much appearance of beaver & other amphibious animals. After following this ¾ miles we descended two miles up these waters. Here to most of us was an unofficial report. An ox had been drown from Norridgwalk by two hands who had no other duty to attend to. He was slain by the first Division, each man taking all, or part as they came up. From the 8ᵗʰ of the month, this poor animal [had] eaten no other food than what the [illegible] etc. afforded him & he swam over the rivr & drove round the ponds & at night contentedly lodged with his drivers.

The water of this riv'r, which is the W. branch of the Kennebec, had a remarkable dark appearance, & scarcely when we entered it to have any motion. Here we found excellent trought [trout] in plenty as we had in most of the ponds we had pass'd.

21ˢᵗ. We had a south west storm through the whole of this day which blew with such violence that we had not ascended but a few miles before the water became so great that it was with greater labour we forced our way against them. Add to this embarrassment, the violence of the increasing wind threw so many trees in to the river that we were momentarily expected to be sunk. We however labored incessantly while night approached & encamped about 15 miles up the stream, but instead of resting we were obliged to watch the provisions part of the night to guard against accidents from the frequent falling of the trees around us.

We here found Col. Greene's Div which could proceed no further for the want of provisions.[471]

By the 20ᵗʰ, most of the rear Division had passed this carrying place, & after passing this [we] reverted near a mile [until] we came in to the Dead River, a western branch of the Kenebec. This stream is about 12 feet wide & for the most part was not very deep. There were much appearance of beaver & other animals of the kind here. When we first entered on this stream, its water appeared almost motionless, till a heavy rain with a violent wind S.W. soon swelled it to that degree that by 4 in the afternoon we had a rapid cur[rent] to oppose, with the addition of a great number of trees, which were by the severity of the wind constantly thrown in & across it.

21. The storm continued to increase. All this day's ascent was accompanied with the same difficulties in a greater degree than yesterday.

Side note: [All these ponds abound with [the] tastiest trought [trout], which are easily taken.

22d. Not a dry thread had any of the army all night & as the morning was serene we were in motion at its dawn. The rivr from being dead now had become so lively that many of our boats lay submerged almost out of sight. By actual measurement it had risen 8 feet during the night & how much in the day we could not definitively ascertain. In many places the land what was dry the day before now was inundated in many places for miles, especially up such creeks & small streams as emptied themselves into it. The land party now suffered hardships equally great as with that [those] which went by water. Since in many instances the men were obliged [to] leave the course of the stream several miles to cross those overflown places, & in several instances they had no other method left them than to fell the trees to pass upon. These difficulties retarded our advance to that degree that in two days of the most severe exertion we [were] not more than 14 miles in advance. [The] Greater part of the way the bateaux were hauled up entirely [with] the assistance we obtained from the projecting inclining branches of small trees. Boats were oversot [with water].[472]

[Here a page seems to be missing]

[The journal resumes].

He [Enos] arriv'd with a part of his officers, while the rest of his party were still below. While in the meantime, the remainder of the invalids were going back. [Based upon] An examining into the state of the two Divisions, it was found that in Enos's [Division] there are no [illegible], while in Greene's they [are] nearly expended. The question [to be decided] being, [with] Enos [as] Pres., whether to proceed or return. The party against going on argued that there was no provisions for the whole army to last for 5 days.[473]

25th. When all the officers present voted in the following manner.

Greene's Division	Enos's Division
For going forward.	
Lt. Col. Greene	*Capt. Williams*[474]
Maj. Bigelow	*Capt. McCobb*[475]
Capt. Topham[476]	*Capt. Scott*[477]
Capt. Thayer[478]	*___ Hyde*[479]
Capt. Ward[480]	*Lt. Pellis*[481]

Col. Enos, who was President, gave his vote for going on.

It has already been [illegible] that in consequences of the greater difficulties the two first Divisions of the Army expected to encounter the less they were encumbered [with] the more weighty & solid provisions. Hence it was [agreed] there were much more pork & flower [flour], & less of the perishable articles in the last party [Enos Division] than in the other. The batteaux however in general [were] full of various things. The boxes of candles, kegs of powder, flint & ball were plentifully laid.

It ought not to escape observation that altho Scott [Enos] voted for a part of the army to proceed, yet it is very understood both by the officers who were of his party, as well by those of Col. Greene's, that he had pledged himself not to go forward. As the matter was now determined by vote what parts of the army would go forward, Colonel Greene provided an order left in this place by the Commander in Chief for an equal partition of the provisions between Greene's & Enos's Divisions & solicited [a] dividend & agreed upon their principles to go on with those only who were willing to risk it. To this, the returning party utterly refused & asserted that there was not sufficient stores to inc[lude] all that part of the army & [to] carry through the party who were determined to go on.

Col. Enos was then call'd upon to give a propitious order for an equal division. He replied that his men were out of his power, & that they had previously determined not to part with any. However, [they] finally concluded to give up 2 1/2 barrels of flower [flour] & this was all that we could do with them. We now quit all our batteaux excepting one to each company, for the purpose of conveying the military & hospital stores. We also left the few tents which we had in the army. Each one took his pack made out of a shirt & proceeded with all the vigor & determination which the desperacy of the occasion demanded. [We] Pursued the River & passed one fall[s] that afternoon & encamped when we could no longer see our way thru these dismal woods.

26th. In Col. Arnold's orders which he had left behind, we were directed to rendezvous on the [illegible] at the head of the Chaudier Lake[482] where all the parties except himself were to wait for us. We passed three carrying places for the batteaux, at [which] there were high precipices & craggy mountains which we were obliged to crawl up on all fours with nothing but rock, moss & trees & shrubs to support us from tumbling down. Passed one point [where] the Rvr ran through beyond these rugged heights, & to encamp with nothing to cover ourselves except [a blanket] for two.

27th. We rose by day light & having no cookery we made the best of our way. In the course of the days march, the Rivr had dwindled away to [become] a small brook. Our course was [illegible] S.W. This day we passed 4 ponds which this brook ran through. *The last of which was very beautiful one on the Apalachian Mts from which this branch of the Kenebec Lake rises. We now proceeded over this chain of mountains, till we came to a descent & then to 7 Mile Stream which heads into the Chaudier Lake. This carrying place was [illegible] 4 [illegible]. The course of this beautiful little riv'r was about N.E. & S.E. Here we found Capt. Morgan's Division with the rest of the advanced party where we were all to be waiting for the rear of the Detachment to come up.*

Here the journal ends.

CHAPTER FOURTEEN

PRIVATE JOSEPH WARE JOURNAL

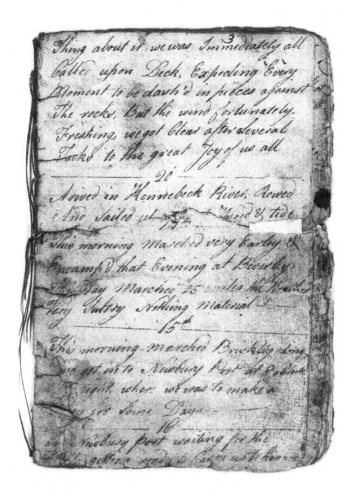

DESCRIPTION.

The Ware journal first surfaced in 1852 when it appeared in the *New England Historical and Genealogical Register* as transcribed by William B. Trask. It was "published for Joseph Ware, grandson of the journalist."

According to the introduction by Justin Winsor, the journal he examined contained the words "Joseph Ware, his book" written on the front page.

The importance of the Ware journal is evidenced by its inclusion of a detailed list of the officers and men, by company, who were killed, wounded or taken prison during the assault on Quebec. The importance of this list in identifying the names of the expedition men in those categories cannot be over emphasized.

There has been a debate about the authorship of the Ware journal as it is identical to one written by Ebenezer Tolman of the same company. Justin Smith argues that Tolman is the original author because, he says, Joseph Ware was not on the expedition. Trask claimed that Ware was on the expedition and that he was the original author. Based on research for *Voices*, the following conclusions about the Ware and Tolman were included in the book on pp. 145-6.

1. The Ware and Tolman journals are, in fact, two different journals written in different handwriting but which are identical in their accounts. There are relevant sources to support the authenticity of both journals.
2. The authenticity of each journal is supported by each author's heirs. Both have supportive statements by heirs and, therefore, have equal value.
3. There is sufficient documentation to confirm that Ware was on the expedition and wrote a journal. (See *Voices* Chapter Three for details).
4. Justin Smith's contention that Ware did not go to Quebec is incorrect and his conclusion that Tolman's journal is the original is also wrong. Ware has the better case.
5. There is ample evidence to conclude that Ware was the original author. The two pension applications are sufficient proof to support this conclusion. None of the evidence favoring Tolman as the original author is as persuasive as the two pension applications that support Ware.

The two relevant pension applications are as follows;

> First, an 1845 deposition by Elijah Clark of Brighton, Massachusetts, located in the pension application of Oliver Edward Clark, which states that he has "an original manuscript which has ever been known by available witnesses to be the handwriting of Joseph Ware of Needham... and that I received the same... of Mrs. Shepard, a daughter of the aforesaid Joseph Ware." His statement goes on to say that the manuscript is "beyond doubt a genuine original and true account."

> Second, a pension application for Joseph Thomas, a 2nd Lt. in Samuel Ward's Company, contains a deposition made by Ebenezer Homan of Boston in 1809 where he states that he has in his possession "an original written document... kept by Joseph Ware... I further certify that I have no doubt the the Journal aforesaid is the true and genuine document which it purports to be."

The original Ware journal is located in the New England Historical and Genealogical Society library. That document is in poor condition with only half of the first two pages still present and the entire journal ripped in half. The entire Ware journal as copied by Peter Force is on a microfilm in the Library of Congress.

PUBLICATION.

The only significant previous publication of the Ware Journal was in *New England Historical and Genealogical Register,* Vol. VI, April 1852, pp. 129-150.

AUTHOR.

Joseph Ware was born in Needham, Massachusetts, on October 15, 1753. Joseph, like his father, was a farmer prior to the Revolution. He enlisted in a company from Needham that marched to Cambridge on

April 19th in response to the Lexington Alarm. Ware then enlisted in a Massachusetts company in early May and may have been involved in the battle of Bunker Hill. Ware joined the Arnold expedition in September of 1775 serving in the Captain Samuel Ward Company. He was captured during the assault on Quebec and was released in August 1776 with the American prisoners being held in Quebec.

In the *History of Wellesley, Mass.*, it states that the Joseph Ware who authored the journal was an orderly sergeant and recruiting officer during his service in the Revolution. He married Esther Smith on June 1, 1780, and had seven children. He died on November 12, 1805, at the age of fifty-two.

JOURNAL

A Journal of a march from Cambridge on an Expedition against Quebec in Colonel Benedict Arnold's Detachment, Sept.13, 1775.

Sept. 13th-. Marched from Cambridge in the evening, and encamped at Malden that Night.

14th- This morning marched very early, and encamped that evening at Beverly. This day marched 25 miles--the weather very sultry. Nothing material.

15th. - This morning marched briskly along and got into Newburyport[483] *at eight o'clock at night, where we were to make a stay for several days.*

16th. - In Newburyport, waiting for the vessels [that were] getting ready to carry us to Kennebec.[484]

17th. - This day had a general review, and our men appeared very well, and in good spirits, and made a grand appearance, and we had the praise of hundreds of spectators, who were very sorry to see so many brave fellows going to be sacrificed for their country.

18th. - Had orders to embark in the evening. Our fleet consisted of eleven sail of vessels, sloops and schooners[485]*; our number of troops consisted of 1300 and eleven companies of musketmen and three of riflemen. We were embarked this evening and lay in the river all night.*

19th. - Early this morning weighed anchor with a pleasant gale, our colors flying, drums and

fifes. This night had like[ed] to have proved fatal to us, for we were close aboard of the rocks, before we knew anything about it. We were immediately all called upon deck, expecting every moment to be dashed to pieces against the rocks, but the wind fortunately freshing we got clear. After several [fifes] a playing, and the hills all around covered with pretty girls weeping for their departing swains, [the vessel] tacks, to the great joy of us all.

20th. - Arrived at Kennebec River, rowed and sailed up against wind and tide.

21st. - Arrived at Fort Weston[486]*, where we halted for some days, and here we were furnished with bateaux and provisions for carrying us up the river.*[487] *Continued here the: 22d, 23d, and 24th.*

25th. - Embarked on board our bateaux, and arrived at Fort Halifax[488] *in the evening of the 26th.*

27th. - Carried over Ticoneck Falls[489] our bateaux and provisions, forty rods land carriage, and pushed up three miles.

28th. - Pushed up eight miles, the water so bad that the bateaux men were obliged to drag the boats up over shoals, and in many places were up to their chins in water.

29th. - Pushed up to the second carrying-place, called Cohiggin[490] Falls.

30th. - Carried over sixty rods, and pushed up 3 miles.

October 1st. - Pushed up over rocks and shoals, where we were many times over head in water, pulling the bateaux over, and we arrived at the third carrying-place in the evening.

2d. - This day carried over Norridgewalk Falls[491], one mile and a quarter, and then encamped very uncomfortable this night after carrying our boats over roots and rocks and mud.

3d. - Pushed up eleven miles on our way. Captain Hendricks' company[492] of riflemen shot a young moose which weighed about 200 pounds; but we had none of it, they being before us. This

day we left all inhabitants, and entered an uncultivated country and a barren wilderness. The timber for the most part is birch, pine and hemlock. [In] Some places on the river side, there are pieces of ground where large sugar trees grow.

4th, - Pushed up eight miles to Tintucket, or Hellgate Falls[493], and carried our boats over forty perches.

5th, 6th and 7th. - Pushed up to the head of the Kennebec, where we carried out into a pond. These three last days we came about twenty miles.[494]

8th. - This day we pushed on very briskly, it being Sunday. The foremost company lying still on account of heavy rains; but we marched all day, it being very wet and cold, and we suffered a good deal from the inclemency of the weather, and came up with some of them at night.

9th, 10th, and 11th.-. Carried to the first pond, three and one-half miles land-carriage, crossed the pond two miles over.

12th and 13th,-. Carried to a second pond three ¾ of a mile, crossed the pond one mile over, then carried two miles to a third pond, and crossed the pond two miles over.

14th, 15th. - Carried into the Dead River[495] three miles and went up one mile, then encamped for the night. This river runs so still, that it can scarcely be perceived which way it runs; it is black water, about four rods wide, and runs southeast.

16th. - The water now being deep and dead, we betook ourselves to our barge [bateaux], and rowed up six miles.

17th. - After carrying over a small carrying-place, about ten rods, rowed up 16 miles.

18th-. Rowed up twenty miles, and carried over a small carrying place.

19th. – Carried over four carrying-places, and rowed up about five miles this day.

I

20th, 21st, and 22d. – [We] Were detained in our tents by heavy rain.[496]

23d. - The water being shallow, we were obliged to lay by our oars and take our setting poles[497]; *We pushed up ten miles.*

24th. - Our provisions growing scanty, and some of our men being sick, held a council, and agreed to send the sick back, and to send a captain and fifty men forward to the inhabitants as soon as possible, that they might send us some provisions, Accordingly the sick were sent back, arid Captain Hanchitt[498], *with fifty men, sent forward. Before this, Colonel Enos, with three captains and their companies, turned back, and took with them large stores of provisions and ammunition, being discouraged [as we supposed] by the difficulties they met with.*[499] *This day got forward nine miles. The water being very rapid, many of our boats were upset, and much of our baggage lost, and provisions and guns.*

25th.-Snowed all night; very cold this morning; pushed over two carrying-places. Got forward eight miles this day.

26th.-. Pushed up four ponds and carried over two carrying-places, one of them a mile over. The ground covered with snow.

27th. - Crossed a pond half of a mile over, and carried fifteen rods to another pond, two miles over, to the Great Carrying-place,[500] *4 miles and 50 perches over. Here it was agreed to leave most of our bateaux, being greatly fatigued by carrying over such hills, rocks, and swamps as were never passed by man before.*

28th.- After carrying over the great carrying-place, we encamped by a small stream, running into Chaudiere Pond[501]*; dealt out to each man four pints of flour and what little meat we had left, which was about four oz. a man.*

29th. - Early this morning set out for the head of Chaudiere River.[502] *This day we suffered greatly by our bateaux passing by us, for we had to wade* *waist-high through swamps and rivers and breaking ice before us. Here we wandered around all day, and came at night to the same place which we left in the morning, where we found a small dry spot, where we made a fire, and we were obliged to stand up all night in order to dry ourselves and keep from freezing. We continued so till next day when a bateaux came up and took us across the river.*

30ᵗʰ. - At noon were relieved from our miserable situation, and we made the best of our way

through the woods for [the] Chaudiere.

31ˢᵗ. - Pushed on for [the] Chaudiere with all speed, in hopes of overtaking our beateaux in order to get some flour, for ours was all expended; but to our great grief and sorrow our bateaux were stove and the flour was lost, and the men barely escaped with their lives; now we were in a miserable situation, not a mouthful of provision; and by account, seventy miles from inhabitants, and we had a wilderness barren and destitute of any sustenance to go through, where we expected to suffer hunger, cold and fatigue. Here the captain with the ablest men pushed forward in order to get provisions to send back for the sick.[503]

November 1ˢᵗ. - This morning started very early and hungry and little satisfied with our night's rest. Travelled all day very briskly, and at night encamped in a miserable situation. Here we killed a dog[504]*, and we made a very great feast without any provisions, and we went to sleep that night a little better satisfied. Our distress was so great that dollars were offered for bits of bread as big as the palm of one's hand.*

2d. This morning when we arose, many of us were so weak that we could hardly stand, and we staggered about like drunken men. However, we made shift to get our packs on our backs, and marched off hoping to see some inhabitants this night. A small stick across the road was sufficient to bring the stoutest to the ground. In the evening we came in sight of the cattle coming up the river side, which were sent by Col. Arnold, who had got in two days before. It was the joyfullest sight that ever I beheld, and some could not refrain from crying for joy.[505] *We were told by the men who came with the cattle that we were yet twenty miles from the nearest inhabitants. Here we killed a creature and we had some course flour served out, with straws in it an inch long. Here we had a noble feast and some of the men were so hungry that before the creature was dead, the hide and flesh were on the fire boiling.*

3d. - Marched this clay twenty miles, wading through several small rivers, some of them up to our middle and very cold. In the evening came in sight of a house, the first we had seen for forty-one days.

4th. - Last night had plenty of beef and potatoes; but little or no bread to be had. Snowed most of the night. In the morning marched down the river to inhabitants [that were] thick[ly] settled.[506]

5th. -- Continued our march down the river. The people very hospitable; provisions plenty, but very dear, milk one shilling sterling per quart, and bread a shilling per loaf, weighing no more than three pounds. Came this day twelve miles.

6th. - Came up with Colonel Arnold and the advance party. Marched off together at two o'clock, and marched till twelve o'clock at night. Roads excessive[ly] bad, most of the way mid-leg deep with mud and water. Marched seventeen miles.

7th. - Marched three miles, then halted till night, when a lieutenant was sent forward with twenty men to see if our way was clear. Accordingly they marched till near two o'clock in the morning, when we halted we were in sight of Quebec, the river St. Lawrence between us and the town.[507]

8th. -Took up our quarters along the river-side, until our troops behind could come up, here we stayed until the 13th. By this time all the men alive had come, several having perished with hunger in the woods. During our stay here, we took a midshipman belonging to a frigate in the harbor, who came on shore with some others in a boat to carry away flour from a mill on our side of the river. The river is about one mile or some better wide. At the city [there are] one twenty-eight-gun frigate and a sloop-of-war with some merchant men in the harbor.[508]

13th. - Crossed the river at night in long boats and canoes.[509] *Some of the canoes overset in the river; but none of the men lost, only some few guns and clothes. Got all over against morning at a place called Wolf's Cove.*[510]

14th.-This morning [we] were fired upon by the frigate, but received no damage; took up our quarters in some good houses near the town, which were forsaken by the owners. Here we remained until the 20th. During which time we were informed that there were not more than 100 regulars in the city, with a number of sailors and other new recruits, in all not exceeding four hundred under arms. The first day we came over the river, we passed close by the walls of the town, and gave three cheers without being molested by the enemy, who fired a few shots from their cannon, but did no harm.

21ˢᵗ. - Marched up the river 20 miles to Point aux Trembles[511], our ammunition being almost expended and too scanty to attack the town with. Here we were joined by Gen'l Montgomery with the York forces from Montreal, who had taken St. John's fort, Chambles, and Montreal.[512] In these places they took a great quantity of provisions, clothing, ammunition and cannon, with 950 prisoners. Remained here till the 5ᵗʰ December, when we marched back to Quebec, and laid siege to the town. Continued the siege until the 20ᵗʰ, during which time we took several prisoners and cannonaded and bombarded each other both day and night. During these transactions the two men who had been left with Lt. McClelland, came to us and informed us that they had buried him at the first inhabitants,[513] after he had been brought down the river by two Indians, hired by Capt. Smith[514] for that purpose.

[Note: The following two entries are taken from the transcription of the journal that was published by NEHGR in 1852. The dates do not make sense because both entries are describing the same event. Some of the wording in the second entry of December 30 and 31 duplicates the wording in the entry for the 29ᵗʰ but reading both together offers a better understanding of the assault.]

29ᵗʰ.-This night prepared to storm the city in two different places, General Montgomery with the York forces on one quarter and Col. Arnold on the other hand. Accordingly about 5 o'clock in the morning began the attack; they could not get to the wall, but retreated back to their quarters; their General and two leading officers killed by the fire from the enemy. Col. Arnold with his party carried on the attack in his quarter, and got possession of their two gun battery, and took 70 prisoners. Our Colonel, being wounded in the beginning of the attack, was carried back. The captains themselves then took the lead, and drove the enemy until overpowered by numbers, and surrounded; we were obliged to surrender ourselves [as] prisoners of war. During the attack, Capt. Hendrick and Capt. Hubbard, with Capt. Morgan's first lieutenant, were killed.

Sunday, Dec. 30ᵗʰ & 31ˢᵗ. It began to thicken up towards night and snowed very much. We were ordered to be in readiness, and at 2 o'clock at night, we were mustered, and got all fit for scaling the walls, and marched near to the city, some with ladders, some with axes, and some with saws. Gen. Montgomery with his forces, on the one quarter, and Col. Arnold on the other hand. Gen. Montgomery was to throw three sky rockets into the air for a signal for each party to strike together. Accordingly, about 4 o'clock, in the morning, [we] began the attack; but they could not get to the walls, but retreated back to their quarters, Gen. Montgomery and two leading officers being killed by the fire from the city. There were three or four false flashes made, for a signal to retreat, but Col. Arnold did not receive them, but carried on the attack on his quarter, and got possession of their two gun battery, and took 70 prisoners. Our colonel, being wounded in the beginning of the attack, was carried back, and the captains themselves then took the lead, and drove the enemy, until overpowered by numbers and surrounded, we were obliged to surrender ourselves prisoners of war. During the attack Capt. Hendrick and Capt. Hubbard, with Capt. Morgan's first Lieutenant, were killed. Likewise they set St. Roche all on fire. We were all put in the French convent, and there they gave us a gill of rum to drink and hard bread to eat.[515]

The following is a list of the killed, wounded and taken prisoner of the American troops at Quebec, on the 31st December 1775.

Officers taken prison'rs
Lt. Col. Green
Major Meigs
Major Bigelow
Adjt Febezer [Febiger]
Capt. Matthew Duncan

York forces killed [came to Canada with Montgomery]
Genl. Montgomery
Capt. Jacob Cheeseman
Aide-de-camp Mc'Pherson
1st Battalion, 8 killed and one wounded
3d Battalion, 2 killed
Capt. John Lamb's Company [with Montgomery]

     Peter Nestle

     David Torrey

Killed
Solomon Russell   *Capt. Daniel Morgan's Company*
Martin Clark

Killed

Wounded

	Lt. Humphrey
Wm Rutlidg	*Cornelius Norris*
Capt. Lamb	*David Wilson*
Barthᵒ Fisher	*Peter Wolf*
Thos. Oliver	*John Moore*
Ely Gladhill	*Matthew Harbinson*
Barns Burns	*Richᵈ Colbert*

Prisoners   *Wounded*

Lt. Andrew Moody	*Benj. Cackley*
Capt. Lockhart, vol.	*Solomn Fitzpatrick*
Joseph Ashton, Sergt	*Daniel Anderson*
Robt. Baird	*Spencer George*
Robt. Barwick	*Daniel Durst*
James Arvin	*Hezekiah Phillips*
John Ashfield	*Adam Hizkill*
Gasper Steyman	*John McQuire*
Moses Brackit	*John Wheeler*
George Carpenter	
Thomas Winter	*Prisoners*
Jacob Bennit	*Capt. Morgan*
Joseph Spencer	*Lt. Wim. Heath 2d.*
Thomas Thorp	*Lt. Bruin 3d.*
John Conet	*Wm. Fickhis serg't*
Joseph Dean	*Charles Porterfield do*
Benj. Vandervert	*John Donaldson do*
John Martin	*John Rogers corp*
John Fisher	*Benj. Grabb do*
	John Burns
[En]listed in the King's service	*Solomon Veal*
James Patten	*Joseph Sperry*

John Poalk

John Wilson

Thomas Dey

William Whitwell

Thos. Morrison

David Stone

John Kelley

John Johnston Benj.

John Lucox

Wm. McLieu

John Ritters

Peter Fenton

Shelly Holland

Daniel Davis

John Brown

John Oram

John Maid

John Harbinson

Jedediah Phillips

Jacob Ware

Absalom Brown

Thomas Chapman [En]listed in the King's service

Charles Secrests

Jeremiah Riddle

William Flood

William Greenway

Rob't Mitchell Daniel Carlisle

[En]listed in the King's service

John Cockran

Curtis Bramingham T

Timothy Feely

Adam Kurts

John Shoults

Charles Grim

Peter Locke

John Stephens

David Griffith

John Pearce

Roderick

Thomas Williams

Gasper de Hart

Benj. McIntire

Jeremiah Gordon

Rowland Jacobs

Tho. Anderson

George Morrison

John Ray

Wm. Kirkpatrick

Wm. Gammel

Henry Crone (Sergt.)

Jacob Mason

Henry Turpentine

Joseph Greer, Sergt.

Barnabas McGuire

Mathew Cunning

Richard Lynch

Philip Maxwell

Peter Burns

homas Winthrup

Thomas Murdock

Edw. Seedes

Patrick Dolton

Robt. Churchill

Capt. Wm. Hendrick's Company

Killed

Capt. Hendrick

Dennis Kelley

John Campbell

Wounded

John Henderson

John Chesney

Abraham Swaggerty

Philip Baker

Prisoners

Lt. Francis Nichols

Thomas Gibson

Wm. McCoy

John Chambers

Robt. Steele

John Blair

Rich^d M'Cluer

James Reed

John McLin

Henry McGowan

Edward Rodden

Daniel North

Mathe^w Taylor

Daniel Grahan

Ingrahart Mortworth

Francis Furlow

Wm. Shannon

Edwd Morton

Roger Casey

Wm. Snell

George Morrow

Daniel M'Cleland

James Ireland

Daniel O'Hara

Michael Young

John Hardy

James Greer

Peter Frainer

James Hogge

William Burns

Wm. O'Hara

Alexander Burns

John Caskey

John Cove

Arch'd McFarlin

Thomas Greer

William Smith

Joseph Wright

John Carswell

John Gardner

Thomas Lisbe

Capt. Smith's Company

Killed

Alexander Elliot

Henry Miller

Peter Heady

James Angles

Wounded
Lt. Rich'd Steele
John Miller
Thomas Silborne
Peter Carbough

Prisoners
Robt. Cunningham
Thomas Boyd, serg.
Sam'l Carbough
Philip Newhouse
Conrad Meyers
Conrad Sheyers
Valentine Willey
John Shafer
Michael Shoaf
Anthony Lebant
John Henry vol.
Edw. Egnew
Patrick Campbell
Joseph Doekerty
Nicholas Nogle
Thomas Gunn

[En]listed in Kings service
Joseph Snodgrass sergt.
Henry Herrigan corp
Henry McAnalley
Michael Fitzpatrick
Edward Cavener J
Timothy Conner

Spencer Merwick
John Morriss
Theophilus Hide

Wounded
David Sage

Prisoners
Capt. Oliver Hanchitt
Lt. Abijah Savage
Benj. Catlin Quart^m
Peletiah Dewey, serg^t
Gabril Hidgkiss do
Gershom Wilcox do
Rosewell Ransom, corp
Jedediah Dewey do
John Risden
Samuel Biggs
Samuel Bliss
Richd Brewer
Saml Burroughs
Nathl Coleman
Stephen Fosbury
Isaac George
Isaac Knapp
Edwd Lawrence
Joel Loveman
Elijah Marshall
Daniel Rice
David Sheldon
Ichabod Swaddle
onathan Taylor
Solomon Way

William Randolph

Robt. Richmond

Alexander McCarter

John Anderson

Hugh Boyd

Thomas Walker

Joseph Higgins

Daniel Crane

Henry Taylor

Thomas Pugh

Ct. Handchitt's Company

Killed

Lt Sam'l Cooper

Nath¹ Goodrich

Wm Goodrich

Joseph Kenyon

Baker Garlin

Prisoners

Ct. John Topham

Lt. Joseph Webb

Lt. Edw. Sloakum

Matthew Cogshall, sergt

John Finch do

Reuben Johnson do

Stephen Tift

Philip Rollins

John Darling

Oliver Dunnel

Wm. Underwood

Wm. Thomas

Noah Whipple

Abner Stocking

Moses White

Simon Winter

[En]listed in the King's service

John Basset, Drumʳ

Patrick Newgent

Capt. Topham's Company

Killed

Charles King

Caleb Hacker

Hugh Blackburn

Wounded

Thomas Law

James Hayden

James Stone

Silas Hooker

Jonathan Jacobs

Stephen Mills

Daniel Lawrence

Elijah Fowler

Bannister Waterman

Jonathan Scott

Cornelius Hagerty

Benj. West

Jesse Turrell

Samuel Ingolds

Andrew Henman

Isaac Beatey

Charles Sherman

Benj. Trim

Benj. Durphy

Wm. Pitman

Wm. Clark

John Bentley

Jeremiah Child

Thomas Price

Samuel Geers Capt.

Anthony Salisbury

[En]listed in King's service
Danl Booth sergt.

Michael Clamsey

John Linden

James Green

Patrick Kelley

Tobias Burke

Captain Thayer's Company

Killed

Daniel Davidson

Patrick Tracy

Wounded

John Rankins

David Wuilliams

Peter Field

Prisoners

Capt. Simon Thayer

[En]listed in King's service

Thomas Page, serg^t

Moses Hemmingway

John Robinson

Wm. Dixon

Wm. Clements

Edw. Conner

Patrick Harrington

Goodrich's Company

Killed

Amos Bridge

Wounded

Noah Cluff

Nathl Lord

Prisoners

Capt. Wm. Goodrich

Lt. John Cumpton

Ashley Goodrich, sergt

Augustus Drake do

Festus Drake

Daniel Doyle

Jabez Chalker

Benj. Buckman

Samuel Buckman

Paul Doran

John Parrot

John Lee

David Peters

Caleb Norhtrup

Lt. Humphreys
Silas Wheeler
Oliver Avery [
Elijah Alden
Benj. Pearce
Abner Day
John Taylor
Josiah Root
Richd Shackley

Capt. Ward's Company

Killed
Bishop Standley
Thomas Shepherd
John Stephens

Wounded
Eng^r James Tisdell
Nathl Brown. Corp.
Jabez Brooks

Prisoners
Capt. Samuel Ward
Lt. John Clark
Lt. Sylvanus Shaw
Amos Boynton, sergt
John Sleeper, corp.
Samuel Halbrooks
John Goodhue
John Shackford
Moses Merrill
Nathl Babson

Roswell Ballard
Rowell Foot
En]listed in King's service
Charles Harkins

Capt. Hubbard's Company

Killed
Cpt. Hubbard
Sergt. Westin

Prisoners
Lt. Samuel Browm
Jonathan Ball, sergt
Minath Farmer. sergt
Luther Fairbanks, do
Thomas Nichols
Oliver Smith
Simon Fobes
David Patch
Thomas McIntire
Benj. Phillips
Timothy Rice
Joseph White
Aaron Heath
Wm. Chamberlain
Anthony Jones
Russel Clark
Paul Clap
Joseph Parsons
Samuel Bates
Luke Nobles
Joseph Burr

Enoch Foot

Jacob True

Josiah George

Ebenezer Tolman

Thomas Gay

John Stickney

Elijah Dole

Elijah Hayden

Jeremiah Greenman

Enos Chillis

Gilbert Caswell

John Gridley

Wm. Dorr

James Rust

Joseph Pool

Isreal Barrit

Bartholomew Foster

Joseph Ware

Thomas Fisher

Joseph Osburn

Wm. Preston

Eben' Tuttle

Moses Kimball

Joseph Smith

James Melvin

James Beverley

Jonathan Smith

Samuel Sias

Thomas Holmes

Moses Folnsby

Charles Hilton

John Morgan

Enos Reynolds

Oliver Edwards

George Mills

[En]listed in King's service

Charles McQuire

Morris Hayward

John Hall

Capt. Dearborn's Company

Prisoners

Capt. Henry Dearborn

Lt. Nath' Hutchins

Lt. Amos Andrews

Lt. Joseph Thomas

John Flanders

Jona. Perkins

Caleb Edes

Jona. Fogge

Wm. Taylor

Eliphas Reed
Robert Heath
Elkaner Danforth
Nath¹ Martin
Jonathan Morris
John Dobbin
John McCalm
Charles Budget
Samuel Hewes
Aaron Serjant

Total Killed 35
Wounded 33
Prisoners 372
Total 440

York Forces

Killed 13
Wounded 1

Total killed, wounded
And Taken 454

January ye 1ˢᵗ, 1776. - *Our allowance of provisions was one pound of bread, one half pound of pork, and one gill of rice for a day, and six ounces of butter a week.*

2d.- *In prison, this day we had a cask of porter sent to us by some gentleman of the town.*

3d & 4ᵗʰ. - *The general [Carleton] sent for a list of our names, of the old countrymen in particular by themselves that were with us, and they chiefly enlistcd in the king's service.*[516]

5ᵗʰ to the 8ᵗʰ-. *The prisoners petitioned to have their packs sent in to them, whereupon they sent out a flag and received them for us.*

15th to 19th. Capt. Hubbard died with the wound he received a coming in.

19th to 22d. - Five of those that listed out of prison and five others deserted the garrison in the night. There were two men put in irons for attempting to break out of prison.

22d to 25th. - There were three vessels and a house burnt by our people. The enemy went into St. Roche after plunder. There were two of our people taken [as they were] going to set fire to the shipping.

25th to 29th-. There were eight men [that] deserted the garrison. The people go out into St. Roche every day and fetch in the remains of the buildings that were burnt.

*29th to 31st.-Two men of Captain Ward's company died of the small-pox*517. *The men are getting well, some of them.*

February lst to the 5th. - There were two men [that] deserted. Seven of our men died with the small-pox and one of our men died with the pleurisy. He was sick but 4 days.

5th to 9th. - Three men deserted. Forty men lay sick in prison.

9th to 12th, --- Very snowy; the storm very heavy. Three men were stifled to death in the night on duty.

12th to 16th. - This morning sixty men went to the hospital with the small-pox. The men have it very favorably.

16th to 20th. - Six of the old countrymen that listed out deserted, and the remainder were put in prison again because [of] those [who] deserted.

20th to 24th. - Five men died with the small-pox. The enemy made an attempt to go out after one of our people's cannon, and got drove back. There was a continual firing after them.

24th to 31st. - Nothing remarkable.

March 1st to 6th. - Three men deserted.

6th to 10th. - One of the prisoners was put in irons for talking with one of the sentries. We hear that Boston is taken by our people.

10th to 13th. - There was an alarm in the city about ten o'clock at night. A large picket was set around the prison, and a field-piece [was set] before the door.

*13th to 18th. The "emigrants" are moved into the artillery barracks, and the rest of us into a stone goal and are locked up at 7 o'clock at night.*518

18th to 25th. Nothing remarkable.

25ᵗʰ to 30ᵗʰ. In the night one of the prisoners got out of prison and ran to our people. We are in a miserable condition, having no wood, we almost freeze.

30ᵗʰ to 31ˢᵗ. Most of the prisoners consulted together to break out of prison, to try their best to take the town, but as one of the persons was cutting away some ice on the cellar door, in order to have it handy to open at a moment, to go out at, the sentry standing nigh, and hearing the cutting, acquainted the officers of the guard, who acquainted some other officers, and they coming in, inquired who was cutting at the door, and what they were [about]. On which, one of the prisoners informed them of all the transactions that were going forward. The officers searched all the rooms in the prison, and every man's pack, to see if they could find any arms or ammunition, for they supposed some of the people in the town had supplied us with arms and ammunition; but they could not find any such thing with us. At this we were put all in to strong irons.

April 1ˢᵗ to 14ᵗʰ. Our people having a battery across the river, at Point Levi, they threw shot into town very merry. The officers of the guard are very particular with us. They call a roll and count us morning and evening.

14ᵗʰ to 27ᵗʰ. It is very sickly with us. The scurvy and lameness rage very much, occasioned by living on salt.

27ᵗʰ to 31ˢᵗ. The town was alarmed in the night.

May the 1ˢᵗ to the 6ᵗʰ. Nothing strange; but in great distress and despair.

6ᵗʰ. This morning three ships came in with reinforcement of about one thousand men. All the bells in town rang for joy most of the day. Then all forces in town marched out on Abraham's Plains to have a battle with our people, but [they] retreated as fast as possible and left a number of sick in the hospital. Likewise some of the canon and ammunition with a number of small arms and packs [were taken].

7ᵗʰ & 8ᵗʰ. The general ordered the irons to be taken off the prisoners. The general likewise gave the "emigrants" their liberty again. This morning two ships came in. The ships have gone down the river, and a number of people by land, for Montreal.

9ᵗʰ to 14ᵗʰ. Three ships and three brigs came in. There were six prisoners put in with us, taken strolling about. One company set out for Montreal.

14ᵗʰ to 19ᵗʰ. Two ships went out. One of them [was] a packet for England.

19ᵗʰ to 23d. One ship and a number of small craft came in. Thirteen prisoners [en]listed into the king's service. One ship sailed out.

23d. - Our allowance is one pound of soft bread and one pound of beef.

24ʰ to 26ʰ. - The militia have laid down their arms. One of those men that went out of prison was put on board a fifty-gun ship; but he did not incline to enter on board, and they put him in irons and threatened to hang him, but he was taken out of irons and put into prison again in the evening. Robert Beard was taken out of prison and has got his liberty. He is going home by water to Ireland.

26ʰ to 30ʰ. -. One ship went out and twenty came in. There were eight or nine prisoners taken out to work; they stayed out one or two days, and were required to swear allegiance to the king, that they would not take up arms against him, and to make known all experiments against him.

30ʰ & 31ˢᵗ. - Four ships came in; one brig and two ships went out.

June lst to the 5ʰ. - Eighteen ships came in with General Burgoyne. There are six thousand Hessians and Hanoverians come to assist the King's troops.[519] *Five hundred marched up the river for Montreal.*

5ʰ. - This day General Carlton[520] *with a number of the officers, came to see us, and inquired of us whether we had fared as well as they promised us we should when we were taken. We told him we fared very well. He said he did not take us as enemies, and likewise said if he could rely upon our honors, he would send us to New England, if we would be quiet and peaceable, and not take up arms any more.*

June ye 6ʰ, A. D.1776. A copy of an answer sent to Gen'l Carleton.

May it please your Excellency:

We, the prisoners in his Majesty's goals, return your Excellency our most happy and unfeigned thanks for your clemency and goodness to us whilst in imprisonment. Being sensible of your humanity, we give your Excellency thanks for your offer made us yesterday, and having a desire to return to our friends and families again, we promise not to take up arms against His Majesty. But remain peaceable and quiet in our respective places of abode, and we further assure your Excellency that you may depend on our fidelity.

So we remain your Excellency's humble servants.

Signed in behalf of the prisoners.

June 7ʰ to 12ʰ. Thirteen of the prisoners were taken out to go a fishing. Two ships sailed. Gov'r Carleton has gone up to Montreal. One regiment has set out from the same place. The French are obliged to send a number out of every parish.

12ʰ to 17ʰ. Two of the prisoners that were out at work, ran away.

209

17th to 21st. A child killed with lightening. Two ships came in.

21st to 25th. Nothing strange.

25th to 30th. The soldiers are cut short their allowances of bread—half a pound a week; likewise the prisoners the same. A company marched for Montreal. One ship came in.

July 1st to 7th. Five ships came in, and three schooners. Two prisoners were put in with us that were taken at Montreal by the Indians.

7th to 14th. Nothing remarkable.

14th to 19th. Col. McLean[521] came from Montreal.

19th to 21st. A ship came in. One of the prisoners, that were taken last, was taken out and confined in close prison in irons for talking saucy to the provost.

21st. This day a number of prisoners that went out to work ran away through the woods. The general has sent after them.

22d. The general has come down from Montreal.

23d to 27th. One ship came in and one went out. One of the prisoners is taken crazy.

27th to 29th. One ship sailed. Two officers came into prison, and enquired if there were not some of us that wanted shirts. They were told there was a number of us who had none. They told us we should all have shirts that wanted [them]. They likewise told us we should be sent home in ten days.

29th to 31st. Our officers have the liberty of the town.

August 1st to 3d. Nothing remarkable.

4th. The General sent for all prisoners to come in, who were out in the country at work, that were minded to go home

5th. This day ninety-five prisoners embarked on board the ship.

6th. This day expected to embark, but were disappointed.

7th. This day the men all in good spirits, and embarked on board the ships. Sixty of the prisoners on board the Mermaid.[522]

8th. This day our provisions are pork, peas and hard bread. The wind [is] in our favor, but [we are] waiting orders to sail. At night [we were] removed from the Mermaid to the John Christopher.

9th. This day our provision is fresh meat and soft bread. The wind [is] in our favor, but no orders to sail.

10th. Last night a brig came down the river with 28 prisoners. At little Wolfe's Cove, the wind blows up the river.

11th. This morning the signal was given for sailing. Weighed anchor and went down about one mile. At night, weighed anchor, and went down the river thirteen miles. The weather cold and stormy.

12th. This morning the signal was given. We weighed anchor and beat down the river about 11 miles, and came to an anchor, the wind being strong against us.

13th. This day we lay by waiting for the wind.

14th. This morning weighed anchor with a pleasant gale of wind. Sailed down the river about 15 miles, and came to an anchor. Then hove up, and with a brisk wind, sailed down the river to the Isle Obeeck, 50 leagues from Quebec.

15th. Having a prosperous gale of wind, we made sail. In the afternoon passed by a frigate, lying in the river, to see if there was no fleet coming up except their own.

16th. This day had a very brief wind.

17th. The wind breezed up in our favor.

18th. Left Gaspy and made St. John's Island.[523]

19th. St. John's Island being eleven leagues long, we sailed by it most of the day. Hove in sight of Cape Breton Island, before we left Saint Johns. Espied a ship in distress, cast away on the end of the island, her foremast, nuzzen mast and bowsprit carried away. A barge was sent on board from our convoy, but we have heard no return.

20th. We were detained by bearing round the island to get letters ashore to the Governor of the island, concerning the wreck that was run ashore.

21st. This day we had a small breeze of wind against us. At night came to an anchor, in order to send a boat ashore with letters to the Governor.

22d. This morning the boat went ashore and returned about sunset. Then hove up with a brisk wind. Sailed all night.

23d. This day went through Canso Gut into Chebucto Bay. Left it this night and came in to the open ocean.[524]

24th. It was our misfortune to have the wind ahead, so that we drifted from our course, and made little to no headway this day.

Sunday, 25th. The wind still ahead. Changed our course N.W., and made Canso Shore that night.

26th. This day the wind got almost fair, and breezed up a very big gale about dark.

27th. The wind held fair and strong till about 2 o'clock this afternoon.

28th. The wind died away and there was a large swell.

29th. This morning the wind quickened up, and the captain of the ship took an observation and found us to be in latitude 42°, which is Boston latitude.

30th. A light breeze, but very fair, and continued so this day.

31st. We were told, by the second mate, that we were abreast of New York, and were afraid to put in for a harbor, for fear our Privateers would give them a beating.

Sunday, Sept. 1st. Were this night informed, that we were south of Pennsylvania.

2d. This day kept our course S.W. until the morning, the wind being yet ahead.

3d. This morning we were almost up with the Virginia Cape.[525] We [turned] about ship and run upon the other tack.

4th. About 3 o'clock this morning, blew up a squall and a heavy shower of rain. We were obliged to shorten sail, and stand before it.

5th. Fortune yet frowning in regard to the wind, we look up within two points.

6th. We were informed by the shipmen, according to reckoning, that we were in the latitudes of Philadelphia. Latitude 39° North.

Appendix to Ware Journal

Justin Winsor describes this as "an account of the distances of the various portages on the Kennebec, Dead and Chaudiere rivers. There seems to be two different accounts, slightly varying. This is the summing up of one account."

	# of Carrying Places	Rods	Miles	Rods	Miles
On the Kennebec	4	99	1	0	0
To Dead River	4	0	$10\,^1/_3$	3	3 ¼
On Dead River	16	125	8	7	$28\,^1/_3$
On Chaudiere 3	7	½	0	0	
Total	27	294	$19\,^5/_6$	10	$31\,^7/_{12}$

CHAPTER FIFTEEN

LOST JOURNALS

There are three additional journals that were written by expedition participants but which have been lost, destroyed or have disappeared and are therefore not available. Since each of these accounts has an interesting story about first being lost and the subsequent discovery of its existence by myself or others, they are included in this separate chapter. The fact that information on three lost journals written by men on the expedition has been uncovered is unusual enough as compared to other military events in the Revolutionary War. However, when considered along with thirty-five journals that are not lost, the total number of men who took the time to record their experiences is extraordinary. The hardships and suffering that these men endured could be part of the explanation as to why so many participants recorded their journey to Quebec and their subsequent experiences including illness, prison or lucky enough to escape either. Who knows what details might have been included in these lost accounts.

PRIVATE JOHN SLEEPER JOURNAL

According to John Sleeper in his 1818 affidavit of support for Caleb Haskell's pension application, he "kept a record of all our proceedings," which refers to the experiences of the men who served along with him in Captain Samuel Ward's Company. The use of the word "our" indicates that he viewed his journal as telling a group story. He further explained that his written record had been "preserved several years but which is now destroyed." The statement contains no details on when or how the journal was destroyed. There is no reason to doubt the truthfulness of Sleeper's assertion as he was writing to support Haskell's successful pension application and not his own. He indicated in his support letter that he knew Haskell because they grew up together and added that he had his own record of the expedition probably in order to give his statements more credibility. Sleeper knew Haskell because both were from Newburyport and both were in the Ward Company. Haskell also wrote a letter of support for Sleeper's pension application which was filed in 1832.[526]

We already know about the extant Ward Company journals written by Joseph Ware, Ebenezer Wild, Ebenezer Tolman, Caleb Haskell and William Dorr. These journals are sometimes referred to as the "collaborative journals" of the Ward Company because some authors claimed that the journals were similar to each other. In *Voices* Chapter Three, details of those journals are offered that dispel the notion of collaborative efforts on the part of all the journalists. Since Sleeper's account has been lost, there is no way to tell whether he wrote a separate and personal journal and what daily entries he included in his account.

John Sleeper was born in Newburyport, Massachusetts, on August 11, 1754. Sleeper was part of a company of minutemen from Newburyport, commanded by Captain Moses Nowell that marched to Cambridge in response to the Lexington Alarm. The company returned home after a few days and Sleeper enlisted in Captain Ezra Lunt's Company which, according to Haskell, participated in the Battle of Bunker Hill. Sleeper's pension application makes no reference that he was in that battle.

On September 10, Sleeper, along with others from Newburyport, enlisted in Captain Samuel Ward's Company for the Quebec expedition. He was among those taken prisoner by the British in the assault on Quebec and was released by the British in August of 1776. After returning home, Sleeper enlisted to serve on board the frigate *Boston* in late 1776 and was on that vessel when it captured a British sloop of war. He served on the frigate for more than a year as the ship's carpenter.

In 1818 while residing in Chester, New Hampshire he submitted a statement in support of Caleb Haskell's pension application. He was awarded his own pension in 1832 and died in Chester on June 27, 1834. His pension papers contain no family information on whether he had a wife or children. Sleeper's lost journal would be unknown had he not written the statement in support of Haskell.[527]

PRIVATES FREEMAN AND DANIEL JUDD JOURNAL

Mark Sullivan, a Department of the Army civilian from Indiana, discovered the Judd Journal as he was doing research on the Old Jefferson

Cemetery in Schoharie County, New York. In the course of his research, Sullivan found grave sites of the Judd family and began doing research on Freeman Judd. He found a reference to a listing in the November 12, 1949, issue of the *Antiquarian Bookman* about a journal written by brothers Freeman and Daniel Judd. According to the *Bookman*, the Judd journal was offered in a listing by the Old Corner Bookstore in Boston with the following description: "Freeman and Daniel Judd. *Journal of the Expedition to Quebec (Under Benedict Arnold, 1776-1776)."* This entry confirms that a copy of an actual journal written by the Judd brothers was offered for sale in 1949 by the now defunct Old Corner Bookstore. Information on the copy's purchaser and its current location remains unknown. We also don't know how many copies of this journal were published.[528]

In addition to the *Bookman* reference, Sullivan found references to the Judd's writing a journal in two letters written by Freeman Judd to James L. Edwards, Commissioner of Pensions, in 1828 and 1830. In the earlier letter, Judd describes his journal as his "woods book" which he had left with John Eaton, Secretary of War. In the later letter he calls it his "1775 journal that my brother and Mr. Stocking kept through the woods when I was with Arnold." The Stocking referred to is journalist Abner Stocking.[529]

In 1857, Sylvester Judd wrote a history of the Judd family in which he states that Freeman and Daniel Judd "kept a journal of their proceedings from Boston to Quebec, which was printed."[530] It is clear that Sylvester Judd had seen the journal and knew about it being printed. Unfortunately, it was not in the fifty-six volumes of his papers which are in the Forbes Library in Northampton, Massachusetts. Despite an extensive search by Sullivan, with some help by this author, of many sources including local historical societies and libraries where the Judd's had lived, as well as museums, university libraries and state historical societies, no copy of the journal has been found.

However, Sullivan found a seven page document titled, "Autobiographical Notes of Freeman Judd: A Diversionary Expedition" in the files of the Niagara County Genealogical Society.[531] This document was written by A. Milne Judd, a great grandson of Freeman, in 1981. In an End Note, the author states that "All dates and places are accurate. Freeman's thoughts are conjectures but in light of circumstances are entirely probable. Memories passed by word of mouth through four generations." It seems apparent the A. Milne Judd took the information in Freeman Judd's pension application and the known histories of the expedition and assault on Quebec to create his short conjectured history of Freeman Judd's experiences. It is clear that this document was not the actual journal.

Mark Sullivan wrote an article for the *Journal of the American Revolution* setting forth his efforts at locating a Judd journal and including information on Freeman Judd's life.[532]

Freeman Judd was born in Waterbury, Connecticut, later called Watertown, on August 10, 1755. According to his pension application, he served in various Connecticut militia companies throughout the war. On April 25, 1775, he enlisted with his two brothers, Daniel and Ebenezer for a term of seven months in the Connecticut Company commanded by Captain Trowbridge, which marched to Boston in response to the Lexington Alarm. In August, he and his brother Daniel enlisted in Captain Oliver Hanchett's Company for the expedition to Quebec. He was not captured in the assault but remained in Canada until he was discharged in June of 1776. He enlisted in July of 1776 as a sergeant in the company of Captain Couch and was discharged in Philadelphia in January 1777. In April of 1777, he was in Captain Peek's Company and in June 1778 he was a sergeant in Captain Matthew's Company in the Battle of Westchester. In 1779 Freeman remained in that company for the British attack on Norwalk, Connecticut. He was in Captain Catlin's Company in the fall of 1779 which was stationed at Horseneck, and later served as recruiting sergeant in Captain Stoddard's Company in 1780 and 1781.

After the Revolutionary War, Freeman Judd lived first in Norwalk, Connecticut, where he married, and then in various towns in New York State. His family moved to Erie County, Pennsylvania in 1818, where he applied for a pension. According to his obituary, he received "a small pension." He also had a claim for the loss of his property during the war that was never paid, despite journeying on horseback to Philadelphia and Washington, DC to argue for it. He moved to Niagara County, New York, in 1838 and died there on March 5, 1840, at the age of 85.[533]

PRIVATE SAMUEL COOK(E) JOURNAL

This author discovered information on a third lost journal while researching pension applications for members of the expedition to Quebec. I found that some of the details contained in a few pension applications provided interesting and new information that was not found in the journals. It seemed to me that these accounts, although much shorter, revealed insights and details which were worth including in this compilation. As a result I began searching for interesting pension applications from members of the expedition.

One of the applicants was sent into the pension office by Samuel Cook of Hadley, Massachusetts. Cook's application begins by identifying the names of some of the officers on the expedition, and then apologizing for any possible mistakes. "As I have lost my diary or journal that I kept from the time I left Hadley in 1775 until I returned there in June 1776, I may have made some errors…" His Declaration was made in 1832 which would have been more than fifty years after the march so it would not be surprising if he had memory problems of the men and details involved in his adventure. In his Declaration he identifies fellow expedition member from Hadley named William Pierce, whose journal is found in Chapter Eleven.

In the papers contained in his pension application is a statement by his son, Denison Cooke, who was then Town Clerk of Morristown, Vermont. His son states, "I have read a written journal or diary which said Samuel Cook said he kept, in which was particularly mentioned the time he set out in said expedition…" The son goes on to summarize the various activities that occurred during the expedition to Quebec and his subsequent service in the Saratoga campaign.

A short biography of Samuel Cook is found in the presentation of his pension application in Chapter Sixteen.

CHAPTER SIXTEEN

PENSION APPLICATIONS

In 1818, thirty-six years after the end of the war, the United States Congress finally provided financial relief to those surviving veterans who were instrumental in obtaining their country's freedom from Great Britain through their participation in the long and grueling war that lasted six and a half years. As a result of the passage of time, a number of the veterans were dead, and many of those still alive were living in a state of poverty due to age and war injuries. After observing the second war with the British in the War of 1812, the surviving veterans of the first war were older and in financial distress and were requesting help from their government. The Congress, for whatever reasons, finally acted and passed legislation for the veterans.

Many of those veterans still alive responded with information on their service during the war to justify obtaining the assistance promised in the legislation. One of the requirements was to submit a sworn Declaration stating their record of service including their units, their commanders, where they served and what battles they fought in. A special office was set up in Washington, D.C. to process the applications. As the deficiencies of the first legislation become clear, additional bills were passed over the years to correct the problems, including allowing widows of Revolutionary soldiers to obtain a small pension.

The following six pension applications were selected for this compilation based on their account of their experience while on the expedition, including the march through the wilderness, the assault on Quebec and, in some cases, their experience as a British prisoner in Quebec in 1776. Two of the applications was submitted in 1818 and the rest were submitted in 1832 following the passage of new legislation. Because each pension request provides interesting and unique experiences which has its own relevant account, none of which is significantly more important than the others, they are arranged in alphabetical order. Since the veteran had to submit a sworn Declaration, the wording was often written by the official, usually a judge or attorney, who took the oath. Therefore, some were written in the third person. For the others, it is difficult to tell whether the words are their own or the official who took the oath.

EDWARD CAVANAUGH or CAVANAGH

Cavanaugh was born in Dublin, Ireland, on February, 1750. He immigrated to the American colonies sometime after that "at an early age," and settled in Cumberland County, Pennsylvania. While living in Pennsylvania before the Revolution, Cavanaugh came to be known as "Honest Ned" by his friends and neighbors. He enlisted on July 1, 1775 as a private in the company commanded by Captain Matthew Smith, in the First Regiment of Pennsylvania Riflemen commanded by Colonel William Thompson. Smith's company, commanded by Captain Matthew Smith, was chosen by Thompson to join Colonel Benedict Arnold's army in the march from Boston through the Maine wilderness to Quebec.

During the march to Quebec, he saved the lives of John Joseph Henry, one of the journalists of the expedition, and of then Lieutenant Michael Simpson, who later became General Simpson. The incident occurred as Henry and Simpson were attempting to swim the Dead River when both were overcome with exhaustion after their bateau capsized and were rescued by Cavanaugh. Henry stated that "we should have drowned but for the assistance of Edward Cavanaugh, an Irishman and an excellent soldier… Cavanaugh was captured by the British during the assault on Quebec, and being a native of the British Empire, or what some of the journals refer to as an "Old Country Man," he was forced to enter the British service. He later escaped and joined Captain Lowdon's Company of the First Pennsylvania Regiment and was discharged at the end of June 1776.

Cavanaugh was awarded a pension on May 6, 1818, when he was a resident of Allen Township in Cumberland County, Pennsylvania. He died on November 14, 1842 in York County, Pennsylvania at the age of ninety-two.

This account is included in this chapter because of Cavanaugh falling into the category of "Old Country Men." His is the best account of the experience of one who, because of his birthplace in the British Empire, was compelled to join the British army under the threat of being tried for treason and sentenced to death. The British stance on the Old Country Men is not well known and Cavanaugh serves as a good example of who those men were and how they responded to the British threat as captives.

Declaration

About the first of the month of July in the year of our Lord One Thousand Seven Hundred and Seventy Five, he entered into the Army of the United States raised for the defense of American Liberty and repelling every hostile invasion thereof, by enlistment as a private soldier in a co[mpany] commanded by Capt. Smith, at Lancaster in the said state in the first regiment of Riflemen in the Pennsylvania line for the term of one year, if not sooner discharged. That after his enlistment aforesaid he was marched in said company to Prospect-Hill near Boston in the State of Massachusetts, where he joined said regiment. That at the last mentioned place, three companies were drafted in the regiment, to wit, those commanded [by] Captains Matthew Smith, Morgan and Hendricks to serve on an expedition to Quebec under the command of Colonel Benedict Arnold.

That said detachment in pursuing its route to Quebec met with extreme hardships and privations. That when he arrived at Quebec, General Montgomery assumed the command of all the American troops that were there. That in the general attack on Quebec on the City of Quebec, this deponent was in the Division headed by Colonel Benedict Arnold, who led it on to the storming of the Lower Town at Palace Gate. That after making a break in the wall and entering the City aforesaid, the three companies of rifle-men, among others and this deponent also were taken captive. That after remaining about ten days in captivity, a proposition was made to the companies in the American service by the commanding officer of the B forces, to either enter the British service or submit to enclosed confinement in the Dungeon until vessels should arrive from England for the purpose [of] taking them there to be tried for treason.

That this deponent with [the] rest of those aforesaid to whom such proposition was made acceded to it by enlisting in the British Army until a reinforcement should arrive from England, when every man who reenlisted was to be sent, each to his particular place of Birth. This deponent being born in Dublin in the Kingdom of Ireland. That he deserted from the British service about two months after his enlistment aforesaid in company with three {men}. That the morning after their said desertion, he was taken before Colonel Arnold aforesaid who succeeded to the command after the fate of General Montgomery. That the said Colonel Arnold, on examining the deponent, gave him a pass and ordered him to join his regiment. That he joined his regiment in Hartford in the State of Connecticut and entered the company commanded by Captain Loudon in said regiment, to wit, the First Pennsylvania regiment. That he continued to serve in said regiment and line until he was discharged in the latter end of the month of June in the year of our Lord One Thousand Seven Hundred and Seventy Six against the common enemy. That by reason of his reduced circumstances in life, he is in need of assistance from his country for support...

SAMUEL COOKE

Samuel Cooke was born in Hadley, Massachusetts on March 18, 1755. He was in a minute man company from Hadley which marched to Lexington on April 18, 1775 in response to the Lexington Alarm. While in Cambridge, he enlisted in the company of Elikin Smith and was in the Battle of Bunker Hill. Cooke was in Captain Jonas Hubbard's Company on the expedition to Quebec. Prior to the assault on Quebec, he had frozen his feet so he did not participate in the actual assault. On January 19, 1776, he enlisted in Captain Joshua Woodbridge's Company. In March of 1776, while still in Canada, he contracted small pox and spent time in the hospital but survived. He left Canada in May ahead of the remnants of the American Army in Canada and arrived home in Hadley in the middle of June.

Cooke married Mehitabel Marsh on May 11, 1781 in Hadley per Town Records. He served in the 1st Connecticut Regiment in 1782 per the Connecticut Comptroller roll, which was placed in his pension file in 1838. He successfully applied for a pension in 1832 . The family moved to Morristown, Vermont, prior to 1832, where he died on December 7, 1834. After his death, his wife was awarded a widow's pension.

His pension application is included in this chapter for five reasons. First, he provides a more detailed account about the expedition and the aftermath of the assault on Quebec than many other pension applicants, including names of officers in the expedition. Second, his declaration states he lost the journal that he kept while on the expedition after he arrived home in Hadley. This confirms another lost journal which is significant because of the number of such journals. Third, he records information about his "mess mate," William Pierce, also of Hadley, whose journal is included in this compilation. There is no mention by Cooke of the existence of a journal kept by William Pierce and no mention in the Pierce journal of his mess mate Samuel Cooke. Fourth, he refers specifically to Major Ogden as a volunteer. Fifth, he has a different listing of the companies in the 1st Division of the expedition which included the rifle companies. Certainly his designations differ significantly from others, including Arnold and Oswald.

Declaration

On the 6th of Sept., orders came from Gen'l Washington for a detachment to march to Quebec under Col. Benedict Arnold. I with several others of our co[mpany] joined in said expedition under Capt. Jonas Hubbard, Lieut. Elihu Lyman & Lt. Brown.

About 13th of Sept. we marched from Cambridge to Newburyport, where we took shipping for [the] Kennebec River, and went up said river to the head of navigation; then took bateaux to convey our provisions. The Army was, as I understood, divided equal into two Divisions. Our company was in the first under Lt. Col. Greene, Maj. Meigs and Bigelow. A Major Ogden accompanied us as a volunteer.

As I have lost my diary or journal that I kept from the time I left Hadley in 1775 until I returned there in June 1776, I may make some errors but I believe that Col. Greene's Division consisted of the following companies: Capt. Morgan's from Virginia, Capt. Hendricks and Capt. Smith from Pennsylvania, called southern troops; Capt. Goodrich. Capt. Hanchett, Capt. Hubbard, Capt. Dearborn, Capt. Thayer and Capt. Topping [Topham]'s companies, New England troops. The rear Division [was] under Lt. Col. Enos.

We made slow progress up the river. Our skiffs or bateaux, being built light and slender for the purpose of being carried by land at Carrying Places, were not well constructed for such a rough stream as the Kennebec River. We left the

Kennebec taking a westerly course across the twelve mile carrying place to Dead River. Proceeded up said River, but before arriving to the Height of Land, Col. Enos returned with his Division. The invalids of our Division were selected and sent back under the care of two officers, one of which was Lt. Lyman of our company. Col. Arnold went forward with a small party.

On arriving at the waters of Chaudiere River, we divided what little provisions we had, took up our march to and down said river, and about the third of Nov., came to an Indian settlement and French Inhabitants said to be ninety miles from Quebec. On the 9th of November came to Point Levi opposite of Quebec. After procuring craft and making preparations, on the night of the 13th [we] crossed the river St. Lawrence at Wolfe's Cove. Went to the Plains of Abraham to the road that leads into the City at Cape Diamond. Saw teams going into market before daylight, Found a square of buildings called Holland House. The next night the remainder of the Army came over the river.

About the 19th, the army left the Plains of Abraham, marched up the River St. Lawrence to a village called Point aux Trembles. Kept on guard at a small river about 10 miles above Quebec.

About the first of December, General Montgomery came down the river [St. Lawrence] and landed at Point aux Trembles where we had given to us a suit of British Regimental clothing. In a few days, the army marched back to Quebec. Gen"l Montgomery made his headquarters at the Holland House on the Plains and Arnold by and in the suburbs of St. Rocks.

In the morning of the last day of December or the morning of the first day of Jan'y the attempt to storm and take Quebec was made. Capt. Hubbard and all his Co. went, and were made prisoners, excepting the mess mate of mine by the name of William Pierce and myself, having my feet frozen to the degree I could not walk without crutches, which happened on the 25th of Dec. while at working building a battery on the Plains of Abraham. Said Pierce being sick and very feeble and myself lame, and our term of enlistment having expired, we left Quebec the 3rd January 1776 and hired our passage to Montreal, where we arrived the 8th. I immediately went to Gen'l or Col. Wooster, the commanding officer. When at his request I gave him a history of our march from Cambridge and what had taken place at Quebec. He said he could not allow any man to leave Canada until recruits shall arrive, which was expected soon, but that we should be taken care of, or if we were willing to enlist for three and a half months, or to 15th April, we should be entitled to the same as those that had so enlisted, with a suit of clothes and a month advanced pay. He then gave me and him to Maj. Brown to see us provided for. He gave us an order to draw provisions and had us provided for in a French family.

On the 14ᵗʰ January we both enlisted in Capt. Woodbridge Co., Col. Elmore and Maj. Brown, for the term as named by Gen'l Wooster. Soon after, rec'd a month's pay and clothes. Soon after Capt. Woodbridge and his Co. went to Quebec and left us in Capt. Roots Co. About the last of March I was taken with the small pox and went to the hospital, and although it was not expected, my life was preserved.

On the 20ᵗʰ May, Capt. Woodbridge came to me, said the army would leave Canada and, if possible, wished to have me get away. I sent and got a suit of clothes. Next morning [I] came into town where Capt. Woodbury informed me that Arnold had ordered that no more soldiers should leave town, but he would take me for a waiter and get me over the river, and I must try to get to Lt. Church who had gone with a Co. up the Sorel river to St. Johns. We crossed the river where he gave a package of papers in which was a quantity of Continental Bills to hand to Lt. Church, and if I did not see him to carry them home. He said he was going up to the Cedars where Maj. Butterfield was cut off by the Indians. This was the last time I saw Capt. Woodbridge.

Not being able to travel, I hired myself carried to Chambly and St. Johns, There found that Lt. Church had left Canada. In 3 or 4 days [I] left St. Johns in company with others in a boat. Stopped at a place called Williams Creek [on the] west side of Lake Complain. Crossed over to the mouth of Otter Creek in Vermont. Proceeded up said creek & through Vermont to Williamstown, Massachusetts, and arrived at Hadley about the middle of June, having been [gone] almost nearly 14 months.

FENNER FOOT

Fenner Foot was born in Colchester, Connecticut on October 5, 1754 to Jonathan and Sarah Foot. His family moved to Lee, Massachusetts prior to the war. On January 3, 1775, he joined the minute man company in Stockbridge, Massachusetts, headed up by Captain William Goodrich from that town. Foot describes the company, which was in Colonel Patterson's Regiment, as 'being drilled immediately and continued in Stockbridge until the first or second of April." The company under Goodrich marched to Cambridge in response to the Lexington Alarm. Obviously he got his dates wrong and would not have left Stockbridge with his company until the 19th of April. He was stationed as a guard near the Battle of Bunker Hill during which he remembered that "balls however fell thick around us being within sight of the battle." His company remained around Boston until September when Goodrich's company volunteered to join the expedition to Quebec.

Foot was not in the assault on Quebec as he was guarding the hospital located in a nunnery on the outskirts of Quebec. Even though his enlistment had expired he stayed on in Quebec until the spring of 1776. He arrived back home in Lee on the first of June 1776. On November 15, 1776, he enlisted in the Regiment of Colonel David Rossiter, where he served for four months at Fort Ticonderoga. He also enlisted for two weeks to respond to the British invasion of New York under General John Burgoyne and went to Bennington, but was not involved in any action.

On March 11, 1779, Fenner Foot married Sarah Wilcox in Lee, Massachusetts, and they had five children. He died on April 27, 1847, in Lee, Massachusetts at the age of ninety three. He is buried in the Fairmount Cemetery in Lee.

Although Foots declaration is short, he provides an interesting and well written narrative of his experiences. His is one of the few accounts which mention the difficulties of sea sickness as a result of a hurricane type storm while the transports were in the Atlantic Ocean. His description of the physical and mental hardship and food running out while in the wilderness provides an unusual perspective of the suffering which is not found in most accounts. At the end, he laments that none of the men who were on the march received any money. There is evidence that some of the men did get paid. However, based on the journal entries by William Heth of Virginia, it is not surprising that Goodrich's men were never paid.

My wife designated Foot's declaration as her top choice among the pension applications included in this chapter. Foot's account is interesting because while he marched through the wilderness under Arnold, he did not participate in the assault on Quebec. He contracted small pox in 1776 while still in Quebec, which is a reminder of how prevalent the pox was among American soldiers in Canada during that period.

Declaration

When volunteers was called for to go with Arnold into Canada by the way of wilderness, Capt. Goodrich, with most of his company enlisted in this service as did myself. We started on the 15th of Sept. and marched to Newburyport. From thence we went by water to the Kennebec River, suffering extremely from [sea] sickness. We landed at a place called Pownal [Maine] after having encountered a tremendous storm on the passage, and having at one time been driven into a [illeg] place called the Four Brothers.

We went up the Kennebec River in bateaux, which had been provided for us, as far as we could. Then we had to carry them and our ammunition and provisions across a carry place of seven miles to another stream [Dead River] and then again frequently over other places, making our march severe in the extreme. Sometimes we had to go back over those carrying places three or four times to bring all of our effects. By this time it was ascertained that our provisions was not sufficient to last the whole party consisting of about 1200. Orders were given for 600 to march back,

We went on and our provisions were at last all consumed but one barrel of meat that we soon had the misfortune to lose in one of the rapids. We were now thirty-eight days in the wilderness during which time we saw no human being except our own party. We suffered from bad cold and hunger all that human nature could suffer. For two weeks we had no more than one pint of flour to ten men, only in twenty-four hours, and this at last failed us. We were now on the Height of Land between the State of Maine and the River St. Lawrence at Chaudiere Pond. At this place the water had flooded to a great distance and we were under the necessity of marching through it mid way in the water, and also to track the ice to the distance of one mile. Now the only inquiry to be heard was what shall we do to keep us alive.

Our captain concluded to take some of our ablest men and go forward to to try to find some inhabitants. We had eaten nothing then for twenty-four hours. The day after Capt. Goodrich left us, Capt. Hendricks Co. overtook us. From them we obtained a dog and it was killed and eaten voraciously. Some of our companions were taken sick and we could do not less than lay them down to die and go on and leave them, being ourselves so emaciated and worn that we could afford them no relief. At last we found inhabitants ninety miles from the place of our destination and found relief.

We then marched on and encamped for a few days opposite the Abraham Plains. Now I was taken sick and did not recover for two or three weeks, as was the case with many of us. We stayed there until one night orders were whispered to us to be ready to move out at a moments warning [to go] on to Abrahams Plains. We soon were in motion and took possession of the heights, where our whole army encamped for that night. The next morning Gen. Arnold paraded his army and marched before the City, gave three cheers and then retired.

When the assault upon Quebec was made and Gen. Montgomery was killed, I was stationed as a guard before the door of a nunnery used as a hospital. We stayed [in Quebec] until the next spring when we left the place. Having had severely the small pox for a while there, I arrived at home the first of June 1776. For our services in this dreadful campaign, we never received a dollar. Our Capt. was taken prisoner in the assault and I never saw him afterwards.

John Gridley

John Gridley was born in Roxbury Massachusetts in November 1752, the son of Deacon Samuel Gridley. He had a twin sister Patience. In 1775, at the age of twenty-three, while residing in Medbury, Massachusetts, he joined a company of minute men from the surrounding towns in Capt. Sabin Mann's Company in Colonel Greaton's Regiment. His company responded to the call to action as a result of the Lexington Alarm and marched to Cambridge in the afternoon of April 19, too late to participate in any action. Gridley remained in Cambridge and then enlisted in Captain John Boyd's Company of Greaton's Regiment and was in the Battle of Bunker Hill. He volunteered to join the expedition to Canada and was assigned to Capt. Samuel Ward's Company. In the assault on Quebec, he was taken prisoner and released with the rest of the prisoners in September of 1776.

On August 20, 1780, he married Anna Rixford in Petersham, Worchester, Massachusetts. They had two children, Anna and John Jr. His widow applied for a pension application in 1839 and was allowed a pension at that time when she was seventy-seven years of age

On January 1, 1777, Gridley enlisted in Captain David Bryant's Company in Colonel John Crane's Regiment of Artillery. In the Battle of

Brandywine, Gridley was injured and Capt. Bryant was killed. He was in the battles of Germantown and Monmouth. In October of 1783 he was commissioned as a captain brevet and served until the end of that year.

Gridley applied for and was approved for a pension in 1818 when he was a resident of Fishkill, New York. He relinquished his pension in 1828 "for the benefit of the act." He died in Middleburgh, Schoharie, New York on September 15, 1824 at the age of seventy-two.

His pension application provides an interesting account, especially of the assault on Quebec and then when he was a prisoner in Quebec, forty-two years after it happened. His involvement in the escape attempt while the American soldiers were in the stone prison contains details that only appear in a limited number of journals.

Declaration

I volunteered with the troops on the Quebec expedition in Capt. Ward's Co. of Rhode Island, under Col. Arnold and Maj. Meigs. Marched to Newburyport, sailed to the mouth of the Kennebec River, then took bateaux for our provisions and baggage, and proceeded for Quebec. Continued up the river and over carrying places. Run till our water craft was destroyed, with the loss of other articles. Then proceeded by land, and after suffering every[thing] but death, arrived at Quebec, having [left] many dead bodies to feed the beasts of the wilderness.

Although I did not arrive with the army, being left with three others of my unfortunate companions in the wilderness to suffer the fate of many others there, lying in the wilderness. But by the assistance of God, after so long a time, we arrived at a small village in the vicinity of Quebec called St Rocks, where our army then lay waiting for Gen'l Montgomery to arrive from Montreal with his troops

After his arrival and matters being managed, on the 31ˢᵗ December orders were received for storming Quebec at night, which was obeyed. We accordingly attacked in two Divisions. Gen'l Montgomery [was] at the upper town with his Division and Col. Arnold with his [Division was] at the lower town. But the Gen'l being killed on his first attempt, and his Division retreating precipitously, left us to their mercy, and being over powered with numbers and within the walls of the city, they, shutting the gates upon us, demanded our surrender. But we, being successful and not knowing our Gen'l was killed nor the defeat of his Division, would not resign. At last, finding ourselves surrounded and receiving a flag, which again demanded our surrender or we should all be put to death by the sword, concluded but to resign. Accordingly. to make up the measure of our misery, we gave our [illeg.] a New Year's gift unto Gen. Carleton of Canada, 1776, and was conveyed under a strong guard to a seminary because the stone jail was not ready to receive us.

After some repose, we were escorted to the dreadful strong burn proof prison. After remaining in this doleful condition, not being content but was still determined for Liberty, we planned a show to send out to the army which lay out one mile or two from the city. A man of ours [was sent] with a letter to acquaint the commander, he promising to assist, that on such a night he being ready, and would come and assist us, we would as yet try to take the city. Accordingly, a letter was voted. A man agreed to convey it with our assistance. We then beat a hole through the very thick stone wall of the prison, cut out blankets in strips, and then let him down not expecting to hear from him again. But to our surprise we received a satisfactory answer.

But having a number of British deserters with us and the British, finding it out, sent a pardon to them [Old Country Men] provided they would return to their duty. A major supporter of the British, being with us, revealed our plan. He was taken from us and returned to duty. We were immediately confined in irons, handcuffs and footlocks, two and two together, and continued in that condition until their reinforcements arrived from Halifax in the month of August. [We were] half starved.

In the month of August, we was put on their shipping and conveyed into New York Harbor in the month of September 1776. After arriving in New York harbor, being then among their fleet, and they also laying siege to New York, [we] were not allowed on shore until they had completed their design. After they had taken New York, we were put on our land of liberty at Elizabethtown [New Jersey], and thus ended our unparalleled distress.

OLIVER SMITH

Smith was born in Hadley, Massachusetts in 1752. (No specific date known.) He joined the Captain Foster Artillery Company from Hadley in April of 1775 and went with that company to Cambridge on April 21st.

In May, while still in Cambridge, he enlisted in Captain Eliahom Smith's Company in the Regiment of Colonel Ward. He subsequently enlisted in the expedition to Quebec and was in the Captain Jonas Hubbard Company. He participated in the assault on Quebec and was taken prisoner. Smith was released with the other prisoners in September of 1776 and was exchanged in January of 1777.

Oliver Smith moved to Bennington, Vermont in the autumn of 1777 and was in the Battle of Bennington for fourteen days as a private in Captain Samuel Robinson's Company of Vermont troops. He married Betsy Rood at a date unknown. He moved to Rome, New York in 1797 and then to Clarendon, Orleans County, New York in 1815. He received a pension in 1833when he was eighty years old. He died in Clarendon, New York at an unknown date.

Oliver Smith's pension application is included in this book because his account states that he heard the words Benedict Arnold uttered after he was wounded and being helped off the field to the hospital. He also provides the names of various officers on the expedition and two volunteers, Matthias Ogden and Aaron Burr. He remembered Ogden being wounded in the assault. The repeating of the words he heard from Arnold is relevant because there are other writers who have provided different words from Arnold at that time. As far as I know, Smith has not been cited as a source.

Declaration

In the summer following (1775), General Washington arrived and took command of the Army. In the latter part of the summer or first of the fall, I engaged to go with Col. Arnold in the expedition to Quebec, and that about one week after such engagement or enlistment, I marched with said party, under the command of Col. Arnold for Quebec, and continued under Col. Arnold and suffered all of the hardships and privation of that campaign until the final surrender of the greater part of Arnold's men at Quebec on the morning of the first of January 1776. The captain under whom I served was Jonas Hubbard, who was wounded in the action and died of his wound. The Lieut. was [Samuel] Brown and the Ensign was [John] Pierce. He, Pierce, was not in the action.

Of field officers, [he] recollects Major [Timothy] Bigelow, Lieut. Col.

[Chistopher] Greene, and [he] thinks Major [Return J.] Meigs; of the Captains, [he] recollects Capt. [Daniel] Morgan of the Riflemen, Capt. [Matthew] Smith of the Riflemen and Capt. [William] Hendricks of the Riflemen, which last was killed. Also Capt.'s of the infantry of the State of Rhode Island, [Samuel] Ward, [Simeon] Thayer and [John] Tolman [Topham], and Capt. of Infantry of Massachusetts was [William] Goodrich & [Jonas] Hubbard; from Connecticut Capt. [Oliver] Hanchet; from New Hampshire Capt. Henry Dearborn. Recollects of [illeg.] with Arnold's command, two young men as volunteers who he thinks got to be staff officers while In Canada. The one was [Aaron] Burr and [Matthias] Ogden the other. Ogden was wounded in the back or shoulder at the battle of Quebec within my reach. Also recollects Lieut. [John] Clark and others.

The last words I recollect to have heard Benedict Arnold say, was in the Battle after he was wounded when he was assisted back by two men, "Rush on my brave boys, the Town is our own, we have got our battery."

I continued a prisoner of war at Quebec until sometime in the summer of 1776 when I, with the rest of the prisoners, was put on board of our transports, who together with the envoy, went down the St. Lawrence and around to New York, and about the first of October 1776, I with [the] rest of the prisoners was discharged in Elizabethtown in New Jersey as prisoner of war on parole; and from his best recollection now thinks it was about the first of January 1777 when he was exchanged and ceased to be a prisoner of war.

RICHARD VINING

Richard Vining was born in East Winsor, Connecticut in about 1752, and became an indentured servant in Enfield, Connecticut, at the age of nine. After the end of his servitude, in about 1771, he moved to Otis, Massachusetts, and married Phebe Langdon in about 1773. They had two children and she died about 1817. He was living in Otis when he enlisted in Captain William Goodrich's Company in Stockbridge, Massachusetts, which was part of Colonel Patterson's Regiment. His company went to Cambridge about May 1, 1775 and he is listed on the company muster roll as of August 1, 1775.

Vining and some of his company joined Capt. Goodrich to enlist for the expedition to Quebec in early September. He was with the company through the wilderness of Maine and Canada but was not in the American assault on Quebec. He became ill while at Point aux Trembles with the army so could not join in the assault. He returned home to Otis on January 28, 1776.

In the summer of 1776, he was a sergeant in Capt. John King's Company, Colonel Lowell's Berkshire Regiment, at Newburgh, New York, for approximately one month to August 5, 1776. According to John C. Dann, his company was "guarding the Hudson at the time of the abortive Vaughan expedition." His family moved to Granby, Connecticut, after the war in about 1784, where he lived for twenty-five years. He then moved again to Salisbury, Ohio, and lived there about fourteen years. He moved back to Granby, Connecticut, in 1824 and stayed there about seven years. In 1831, he made his final move to Boonville, Oneida County, New York. He was approved for a pension as an invalid in 1833 at the age of eighty years old. He died in Boonville at an unknown date.

Vining's account includes much detail about the difficulties encountered in the remarkable march through the wilderness, as stated by John C. Dann in his book which published Vining's declaration for the first time. Vining also includes details of how he resolved the problems he encountered as a result of his illness in Quebec prior to the assault. Dann reminds his readers that the "previously known narratives of the expedition, which support the accuracy of Vining's detail, were collected in Kenneth Roberts's March to Quebec (1938) and were used as sources for his novel Arundel (1930)."

Declaration

About the first of September (1775), General Arnold had orders to march to Quebec, when deponent volunteered his services into the same company under the same officers, except the Colonel whose name he does not now recollect. After they had started, he got acquainted with Lieut. Colonel [Christopher] Greene and Major [Return J.] Meigs. [He] Does not recollect their Christian names. The orders then came to [march to] Newburyport, which they did and lay some days in preparing sloops to carry the Army over into the bay of Fundy into the mouth of the Kennebec River. They set sail & went up the Kennebec River as far as an Indian fort called Fort Western. They there landed and lay some days making preparations for marching through the woods. There they took up the line of march up the river aforesaid until the stream got so small that trees reached across, so they crossed and left the Kennebec, and went through the woods [to] Chaudiere [actually Dead] River, [I] should think about fifteen miles from [the] Kennebec.

Previous to this time, by undertaking to round a creek which was not fordable 9the company with me0, I, having occasion to stop, was left by my company and got lost and was in the woods alone [for] three days without a mouthful of provisions. In that time I did not travel much as I thought I should not gain the River by traveling until the sun could be seen. It was cloudy. When the sun shone again I then struck for the River and came up with the rear company of the army, and there I got half allowance which was allotted to the army on account of the scarcity of provisions. The day after, I came up with the company aforesaid. I started out at sunrise and overtook my own company.

I continued on half rations for nine days, when I came to [the] Chaudiere River. Then we went down Chaudiere River until we came to a marsh which by [the] previous rain had been overflown. We waded the marsh, some places to our middles, and the ice as thick as window glass. After we got across the marsh we came onto a rise of ground and a creek which we could not cross presented itself, and the company was ordered to fire three rounds as a signal of distress. Major Meigs procured from some Indians a bark canoe [and] on hearing the firing and crossed a pond which lay upon the west side of us and took Capt. Goodrich and went back to where the bateaux was which belonged to the army and carried our company across.

General Arnold took 5 or 6 mean, pushed on to the French Inhabitants as fast as possible to provide provisions for us. The General on coming to the first Inhabitants procured a cow and sent [it] back to relieve the Army. Previous to this our company was obliged to kill a dog and eat it for our breakfast, and in the course of that day I killed an owl and two of my mess mates & myself fared in the repast. However, we came up for the cow and cooked a portion of it and drank the broth of the owl and cooked together and the next day ate the meat. The second day after we got the beef, it rained heavily and turned to a snow storm and the snow fell [to] a middle deep. The day following we waded a river thirty rods wide. We came soon to a house where we drew a pound of beef and 3 potatoes each. Do not recollect the name of the man owning the house. *Went from the house into the woods and found an Indian camp and lodged for the night*

Next day started and I was taken sick of a kind of camp disruption. Could not walk far in a day. Went on five miles and came to another house where we got our pound of beef, 3 potatoes and a pint of oatmeal each. We then went on when I became so feeble that myself and two more hired a Frenchman to carry us on over, but our own expense, for 13 miles. There we found common rations. We then went on all being very much enfeebled by reason of sickness and hardship for four or five days until we reached Quebec.

At Quebec we lay on the opposite side of the river [St. Lawrence] from the town about one week. Then General Arnold ordered all who were fit for duty to cross the river, who crossed and presented themselves in front of the fort when the British fired upon them. No injury done except that one man had a leg shot off by a cannon ball. The General then ordered a retreat. We retreated up the river towards Montreal to a place called Point aux Tremble, 24 miles from Quebec. We lay there about four weeks until Gen'l Montgomery had secured Montreal, when he came and found us and we returned to Quebec.

I was sick and left at Point aux Trembles, and left in a hospital at that place. Stayed at that place about two weeks. Then my physician told me that he would give me a recommend for a discharge, as did other physicians when I got to Quebec. But [I] refused it as I thought I might get better. I went to Quebec and my Capt. went with me to the physicians who gave me recommend for discharge which I presented to General Arnold, who told me I had not better take a discharge but had better take a furlough until I gained health and soundness, which furlough he gave me, which furlough is lost. The General have gave me five dollars to bear my expenses, I bought a horse off my Capt, for which I was to let him have ten dollars out of my wages. After I left, the captain was taken prisoner in an attempt to scale the walls of Quebec, as I understood. My Lieutenant rec'd the pay for the company to which I belonged and sent word to me that your money was ready. I went to Stockbridge in Massachusetts and received my pay; This was after the Lieutenant had returned home. I then went and paid the ten dollars due my Capt. for the horse to his wife for which I took her receipt which I have kept and herewith present. I returned home the 28th day of January 1776 but was not discharged until the first of May following.

APPENDIX A. COMPLETE LIST
OF EXPEDITION JOURNALS

JOURNALIST'S NAME		RANK	COMPANY	HOMETOWN	DATE 1ST PUB	NAME OF PUBLICATION
ARNOLD, BENEDICT	1	COL	COMMAND	NEW HAVEN, CT	1835	LIFE OF AARON BURR
BARNEY, SAMUEL	2	PVT	HANCHETT	NEW HAVEN, CT	2011	VOICES FROM WILD EXPEDITION
DEARBORN, HENRY	3	CPT	REVISED	NOTTINGHAM, NH	1886	PROC MASS HIST SOC, VOL 2
DEARBORN, HENRY	4	CPT	ORIGINAL	NOTTINGHAM, NH	2011	VOICES FROM WILD EXPEDITION
DORR, WILLIAM	5	PVT	WARD	DOVER, NH	2000	DORR'S MARCH TO QUEBEC
DURBEN ANON 2	6	UNK	UNKNOWN	UNKNOWN	2011	VOICES FROM WILD EXPEDITION
DURBEN ANON 3	7	UNK	UNKNOWN	UNKNOWN	2011	VOICES FROM WILD EXPEDITION
FOBES, SIMON	8	PVT	HUBBARD	AMHERST, MA	1878	HIST COLL MAHONING VALLEY, Vol 1
FLANDERS, JOHN	9	PVT	DEARBORN	BOSCAWEN, NH	1881	HIST BOSCAWEN NH
GREENMAN, JEREMIAH	10	PVT	WARD	PROVIDENCE, RI	1978	DIARY OF COMMON SOLDIER
HASKELL, CALEB	11	PVT	WARD	NEWBURYPORT, MA	1881	CALEB HASKELL'S DIARY
HENRY, JOHN JOSEPH	12	PVT	SMITH	LANCASTER, PA	1812	ACCURATE INTERESTING ACCT
HETH, WILLIAM	13	LT	MORGAN	WINCHESTER, VA	1931	PAPERS WINCHESTER VA HS, VOL 1
HUMPHREY, WILLIAM	14	LT	THAYER	PROVIDENCE, RI	1931	MAGAZINE OF HISTORY, EXTRA 166
KIMBALL, MOSES	15	PVT	DEARBORN	HAMPSTEAD, NH	2011	VOICES FROM WILD EXPEDITION
MCCOY, WILLIAM	16	SGT	HENDRICKS	CUMBERLAND, PA	1776	JOURNAL BODY PROVINCIALS
MEIGS, RETURN J	17	MAJ	DIVISION	MIDDLETOWN, CT	1776	JOURNAL OF OCCURRENCES
MELVIN, JAMES	18	PVT	DEARBORN	HUBBARDSTON, MA	1857	JOURNAL OF EXP TO QUEBEC
MORISON, GEORGE	19	PVT	HENDRICKS	SHERMAN VALLEY, PA	1803	INT JOUR OF OCCURRENCES

NICHOLS, FRANCIS	20	LT	HENDRICKS	CARLISLE, PA	1896	PA MAG HIST & BIOGRAPHY, Vol 20
OGDEN, MATTHIAS	21	CPT	VOLUNTEER	ELIZABETH, NJ	1928	PROC NJ HISTORICAL SOC, Vol 13
OSWALD, ELEAZER	22	VOL	HQ	NEW HAVEN, CT	1846	FORCE, AMERICAN ARCHIVES
UNKNOWN	23	UNK	UNKNOWN	PENNSYLVANIA	1779	PENNSYLVANIA PACKET
PIERCE, JOHN	24	SGT	HUBBARD	WORCESTER, MA	1946	MARCH TO QUEBEC
PIERCE, WILLIAM	25	PVT	HUBBARD	HADLEY, MA	1900	AMER ANTIQ & ORIEN JOUR, Vol 22
PORTERFIELD, CHARLES	26	VOL	MORGAN	WINCHESTER, VA	1901	MAG AMERICAN HISTORY, Vol 21
PRESTON, WILLIAM	27	PVT	DEARBORN	CHESTER, NH	N/A	NONE
SENTER, ISAAC	28	SUR	HQ	NEWPORT, RI	1846	BULLETIN HIST SOC OF PA, Vol 1
SENTER, ISAAC 2ND	29	SUR	HQ	NEWPORT, RI	2011	VOICES FROM WILD EXPEDITION
SQUIER, EPHRAIM	30	PVT	SCOTT	ASHFORD, CT	1878	MAGAZINE OF AMER HISTORY, Vol 2
STOCKING, ABNER	31	PVT	HANCHETT	HADDAM, CT	1810	JOURNAL OF ABNER STOCKING
THAYER, SIMEON	32	CPT	THAYER	PROVIDENCE, RI	1867	INVASION OF CANADA IN 1775
TOLMAN, EBENEZER	33	PVT	WARD	FITZWILLIAM, NH	1917	150 ANNIV OF NELSON, NH
TOPHAM, JOHN	34	CPT	TOPHAM	NEWPORT, RI	1897	NEWPORT MERCURY NEWSPAPER
WARE, JOSEPH	35	PVT	WARD	NEEDHAM, MA	1852	NE HIST & GEN SOCIETY, Vol 11
SLEEPER, JOHN	36	PVT	WARD	NEWBURYPORT, MA	N/A	AFFIDAVIT FOR PENS APP
JUDD, FREEMAN	37	PVT	HANCHETT	WATERBURY, CT	N/A	SOLD AT OLD CORNER BKSTORE
SAMUEL COOK	38	PVT	HUBBARD	HADLEY, MA	N/A	PENSION APPLICATION

GENERAL NOTES

These general notes are added just before the End Notes because the majority of these entries are referred to in at least one, and sometimes all, of the journals. While each journal has its own annotations, it will be more efficient to include the common references in the journals in this category with some helpful details on each listed item. The General Notes include information on important geographical references and town names, the significant events that took place and the names of significant people associated with Arnold's expedition to Quebec. These notes will help the reader to better understand the invasion of Canada and the Arnold expedition. The notes will also help to illuminate the common journal references and will eliminate the need for a separate and repetitive reference at the end of each journal. These notes are divided into four categories: People, Places, Events and Subjects.

The General Notes will be referenced in the End Notes as GN (specific number). No page number.

PEOPLE

1. **Colonel Benedict Arnold**. Arnold is one of the most well-known American officers of the American Revolution. More books (there are at least fifty-two volumes) have been written about his life and military service than any other American officer except George Washington. His exploits in the first two years of the war are unmatched by any other American officer. One of his most extraordinary achievements was leading the men who volunteered to participate in the secret mission to take Quebec described in the journals in this book.

   In order for the reader to understand the extent of Arnold's leadership in the planning and execution of the march to Quebec, this profile will not include the usual biographical details of Arnold's life. Instead, the specific details offered below show his exemplary leadership in leading the Quebec expedition on assignment from General George Washington. It should be noted that he had no formal military training prior to the Revolutionary War.

Benedict Arnold's military leadership achievements:
- Only accepted volunteers. No man was ordered to participate because the march was through an unknown wilderness.
- Followed Washington's warning to maintain strict discipline to ensure that his troops did not "plunder or insult" any Canadian citizens that the expedition encountered and that he pay "full Value for all Provisions." Washington also instructed Arnold to "avoid all Disrespect or Contempt of the Religion of the Country." There is no evidence that Arnold did any of the negative actions or failed to do the affirmative actions that were set out by Washington in his letter of instructions. In fact, the local inhabitants said Arnold's men were "a good sort of men who take nothing by force," and who "pay liberally for everything they purchase."
- Provided Reuben Colburn, the boat builder, with details about the construction of the bateaux in a letter dated August 21, 1775. In it he spells out important details about the boats he and Washington wanted Colburn to build. There were few, if any, American officers who had sufficient knowledge about boats to write these specifications.
- Correctly estimated the time it would take for the expedition to get from Cambridge to Quebec. He instructed Colburn to provide forty days of food supplies per man. The actual expedition took 45 days.
- Arranged for provisions be waiting in Newburyport and Fort Western.
- Through his friend and trader Nathaniel Tracy, arranged for vessels to transport the troops from Newburyport. Arnold's experience owning his own trading company before the war enabled him to make easy connections with other traders.
- Divided his companies into four divisions at Fort Western to keep the men in the companies sufficiently spaced out so they would not get in each other's way.

- Sent scouting parties ahead of the main body to report on the route and any difficulties that might be avoided. Unfortunately, his scouts did not explore the route in Canada as he instructed making their report unhelpful.
- Led his men by example from the front and experienced the same hardships and difficulties that they encountered. Moved up and down his column of troops as they made their way through Maine to offer encouragement and instructions.
- After leaving the Kennebec River, instructed that a log house be built to store food and other supplies in case his men had to retreat.
- Ordered a log hospital to be built in the wilderness as a shelter so that when his men became sick and exhausted they would have a place to shelter.
- Sent back those too sick to continue, with an escort, so that no one was left alone in the wilderness.
- Left handwritten notes at various locations containing instructions for his men when necessary.
- Led a small group of men to hurry ahead of the rest of his men to the first Canadian settlement to procure food for the men when severe food shortages became apparent. This action undoubtedly saved his men from starvation. One report said that Arnold's men who made it to Sartigan appeared "more like ghosts than men."
- Purchased boats and canoes from the inhabitants for future use when the expedition went along the Chaudière River. Without this action, there would have been no way for the men to cross the St. Lawrence River as the British had removed all boats before he got there.
- Led the expedition across the St. Lawrence between two British warships in the middle of the night without being discovered or losing a man.
- Spent 15,000 pounds of his own personal money to obtain food for his men while in Canada. He never got reimbursed by Congress for those expenditures.
- Despite all the hardships and the early return of the Enos division, he was able to get 675 men through the unknown wilderness to

Quebec. This epic feat has been compared to Hannibal's march across the Alps.

- Removed his men waiting outside the walls of Quebec to Point aux Trembles which was twenty miles away after reports from a spy that the British were planning to lead an attack against him from the city.
- Participated in the planning and led one of the two detachments in the assault on the city and was wounded at the first barricade. Arnold was wounded in his left leg by a musket ball which entered just below the knee. Dr. Senter removed the ball but it was not until the end of February that Arnold could walk on his leg.
- Worked to establish a blockade of supplies coming to Quebec from the Point Levi side of the St. Lawrence so that during the months of November and December "not a single canoe crossed with food from there."
- Was promoted to Brigadier General on January 10, 1776, by the Continental Congress as a result of the positive reports of his leadership of the expedition.
- Stayed on in Canada in a command position during recuperation from his wound where he continued the blockade of Quebec. He continued to lead his men first at Quebec and then at Montreal until the dispirited American army retreated in June. Captain James Wilkinson, then an aide to Arnold, claimed in his memoirs that he and Arnold were the last Americans to leave Canadian soil when they jumped into a canoe at St. Johns on May 16, 1776, when the approaching British Army was sighted.

Although there have been numerous books and articles written about Benedict Arnold, the best and most accurate biography is the one written by James Kirby Martin, *Benedict Arnold, Revolutionary Hero: An American Warrior Reconsidered*. New York University Press, 1997.

2. **Major General Philip Schuyler.** Schuyler was from Albany, New York, and was a member of the Hudson Valley Dutch aristocracy who owned a large estate and had significant wealth. He served as

the on again, off again commander of the Northern Continental Army, sharing that honor with Major General Horatio Gates. Schuyler was supposed to head up the second prong of the invasion of Canada in 1775 but he bowed out because of poor health and gave his command to General Richard Montgomery. Many New Englanders viewed him with suspicion because of his wealth and land holdings. He was not a fighting general but was a capable administrator for Washington during the times he had the command. See Don Gerlach. *Proud Patriot: Philip Schuyler and the War of Independence, 1775-1783.* Syracuse University Press, 1987.

3. **Brigadier General Richard Montgomery.** Montgomery was born in Ireland and served in the British Army in the French and Indian War. After coming back to America, he married Janet Livingston of the Hudson Valley Livingston family. Her family was very wealthy and she was a close relative of General Philip Schuyler, who Montgomery replaced as the commander of the Lake Champlain and Richelieu River prong of the invasion of Canada. He led a separate army up the Richelieu River to capture St. John, Fort Chambly and Montreal. He was killed in the assault on Quebec on the night of December 31, 1775. See Death of Montgomery in General Notes 100. The best biography is *Major General Richard Montgomery, The Making of an American Hero*, by Michael P. Gabriel. Farleigh Dickenson University Press, 2002.

4. **James Livingston.** Livingston was a relative of General Montgomery's wife Janet and was born in Chambly, Canada.. He joined Montgomery's forces with a company of Canadians to help take Fort Chambly. He was with Montgomery when he joined up with Arnold near Quebec and was with Montgomery when the general was killed. In 1777, Livingston's 1st Canadian Regiment was part of the relief of Fort Stanwix and in the Battle of Saratoga. In 1780, his unit was at Verplank's Point when Major Andre came up the Hudson River to meet Arnold.

5. **Lieutenant Colonel Donald Campbell.** He was second in command under General Montgomery in the assault and took over command of the forces when Montgomery was killed. He was strongly criticized for retreating after the death of Montgomery instead of continuing the assault.

6. **Captain Jacob Cheeseman.** An Aide-de-Camp to General Montgomery who died at his side in the assault on Quebec.

7. **Lieutenant Colonel Christopher Greene.** Although he was the 2nd Division commander on the expedition, he did not distinguish himself so he is rarely mentioned in any journals. Greene was born in Warwick, Rhode Island, and was a friend and relative to General Nathaniel Greene. He was captured in the assault on Quebec and released in August of 1776. After being exchanged, he was promoted to the rank of Colonel and distinguished himself at the defense of Fort Mercer, or Red Bank, in 1777. He was killed in Westchester County, New York by a group of Loyalist insurgents on May 13, 1781. Smith described him as "most highly esteemed." See Stone, Appendix, pp. 52-57; *Col. Marcus Denison Raymond. Col. Christopher Greene of Rhode Island. Address to Rhode Island Historical Society, April 26, 1902.*

8. **Lieutenant Colonel Roger Enos.** The commander of the expedition's 4th Division was born in Simsbury, Connecticut in 1729 and served in the French and Indian War in the Regiment of Major General Phineas Lyman. In April of 1775, after the Lexington Alarm, he was appointed by the Connecticut General Assembly as a captain in the 3rd Company of Colonel Joseph Spencer's 2nd Regiment. He was promoted up the ranks to become a lieutenant colonel in Spencer's Regiment. It is likely that Arnold selected Enos for his expedition based on his F & I War experience and it is likely they knew each other because of the Connecticut connection. Enos led the three companies in his division to leave the expedition in late October of 1775 and return to Cambridge without Arnold's approval. The Enos Division being the last

division on the march was obliged to carry most of the food for the entire detachment. When they left the expedition to return to headquarters, most of the food they were carrying went with them. For a more detailed biography of Enos, see *Voices*, pp. 203-210.

9. **Eleazer Oswald.** Oswald was born in England and came to American in 1770. He opened a printing business in New Haven, Connecticut in 1771 and organized a military company with Benedict Arnold. Oswald went to Cambridge right after the Lexington Alarm with the company he and Arnold helped to establish. Oswald was with Arnold as his aide-de-camp at Fort Ticonderoga and the capture of Fort St. Johns. Oswald accompanied Arnold as his aide on the expedition to Quebec and wrote a journal of short duration. He was the leader of the "Forlorn Hope" in the Arnold detachment's assault on the barricades on December 31, 1775.

Oswald was taken prisoner during the assault and after he was exchanged he joined Colonel John Lamb's artillery regiment where he was promoted to lieutenant colonel. He was in the Battle at Compo Beach in April of 1777 and in the Battle of Monmouth with Lamb's artillery. After his army service he became a printer in Baltimore at the *Maryland Journal* and in Philadelphia as editor of the *Independent Gazetteer*. Oswald was an avid anti-federalist and opposed the new Constitution but supported the Bill of Rights. In 1793 he went to France to participate in the French Revolution and died of yellow fever back in America in 1795.

10. **Adjutant Christian Febiger.** Febiger was born in Denmark and joined the American Army in the late spring of 1775. He served as Arnold's adjutant on the expedition and was captured at the assault on Quebec. He served in many battles and campaigns during the Revolution earning the nickname "Old Denmark." When he left the service, he was serving as a brevet brigadier general. He became the Treasurer for the State of Pennsylvania in 1791 and died while serving in that office in 1796.

11. **Captain Daniel Morgan.** Morgan commanded a company of riflemen from Winchester County, Virginia. He was selected to be the 1st Division commander of the three rifle companies when Arnold divided his force into four divisions. Morgan is probably the most notable and praised officer from the expedition after Arnold. He attained more fame later in the war in the Battle of Saratoga and then in the Battle of Cowpens in South Carolina where he beat back the detachment under Colonel Banastre Tarleton, who headed a Loyalist force that was well known for its fighting ability. A good Morgan biography is *Daniel Morgan, Ranger of the Revolution*, by North Callahan.[534]

12. **Major Return J. Meigs.** Meigs was born in Middletown, Connecticut on December 16, 1740. His journal of the expedition was the first one published sometime in 1776. He served in 6th Connecticut Regiment as a lieutenant and then was promoted to captain in 1774. His company responded to the Lexington Alarm and he was subsequently promoted to Major in Colonel Joseph Spencer's 2nd Connecticut Regiment. Arnold selected him for the expedition and appointed him to command the 3rd Division. He was taken prisoner in the assault on Quebec but was one of two officers released early on parole in May of 1776. A recently written and interesting biography is by Richard A. Mason, *The Quiet Patriot, Colonel Return Jonathan Meigs.*[535]

In a letter to Washington on July 15th, Meigs explained why he got an early release. "I am to represent to your Excellency the situation of the unfortunate detachment that were made prisoners on the 31st December last…The prisoners… are anxious for an exchange of Prisoners…In February last, the officers, prisoners in Quebec, petitioned General Carleton for an exchange of prisoners." Meigs acted as an envoy from the Quebec prisoners to convince Washington to arrange an exchange so they could go home.

13. **Major Timothy Bigelow.** Bigelow was born in Worcester, Massachusetts, and in 1773, he was a member of the Worcester

Committee of Correspondence. He was instrumental in forming a local branch of the Sons of Liberty in 1774 and was a delegate to the Provincial Congress. When the minutemen formed in Worcester, Bigelow was selected as the commander and led the company to respond to the Lexington Alarm. He was promoted to major and volunteered to accompany the Arnold expedition to Quebec. While still in the Maine wilderness, Bigelow and a small party of men were ordered by Arnold to ascend a mountain near the headwaters of the Kennebec. The mountain, now Bigelow Mt., was named after him. He was taken prisoner at Quebec and when he was exchanged he served at Saratoga, Peekskill, and Valley Forge. His bio in *Massachusetts Soldiers and Sailors in the War of the Revolution*, p. 27, states that he was "reported deranged Jan. 1, 1781."

After the war, he became ill and could not take up any occupation. His property and business were damaged and he was heavily in debt. The sad end to his story is that by 1787 he was so deeply in debt to so many people that he was confined to debtors' prison in Worcester where he died on March 31, 1790. Despite his service in the war, no one stepped up to help him out while he languished in prison. The City of Worcester, in a belated recognition, later placed his statue in the center of town.

14. **Captain Henry Dearborn.** Dearborn achieved the highest rank of any Arnold expedition alumnus because of the positions he held subsequent to the Revolutionary War. In 1801, President Thomas Jefferson appointed him as Secretary of War where he served until 1808. In the war of 1812, President James Madison appointed him as the Senior Major General in the United States Army and placed him in command of the northeast sector but by 1813 he was relieved of command and assigned to an administrative position with the army. He was honorably discharged from the army on June 15, 1815, with less than a stellar reputation. Dearborn was nominated as Secretary of War by President Madison but he was rejected by the Senate. He served as Minister Plenipotentiary

to Portugal from 1822 to 1824. He then retired to his home in Roxbury, Massachusetts, where he died on June 6, 1829. There is more about Dearborn in the chapter on his original journal from *Voices*, pp. 95-137, including the fact that he was released early on parole in May along with Meigs. The only biography of his life is by Charles Coffin. *The Life and Services of Major General Henry Dearborn*.[536] Also see Chapter Four of this book.

15. **Captain Simeon Thayer.** Thayer was born in Massachusetts but moved to Rhode Island where he joined a regiment to fight in the French and Indian War. In May of 1775, he raised a company and was appointed its captain and then marched to Cambridge. Thayer joined the expedition as a company commander and was captured in the assault on Quebec. After he was exchanged, he was promoted to major and led his regiment to Red Bank where they defended that position in the face of an attack by 1200 Hessians. He participated in the assault on Stony Point and was in the Battle of Monmouth and then in Battle of Rhode Island. He retired from the service in 1780 and was appointed as a Brigadier General in the Rhode Island militia. In 1800, Thayer was thrown from his horse and killed while returning to his home. His journal has been described as "a careful and well-written account of the invasion of Canada." A Thayer bio can be found in Edwin M. Stone, ed. *The Invasion of Canada in 1776: including the journal of Captain Simeon Thayer*. Appendix, pp. 70-80.

16. **Captain John Topham.** Topham, who was from Newport, Rhode Island, was commissioned a lieutenant-captain in the 3rd Rhode Island Regiment and went to Cambridge with his company. Arnold appointed him to command a company in the 2nd Division and he and his company were captured during the assault on Quebec. In 1777, he was promoted to Lieutenant Colonel in the State Brigade. He was in the Battle of Rhode Island in August of 1778. In 1780 his regiment was discharged by the state with thanks to Topham for the "great fidelity and ability' with which he discharged his

duties during the war. Topham wrote a journal of the expedition that is very similar to Thayer's. See his bio in *Voices*, pp. 32-34.

17. **Captain Oliver Hanchett.** Hanchett was from Suffield, Connecticut and commanded a company on the expedition. He was a sergeant in General Phineas Lyman's regiment in the French and Indian War. In 1775, he commanded one of the companies authorized by the Connecticut legislature to respond to the Lexington Alarm. He was taken prisoner in Quebec and was exchanged on January 10, 1777. There is no record of his service after the expedition. For more about how Hanchett was a ringleader in opposing Arnold and Montgomery's plan to assault Quebec, see Hanchett's biography in *Voices*, pp. 192-195.

18. **Captain Samuel Ward, Jr.** Ward was a company commander from Westerly, Rhode Island. He joined the army in May of 1775 as a captain in a Rhode Island company and went to Cambridge. He was promoted to Lieutenant Colonel after Quebec. After the war, he became a merchant and settled in New York. He was the grandfather of Julia Ward Howe. See Stone, Appendix, pp.83-9.

19. **Captain William Hendricks**. On the expedition he commanded a company of riflemen from Cumberland County, Pennsylvania. He was killed in the assault on Quebec and was buried in Quebec in the same grave as General Montgomery. See his biography in *Voices*, pp. 187-190, and Robert G. Christ. *Captain William Hendricks and the March to Quebec, 1775*, Hamilton Library and Historical Association of Cumberland County, 1960.

20. **Captain Jonas Hubbard** was from Worcester, Massachusetts. In 1775 he was in Captain Timothy Bigelow's company of minutemen at Cambridge after the Lexington Alarm. The company marched to Cambridge where it served for five days and returned home. On May 23, 1775, Hubbard was appointed the captain of a company in the regiment of Jonathan Ward. Hubbard's company went to Cambridge after his commission and it served there during

June, July and August. He was selected by Arnold to command a company on the expedition in September of 1775. He was wounded while leading his company's storming of a barrier in the assault on Quebec and died fourteen days later in the hospital at Quebec. See his biography in *Voices*, pp. 190-192.

21. **Captain William Goodrich.** Goodrich was a company commander but very little is known or published about his life. Until 2010, he was an enigma to researchers of the expedition as no one had been able to identify the real William Goodrich. Based on additional and focused research by this author it was discovered that he played a role in the dissention in the ranks of Arnold's troops prior to the assault on Quebec. He was described in a footnote to Heth's journal as "a trouble maker in Arnold's army" because he objected to the assault and asked to be withdrawn from Arnold's command.

Goodrich, who lived in Stockbridge, Massachusetts, was a tavern keeper and captain of a company of Stockbridge Indians that marched to Boston on April 22, 1775. After his service in the Revolution he moved to Vermont but there is no credible information about his death. The only extensive biography of Goodrich is found in *Voices*, pp. 195-202, and in my article on William Goodrich in *Berkshire Genealogist*, Vol. 33, No. 2, Spring 2012, pp. 41-45.

22. **Captain Thomas Williams** of Stockbridge, Massachusetts commanded a company in Enos's 4th Division. He voted to return to Cambridge on October 25, 1775. Little additional information exists about him but see *Voices*, p. 212 for a short biography and *Massachusetts Soldiers and Sailors of the Revolutionary War, Boston*, 1908, p. 483.

23. **Captain Samuel McCobb** was born in Georgetown, Maine and in June of 1775, he enlisted a company from Georgetown using his own money. He then led the company to Cambridge and

participated in the Battle of Bunker Hill. In August of 1775, he was assigned to command a company in Arnold's expedition. Consisting mostly of men from Georgetown, McCobb's company was placed in the 4th Division. There is no pension application for him and no written biography. There were nine men from Georgetown, Maine in McCobb's company. See short bio in *Voices*, 211-12

24. **Captain Matthew Smith.** Smith was from Lancaster County, Pennsylvania. He was a member of the infamous "Paxtang Boys' during the French and Indian War. In June of 1775, he enlisted in a company of rifleman to go to Cambridge. He was commander of a rifle company on Arnold's expedition. Although he did not show up on time, he was captured during the assault on Quebec, probably in the location where he was residing. For some reason, Smith was not exchanged until 1778. Henry J. Young, *The Spirit of 1775, John and Mary's Journal*, March, 1075, p. 46, explaining Smith's absence from the assault, says that "Captain Smith was absent without leave on the Ile d'Orleans 'for particular reasons' meaning probably that he was drunk." After he left the army, he was on the Supreme Executive Council representing Lancaster County in 1778-9, and then became the prothonotary for Northumberland County from 1780-1783. He died in Milton, Pennsylvania on July 22, 1793.

25. **Captain William Scott.** All references to this commander of a company in Enos's division prior to 2010 mentioned only his surname. (See two books on the expedition: Robert McConnell Hatch. *Thrust for Canada: The American Attempt on Quebec in 1775-1776*. Houghton Mifflin, 1979; and Thomas A. Desjardin. *Through a Howling Wilderness, Benedict Arnold's March to Quebec in 1775*. St. Martin's Press, 2006). The lack of information about Scott's name is surprising when one considers how much time has passed since the expedition. As a result, a major effort was undertaken by this author to unravel the mystery of Scott's identity and the story of his life. I found that he was William Scott from

Peterborough, New Hampshire. He was born in Ireland and his local nickname was "Short Bill," to distinguish him from his cousin "Long Bill" Scott. There is a chapter in *Voices* devoted to findings about the identity of Captain William Scott, pp. 212-217. Author John Shy has a chapter on his cousin Long Bill Scott in *A People Numerous and Armed.*

26. **Reuben Colburn.** When the Revolutionary War began, Colburn was running a ship building yard in what was then Gardinerston, Maine. In 1775 after the Lexington Alarm, Colburn led a group of Abenaki Indians to Cambridge to meet with General Washington. While there he was selected by Washington to build the 200 bateaux that would be needed for the Arnold expedition. After he was employed for that purpose, he hurried back to his boatyard to begin construction of the boats. He also bought food supplies from the local inhabitants and sent three scouts to examine the route of the expedition from his boatyard to the upper Dead River. Colburn made three trips to Cambridge during the period of the boat construction. He did build the number of bateaux requested but the short time deadline resulted in bateaux with problems as outlined in General Note 109.

Despite the fact that Colburn did his best to assist the expedition with boats, repairs, food and other matters, when he contacted Washington and the Continental Congress in the winter of 1776 with a detailed bill to get paid for his services, he ran into difficulty. At some point the Treasury Department lost his receipts and for twenty years they were unknown resting in a box in New York. Colburn's expenses as of 1819 were 523 pounds with a 159 pound credit to the government. Sadly the dispute over the Colburn claims lasted until 1856 when his family finally gave up trying to get payment. Colburn died in 1818 having endured many years of economic hardship due to his unpaid expenses.

27. **Lieutenant Archibald Steele.** Steele was born in Lancaster County, Pennsylvania, and joined Captain Matthew Smith's rifle

company as a lieutenant. Arnold selected Steele to lead a group of eight men from various companies to scout out the proposed route to Canada. Captain Smith did not show up for the assault on Quebec so Steele took command of his rifle company during the battle. Steele was captured by the British but escaped and returned to Washington's army, which was then in New Jersey, after a long and trying march back through the wilderness. As a result of the march back home, he "had broken his health to such an extent that Washington assigned him to the commissary department." He served in that department until 1821 having served forty-six years.

28. **Lieutenant Nathaniel Church.** Church was another expedition person who was only identified by his last name. I did extensive research on Church and concluded that the best supporting evidence is that he was Nathaniel Church from Captain Topham's Rhode Island Company. He joined the army in May of 1775 and served as 1st Lieutenant in the Rhode Island Regiment of Colonel Thomas Church. His company marched to Cambridge in May of 1775 and he volunteered to serve with Topham in the expedition to Quebec. See *Voices*, pp. 258-260 for his bio.

29. **Lieutenant Nathaniel Hutchins.** Hutchins was from Hopkinton, New Hampshire, joined Captain Henry Dearborn's Company after Lexington and was in the Battle of Bunker Hill. He was on the expedition as a lieutenant in Dearborn's company. After being released, he served in two New Hampshire Regiments before he retired in 1781. He subsequently moved to Fryeburg, Maine where he died in 1832.

30. **Lieutenant John McLellan.** Lieutenant in Captain Hendrick's Company of riflemen. He died in the wilderness in Canada and is mentioned in many of the journals. He was left behind with two guards until he died. The guards continued on to Quebec and rejoined the expedition.

31. **Chaplain Samuel Spring.** Samuel Spring was selected as the chaplain for Arnold's expedition and is said to be one of the men who escorted Arnold to the hospital when he was shot in his left leg. He was born on February 27, 1746 in Northbridge, Massachusetts and attended College of New Jersey, now Princeton, where he studied religion under Dr. Witherspoon. He became licensed to preach in 1774. He became an army chaplain on May 19, 1775 with the Massachusetts Bay Provincials. At the end of 1776, he left the army and became a pastor at Newburyport in 1777. In 1806, he was awarded the degree of Doctor of Divinity from the College of New Jersey. He died in Newburyport on March 4, 1810.

32. **Aaron Burr.** Aaron Burr served as Vice President in the first term of the Presidency of Thomas Jefferson (1800-1804). After he left office in 1804, Burr fired a shot that ultimately killed Alexander Hamilton during a famous duel. As a result of the office and later the duel, Burr is probably the most famous alumnus of the Arnold expedition.

In his 1829 pension application, Burr says that he "entered the Continental Army during the Revolutionary War as a volunteer in the summer of 1775." He volunteered for the Quebec expedition and served under Arnold until December of 1775. At that time he was appointed as an Aide-de-Camp to General Richard Montgomery. After Montgomery's death, he continued to serve under Arnold in Canada. After returning in the summer of 1776, he was appointed as Aide-de-Camp to General Israel Putnam. In 1777, he was promoted to Lieutenant Colonel in Malcom's Regiment. He was in the Battle of Monmouth and served in Westchester County, New York in 1779. He resigned from the Army in 1779 due to continuing ill health.

Burr served two terms in the New York State Assembly and was appointed Attorney General from New York in 1789. He was elected as a United States Senator from New York in 1791 and served until 1797. While Vice President, Burr served as President of the Senate. He died on September 14, 1836 at the age of eighty in Staten Island, New York. There are many biographies of Aaron Burr.

33. **Natanis.** The expedition passed by the wigwam of the Norridgewock Indian, Natanis, in the Dead River Valley. This event was noted by various journalists. Dennis Getchell and Samuel Berry, two scouts for the expedition traveled ahead of the advance column and found Natanis because they knew him and his location. Henry's journal states that Natanis was "well known to the white inhabitants of the lower country; they knew from him the geographical position of his residence."

Getchell and Berry's written report to Arnold states, "30 Miles up Dead River; here we got intelligence of an Indian [Natanis], that he was Stationed there by Governour Charleton, as a Spy, to watch the motions of an Army..." Despite the revelation from Natanis about being a spy, they hired him to lead them up the Dead River for two days. Arnold referred to Natanis as a "noted Villain" and a spy; however, he later, at Sartigan, allowed Natanis to volunteer to help the expedition reach Quebec. There are stories that Natanis participated in the storming of Quebec. See a biography of Natanis at www.nedoba.org/bio_natanis01.html.

In the middle of the 19th century, George Lippard, a well-known and best-selling fiction writer of the time, presented the often repeated and generally accepted legend about the Dark Eagle. In it chief Natanis proclaimed the famous Dark Eagle prediction upon meeting Benedict Arnold in the wilderness. Lippard published the following quote in his book, *The Legends of the American Revolution*.

"The Dark Eagle comes to claim the wilderness...The Dark Eagle will soar aloft to the sun. Nations will behold him and sound his praises. Yet when he soars the highest his fall is most certain. When his wings brush the sky then the arrow will pierce his heart."

Although it was fictional writing, the quote was accepted and used by various Arnold biographers in the twentieth century, including Willard Sterne Randall in his 21ˢᵗ century biography of Benedict Arnold. Those who repeated this story used it to show how the Indian Chief Natanis correctly predicted Arnold's future life including a fall which they asserted was his treason. (See my article "The Dark Eagle: How Fiction Became Historical Fact", in *Early America Review* refuting the accuracy of this story).

34. **Major General Guy Carleton.** Carleton, who was the 1ˢᵗ Baron Dorchester, was born in Ireland and was commissioned as an Ensign in the British Army in 1742. He served as Quarter Master General to General James Wolfe in his attack on Quebec in 1759. He was appointed as the Governor of the Province of Quebec from 1768 to 1778. In the summer of 1775, Carleton directed the preparation of Quebec's defenses, including the forts along the Richelieu River and Montreal. Carleton led the British forces in the fall of 1776 when they invaded the Lake Champlain region in response to the American invasion of Canada in 1775.

Carleton was replaced as Governor of Canada and military commander in 1778, but was appointed to succeed Sir Henry Clinton in 1782 as commander-in-chief of the British Army in America. He was in charge during the evacuation of New York in 1783 after the treaty ending the war was signed. In 1786, he was appointed Governor-in-chief 0f Quebec where he served until 1791. He died in England in 1808. See Paul David Nelson., *General Sir Guy Carleton, Lord Dorchester: Soldier-Statesman of Early British Canada.* Associated University Presses, 2000.

35. **Colonel Allan MacLean** was born in Scotland in 1725 and was a lieutenant in the 62ⁿᵈ Regiment of Foot during the French and Indian War. He remained in America for a time and then went

back to Scotland. On June 12, 1775, he was back in Canada and empowered to raise a Regiment from disbanded soldiers living in Canada called the Royal Highland Emigrants. MacLean was recruiting members of his regiment in southern Canada when he learned of the American invasion. Most historians credit MacLean with arriving just early enough before the American assault to take temporary command and then to arrange what proved to be a successful defense of Quebec. Author Mark Anderson states that Maclean worked with "energy and dedication" to build up Quebec's defensive needs. On May 11, 1776, he was appointed Adjutant General of the British Army in North America. He returned home after the war and retired from the army in 1784. He died in London on February 18, 1798.

36. **Major Henry Caldwell.** Caldwell was a British officer born in Ireland in 1735. He rose up the ladder to captain during the French and Indian War in the 29th Regiment of Foot. He was Assistant Quartermaster to Guy Carleton in 1759. After the war he stayed in Canada and was promoted to major in 1772 but retired in 1774. During the American invasion of Canada, he took part in defending Quebec as a brevet lieutenant colonel commanding the militia. After the Revolutionary War ended, he began to buy up land in Quebec and by the early nineteenth century was a significant land owner. He died in 1810 at his residence in Quebec.

Caldwell had a mill on the Point Levis side of the St. Lawrence River that was used by Arnold's men while they waited to cross over to Quebec. Benedict Arnold took up residence in Caldwell's manor house outside the walls of the city when his expedition first arrived at Quebec in November of 1775. At that time, Caldwell was inside the walls defending the city.

37. **Major Murray.** Barracks Master for the British Army in Quebec. He is mentioned in several journals. His assistant, Captain Prentice, is also mentioned. According to a letter written by journalist John Joseph Henry, Sergeant McCoy gave "a genuine

copy of his journal" to Major Murray, who he describes as "of the Quebec garrison." The most reasonable assumption is that Murray, who was a Scotsman, sent the journal to someone in Scotland, where it was published in 1776.

38. **Old Country Men.** This name was given by some journalists to American prisoners taken during the assault on Quebec who were born in England or Ireland. These were men who immigrated to the colonies and subsequently joined the American Army. Carleton and the British government considered these men as being from "the old country", and thereby were citizens of that country. The British felt that these men owed allegiance to the British crown. Early in their imprisonment, Carleton asked each American prisoner to list the place he had been born. Based on the responses, he put those who were born in "the old country" in a separate location so they could enlist in the British Army. Many of them did enlist and some later escaped. Some were apparently deported back to their original country. There is no record that accounts for the disposition of each man who was in this category.

39. **Captain Jeremiah Duggan.** Duggan was a Chambly barber acquaintance of James Livingston and was one of the men recruited by him prior to the taking of Fort Chambly. He was with Ethan Allen in the failed attempt to take Montreal. According to Kenneth Roberts, Duggan was "heartily disliked by Arnold's enemies, particularly by Colonel Hazen." Robert Hatch says Hazen "engaged in a running quarrel with Jeremiah Duggan."

40. **Colonel David Wooster.** Wooster was from Connecticut and commanded a regiment under General Richard Montgomery on his expedition to Canada. After Montgomery's forces captured Montreal, Wooster was left in charge of that city while Montgomery went on to join Arnold in Quebec. When Arnold recovered from his wound, he requested that Wooster relieve him as commander of the American forces at Quebec. After some delay, Wooster did so. A Continental Congress Committee was sent to Canada in the

spring of 1776 consisting of Benjamin Franklin, Charles Carrol of Carrollton and Samuel Chase. The Committee recommended that Wooster be replaced for questionable conduct. Wooster was later found innocent by a court martial and then became the commander of the State of Connecticut militia. He was killed in the Danbury raid in April 1777. See the bio in Stephen Darley. *Call to Arms: The Patriot Militia in the 1777 British Raid on Danbury, Connecticut.* CreateSpace, 2015. Chapter Two, pp. 37-70.

PLACES

41. **Newburyport**. This refers to the modern seaport town of Newburyport, Massachusetts. In 1775, this was a thriving seaport with several shipyards and two thousand residents. It was an important trading center in the eighteenth century. Arnold used this location as a starting off point for the transport vessels that would carry his forces in the Atlantic Ocean and then on up the Kennebec River in Maine to pick up the bateaux that would be used by the expedition to navigate the rest of the route to Quebec.

    Arnold and his officers were entertained in Newburyport by Nathaniel Tracy, the town's most prominent resident and an acquaintance of Arnold. The expedition spent five days here loading the transports with food and other supplies which Tracy acquired. On Monday, September 18th, the troops boarded the eleven vessels that would transport them to their bateaux near Fort Western.

42. **Kennebec River**. A 170 mile river in Maine that runs from its headwaters at Moosehead Lake in west central Maine to the Gulf of Maine in the Atlantic Ocean. The expedition's route was to ascend the river to the boatyard of Rueben Colburn in what is now Pittston, Maine, where the men would pick up the bateaux. Tributaries that feed the Kennebec include the Dead River, the Carrabassett River, Sandy River and Sebasticook River.

While the Kennebec River is navigable for larger vessels from its headwaters to Augusta/Fort Western, it becomes navigable only by shallow boats from there north. That portion of the river north of Fort Western had a number of rapids, boulders and falls which caused the men to portage their bateaux on their shoulders. The river was not easy going for the men and they soon became exhausted transporting their boats overland. The Kennebec was also where a number of bateaux over turned and spilled the contents into the water. The river caused damage and leaking as well as destruction to the bateaux. Leaking boats became such a serious problem that a group of men from Colburn's shipyard were sent to Norridgewalk Falls to make repairs to the boats they had built.

43. **Georgetown, Maine.** Located on an island near the mouth of the Kennebec River. During the 19th and 20th centuries it became a summer resort area which was home to several prominent artists. There were eight men from Georgetown, including Captain Samuel McCobb, in his company of musketmen.

44. **Vassalborough/Vassalboro.** This town in Maine just north of Augusta and Fort Western, was home to five of the men who served as Arnold's guides through the Maine wilderness, including three members of the Getchell family. Two Vassalboro guides, Dennis Getchell and Samuel Berry, were sent on the proposed route of the expedition by Arnold to "see what obstacles Colonel Arnold would be likely to meet." That route was up the Kennebec River, then on the Dead River and then along the Chaudière River in Canada to the St Lawrence River. Unfortunately they did not make it further than the Dead River and then returned to make their report. They reported that the carrying places were "pretty passable," the rivers "pretty Shoal" and the tress blazed by Indians making the route "pretty direct." In fact, none of this description was accurate, so it did not help Arnold or his men understand the difficulties they would be facing.

45. **Gardinerston.** A town in Maine that was settled by Sylvester Gardiner and, according to Justin Smith, *Arnold's March from Cambridge to Quebec: A Critical Study*, G.P. Putnam's Sons, 1903, it included "at one time probably not less than one hundred thousand acres...and the name of Gardinerston covered not only what we know as Gardiner, but half a dozen other towns as well." The Reuben Colburn shipyard is located in what is now Pittston, which was one of the towns that originally made up Gardinerston. Today the old Colburn House in Pittston is still standing and it is owned by the State of Maine as an historic site. It serves as the headquarters for the Arnold Expedition Historical Society, which has a number of artifacts and other items in the house related to the Arnold expedition.

46. **Cobercanta/ Cobbossee Contee River.** The name of a river that flows into the Kennebec River from the west near Gardinerston, Maine. The name is so uncommon that it is only mentioned in one or two journals.

47. **Hallowell.** A town in Maine on the west bank of the Kennebec River about two miles below Augusta, Maine/Fort Western. There were seven men from Hallowell on the expedition in Captain Samuel McCobb's Company. The transports did not go up the Kennebec River beyond Hallowell.

48. **Fort Western.** A French and Indian War fort on the east side of the Kennebec River in Augusta, Maine. Various spellings are used in the journals to identify this site. It is about forty-three miles from the mouth of the Kennebec. According to Stephen Clark, "In the 1600's, this place was known as Cushnoc, and it was a pilgrim trading post...The fort was constructed to be a supply facility for Fort Halifax..." In 1759, the need for Fort Western was gone and portions of it were dismantled and its garrison dismissed. However, its commander, James Howard, remained in the area as a settler building a house about a mile above the fort on the Kennebec River.

One man, Charles Bourget, signed up for the expedition at Fort Western. He was in Captain Dearborn's Company and was captured in assault on Quebec. He later served in the 3rd New Hampshire Regiment and in the 2nd Light Regiments of Dragoons.

Justin Smith described the barracks as lodging very suitable for a good number of Arnold's men." Senter called the Howard family, in whose residence Arnold apparently stayed, as being an "exceeding hospitable, opulent, polite family." Fort Western was the setting off point for the expedition with the men using only the bateaux instead of the transports because "just above begins a half-mile of rapids." The fort's original main barracks and the commissary building are still standing but the rest of the original fort has been reconstructed as a tourist attraction that is now called Old Fort Western and is located on Cony Street in Augusta.

49. **Fort Halifax**. This French and Indian War fort is located about eighteen miles north of Fort Western on the east side of the Kennebec River in Winslow, Maine. It is on a plateau near the confluence of the Kennebec and Sabasticook Rivers. Today there is one rebuilt block house that remains on the site, although the town is raising money to improve the area around the fort, which is now a park. Fort Halifax was built in 1754 as part of a series of forts planned by the British to protect frontier settlers from Indian raids. Stephen Clark, in his excellent book, *Following Their Footsteps*, says, "When built, the fort consisted of a large barracks, two large blockhouses, and a smaller watch house at each of the corners." At the time of the expedition, the men found entertainment at a tavern operated in the officer's quarters of the fort.

In its heyday, Fort Halifax was the largest frontier fort in Maine and was garrisoned until 1767. By 1798, the only remains of the fort was a lone blockhouse on the Sabasticook River. In 1987 a flood swept the entire blockhouse away but the original timbers were recovered and the blockhouse was rebuilt the next year using those timbers. Extensive archaeological investigations have been conducted at the site by the Maine State Historic Preservation Commission.

50. **Ticonic Falls.** Per Justin Smith, "Half a mile above Fort Halifax the Kennebec ran over a series of ledges and broke into what we call Ticonic Falls." There are many different spellings used to designate this landmark in the journals. Smith went on to say, "No boat could possibly ascend the stream here and so this becomes the first carrying place."

51. **Skowhegan Falls.** This falls is located in the town of Skowhegan, Maine about twenty-one miles above Fort Halifax. Every journalist had his own spelling for this landmark. Stephen Clark says "below the falls, the river forms a large, round pool now called 'the Great Eddy'. Upstream from this eddy was a narrow, half-mile long gorge containing rapids leading up to the base of the falls…At the end of the gorge, a rocky island divided the river into two channels, both with high falls." Justin Smith says the local Indians "were accustomed to take their canoes up through a slight break in the almost vertical wall at the lower end of the islet, twenty-five or thirty feet high." He points out that even carrying a canoe would have been a difficult task but it was "far worse to transport the heavy bateaux of green pine by such a route."

52. **Norridgewock Falls.** This falls is actually not located in Norridgewock but in present day Madison, Maine. Arnold's journal states that the falls is approximately fifty-eight miles above Fort Western. Norridgewock is a series of falls with very heavy rapids and Justin Smith concludes that no boat could survive in the rapids. He declares that the "total drop of the river in the course of a mile or so is given at ninety feet." Clearly this carrying place that would require tremendous effort.

Smith says that Arnold remained at the falls for a week to oversee the repair and overhaul of the now leaky bateaux. Reuben Colburn, the boat maker, sent some men from his boatyard to Norridgewock to help the troops repair and caulk the boats. Not only was the leakage a problem for the men, it created a larger problem for the provisions. A large portion of provisions was affected by the leaking water and had to be discarded due to spoilage.

Near Norridgewock Falls was an old Indian town established by Father Sebastien Rale, a Jesuit Priest, who made it his life work converting the Indians in northern Maine. He was killed in 1724 by English colonists who then sacked his mission and closed his church. At the time of the expedition, some remains of the town were visible to the men and some referenced it in their journals.

According to Justin Smith, "two or three families had recently settled in this vicinity," and one of the families had a young baby. This location was the last settled area that the expedition encountered on the route until they reached the first village in Canada.

53. **Carratunk Falls, also known as Hells Gate Falls and Devils Falls**. Many of the journalists mention these falls which are located in the present town of Solon, Maine. Clark says, "The entire volume of the river shot through a narrow gap in the cliffs in a drop of more than fifteen feet." Although no settlement was present here in 1775, because of the difficulty of the portage it was a much remembered point. Smith remarks that 'this point marks now, and marked then, the entrance to the real wilderness." Whatever difficulties the expedition had encountered by the time they reached these falls, they would find that much worse problems were coming.

54. **Great Carrying Place**. This is the location where the expedition left the Kennebec River at a small cove where the Carrying Place Stream begins. It was 135 miles from the mouth of the Kennebec River. The Great Carrying Place runs thirteen miles from the Kennebec River to the Dead River. It was primarily a land portage interrupted by three small ponds. The expedition used this as their

jumping off place from the Kennebec River primarily because it was spelled out on the route followed by Major John Montresor, a British officer, who made the trek from Quebec to Maine in 1761. According to Henry's journal, the trail consisting of the Great Carrying Place was "tolerably distinct," and the advance party made it better by marking the trail and clearing some of its bushes and trees.

Clark describes the work that was needed to widen the portage trail which when the expedition arrived it was "only wide enough for men to pass single file carrying a light canoe." Morgan's Division cut down trees with axes to widen the path enough for "men to line along the sides of the bateaux to carry them", which was about eight to ten feet wide. The widening left tree stumps all along the path which made it difficult for the men to portage the heavy bateaux. Clark concludes that the men were in a line carrying the boats by "slogging up the muddy, stump-infested path to the first pond.

As early as the 1600's, Native Americans used the name The Great Carrying Place to refer to this area which allowed them to avoid the problematic stretch of rapids and waterfalls above this cutoff on the Kennebec River. . This route was more easily passable and it led to the West Branch of the Kennebec, called the Dead River. Although this was easier and more passable, it was but by no means easy.

The Great Carrying place begins with a portage up a steep mountain which Arnold describes in his journal as being "in the shape of a shugar loaf" which "seems to rise out of the middle of the river." Clark describes the steepness of the mountains in this area. "The rise in elevation from the Great Carrying Place to the first carrying pond is about 800 feet." The first pond is about three miles from the Kennebec and the men had to carry their bateaux and provisions over this distance seven or eight times according to Senter's journal. The members of each bateau would have to repeat this portage multiple times to get all of their provisions up to the first pond. The route continued over three ponds which resulted in an additional rise in elevation of 400 feet until it reached the Dead River.

The Arnold Expedition Historical Society booklet describes this trail as being "heavily forested, blocking all view of the surrounding country, except for three small ponds that were part of the portage." It goes on to state that the final segment of the route "broke out of the confinement of the woods into an open area, "called by some of the journalists as "the savanna." This area was a spruce bog "about a half mile from the west end of the portage at Bog Brook," which caused the men to sink into the muck, sometimes up to their waist. It was very difficult going and it greatly weakened and injured the men and damaged the boats.

55. **Log Hospital**. Arnold stayed at the Great Carrying Place for five days and during that time he ordered the construction of a log hospital on the second portage. Eight or ten sick men took immediate possession of the hospital and that number soon increased.

The journalists had various names for the hospital including "Arnold Hospital" and "Fort Meigs."

56. **Log House**. Arnold ordered a small log house to be constructed on the Great Carrying Place near the Kennebec River while he was at that location supervising the removal of boats and provisions from the Kennebec. The purpose of the log house was to serve as a depot for "men and provisions," which would constitute a reserve for an emergency in case his force had to retreat. Men were hired by Arnold's commissary to bring the provisions that were still at the Kennebec River to the hut. Establishing a reserve of supplies shows Arnold's clear thinking about the potential dangers for the expedition.

57. **Dead River.** This 42 mile long river was so named because it was an extremely slow moving river which seemed almost dead to the men on the expedition. The river was also called the West Branch [of the Kennebec] because it flows east into the Kennebec River at The Forks, Maine. The river today is not the same as it was in 1775 due to the construction of the Long Fall Dam which created Flagstaff Lake. The expedition traveled on this river starting about twelve miles from the Great Carrying Place and then proceeding up the North Branch of the river, through the Chain of Ponds and then to the Arnold Pond, located at today's Coburn Gore, Maine.

While the men were ascending the Dead River, a hurricane struck and caused the river to rise significantly. Although there is not unanimity in the journals regarding the dimensions of the rise of the water, most reported that it rose at least eight feet. Because the topography was so changed with water everywhere, the difficulty of finding the way north to the Chaudière River increased exponentially. The unanticipated hurricane arguably created one of the most significant challenges the expedition faced.

58. **Chain of Ponds.** Stephen Clark describes this portion of the route as a series of six interconnected ponds about five miles in length. The ponds are surrounded by high mountain peaks which then steeply slope down to the ponds creating very high cliffs. Marching through this section would have required both land portage and traveling by water. The designation of this area as "the chain of ponds" first appeared in British Captain John Montresor's journal of his trip from Quebec to Maine in 1761. He called this section "the chain of Lakes" and that designation was modified by later historians of the expedition.

59. **Bigelow Mountain.** As the expedition reached the chain of ponds, the men observed a high mountain range to the northwest. The range's highest point is over 4000 feet and, at the time, it had no name. It was later named Mt. Bigelow, after Major Timothy Bigelow, an officer in Colonel Green's 2nd Division. Local tradition

says the Major Bigelow climbed this mountain to see the City of Quebec. There is no record of his climb but it is certain that the name came from this tradition.

60. **Height of Land.** The height of land area begins near the Maine and Canada border at what is now called Arnold Pond. It marks the dividing point between opposite flows of water. The division was: 1) the waters in Maine that flow south into the Kennebec River and ultimately to the Atlantic Ocean; 2) the waters that flow north through Canada to the St. Lawrence River. The flow north, which is the height of land route used by the expedition, began with what is now the Arnold River, which flows north, first through a meadow and then through a swamp to Lake Megantic. The Arnold River was a "small, rocky steam flowing out of nearby mountains for eight miles." The swamp is at the south end of Lake Megantic, and is several miles wide. The river and the swamp were tough going for the men. The designation of this geographical area was first mentioned in Montresor's journal and was later picked up and used by successive historians of the expedition.

61. **Chaudière Pond/ Lake Megantic.** This lake is located north of the Height of Land at the headwaters of the Chaudière River. The present lake, known as Lake Megantic, is fourteen miles long and between one and two miles wide. Stephen Clark states that the lake is on a plateau approximately 1100 feet above sea level. It is located a few miles from the present town of Lac-Megantic, Canada. Almost all of the journals refer to this lake with one or the other name.

62. **Chaudière River.** The river begins at Lake Megantic and empties into the St. Lawrence River 109 miles north, near the town of Levis, Quebec. Levis is about six miles above Quebec City on the opposite side of the St. Lawrence River. According to Steve Clark the greatest portion of the river's descent in elevation is in the first fifty miles which descends more than 600 feet as it makes its way to the St. Lawrence. Many journalists mention this river.

63. **Sartigan, now St-Georges**. This is the name that most of the journalists used to identify the first French settlement they encountered on their way to Quebec, It is spelled differently in the journals but it always refers to the first Canadian settlement. According to Justin Smith, the name comes from St. Igan which was an early French designation. It is located seventy-five miles from Quebec and is now the town of Saint-Georges, in the Beauce-Sartigan Regional County Municipality. Although the Americans referred to it as a specific settlement in 1775, the Canadians gave the name to the entire region.

64. **Pere St. Joses.** This is the present town of Saint-Joseph-de-Beauce, a small incorporated town on the Chaudière River, 38 miles south of Quebec City. The expedition passed through this town on its way to Point Levis and used the more English name to describe it.

65. **Saint Marie or Mary's, now Ste-Marie.** This is the present town of Ste-Marie, which is approximately thirty-three miles north from Saint-Georges (Sartigan) and twenty-seven miles south from Point Levis. It is the home of the Taschereau Manor which belonged to a patrician French family. The expedition bivouacked in the original manor house. The town has since replaced the old manor house with a newer manor house.

66. **Point Levis.** A point of land projecting into the water on the heights along the south side of the St. Lawrence River across from Quebec. This point is not the present town of Levis. The journalists referred to their destination on the St. Lawrence as Levi, Levis or Point Levis. Arnold did not want to place his encampment directly across from armed fortress of Quebec so he directed his army to follow the Etchemin River north. They encamped on the shore of the river near Caldwell's Mill and Point Levis at the mouth of the Etchemin River. Caldwell's Mill was owned by Major Henry Caldwell, a retired British officer, who is described in detail in GN 36.

Through his scouts, Arnold was aware that the British knew about his expedition and had "destroyed all the canoes" on the south side of the St. Lawrence. He had the foresight to purchase all the canoes and small boats he could find along the Chaudière River between Sartigan and the St. Lawrence and kept them in a cove about three miles up the river from Caldwell's Mill. Without these captured or purchased boats, the expedition could not have crossed the St. Lawrence to assist in the attack on Quebec.

67. **Wolfe's Cove**. The location where the Arnold expedition landed after crossing the St. Lawrence River the night of November 13-14. They crossed by navigating between two British war ships that were anchored in the river. After landing at the cove, Arnold led his men up the steep slope to the plains repeating the path of General James Wolfe of the British army. It was the site where British General James Wolfe landed his men in 1759 when he led an assault on Quebec during the French and Indian War. Despite the French notion that no army could get from the St. Lawrence to the heights of Quebec, Wolfe's army was able to ascend to the Plains of Abraham and then defeated the French army to secure Quebec for the British. Arnold looked at various possible landing places on the St. Lawrence and ultimately chose this one realizing that it had worked for Wolfe and it could work for him. Justin Smith describes the cove as a place "where, since the French war, a fair road had been constructed to the plains above."

68. **Plains of Abraham/Heights of Abraham.** This Quebec landmark is part of a 242 acre national park that extends from the Citadel in Quebec City along a plateau above the St. Lawrence River. The original Plains, which are only a portion of the park, are named after Abraham Martin who moved to Quebec in 1635 and settled on some of the land. The Plains of Abraham was the site of the battle between the British army under Wolfe and the French defenders under General Montcalm on September 13, 1759. It is now an historic area within the Battlefields Park and is visited by 4 million visitors and tourists annually. The park

has an Interpretation Center that provides information on the history of Quebec and the various battles that have taken place there, including the American attack on Quebec on the 31st of December, 1775.

69. **Saint Foy, now Sainte-Foy**. A former town on the St. Lawrence River that was incorporated into Quebec City as of 2002. In 1775, it was about four miles west of the walled city of Quebec. Arnold's men stayed there for a time while waiting for the arrival of Major General Richard Montgomery. Some of the men who were not taken prisoner also stayed there after the assault.

70. **Point aux Trembles**. A small town about twenty-one miles up the St. Lawrence River from Quebec which was first settled in 1684. The town was located on the Chemin du Roy, which was the first road built between Quebec and Montreal, and was used by the expedition. In a note to his transcription of the original Dearborn journal, Dr. Robertson called it a "paltry struggling village." The area was a civil parish in 1684 and became known as Point aux Trembles because the point where the town church was built was covered with quacking aspen and birch.

While waiting for Montgomery, Arnold moved his troops to this site when he got news from a Canadian deserter that the British were planning to come in force to attack his encampment at Saint Foy. He moved because his troops were almost out of ammunition, were poorly clothed and would not have been able to withstand a concentrated British attack. According to one source, when Arnold's men departed for Point-aux-Trembles on November 19th, they were "attended by the regrets of a host of well-wishers among the peasantry." Arnold and Montgomery met up together on December 1, 1775 at Point aux Trembles.

The town is now called Neuville, which is described as "a lovely little town on the northern bank of the St. Lawrence River" west of

Quebec. In 1996, the village of Neuville and the parish of Pointe-aux-Trembles merged to form the City of Neuville.

71. **St. Roch, also called "Saint Rocks"**. A Quebec suburb in 1775 that was located beyond the northwest corner of Quebec's fortified wall. It had houses located only two hundred yards from the wall. These were inviting targets when the Americans moved in to occupy them in early December of 1775. At that point in time, Montgomery made his headquarters at Holland House. During December, the Americans conducted a blockade of Quebec from their position in St. Roch. On December 5th, a Canadian militia company supporting the Americans, led the effort to disarm the citizens of St. Roch. Also in December, Arnold's riflemen sniped at British sentries on the walls.

    The American soldiers who were not killed or captured in the assault on Quebec encamped here after the battle. Those in St. Roch used their cannons to bombard the British inside Quebec. The British, with even more cannons, constantly fired at the Americans in St. Roch causing some of the houses to burn. Caleb Haskell reports in his journal that on February 1st, "some of our guards at St. Roche's set some of the buildings on fire." It turns out that Arnold had ordered empty buildings in St. Roch to be burned to keep the British from sending out foraging parties to collect fire wood from the empty buildings. This action was part of Arnold's effort to keep up a blockade. St-Roch is now incorporated into Quebec City.

72. **Palace Gate**. Known as Porte du Palais. This is one of the gates entering the walled city of Quebec which "looks down upon the Charles River bluff toward the Intendant's Palace." This gate was poorly defended when the American Army attacked Quebec. Arnold's force, which was responsible for attacking through the Lower Town from the suburb of St. Roch, was supposed to join up with Montgomery's forces to attack the Upper Town. Arnold moved his men from St. Roch along the Charles River and entered

the city by skirting the Palace Gate unobserved by the British until they came upon the barricade at Sault au Matelot, where they first met British resistance.

It was called the Palace Gate because it was adjacent to the palatial mansion constructed by Francois Bigot, the corrupt Intendant appointed by King Charles in 1748. Bigot left Quebec in disgrace in 1760. In 1775, the gate was in a deteriorated condition but still standing. The British set the Palace on fire during the siege to prevent the Americans from occupying it. By 1791 the gate was in a "ruinous condition" and was demolished in the late nineteenth century.

73. **Saint John's Gate**. One of the three main gates leading into the old walled city of Quebec that was first constructed in 1694. It was enlarged in 1868 as the original gate was too narrow for vehicular traffic entering and leaving the city. The gate entrance is still there today on the western side of the wall on St John Street, but the gate is gone. In 1775, it was a well-known and important location for the residents because of its use as an entrance to the city and was quickly picked out by the Americans as a major landmark.

The St. John's Gate was the target of two feints that General Montgomery planned for the night of the assault to divert the British attention from the actual areas of the assault. Unfortunately, the feints did not accomplish their objective. The British soldiers positioned in the city did not leave their positions to rush to the St. John's Gate when it was attacked.

74. **Pres de Ville**. A small village on the banks of the St. Lawrence River at the southern end of the Lower Town right under the cliffs of Cape Diamond. Montgomery passed through this town on his route to assault the Lower Town.

75. **Sault au Matelot**. A street in the Lower Town of Quebec that was along the path of Arnold's assault on Quebec. In 1775, it was a narrow winding street under the cliff of Upper Town, leading from

the Palace Gate to the Lower Town. The British erected a barricade on this street which ran from the cliff to the river along the line of present day St. James Street. The barricade was the first encounter with British forces by Arnold's men. It was in that location that Arnold was wounded and had to be escorted to the hospital.

76. **Prisons in Quebec.** The American troops who were captured by the British in the assault on Quebec were taken prisoners of war and incarcerated in three known facilities:

Quebec Seminary. This building is now called Seminaire de Quebec, which was founded in 1663 by Bishop Francois de Laval, first Bishop of Quebec. Today, the historical site of the seminary includes a number of buildings, some of which date back to the 17th century. It is now a private Catholic secondary school. The seminary was designated as a National Historic Site of Canada in 1929. Only the officers were incarcerated in this location according to Justin Smith.

According to Dearborn's MHS journal, "we [the officers] were Carry'd to a large Seminary, and put in a large room in the fourth story from the ground." In early January, Carleton allowed Major Meigs to go out to the American encampment in St. Roch to bring in clothes and baggage for the officers. Meigs says "the officers were confined in the Seminary, and well accommodated with bedding." Captain Simeon Thayer has the most complete description of the officer's quarters. "We were log'd in two separate Rooms. But on one Mr. Hutchins saying that there was a number of our men outside, in the hearing of one of the sentries, we were instantly oblig'd to lodge in one Room, which was disagreeable, as some of us were ill, besides being 36 officers of us, and 3 boys, in a small room about 30 feet square."

Recollet Convent or Monastery. Major Return J. Meigs says the captured enlisted men were given quarters in the Recollets, or Jesuit College, which Justin Smith called a Monastery. The journal of James Melvin describes the quarters as containing "a straw bed between two, and a blanket each man." Abner Stocking said the enlisted men were "confined in a large building called the Regules, where we had but very little fire or provision." Sometime in March, the prisoners were transferred to the Dauphin Barracks. The Recollets were an order of friars or monks who came to Quebec in 1620 and built their friary or monastery.

Dauphin Barracks. This was a stone building with a basement that was located "maybe three hundred yards from St. John's Gate." The prisoners were moved to that more secure location because the British were concerned that the prisoners might try to provide assistance to the American forces if they tried to attack the City again. Henry in his journal described the barracks as "capacious and well supplied with berths or bulks." Justin Smith describes it as follows:

> *Fully three feet of solid stone…heavy iron bars darkening the small windows; and a wall twenty feet high, bristling with spikes along the top, shut in the small yard behind. There were two floors, with four non-communicating rooms on each, and at night every room was carefully locked; while the door into the street, a very solid affair, had fastenings on the outside.*

The Dauphin Barracks is still standing and is now called the Dauphine Redoubt. It was built in 1712 and is now part of Artillery Park, a National Historic Site of Canada. It is located on the corner of D'Auteuil Street and Saint-Jean Street in Old Quebec.

77. **General Hospital of Quebec, now Hopital-General de Quebec.** This hospital was built in 1692 by the second Bishop of Quebec to provide health care services to the poor and elderly residents of Quebec. By 1698, the hospital had been turned over Sisters of St. Augustine of the Mercy of Jesus and it was those sisters who administered to the needs of Arnold's sick and wounded men. Arnold himself was treated there after he was wounded in the

assault. It was also the hospital that treated small pox victims in the American Army both before and after the assault. It is located in a meadow above the St. Roch suburb outside the walls of Quebec on the St. Charles River.

Senter describes it in his journal as "an elegant building situate upon St. Charles River, half a mile from St. Roques gate [Palace Gate]. A chapel, nunnery and hospital all under one roof."

Surrounding the hospital is a cemetery where many of the French nobility and military personnel, including General Montcalm are buried. The current hospital building has a museum which houses relics from the early days of Quebec and is now a monastery with the L'Eglise de Notre-Dame des Anges church nearby. Any reference to a hospital in the journals refers to this location.

78. **St. Lawrence River.** A very large and important waterway that runs through the U.S. and Canada. It begins at Lake Ontario and runs 744 miles until it empties into the Atlantic Ocean. It has a number of tributaries including the Richelieu River and the St. Charles River at Quebec and provides water access to Quebec and Montreal. It was, and still is, the only water route for large vessels to reach Quebec.

79. **St. Charles River.** This river begins north of Quebec at St. Charles Lake and runs along the north side of Quebec and empties into the St. Lawrence River. It is the main river in Quebec City and has a series of rapids and waterfalls before it reaches the city. Arnold led his forces along this river the night of the assault on Quebec.

80. **Richelieu River.** This seventy-seven mile long river begins at Lake Champlain and flows north through Quebec Province and empties into the St. Lawrence River about twenty-five miles west of Montreal. This is the river route that Montgomery's forces followed when they invaded Canada passing along Fort St. Johns, Fort Chambly and Montreal.

81. **Sebasticook River.** A 76 mile long river in central Maine running from Dexter, Maine south to the Kennebec River at Winslow, Maine, near Fort Halifax.

82. **Three Rivers, now Trois-Rivieres.** A point about half way between Montreal and Quebec at the confluence of the St. Maurice and St. Lawrence Rivers. The area is so named because the St. Maurice River has three openings into the St. Lawrence River. In 1634, a permanent settlement was established here which is today the city of Trois-Rivieres. In 1775, according to Anderson, "the only substantial structures were the parish church, the 'government house' barracks, and the recollect and Ursuline Convents."

83. **Cape Diamond.** This is the official name of the cape and promontory on which both the old and current city of Quebec is located. It is part of a larger plateau that rises above the confluence of the St. Lawrence River and the St. Charles River. The crest of Cape Diamond is 333 feet above the river. At the bottom of Cape Diamond is the lower town and on top is the upper town. It was an ideal location for a walled city that was destined to be the headquarters of the British army in Canada during the latter half of the 18th century.

84. **Citadel.** Today this is the military fortification built on Cape Diamond. It is a significant Quebec landmark built between 1820 and 1831. References to the Citadel in the journals would refer to the fortified walls that surrounded Quebec in 1775 and not to the present military fortification of today.

85. **Waterway Landmarks from Journals**

A. Newburyport to Fort Western, September 1775. American Transports.

- Isles of Shoals. A group of small islands in Gulf of Maine, 6 miles off the U.S. coast at the border between New Hampshire and Maine.

- Boone Island. A small barren island in Gulf of Maine off York on the Maine coast.
- Seguin Island. A 64 acre island located of Fort Popham in the Gulf of Maine, south of the mouth of the Kennebec River. Has the highest lighthouse on the Maine coast.

B. Quebec to New York, August and Sept, 1776. British Vessels.

- Island of Orleans (Ile d'Orleans). An island in the St. Lawrence River about 3 miles east of Quebec City. The island is 21 miles long and 5 miles wide with a maximum elevation of 490 feet. It marks the boundary between the St. Lawrence and its estuary where salt water begins to mix with fresh water.
- Isle of Bic. An island near the south shore of the St. Lawrence off the Village of Bic. 3 miles long and ¾ miles wide.
- Gaspe Point. Peninsula along the south shore of the St. Lawrence River that extends into the Gulf of St. Lawrence. 400 miles northeast of Quebec City.
- St. Johns Island. Now Prince Edward Island which is a Province of Canada.
- Cape Breton. Island at the extreme northeast tip of Nova Scotia consisting of 3981 square miles.
- Nova Scotia. A peninsula surrounded by the Atlantic Ocean including numerous bays and estuaries. Second smallest Province of Canada consisting of 21,300 square miles.
- Gut of Canso. A 17 mile channel separating Cape Breton from Nova Scotia.

EVENTS

86. **Killing at Fort Western**. An incident occurred on the evening of September 23rd while the expedition was at Fort Western .It involved one man from the expedition killing another. Pvt. James

McCormick of Captain Goodrich's Company killed Sergeant Reuben Bishop of Captain William's Company in a dispute. He was condemned to death by a court-martial held at Fort Western and then, instead of an immediate hanging, the case was sent to George Washington in Cambridge to determine the final judgement. Some journals describe the deferred sentence as waiting until "Washington's pleasure was known." This incident involved the first man killed on the expedition.

87. **Arnold's Detachment Divided into Four Divisions.** Before he left Fort Western, Arnold divided his forces into four divisions. The first was commanded by Captain Daniel Morgan of the Virginia rifle company with the three rifle companies of Morgan, Smith and Hendricks, and was the division that led the way on the route; the second division was led by Lieutenant Colonel Christopher Greene with the companies of Captains Thayer, Topham and Hubbard; the third division was commanded by Major Return J. Meigs which included the companies of Captains Dearborn, Ward, Hanchett and Goodrich; the fourth division, which brought up the rear, was under Lieutenant Colonel Roger Enos with the companies of Captains Williams, Scott and McCobb, and was the division that turned back while on the Dead River. See the General Notes for information on each of these officers.

88. **Hurricane.** No one could have anticipated that the expedition would encounter a hurricane in the Maine wilderness. Hurricanes could have been anticipated when the transports were sailing on the Atlantic Ocean. However, a hurricane did occur in the Maine wilderness. The expedition survived the ocean hurricane with minimal damage and continued on its way. Much to the surprise of those involved, another hurricane hit the army after it made its way from the Kennebec River and onto the Dead River.

The Dead River drains a large number of ponds. The expedition had to cross these ponds, often referred to as the Chain of Ponds. When the expedition began to navigate the Dead River it was shallow and not very threatening, even though it was difficult to navigate. Beginning on October 19th and continuing through the 21st, an intense rainstorm, which some writers have likened to a hurricane, caused the river to rise and completely changed the landscape along the route. Seven journals, including Arnold's, describe the unusual rising of the water in the river on the 21st. Ephraim Squier's description is best, "A windier or rainer day I never see." Stephen Clark rightfully calls the rain storm a "late season hurricane" and not just a normal rainstorm.

89. **Relief Party.** Arnold and a detachment of men, including Captain Eleazer Oswald, Lieutenants Steele and Church and thirteen men left the expedition on October 27th to rush toward the first settlement in Canada to procure food for the starving expedition troops. Arnold made the journey in three days arriving at the first house on the Chaudière on October 30th. He used the expedition's money to buy food and sent it back with a relief party of Canadians to the main party of the expedition which was coming up the Chaudière River.

On November 2nd, the relief party, with cattle and other food, met the head of the expedition column and, after leaving food with them, went on to feed the entire army straggling behind. Arnold's effort prevented the troops still along the Chaudière from starving to death before they reached the first settlement. It should be noted that various journals described the meeting of the relief party in a variety of ways but all expressed relief and joy at the sight of cattle.

90. **Food.** The majority of the journals have entries describing the slow deterioration of the food supply. Despite this, several historical authors have questioned the extent to which the men really suffered from scarcity of food. Several have also accused Arnold of poor planning and under estimating the time it would take to reach Quebec. In fact, Arnold's original estimate of the number of days the journey would take was surprisingly accurate. He ordered the commissary in Cambridge to issue provisions to each company

for forty-five days. The expedition arrived on the bank of the St. Lawrence River in forty-four days after leaving Fort Western.

The real cause of the decline in food supply lies with various external factors including the hurricane, the overturning of boats and loss of provisions in rough currents and on rocky ground, the return of the Enos Division with a disproportionate share of food and the leaky boats which resulted in food being destroyed by water leakage even without being overturned. The severe shortage of food is evidenced by the relevant entries in various journals. Many of the journalists, both officers and men, state that there was a serious lack of food around the time they entered the Chaudière River.

91. **Council of War.** Arnold's journal reports that on October 24th he called a council of war to discuss the situation facing the expedition. His journal reports it as follows: "…the River continues high & rapid, & as our Provisions are but short & no intelligence from Canada, I ordered a Counsell of Warr, summoned of such officers as were Present." Apparently there were twenty-three officers at the council. Arnold solicited opinions as to whether the men wanted to go back because of the hardships encountered but the officers present agreed with Arnold's preference to continue on. It was decided to send back to the settlements all the sick men being treated by a doctor or lying in the log hospital. They also voted to send Captain Hanchett with fifty men forward to the Chaudière River "as an advanced party," in order to reach the Canadian settlements and obtain food for the men.

92. **Eating Dogs.** Some of the journals make references to the troops eating dogs after the food supply ran low. One of the dogs belonged to Captain Henry Dearborn.

93. **Enos Division Returns.** On the 25th of October, three companies of the 233 men of the 4th Division commanded by Lieutenant Col. Roger Enos made the decision to return to Cambridge without

Benedict Arnold's permission. The day had a significant snowfall. According to the account written by Doctor Isaac Senter, a vote was taken in which the officers in that division voted to return. The officers of Greene's Division also had a vote and they voted to continue on. Although Enos personally voted to go on, when the three companies in his division left to return, Roger Enos went with them. Enos was later court-martialed after he reached Cambridge. However, since only his own officers were available to testify and no one testified against him, he was acquitted.

Arnold originally placed the bulk of his food supplies with the 4th Division on the assumption that the last division to travel the route would have an easier time because the others would have made a trail for them to follow. When Enos and his division left the expedition to return back, most of the food they were carrying went with them. Based on the information in the journals, the Enos division left two barrels of flour and no pork behind for the other divisions. There is no specific list of food that the 4th division took back with them. Only the amount of flour left behind is identified in the journals. Some of the men who continued on to Quebec were convinced that Enos had more food for his three companies than they did for the ten companies going forward. If true, Enos' action was worthy of court martial.

It also needs to be clarified that Arnold had a relief force with food from the Canadian settlement which reached the forward contingent of Arnold's soldiers on November 2nd. This was one week after the Enos companies began their return. This food would have arrived to Arnold's soldiers before the returning Enos Division reached Fort Western. Of course with only 233 men, the Enos party had lesser need for food.

94. **Arnold's Letter to John Dyer Mercier.** While he was at the Great Carrying Place, Arnold wrote a letter to John Dyer Mercier, a merchant in Quebec whom he met while carrying on his trading business prior to the Revolution. His letter alerted Mercier that

he was leading a detachment to Quebec and requested Mercier to provide information to him regarding the size of the British garrison, the ships that were stationed in the harbor and the British state of readiness. He employed two of the Indians guiding his expedition to deliver the letter. Unfortunately, the Indians were discovered and the letters were confiscated by the British alerting them of Arnold's advancing into Canada. Mercier immediately came under suspicion by the British government in Quebec and his future as a Quebec merchant became untenable so he left Quebec.

After leaving Quebec, Mercier was later recommended by Arnold for a position in the Continental Congress. Mercier obtained a position and was responsible for reviewing Arnold's request to the Congress for reimbursement of the personal funds he expended during his Quebec expedition. Mercier significantly delayed his request by asking for additional information. Mercier later discounted almost the entire request and referred it to Congress. No motive for Mercier to subvert Arnold's request the way he did has been revealed. The end result is that Arnold never received any reimbursement from Congress and this was one of the reasons he decided to change sides in 1780.

95. **Capture of British Midshipman.** According to Senter, on November 11th, Arnold's forces captured a fifteen year old midshipman named McKenzie from one of the British vessels on the St. Lawrence "who came ashore on the Point Levi side." Thayer says that the midshipman was from "the *Hunter*, Sloop of War," and was sent ashore in a boat to obtain oars. As the British boat neared the shore, the Americans fired on it and the boat retreated in confusion leaving behind the midshipman, according to Captain Topham's journal. The midshipman tried to swim away but was captured and taken prisoner. Justin Smith says that after the capture the "Hunter opened fire on the Americans, but without much effect."

96. **Crossing the St. Lawrence River.** On November 13th, Arnold began the crossing of the river in the various small boats and canoes that had been kept in the cove on the St. Lawrence for this use. Arnold wrote to Montgomery on November 14th that the crossing was "effected between 9 and 4." The route that Arnold followed involved the boats passing between two British vessels, *Lizard* and *Hunter,* which were anchored near each other in the St. Lawrence River. This was a tricky approach because the British were periodically running guard boats between the two vessels. The Americans made this run without lights and eliminated any noise so in three different trips they were not discovered. Some have speculated that this could only have worked in the dark. Justin Smith had an astronomer investigate when the moon rose on that night. Based on the report he received, Smith concluded the "the only possible conclusion seems to be that the sky was heavily clouded until about four o'clock the next morning" This conclusion makes sense based on the available evidence. The journal with the most detailed description of the crossing is Matthias Ogden's journal.

97. **American Flags of Truce.** On November 15th, Arnold wrote a letter to Lt. Governor Hector Cramahe, the administrative officer in charge of Quebec in Carleton's absence, complaining about the British firing on a flag of truce that he had sent to the walls of Quebec, calling it "contrary to humanity and the laws of nations." In his letter, Arnold accuses the British of firing at his officer bearing the flag of truce two times, on November 14 and 15. Arnold called it "an insult I could not have expected from a private soldier; much more from an officer of your rank; and through me, offered to the United Colonies, will be deeply resented." As a result of the British actions, Arnold stopped sending flags of truce to the British walls. Some of the journals mention this incident.

98. **Arnold and Montgomery Meet Up.** On December 1st, General Montgomery arrived at Point aux Trembles where Arnold's force was waiting and the two commanders finally met up with each

other. Many journal express how they and all of the men felt great joy at the arrival of Montgomery as he brought food, clothes, ammunition and cannons with him. Because of the condition of his men, Arnold was unable to make any moves on the city without the support of Montgomery. In his move up the Richelieu River and into Canada, Montgomery had captured Fort St. John's, Fort Chambly and Montreal including British uniforms and great coats. Although Montgomery was able to complete most of his route in boats, he met with serious opposition from the British at each of the three forts that he captured. Montgomery was detained for a time in Montreal setting up an administrative framework for his army. While there he also tried to persuade the local inhabitants to support the American side. He left Colonel Wooster in charge of Montreal when he departed.

99. **Assault on Quebec.** The initial American plans for assaulting the city were planned at a council of war organized by Montgomery in the middle of December. On December 23rd, Montgomery presented his plan for the assault to his entire army and received their support. Montgomery tried to initiate his assault on various nights beginning on Christmas Eve but changed his mind at the last moment for various reasons. Mark R. Anderson, author of *The Battle for the War of Fourteenth Colony: America's Liberation in Canada, 1774-1776*, University Press of New England, 2013, says that Montgomery's prospects were not looking good by the end of December and that "Continental discipline was tenuous." Upon learning that some of Arnold's men were against an assault, Montgomery again met with all of his men on December 27th. As a result of the meeting they agreed to participate in an assault. Montgomery was pressed for time because enlistments of some of his men would expire on January 1, 1776.

According to General Carleton, in the early morning at four or five o'clock on December 31, 1775, the American army in Canada under the command of Brigadier General Richard Montgomery made an assault on Quebec. The assault took place on a cold and snowy day in the form of a two prong surprise attack on the City of Quebec. The Americans also ordered a feint attack on the St. John's Gate and one on Cape Diamond, neither of which were successful in luring any significant British defenders to that site.

Montgomery himself was leading one detachment which would attack the Lower Town along a "narrow defile," or pass, that could only accommodate a few lines of soldiers at a time. Their first objective was to force the barricade, or barrier, at Pres-de-Ville. That barricade ran from the cliff at Cape Diamond down to the river just under the present Citadel, and had a "battery of four 3-pounders and one 4-pounder" which was placed in a small out building and which "completely commanded the pass." The barricade was defended by a Canadian militia officer with thirty Canadian and eight British militia members. This assault failed when the British spotted the Americans before they reached a blockade house and proceeded to fire its muskets and cannons with grape and musket balls. The British gun fire killed Montgomery and some of his men. The successor to Montgomery did not continue the attack and, instead, ordered retreat. The Montgomery attack, which needed total surprise, failed.

Starting at the same time as Montgomery's attack, Arnold's detachment forced an entry into the Lower Town along the Sault-au-Matelot, still a street in present day Quebec, which had two barricades and then proceeded to the rest of the Lower Town. Arnold's force attacked the first barricade, at the eastern end of Sault-au-Marie Street near the corner of Saint James Street, with success because they approached it without being discovered and the attack was "vigorously" pursued. Unfortunately, at this barricade Arnold was wounded in the leg and had to be carried to the General Hospital. The command of Arnold's troops was then taken by Captain Morgan who led the men to the second barricade. The advance required them to move along a street that was surrounded on each side by multi-story houses from which the British soldiers had clear fire on the Americans with muskets and cannon. When the fire from the British continued, there was some hesitation by the men at the second barricade. The British who were defending Matelot Street and the second barricade were joined by the troops that were defending the area where Montgomery had been killed and his men had retreated. The Arnold forces were being fired upon both in front and in their rear with muskets and cannon and were hopelessly outnumbered and surrounded so they finally had to surrender.

Professor Anthony Nardini of Villanova University in his 2005 article, "The American Defeat at Quebec", sums up the American defeat as follows.

> In the immediate sense, the attack failed due to lack of cohesion and the loss of leadership. Montgomery's plan depended on speed and coordination, both difficult to achieve in a dark, driving snowstorm, over unknown, icy territory. Montgomery's assault fell apart when he was killed and his subordinates were unable to operate on their own. With Arnold wounded, his assault slowed, leading to indecision at the second barricade. Without Montgomery and Arnold, the men were left without dynamic leadership and ability. Their effectiveness crumbled.

Although the Americans fought hard, the assault failed and the American forces that were not killed or captured went back to the suburbs about eight miles from the city. This area was now under the command of Arnold, who was in the hospital. They continued their blockade of the city while waiting for sufficient reinforcements for another attack on Quebec. The leaders in America could never amass enough men or weapons to make another attack on Quebec. So the entire army retreated from Canada in June of 1776.

100. **Death of Montgomery.** General Richard Montgomery was killed while he was leading his detachment in the assault at the barricade at Pres-de-Ville which was a barrier that ran from the cliffs above the river down to the river under the present Citadel.

Having already passed through two barriers, Montgomery led his men toward a blockhouse containing British troops. The British opened fire with muskets and cannon directed toward the head of the column, which had a devastating impact. In the burst of firepower, Montgomery and his two aides, Captain Jacob Cheeseman and Captain John MacPherson, were killed. There is a marker on the cliff at the location where Montgomery was killed.

Montgomery's body was found the next day frozen stiff and buried in the snow where he fell. His body was not recognized until it was identified by some of the American officers who were taken prisoner. Carleton gave instructions to have Montgomery's body privately buried and this was accomplished with a "suitable coffin" covered "with fine black cloth and lined with flannel." According to Mr. Thompson, who was in charge of the burial, Montgomery's body was buried "within and near the surrounding wall of the powder magazine, in the gorge of the St. Louis Bastion." When the burial was completed, Thompson reported back to General Carleton. Montgomery's body was exhumed in 1818 and was brought back to New York where he was reburied at St. Paul's Chapel in New York City.

101. **Carleton's List of Prisoners.** Shortly after the battle, Carleton ordered the American prisoners to provide the British with their name, places of birth, age and other details. One of the pieces of information elicited by place of birth was whether any of the men were born in England, Scotland, Ireland or Wales. The journals refer to men who fell into that category as "old country men." The British position was that these men were British citizens and must therefore enlist in the British army. Most of them did so, although some did not but were later able to escape. The list, which was published by Carleton, is helpful today in verifying the names of the Americans who were taken prisoner by the British. The list is available from the "Return of Rebel Prisoners Taken at Quebec, Dec'r 31st 1775." *Colonial Office 42/35:139-143. British National Archives.*

102. **American Reinforcements for Quebec.** After the failed assault, the first contingent of reinforcements from Massachusetts, Connecticut and New Hampshire arrived on January 25th, 1776, and troops continued to arrive through February and early March. Toward the end of March, the promised additional American reinforcements from Pennsylvania, New York and New Jersey began arriving at Quebec. As of the March 30th, *Return of Troops*, there were 2505 men in Canada, including 329 Canadian Continentals. Of the total, almost one-third were hospitalized, presumably with small pox. When General David Wooster took command in Quebec on April 1st, he found that the American army had inadequate provisions of food and ammunition and no funds with which to purchase them. He also realized that enlistments would expire on April 15th for approximately 60% of his troops. . The reinforcements that appeared in Canada were never sufficient to meet the needs of the army trying to capture Quebec.

103. **British Reinforcements for Quebec.** On June 1, 1776, an 11,000 man reinforcement of British troops arrived in Quebec under the command of General John Burgoyne, consisting of seven British regiments, British and Hessian artillery and three thousand Hessian troops. The size of the reinforcements dwarfed the American presence in Canada and forced a retreat back to Fort Ticonderoga in New York. The Burgoyne troops followed the Americans in the fall of 1776 which later resulted in the Battle of Velour Island, another example of Arnold's leadership abilities. (See Stephen Darley, *Battle of Valcour Island: The Participants and Vessels of Benedict Arnold's 1776 Defense of Lake Champlain*).

104. **Carleton's Parole.** In August of 1776, Carleton showed up at the building where the American prisoners were housed to discuss his conditions for release. Having a large number of prisoners in Quebec was a hardship for Carleton so he wanted to release them. They would then cease to be his responsibility. Various journals described the meetings with the prisoners. Each has a different

narrative and perspective. Carleton wanted the prisoners to sign a document that was called a "parole", by which they made a commitment not to take up arms against the British when they arrived home. Carleton was insistent that each man to be released sign the document that he prepared. The men agreed to the terms and signed the document prior to boarding the vessels that took them home.

The Durben/Dearborn journal in the University of Glasgow Library has a handwritten copy of the parole included in its papers. The text of that parole is as follows:

I, (Name)___ ____ in the Province [colony] hereby pledge my Faith & Word of Honour to General Carleton that I will not do or say anything contrary to the Interest of His Majesty or His Government; and whenever Required to so do, I shall repair to whatever place General Carleton, or any of His Majesty's Commanders in Chief in America shall judge expedient to order me.

Given under my hand, this 3d Day of August 1776.

Signature_____

On January 10, 1777, a letter was released to newspapers by Washington's headquarters stating that "the following list of gentlemen, officers and volunteers, who are released from their paroles, which they gave to General Carleton, by an exchange of others of the same rank and number belonging to the British Army." A total of twenty-four officers were on the list but interestingly it did not include Dearborn, who was released earlier and went home with Major Meigs in May of 1776.

105. **Release of Quebec Prisoners.** The journalists report that around the beginning of August 1776, word came down from British headquarters that the prisoners were going to be released. Anticipation ran high as the men waited to see if that would

happen. Rumors about their impending release had circulated in the previous months but nothing had happened. Signing the parole was a condition of release and that did not happen until August, 3rd. The journalists are unanimous in reporting that, much to their joy, on August 7th all of the officers and men who were prisoners in Quebec were put on board four British vessels in which they would be returning to New York. On August 11th, the vessels set sail down the St. Lawrence River. The prisoners were released at Elizabethtown, New Jersey on September 24, 1776.

106. **Schooner _Magdalen_.** According to Thayer, Major Meigs and Captain Dearborn were the two officers who were released early and traveled home on "the schooner Magdalen." Neither Meigs nor Dearborn in their journals provides the name of the schooner on which they sailed home.

107. **Elizabethtown, New Jersey.** This is the location where the British left the officers and men released from the Quebec prisons on September 24, 1776. They could not land in New York City because a battle between the two armies caused a great fire which resulted in a number of burning buildings. The burning of New York could be seen from the transports carrying the Americans, as some journalists reported.

SUBJECTS

108. **1775 Invasion of Canada.** Shortly after he took command of the Continental Army, George Washington became convinced of the desirability of invading Canada to try to take the British headquarters and forces in Quebec and, in effect, turn Canada into our 14th colony. As his plans took shape, a two prong effort was planned and ultimately implemented. The two armies would meet and storm Quebec together. It was expected that the British would know about the army advancing up the Richelieu River. However, Arnold's expedition was to be conducted in secret in order to take the British by surprise.

One of the prongs would begin at Fort Ticonderoga and go north through Lake Champlain and then along the Richelieu River to the St. Lawrence and then to Quebec. Along the way, this force would take the British forts at St. Johns, Chambly and Montreal. This invasion route was to consist of mostly New York troops and was to be commanded by Major General Philip Schuyler. As the departure day arose, Schuyler decided that he was too sick to undertake this expedition and instead gave the command to Brigadier General Richard Montgomery.

The second prong was Arnold's secret expedition through the wilderness of Maine and Canada along the Kennebec River, the Dead River and the Chaudière River to the St. Lawrence River near Quebec. It is this force that the journals in this book represent.

109. **Bateaux**. This word, describing the type of boats used on the expedition, is spelled many different ways in the various journals. The boats were flat bottomed and about twenty-two to thirty feet long with flared sides. They were used in various American locations in the eighteenth century to transport both men and supplies on rivers. The design of the boats gave them very good stability in rough water, and the long narrow bow and stern made them maneuverable in swift running water. Washington and Arnold were both familiar with the capability of bateaux and their decision to use them for this expedition would have been a good one, if the situation had been normal. These boats were the only way that over eleven hundred men could traverse the rivers and streams they would encounter on the way to Quebec carrying their supplies of food and clothing.

Arnold wrote to Reuben Colburn, a boat builder from Maine on August 21, 1775, spelling out the specifications for the bateaux he was to construct. "Two hundred light Bateaux Capable of Carrying Six or Seven men each, with their Provisions & Baggage (say 100 wt. to each man) the Boats to be furnished four Oars, two paddles & two setting poles." There is some indication that when

Arnold arrived at Colburn's boatyard he ordered an additional twenty boats.

After arriving at Colburn's boatyard, in what is now Pittston, Maine, and inspecting the bateaux, Arnold wrote to Washington about the bateaux which he described as "many of them smaller than the Directions given, & very badly built." Chase, *Papers of George Washington*, vol. 2, p. 40. Arnold was a very experienced sailor who had operated his own shipping business for many years. He was familiar with the quality of construction for all manner of seagoing vessels and boats. The expedition's starting date was delayed at the boatyard when Arnold ordered various improvements to the bateaux. Due to the timing of the expedition, Arnold did not have the luxury of rejecting all of the bateaux so he did what he could to make fixes.

Modern explorer Hodding Carter III and three companions reenacted the march to Quebec in 2017 using a bateau constructed by Robert Stevens, one of the participants. The members of that Group estimated their boat weighed 400 pounds. Professor Anthony Nardini of Villanova University estimated the weight of the bateaux constructed by Colburn to be "nearly 400 pounds apiece." If these numbers are close to an accurate indication of the weight of the bateaux used by Arnold, the difficulty of making the march along the chosen route is even more clearly demonstrated. The ability of three or four men to carry boats this heavy on some of the lengthy portages over the barriers of topography, water rapids and falls encountered on the actual march in 1775 is beyond comprehension. Carter's group became so exhausted that they had to rely on truck transport and rolling their bateau on logs to complete their march.

Unfortunately, in the case of the Arnold expedition, the Colburn boatyard had less than twenty days to make the two hundred boats needed for the expedition. He received his written instructions regarding the building of the bateaux from Washington on

September 3rd while he was still in Cambridge, and Arnold's expedition arrived at Colburn's boatyard on September 23rd. The fact that Colburn completed on average more than ten bateaux per day is astonishing. Having no time to properly cure, the wood was green, heavier than normal and leaked extensively. Green wood shrinks and causes the wood planks to separate. This would cause obvious problems with water seepage. Depending on how much the planks separated, water would pour into the boats. Most of the damage to the food supply resulted from water in the bottom of the boats, which seeped into the wooden storage barrels and contaminated the food. Stephen Clark points out that because of the leakage the men had to "constantly bail water out of the boats, a persistent inconvenience."

Green wood is much heavier to carry then a boat of properly cured wood. Freshly cut wood can contain 40-60% moisture by weight, whereas cured wood contains 15-20%. This would have been a significant factor to the men because of the number of portages they encountered. This obviously caused the troops serious difficulties and severe exhaustion. In many respects, the boats became a hindrance rather than a help. Arnold finally ordered all of the bateaux to be abandoned when they reached the Chaudière River. Journal entries suggest that one or two bateaux continued on with the expedition.

110. **Transports.** The Arnold forces were carried by American transport vessels from Newburyport on the Atlantic Ocean up the Kennebec River to the Colburn boatyard in Pittston, Maine. Those journalists who provided the number of transport vessel agreed that there were eleven. Senter states that the fleet "consisted of 11 sail of shipping, sloops and schooners, containing, upon an average, 100 troops." Thayer called them "eleven small vessels."

Because a hurricane like storm occurred before the transports reached the Kennebec River, two of the transports went missing from the rest of the fleet. After waiting for six hours, Arnold decided to go up the Kennebec without them. They later joined the expedition near Bath, Maine.

111. **Row Galleys.** Small wooden boats that have sails and also oars so that the vessel can be moved ahead by rowing. The row galleys in Canada were effectively used by Arnold and the American Army to transport men and supplies on the rivers around Quebec. Arnold was a knowledgeable and skilled practitioner of amphibious warfare as he demonstrated on Lake Champlain and in Virginia in 1781.

112. **Barrels.** The food, powder and other supplies for the expedition were stored in large wooden barrels which were carried on the bateaux. The barrels were obviously not waterproof so they were vulnerable to water seepage which could, and eventually did, render the food inside not fit to eat. In time, the barrels were either destroyed or discorded and provisions were carried in smaller cloth bags which were easier to carry.

113. **Extremely Cold Weather.** David Ludlum, *Early American Winters, 1604-1820.* American Meteorological Society, 1966:90, says that the expedition was subject "to an unusually early onset of winter with late October cold, ice and snow adding to the twin hardships of semi-starvation and physical exhaustion. Some journals describe the first snow falling on October 25th. Arnold says that it "Snowed and blowed very hard on the 25th." Senter says, "A storm of snow had covered the ground nigh six inches deep, attended with very severe weather." The snow and cold weather likely influenced the October 25th decision of the Enos Division to turn back.

Rev. Thomas Smith of Portland, Maine, wrote in his diary about the extreme winter weather of 1775-76. "The winter past has been the coldest, in the whole, that has been known." Cash called that winter "the severest in at least a decade with the temperature dipping to 28 below and snow drifts at 7 feet." William Willis.

Journals of the Rev. Thomas Smith. Portland: Joseph F. Bailey, 1949: 90. From a weather perspective, the Arnold expedition could not have been conducted at a more problematic time. The impact of the hurricane and the unusually cold weather took its toll. As a result the army arrived in Canada with exhausted men and too few troops to mount an effective siege on the fortress of Quebec.

114. **Terrain.** In Maine the expedition started off at sea level when it left Fort Western. After Fort Western, the Kennebec River ascends at a gradual incline until it reaches Taconic Falls. From that point, it ascends at a much steeper grade until the Great Carrying Place. It is at this point that the terrain undergoes a significant change.

The upward descent from the Great Carrying Place to the Dead River is six hundred feet. Clark maintains that the expedition actually ascended an additional three hundred feet due to "several high ridges to overcome to reach the Dead River." He describes the route as "constantly going up." The route from the Dead River over the Height of Land, through the Chain of Ponds, and on to Lake Megantic involves portages that covered thirteen kilometers. Due to the hurricane and the changes in the various water courses and ponds as a result of rising water, the route in that section was nothing like the map Arnold was using or the scouting reports that he received.

The route from Lake Megantic down the Chaudière River was probably the most difficult portion of the trek. Geologist Bruce Rueger of Colby College states that the Chaudière River "drops 180 meters in 80 kilometers in a series of continuous rapids with several large falls." Bruce F. Rueger. *Geologic Influences on Benedict Arnold's March to Quebec, 1775.* The Geological Society of America. Abstract of paper presented at 2006 Philadelphia Annual Meeting. All along the Chaudière River there were locations where the men had to portage whatever boats were still functioning or risk running difficult rapids or descending dangerous waterfalls.

115. **Reduction in Force Due to Sickness, Disease, and Death.**
As the expedition went on its route, sickness, cold weather and
hunger became great obstacles. Many of the journals mention
these factors which resulted in men being sent back or dying
along the way. My roster of men published in *Voices* revealed
that 156 men returned home from the expedition before they
reached Quebec due to illness, exhaustion or injury. This number
represents a 15% reduction in the force that left Newburyport.
This figure does not include the 233 men in the Enos Division
who left the expedition on October 25th. Most of the Enos men
were not sick or exhausted enough to be directed to return and,
in fact, were no different in that regard to those who went on. The
expedition started out from Newburyport with 1130 men and
reached Quebec with 675 men, which was a reduction of 40%.

116. **Small Pox.** By the time the expedition left Cambridge, small pox
was breaking out in the American camp. Fortunately, no members
of the expedition caught the disease while traveling through the
wilderness of Maine and Canada. The first mention of small pox
among the American army was recorded in Caleb Haskell's Diary
on December 6th stating that "the small pox is all around us."
Doctor Senter records in his journal that "small pox broke out in
the army" on the 17th of December." By the 18th, five men were
in the hospital with small pox. By the 27th of February, Arnold
reported to Washington that there were one hundred of his eight
hundred men in the small pox hospital.

Small pox was a problem for both the American and British armies
in Canada during the first six months of 1776. In his journal
Simon Fobes describes how, while confined in prison, he and
seventy or eighty of the enlisted men caught small pox and that his
pox was "not coming out well." Most of those who contracted the
disease apparently recovered. Pierce states in his journal that on
January 13, 1776, "we had one more Died with the Small Pox and
Several more very Dangerous indeed." In his letter to Washington
on February 27, 1776, Arnold gave Washington the bad news. "I

am very sorry to inform you, notwithstanding every precaution that could be used, the small-pox has crept in among the troops; we have near one hundred men in the Hospital; in general it is favorable, very few have died."

General Montgomery's replacement to lead the American forces in Canada was Major General John Thomas. After he arrived in Canada, he caught the small pox virus and died on June 2nd in the fort at Chambly. He was the highest ranking officer to die of small pox in the Revolutionary War.

117. **Few Cannons and Little Ammunition.** This describes the situation Arnold faced when his expedition finally arrived at Quebec and he was facing the British who were inside the walls of the city. It would have been impossible to carry cannons on the expedition through the Maine wilderness due to the conditions that were encountered. Cannons would have brought the expedition to a standstill. Credit is due to Arnold and Washington for not trying to force the presence of cannon on the wilderness army of the invasion.

The amount of ammunition, including musket balls and powder, that the expedition started out with was seriously diminished by the leaky boats, the presence of water and the consistently difficult terrain which caused boats to overturn or break apart. In addition to losing balls and powder, some of the men also lost their weapons. A few who lost their weapons subsequently submitted claims for reimbursement.

General Montgomery did bring cannons with him when he arrived near Quebec. However, the cannons that he had were not sufficient in number or powerful enough to seriously threaten the British behind the Quebec walls. Montgomery also brought powder and balls with him which was a huge boost for Arnold's troops, and was of critical importance in the assault on Quebec. After the American defeat, reinforcements were sent by Congress but they still lacked the firepower that would have been necessary to reduce the fortified city. In hindsight it is clear that Congress and Washington could not produce the number and size of cannon, the number of troops or the money to purchase the food, clothing, winter coats, ammunition and cannons that would have been needed to obtain a victory for the Americans in Canada.

118. **British Ships *Hunter* and *Lizard* on the St. Lawrence River.**

Hunter. British sloop of war that was anchored in the St. Lawrence River when the expedition arrived. It had ten guns and a crew of eighty men.

Lizard. British frigate having twenty guns and a crew of 130 men.

Both vessels were anchored in the river "to prevent Rebels from bringing down cannon." They arrived at Quebec on November 5, 1775, with other vessels.

119. **Expiring Enlistments of Arnold's Men.** All of Arnold's men who joined the expedition in August and September, 1775, enlisted until January 1, 1776. At that point in time, their enlistments expired and they were free to return home. The expiring enlistments were a major factor in the timing of Montgomery's plan to accomplish an assault on Quebec. If he delayed past that date, approximately 675 men from Arnold's Army would be eligible to return home. There is no doubt that the expiring enlistments caused Montgomery to plan to make his attack before January 1, 1776.

120. **American Prisoners.** Based on the roster of officers and men who were on the expedition in *Voices,* 383 men were taken prisoner by the British. Of the total, there were twenty-six officers and 357 enlisted men. As of November 29th, a total of 675 men made it to Quebec. Some of that total died from various causes. A smaller number avoided being taken prisoner. The large number of prisoners was a headache for the British and left the American

forces too small to effect any real opposition in the days following the defeat on New Year's Eve. General Carleton released all of the American prisoners in August of 1776 after they signed his parole. See GN 99.

121. **Rumors Among the Prisoners.** There were numerous rumors among the Americans in the Quebec prisons about the status of British and American forces engaged in the war. The vast majority of these rumors were false. Most of these rumors proclaimed British victories so they were discouraging to the prisoners. Some rumors were probably intentional on the part of the British command to keep the prisoners in line.

122. **Provost, Provost Master, Provost Marshall.** Various designations for the head of the military police in the British and American armies. In Quebec in 1775 it also referred to the head of the prisons and prison guards. The position was held by a British officer.

END NOTES

1   Roberts' two Benedict Arnold novels are *Arundel* and *Rabble in Arms*. His journal compilation is *March to Quebec: Journals of the Members of Arnold's Expedition*. Compiled and Annotated by Kenneth Roberts During the Writing of Arundel. New York: Doubleday & Company, Inc., 1938.

2   Stephen Darley. *Voices from a Wilderness Expedition: The Journals and Men in Benedict Arnold's Expedition to Quebec in 1775*. Bloomington, IN: AuthorHouse, 2011.

3   Justin H. Smith. *Arnold's March from Cambridge to Quebec: A Critical Study*. New York and London: G.P. Putnam's Sons, 1903.

4   *Voices,* p. 146.

5   See Chapter Ten, page 89.

6   *Voices* pp. 65-67.

7   GN 108

8   GN 113, GN 114, GN 90, GN 93, GN 115

9   Philip Schuyler to John Hancock, Pres. of Congress, Nov. 22, 1775. *Naval Documents of the American Revolution*, ed. William Bell Clark, Wash., D.C., 2:1100

10 James Warren to Samuel Adams, Dec. 5, 1775, *The Warren-Adams Letters,* Mass. Hist. Soc. Collections, 2:428.

11 George Washington to Philip Schuyler, Dec. 5, 1775. *Papers of George Washington, Revolutionary War Series*, Ed. Philander D. Chase. Charlottesville, VA, 1985-, 2: 498.

12 Roberts, 65.

13 John Codman, 5. See End note 18.

14 Justin H. Smith. *Our Struggle for the Fourteenth Colony: Canada in the American Revolution*. New York: G.P. Putnam's Sons, 1907. 2 Vols.

15 Stephen Clark. *Following in Their Footsteps: A Travel Guide & History of the 1775 Secret Expedition to Capture Quebec*. Shapleigh, Maine: Stephen Clark, 2003.

16 Charles E. Banks. *Papers and research material regarding Benedict Arnold's Expedition to Quebec*. Mass. Hist. Soc., Ms. N-1782, 1922.

17 Christopher Ward. *The War of the Revolution*. New York: The MacMillan Company, 1962.Page 448, Introduction to notes on Chapter 13.

18 Frederick Cook, comp., *Journals of the Expedition of Major-General John Sullivan against the Six Nations of Indians, 1779*. Auburn, N.Y.: Knapp, Peck & Thompson, 1887.

19 John Codman. *Arnold's Expedition to Quebec*. New York: The Macmillan Company, 1902.

20 Smith, 55.

21 Return J. Meigs. *A Journal of Occurrences which Happened Within the Circle of Observation in the Detachment Commanded by Colonel Benedictine Arnold, Consisting of Two Battalions, which were Detached from the Army at Cambridge, in the year 1775*. Referenced in Rich's Bibliotheca Americana Nova, 1835, Vol. 1, page 211 which describes it as having "no place, date or printer's name." The original of the 1ˢᵗ printing can be found in the Harvard Library with a total of eleven pages and an ink notation. See pages 17-22 of *Voices*.

22 In Newburyport, Barney bought the small book in which he wrote his journal.

23 All of the names listed were in Captain Oliver Hanchett's Company, GN 17.

24 GN 41

25 Sloop *Britania* was one of the transports used to take the men to from Newburyport to Colburn's shipyard. GN 110

26 GN 85A

27 GN 85A

28 GN 45

29 This number was wrong about distance to Quebec.

30 GN 109, GN 26

31 GN 48

32 GN 112

33 GN 86

34 GN 22

35 Ibid.

36 GN 44

37 GN 49, GN 109

38 GN 109, GN 26

39 GN 52

40 GN 54

41 All three were from Capt. Hanchett's Company, GN 17.The only comprehensive source for names of men who were sent back are in Appendix Two of *Voices* where 140 men are identified with references.

42 GN 57

43 GN 33

44 GN 96

45 GN 61

46 GN 62

47 GN 89

48 Pistareen was a small Spanish silver coin from the West Indies.

49 GN 65

50 GN 95

51 GN 96, GN 67, GN 117

52 GN 12
53 GN 98
54 GN 97
55 GN 31
56 GN 99, GN 119, GN 120, GN 3
57 GN 1
58 GN 110
59 GN 42
60 GN 109, GN 26
61 GN 48
62 GN 49
63 GN 81
64 GN 50
65 GN 51
66 GN 52
67 GN 53
68 GN 54
69 GN 11
70 GN 27
71 GN 33
72 GN 57
73 GN 90
74 GN 91
75 GN 17
76 GN 21
77 GN 1
78 GN 7
79 GN 13
80 GN 61
81 GN 62
82 GN 90
83 GN 89
84 GN 63
85 GN 66, GN 117
86 GN 2
87 GN 36
88 GN 1
89 GN 34
90 GN 11, GN 7
91 GN11
92 GN 25

93 GN 70

94 See *Voices,* pages 97-99.

95 GN 41

96 GN 42

97 GN 45

98 GN 109, GN 26

99 This was present day Pittston, Maine GN 45, Colburn GN 26.

100 GN 48

101 GN 86

102 GN 49

103 GN 12

104 GN 51

105 GN 52

106 An Indian town established by Father Rale, a Jesuit Catholic priest who made his life work converting the Indians in northern Maine. He was killed in 1724 by English colonists who sacked his mission and closed his church.

107 GN 53.

108 GN 54

109 GN 55, GN 56

110 GN 57

111 GN 88

112 GN 93, GN 8

113 Justin Smith calls this the Boundary Portage.

114 GN 61

115 GN 21

116 GN 33

117 GN 24

118 GN 89

119 GN 29

120 GN 65

121 GN 66. GN 117

122 GN 95

123 GN 68

124 GN 36

125 See Chapter Eight; GN 97.

126 GN 3

127 GN 70

128 GN 111

129 GN 35

130 GN 118

131 Jacques-Cartier. Presumably the point where the river named for the famous explorer empties into the St. Lawrence River above Quebec.

132 GN 11

133 GN 39

134 GN 69

135 A town five miles up the St. Lawrence River from Quebec.

136 GN 77

137 GN 72

138 GN 63

139 GN 84

140 GN 73

141 GN 71

142 Must have been the houses that were built just outside St. John's Gate.

143 GN 77

144 Presumably Major Caldwell's house.

145 GN 31

146 GN 79

147 GN 99, GN 119, GN 120

148 GN 74

149 GN 72

150 GN 75

151 GN 4

152 GN 6

153 GN 5

154 This defensive works ran from the cliff to the river along the line of present day St. James Street.

155 GN 75

156 Obviously this rumor was not true as Arnold's men never had control of the Lower Town.

157 GN 76

158 GN 12

159 GN 116

160 Roberts identifies him as Judge Peter Livius of Portsmouth, New Hampshire. He was a Loyalist who was thrown out of his home town by the Patriots for holding Loyalist views. He arrived in Quebec in May of 1775 and was recommended to Carleton by Lord Dartmouth to be a judge of the court of Common Pleas and that he should be approved as an appointee to the Council. It seems from his journal that Dearborn knew Livius when both were living in New Hampshire.

161 GN 20

162 Captain Hamilton of the *Lizzard*. According to W.H. Whitely in The British Navy and the Siege of Quebec, 1775-6, he was the "senior naval officer in the St. Lawrence".

163 GN 116

164 Halifax, Nova Scotia.

165 Son of Sir William Johnson, who was one a small number of title holders handed out by the King during the French and Indian War. The Johnson family members, both father and son, were sympathetic Tories. Sir William died on the eve of the start of the Revolution and after the war started, Sir John, who inherited the title from his father, left his home and went to Canada with his Scotch-Irish and Indian followers. He was believed by the colonists to be the leader of a large band of Tories and Indians that were raiding white settlements in upstate New York during the early years of the Revolution. He settled in Canada after the war and his property in New York was confiscated by the patriots.

166 GN 2

167 General Charles Lee was suggested as a replacement for Montgomery by Benedict Arnold after the failed attack. Based on Washington's recommendation, Lee was appointed by Congress to replace Schuyler as commander of the Northern Army and take charge of the operation in Canada. However, the order was countermanded on March 1st and he was instead sent to command the Southern Army.

168   155 GN 15

169 GN 36, GN 35

170 Captain Samuel Lockwood of Greenwich, Connecticut. In April of 1775, he was appointed as a 2nd lieutenant in the 3rd company of the regiment commanded by Colonel David Waterbury. He joined Montgomery's army and was with Montgomery through the attack on Quebec when he was taken prisoner. After being released in May of 1776, he joined Colonel Lamb's regiment of artillery as a Captain. In 1778, he was in the raid on Long Island by boat and was also involved in the raid on Stony brook in 1780. He was a captain of a company in the Connecticut line from 1780 until 1782. He drowned while fishing near Greenwich Point on August 26, 1807, at age seventy.

171 GN 17

172 GN 40

173 When the British troops left Boston, the Americans assumed they were headed to either Halifax or New York.

174 GN 104

175 According to Captain Thayer, they went home on the schooner *Magdalen*. Robertson does not give a name for the Schooner.

176 *Diary of a Common Soldier in the American Revolution, 1775-1783. An Annotated Edition of the Military Journal of Jeremiah Greenman.* Edited by Robert Bray and Paul Bushnell. DeKalb, Illinois: Northern Illinois University Press, 1978.

177 Although Greenman doesn't specify, when his journal begins the expedition was located in Newburyport, Massachusetts, GN 41.

178 GN 42

179 GN 110

180 GN 43; GN 23.

181 Cobercanta is Greenman's term for the name of a river called the Cobbossee Conte, GN 46.

182 GN 47.

183 GN 48.

184 GN 21

185 GN 86

186 GN 22

187 GN 109, GN 26

188 GN 49

189 The town of Winslow, Maine.

190 Goshen as designated in Greenman's journal has not been identified as it has no known location.

191 GN 51.

192 GN 19

193 GN 52.

194 GN 53.

195 GN 54.

196 GN 57.

197 GN 16

198 Freshet is a sudden overflow of a river or stream resulting from heavy rains.

199 GN 91, GN 109.GN 26.

200 GN 8

201 GN 90

202 GN 62

203 GN 61

204 Lieutenant Sylvanus Shaw of Captain Ward's Company from Newport, Rhode Island.

205 GN 90

206 GN 89

207 GN 61.

208 GN 65.

209 GN 66. GN 117

210 GN 91

211 GN 67.

212 GN 68.

213 GN 36

214 GN 69.

215 GN 70.

216 GN 98

217 GN 31

218 GN 79

219 A bundle of sticks bound together for use in constructing earthworks or reinforced trenches.

220 GN 71

221 GN 116

222 GN 99, GN 119, GN 120, GN 76

223 GN 38

224 GN 20

225 GN 116, GN 68, GN 77

226 Captain James Frost was a Loyalist commanding one of the British vessels, probably a privateer. He was from Rhode Island and was a partner of Newport Loyalist Simeon Pease. Frost knew Greenman's father because the Frosts and the Greenmans lived in Newport before the war, which likely explains his interest in helping Greenman with money and clothing.

227 GN 76

228 GN 103

229 GN 104

230 GN 37, GN 122

231 Major General Sir William Howe was the Commander in Chief of the British forces in America in 1775.

232 GN 104

233 GN 105

234 GN 85B

235 Perth Amboy, New Jersey.

236 GN 107

237 GN 1

238 GN 42

239 GN 48

240 GN 86

241 GN 109, GN 26

242 GN 49

243 GN 51

244 GN 52

245 GN 53

246 GN 54

247 GN 58

248 GN 55

249 GN 112

250 GN 57

251   248 GN 7

252   249 GN 31, GN 32

253 GN 109, GN 26, GN 90

254 GN 93

255 GN 17

256 GN 62

257 GN 90, GN 92

258 GN 89, GN 63.

259 GN 95

260 GN 36, GN 96

261 GN 70

262 GN 77

263 GN 79

264 GN 71, GN 99

265 GN 3, GN 83

266 GN 99, GN 119, GN 120, GN 76

267 *Return of Rebel Prisoners Taken in Quebec, Dec'r 31, 1775.* Return dated July 27, 1776. British National Archives. Colonial Officers, 42/35: 139-143.

268 GN 38

269 GN 77

270 GN 76

271 GN 12 & GN 14.

272 GN 103

273 GN 37, GN 122

274 GN 34

275 GN 104

276 GN 21, GN 13

277 GN 85B

278 GN 85B

279 GN 85B

280 GN 85B

281 GN 107

282 GN 41

283 GN 110

284 GN 42

285 GN 48

286 GN 49
287 GN 50
288 GN 51
289 GN 52
290 GN 53
291 GN 54
292 GN 58
293 GN 57
294 GN 90, GN 93, GN 17.
295 GN 62
296 GN 61
297 GN 60
298 GN 30, GN 11, GN 24
299 GN 90, GN 92
300 GN 89
301 GN 66, GN 95, GN 117
302 GN 96, GN 67
303 GN 70, GN 98, GN 30
304 GN 99, GN 119, GN 120
305 *The March to Quebec: A Mystery Solved.* Marie E. Blades, Morristown, New
   Jersey: Morris County Historical Society, 1980. 24 pages.
306 GN 61
307 GN 1
308 GN 60
309 GN 62
310 GN 7
311 GN 32,GN 15
312 GN 11, GN 24
313 GN 18
314 GN 21
315 GN 92
316 GN 14
317 GN 109, GN 26
318 GN 89
319 GN 63
320 GN 65
321 GN 66, GN 117
322 GN 2
323 GN 118
324 GN 94
325 GN 95

326 GN 118, GN 121

327 GN 12

328 GN 67

329 GN 96

330 GN 35

331 GN 68

332 GN 36

333 GN 13

334 GN 97, GN 73

335 GN 110, *Swallow* and *Broadbay* were names of two transports

336 GN 43

337 GN 45

338 GN 48

339 GN 27

340 GN 87, GN 86. See bios of Arnold's officers in GN 7-25.

341 GN 44

342 GN 49

343 GN 51

344 GN 52

345 GN 109, GN 26

346 GN 90

347 GN 53

348 GN 54

349 GN 61

350 GN 2

351 GN 42

352 GN 1

353 The troops in the ten musket companies were from Massachusetts, New Hampshire, Connecticut, Rhode Island and Maine. See Appendix II in *Voices*.

354 GN 11

355 The two Pennsylvania rife companies were from Colonel William Thompson's Regiment and were under the command of Captain William Hendricks, GN 19, and Captain Matthew Smith, GN 24

356 Known volunteers were Aaron Burr, Matthias Ogden, Matthew Duncan, John Coates and Isaac Melchior from Pennsylvania and Eleazer Oswald from Connecticut.

357 GN 41

358 GN 110

359 GN 42

360 GN 46

361 GN 109, GN 26

362 GN 48

363 GN 87

364 GN 86

365 GN 49

366 GN 81

367 GN 50

368 GN 51

369 GN 52

370 GN 53

371 GN 54

372 GN 109, GN 26, GN 90

373 GN 58

374 GN 55

375 GN 27

376 GN 62

377 GN 57

378 GN 33

379 GN 88

380 GN 88

381 GN 90

382 GN 91

383 GN 61

384 GN 60

385 GN 8, GN 93

386 GN 30, GN 90

387 GN 63

388 GN 92

389 GN 89

390 "Diary of Arnold's March to Quebec by a Soldier of the American Revolution." *American Antiquarian & Oriental Journal.* Rev Stephen D. Peet, Editor. Volume XXII, January-December, Chicago, 1900, pp. 224-228.

391 "Anonymous Journalist on Arnold's March to Quebec: Soldiers Identity Uncovered after 237 Years." Stephen Burke and Stephen Darley. *Early America Review,* Vol. 11, No. 2, Winter/Spring, 2013.

392 GN 20

393 GN 41

394 GN 42

395 GN 48

396 GN 86

397 GN 49

398 GN 109, GN 26

399 GN 52

400 GN 54

401 GN 57

402 GN 58

403 GN 15

404 GN 16

405 GN 62

406 GN 89

407 GN 78

408 GN 67, GN 117

409 GN 68

410 GN 70

411 GN 3

412 GN 99, GN 119, GN 120

413 GN 19

414 GN 1

415 GN 82

416 GN 48

417 GN 86

418 "Washington's pleasure shall be known" is a phrase used by some journalists to describe why the man who killed another man at Fort Western was not executed after being convicted. See GN 86.

419 GN 90

420 GN 49

421 GN 51

422 GN 52

423 GN 54

424 GN 55

425 GN 31, GN 58.

426 GN 57

427 GN 7

428 GN 109, GN 26

429 GN 63

430 GN 66, GN 117

431 GN 67

432 GN 70, GN 98

433 GN 79,GN 77

434 GN 99, GN 120, GN 119, GN 76

435 See GN 263.

436 GN 38

437 GN 116

438 GN 121

439 GN 76
440 GN 11.
441 GN 35, GN 121
442 GN 34
443 GN 37, GN 121, GN 122
444 GN 105, GN 104, GN 13, GN 21
445 GN 85B
446 GN 85B
447 GN 85B
448 GN 85B
449 GN 85B
450 GN 2
451 GN 3
452 GN 1
453 GN 41
454 GN 42
455 GN 48
456 GN 109, GN 26
457 GN 11
458 GN 7
459 GN 8
460 GN 49
461 GN 50
462 GN 52
463 GN 51
464 GN 109, GN 26
465 GN 90
466 GN 53
467 GN 54
468 GN 13
469 GN 17
470 GN 58
471 GN 7
472 GN 88
473 GN 93
474 GN 22
475 GN 23
476 GN 16
477 GN 25
478 GN 15
479 LT Jedediah Hyde of Norwich, Connecticut.

480 GN 18

481 No one by that name was on the expedition. It must be a mistake by Senter.

482 GN 61

483 GN 41

484 GN 42

485 GN 110

486 GN 48

487 GN 109, GN 26

488 GN 49

489 GN 50

490 GN 51

491 GN 52

492 GN 19

493 GN 53

494 GN 54

495 GN 57

496 GN 88

497 Setting poles. The bateaux were provided with long poles which could be placed on the river bottom and then used to push the boat forward in sections where the water flowed slowly enough.

498 GN 17

499 GN 93

500 This is actually known as Height of Land, GN 60

501 GN 61

502 GN 62

503 GN 90

504 GN 92

505 GN 89

506 GN 63

507 GN 66

508 GN 95

509 GN 96

510 GN 67, GN 117

511 GN 70

512 GN 98

513 GN 30

514 GN 24

515 GN 99, GN 119

516 GN 38

517 GN 116

518 GN 76

519 GN 102, GN 103

520 GN 34

521 GN 35

522 GN 105

523 GN 85B

524 GN 85B

525 Presumably Chesapeake Bay.

526 Sleeper's statement is found in Caleb Haskell's pension application. National Records and Archives Administration, M804, Record Group 15. Also www. footnote.com.

527 *Voices*, 49-50.

528 *Antiquarian Bookman*, Vol. 4, 1949. R.R. Bowker Company, Newark, New Jersey. Listing from Old Corner Bookstore in Boston.

529 Freeman Judd pension application, NARA, W21500.

530 Sylvester Judd. *Thomas Judd and His Descendants*. Northampton, MA: J. & L. Metcalf, 1856.

531 A. Milne Judd. *Autobiographical Notes of Freeman Judd: A Diversionary Expedition*. Niagara County Genealogical Society, October 31, 1981.

532 Mark Sullivan. *The Lost Journal of Private Freeman Judd*. Journal of the American Revolution, September 25, 2018.

533 Ibid. See End Notes 530 & 531; Freeman Judd obituary, *Union-Sun and Journal*.

WORKS CONSULTED

PRIMARY SOURCES

Arnold, Benedict. "Arnold's Address to the Inhabitants of Quebec". *The Canadian Antiquarian and Numismatic Journal,* vol. II, July 1873: 79-80.

Arnold, Benedict. "Arnold's Letters on his expedition to Canada in 1775." In *Maine Historical Society Collections.* vol. 1, 341-416. Portland, Maine: Maine Historical Society, 1831. Also in Kenneth Roberts *March to Quebec.*

Arnold, Benedict. Day Book and Ledger, 1777-1779. *American Historical Record,* vol. 3, May 1874: 220-222.

Bigelow, Timothy. Letters. *Proceedings of the Worcester Society of Antiquity,* vol. XXV, 1912: 81-113.

Bray, Robert and Paul Bushnell, ed. Diary of a Common Soldier in the American Revolution, 1775-1783. An Annotated Edition of the Military Journal of Jeremiah Greenman. DeKalb, Illinois: Northern Illinois University Press, 1978.

Chase, Philander D., ed. *The Papers of George Washington, Rev War Series,* Vols 2 & 3. Charlottesville: University Press of Virginia, 1987-1988.

Clark, William Bell, ed. *Naval Documents of the American Revolution.* vols 1-3. Washington, DC: Government Printing Office, 1964-1973.

"Committee of Safety Records." *Collections of the New Hampshire Historical Society,* Vol. III, 1868: 18-20; 64; 71; 78-79. [Roger Enos].

Dearborn, General Henry. *Arnold's Expedition to Quebec, manuscript, 23 pages.* New York Public Library, Harkness Manuscript Collection, 1816.

"Diary of Arnold's March to Quebec by a Soldier of the American Revolution." *The American Antiquarian and Oriental Journal.* Vol. XXII. January-December, 1900. [William Pierce journal].

Egle, William Henry, ed. *Provincial Papers. State & Supply Transcripts of the County of Cumberland. Toboyne Township Taxables.* Harrisburg: State of Pennsylvania, 1898.

Force, Peter, ed. *American Archives. 9 vols.* Washington, D.C., 1837-1853. Also at American Archives Documents of the American Revolution 1774-1776. Northern Illinois University. www.dig.lib.niu.edu/amarch.

--- *A Journal of an Intended Tour from Cambridge to Quebeck, via Kennebeck with a detachment of two Regiments of Musketeers and three Companies of Riflers, consisting of about eleven hundred effective men.* [Eleazer Oswald Journal].
--- *Report of Dennis Getchall and Samuel Berry.* [Scouting Report] 4th Series, vol. 3: 961-962. Original is in Maine State Archives. Maine Memory Network, Maine's Online Museum, Rueben Colburn Letter about Benedict Arnold's March, 1775. www.mainememory.net.
--- *Colonel Enos to General Washington.* 4th Series, vol. 3, 1610.
--- *Colonel Roger Enos to the Publick.* 4th Series, vol. 3, 1708.
--- *Court of Inquiry and Court-Martial on Lieutenant-Colonel Enos.* 4th Series, vol. 3, 1710.
--- *Proceedings of a Court-Martial for the Trial of Lieutenant-Colonel Enos.* 4th Series, vol. 4, 238.
--- *Letter from Colonel Enos to General Washington.* 4th Series, vol. 4, 768.

Ford, Worthington C. et al, ed. *Journals of the Continental Congress.* Washington, D.C., 1904-1937. www.memory.loc.gov/ammem/amlaw/lwjc.html.

Ford, Worthington C., coll. & ed. *The Writings of George Washington.* Vol. III, 1775-1776. New York and London: G.P. Putnam's Sons, 1889.

Heitman, Francis B. *Historical Register of Officers of the Continental Army During the War of the Revolution, April, 1775 to Dec. 1783*. Washington, D.C.: Francis B. Heitman, 1893.

Henry, John Joseph. "Letters of Hon. John Joseph Henry." *Pennsylvania Magazine of History and Biography*, vol. 20, 1896: 568-570.

Hinman, Royal Ralph, comp. *A Historical Collection from Official Records, Files & c. of the Part Sustained by Connecticut During the War of the Revolution*. Hartford: E. Gleason, 1842.

Hoadly, Charles J. *The Public Records of the State of Connecticut, From October, 1776 to February, 1778*. Hartford: Case, Lockwood & Brainard Company, 1894.

Hodgkinson, Samuel. "Before Quebec, 1776". [Letter to Parents]. *Pennsylvania Magazine of History and Biography*, vol. X, 1886: 158-162.

"Letter of James Livingston to Unknown". [Conditions in Quebec]. *American Historical Record and Repertory of Notes and Queries*, vol. 3, April 1874: 181-183.

"Letters and Certificates From the Revolutionary Papers of Col. Francis Nichols." *The Pennsylvania Magazine of History and Biography*, vol. 32, 1908: 108-112.

Lincoln, William. *The Journals of the Provincial Congress of Massachusetts in 1774 and 1775*. Boston: State of Massachusetts, 1838.

McCoy, William. *Journal of Sergeant William McCoy of the March from Pennsylvania to Quebec July 13, 1775 to December 31, 1775*. Ed by Raymond M. Bell and Chauncey E. McCoy. Bell and McCoy, 1991, 16 typewritten pages.

Ogden, Matthias. "Journal of Major Matthias Ogden in Arnold's Campaign against Quebec 1775." *Proceedings of the New Jersey Historical Society*, vol. XIII. No. 1. January 1928.

Revolutionary War Pension Files. National Records and Archives Administration, M804, Record Group 15, Records of the Veterans Administration. Includes over 80,000 application files. Also on www.footnote.com.

Roberts, Kenneth, Comp. and Ann. *March to Quebec: Journals of the Members of Arnold's Expedition.* Garden City, New York: Doubleday & Company, Inc, 1946.

Stone, Edwin Martin. *The Invasion of Canada in 1775: Including the Journal of Captain Simeon Thayer.* Providence, R.I.: Hammond, Angell & Co., Printers, 1867.

Ward, Samuel. *Letters of Governor Ward and His Son, Samuel.* American Annual Register of Public Events for the Year 1831-32. Brattleboro, VT: Fessenden and Company, 1833, 405-408.

Warren-Adams Letters, vol. I. Boston: The Massachusetts Historical Society, 1917.
[James Warren to John Adams, November 14, 1775, 181-182].

Washington Papers. *Library of Congress, Manuscript Division, 1741-1799. Series 4. GeneralCorrespondence.1697-1799.*
www.memory.gov.gov/ammem/gwhtml/gwhome.html.

Willis, William. *Journals of the Rev. Thomas Smith and the Rev. Samuel Deane, Pastors of the First Church in Portland.* Portland: Joseph s. Bailey, 1949.

SECONDARY SOURCES

Abbatt, William. "A Neglected Name: Dr. Isaac Senter." *Annals of Medical History,* vol. II, 1920: 381-383.

Abbatt, William. "Arnold and Montgomery at Quebec." *The Magazine of History with Notes and Queries,* Vol. 1, 1905: 13-17.

Abbatt, William. "Dr. Senter and His Descendants, [Introductory Note to Senter's Journal]." *The Magazine of History with Notes and Queries, Extra # 41-44*, 1916: i-ix.

Abbott, William. *The Magazine of History with Notes and Queries.* [Reprints of Quebec Expedition Journals].
--- Dearborn, Extra 135, 1928.
--- Fobs, Extra 130, 1927.
--- Haskell, Extra 86, 1922.
--- Humphrey, Extra 166, 1931.
--- *Memorable Attack on Quebec, December 21, 1775.* Porterfield, Vol. XXI, 1889.
--- Morison, Extra 52, 1916.
--- Senter, Extra 42, 1916.
--- Squire, Extra 160, 1930.
--- Stocking, Extra 75, 1921.
--- Topham, Extra 50, 1916.
--- Wild, Extra 134, 1927.

Alden, Rev. Timothy. *A Collection of American Epitaphs and Inscriptions with Occasional Notes, vol. III,* [Isaac Senter]. New York, 1814.

Allen, Barbara. *Report to Stephen Darley on Captain William Goodrich From Records in the Library.* Stockbridge Library, Museum and Local Archives, January 2010.

Allen, William. "Account of Arnold's Expedition." *Collections of the Maine Historical Society,* vol. 1, 1831: 386-416.

Americana Exchange. A rare book bibliographical database of entries from book collector and bookseller catalogs and rare book auctions. www. americanaexchange.com.

Anderson, Mark R. *The Battle for the Fourteenth Colony: America's War of Liberation in Canada 1774-1776.* Hanover and London: University Press of New England, 2013.

Arnold Expedition Historical Society. Pittston, Maine.

--- *Arnold Expedition Historical Society Newsletter,* 1975-2020.

--- *The Research Room. www.arnold'smarch.com/research.html.* Journals and other documents reproduced.

--- *The Great Carrying Place Portage Trail.* Written by Stephen Clark, 2014.

--- *Arnold's Wilderness March: Kennebec River Maine to Lac Megantic, Quebec.* Map and Guide, 2009.

Banks, Charles E. "Captain Scott of Enos' Detachment." *The Magazine of History with Notes and Queries,* vol. XVIII, January-June 1914: 271-273.

—. *Papers and research material regarding Benedict Arnold's Expedition against Quebec, 1775-1776. Includes handwritten copies of letters and jouornals, including Hendricks, Ware and Heth; newspaper clippings and portions of published articles; copies of maps; and correspondence regarding research with other scholars and institutions.* Ms. N-1782. 1 narrow box and 9 vols in cases. Boston: Massachusetts Historical Society, 1922.

---"Arnold's Expedition to Quebec in 1775; a preliminary note on the personnel of detachment." *Magazine of History with Notes and Queries,* Extra # 50, 1916: 10 pages.

Alex. Harris. *Biographical History of Lancaster County, Pennsylvania.* Lancaster, Pa.: Elias Barr & Co., 1872. [Steele, 561-562].

Bird, Harrison. *Attack on Quebec; the American Invasion of Canada, 1775.* New York: Oxford University Press, 1968.

Blades, Marie E. *The March to Quebec: A Mystery Solved.* Morristown, New Jersey: Morris County Historical Society, 1980.

Blanco, Richard L. Ed. *The American Revolution 1775-1783: An Encyclopedia.* 2 vols. New York and London: Garland Publishing, Inc., 1993.

Boatner, Mark H. *Encyclopedia of the American Revolution.* New York: David McKay Company, Inc, 1975.

Bugbee, James M. "Report of Letter regarding Wild Journal." *Proceedings of Massachusetts Historical Society, vol. XLVI*, October, 1912-June, 1913: 305-306.

Campbell, Frederic L. "Benedict Arnold In Maine." *Sun Up, Maines Own Magazine*, May 1931: 16, 29.

Case, Lafayette Wallace, ed. *The Goodrich Family in America*. Chicago: Goodrich Family Memorial Association, 1889.

Cash, Philip. "The Canadian Military Campaign of 1775-1776: Medical Problems and Effects of Disease." *Journal of the American Medical Association*, July 5, 1976: 52-56.

Celebration of the One Hundred and Fiftieth Anniversary of the First Settlement of Nelson, New Hampshire 1767-1917. Nelson, N.H.: Nelson Picnic Association, 1917.

Chandler, Lorraine. *Lt. Jeremiah Greenman*. www.familytreemaker. genealogy.com/user/c/h/a/Lorraine-Chandler/WEBSITE-0001/u.

Clark, Stephen. *Following Their Footsteps, A Travel Guide & History of the 1775 Secret Expedition to Capture Quebec*. Shapleigh, ME: Stephen Clark, 2003.

Clarke, George Kuhn. *History of Needham Massachusetts, 1711-1911*. Needham: George Kuhn Clarke, 1912.

Coburn, Louise Helen. *The Passage of Arnold Through Skowhegan*. Skowhegan, ME: Louise H. Coburn, 1922.

Codman, John. *Arnold's Expedition to Quebec*. New York: The Macmillan Company, 1902.

Coffin, Charles, comp. *The Lives and Services of Major General John Thomas; Colonel Thomas Knowlton; Colonel Alexander Scammell; Major General Henry Dearborn*. New York: Robert, Hovey & King, 1845.

Coffin, Victor. *The Province of Quebec and the Early American Revolution.* Madison: University of Wisconsin, 1896.

Collins, W.E. "Arnold's Expedition to Quebec." *Collections of the Berkshire Historical & Scientific Society,* vol. I, 1894: 57-67.

Commemorative Biographical Encyclopedia of the Juniata Valley. Chambersburg, PA: J.M. Runk & Co., 1897.

Cowell, Benjamin. *The Spirit of 76 in Rhode Island.* Boston: A.J. Wright, 1850.
--- Captain Simeon Thayer
--- Captain John Topham

Crist, Robert G. and Joseph P. Cullen. "Arnold's March to Quebec." *American History Illustrated,* November 1968: 4-11.

Crist, Robert G. *Captain William Hendricks and the March to Quebec, 1775.* Carlisle, PA: Hamilton Library and Historical Association of Cumberland County, 1960.

Darley, Stephen. *Voices from a Wilderness Expedition: The Journals and Men of Benedict Arnold's Expedition to Quebec in 1775.* Bloomington, IN: AuthorHouse, 2011. [1st Publication of Dearborn's original journal, Anonymous # 2, Barney, Senter 2nd journal, Kimball].

Darley, Stephen and Stephen Burk. "Anonymous Journal on Arnold's March to Quebec: Soldier's Identity Uncovered After 237 Years." *Early American Review,* vol. 11, No. 2, Winter/Spring, 2012. [William Pierce Journal].

Darley, Stephen. "What's in a Name: How Durben in Glasgow Became Dearborn in Quebec." *CommonPlace,* vol. 14, No. 3, Spring 2014. [Capt. Henry Dearborn's Original Journal].

Darley, Stephen. "Dr. Isaac Senter and His Other Revolutionary War Journal." *Rhode Island Genealogy Society,* vol. 38, No. 3. Sept. 2013.

Darley, Stephen. "The Authenticity of Joseph Ware's Journal: A Historical Argument Revisited." *America Ancestors Magazine, New England Historic Genealogical Society*, vol. 13, No. 4. Fall, 2012.

Darley, Stephen. "William Goodrich: A Little Known Revolutionary War Officer from Stockbridge." *Berkshire Genealogist*, vol. 32, No. 2. Spring 2012.

Darley, Stephen. "A Test of Endurance: Benedict Arnold's March to Quebec." *Patriots of the American Revolution Magazine*, vol. 5, No. 1. Jan/Feb 2012.

Davenport, John Scott. *The Frontier Hendricks*. Dorothy N. Lloyd Memorial Hendricks Research. April 10, 1993 letter to Col. Meredith E. Hendricks.

Davis, Curtis Carroll. "Mrs. Warner's Winter Warfare, A Momemto of Arnold's Campaign." *Lancaster County Historical Society Journal*, 1980: 125-131.

Davis, Matthew L. *Memoirs of Aaron Burr*, 2 vols. New York: Harper & Brothers, 1836.

Dawson, Henry B. *Battles of the United States By Sea and Land*. New York: Johnson, Fry, and Company, 1858.

Decker, Peter. *Trekking Arnold's Trail to Quebec*. Lakeville, CT: The Lakeville Journal, 1976.

Desjardin, Thomas A. *Through a Howling Wilderness, Benedict Arnold's March to Quebec in 1775*. New York: St. Martin's Press, 2006.

Dodge, Mary Cochran, comp. A List of Soldiers in the War of the Revolution from Worcester, Mass. Worcester: Worcester D.A.R., 1902, [Captain Jonas Hubbard, 17-18].

Egle, William Henry. Col. Matthew Smith. *Historical Register: Notes and Queries, Historical and Genealogical Relating to Interior Pennsylvania for the Year 1884,* vol. I. 1883: 230-231.

Egle, William Henry, ed. "The Pattang Company Before Quebec, 1775." *Notes and Queries: Historical, Biographical and Genealogical, 3rd ser.,* vol. I, 1887: 249-250.

Evans, Charles. *American Bibliography: A Chronological Dictionary of all Books Pamphlets and Periodical Publications in the United States of America Down to and Including the Year 1820.* 12 vols. Chicago: Charles Evans, 1903-1934.

Fenn, Elizabeth A. *Pox Americana, The Great Smallpox Epidemic of 1775-82.* New York: Hill and Wang, 2001.

French, Allen. *The First Year of the American Revolution.* New York: Octagon Books, 1968.

Gabriel, Michael P. *Major General Richard Montgomery, The Making of an American Hero.* Madison, Teaneck: Fairleigh Dickenson University Press, 2002.

Gardner, Frank A. "The Organization and Personnel of the Expedition." *Danvers Historical Society, Historical Collections.* vol.13, 1925: 38-50.

Gephart, Ronald M, comp. *Revolutionary America 1763-1789, A Bibliography.* 2 vols. Washington, D.C.: Library of Congress, 1964

Gerlach, Don R. Proud Patriot, *Philip Schuyler and the War of independence 1775-1783.* Syracuse: Syracuse University Press, 1987.

Goelet, Ogden. *The Library of the Late Ogden Goelet of New York.* New York: American Art Association Anderson Galleries, Inc., 1935
--- Part One. Benedict Arnold Manuscript Journal, 10-15.
--- Part Two. John Pierce Manuscript Journal, 149-154.

Goetz, Rebecca Anne. *Private William Dorr's March to Quebec: A Study in Historical Ambiguity*. An Honors Thesis to Department of History, Bates College, 17 March 2000.

Goodwin, Daniel, Jr. "The Dearborns." *Chicago Historical Society's Proceedings*, 1884: 20-40.

Hadley, E.D. "General Henry Dearborn." *The Granite Monthly*, Vol. XLVII, 1915: 409-412.

Handley, Christopher Simpson, comp. *Annotated Bibliography of Diaries Printed in English, 3rd Edition. Vol. IV, Diaries 1780 to 1817*. Tyne and Wear, England: Hanover Press, 2002.

Harrell, Mary Edith. *The Scott Family: An Account of Lieutenant Colonel William Scott of Peterborough, N.H. and His Descendants*. Cincinnati: Mary Edith Harrell, 1967.

Hatch, Robert M. *Thrust for Canada: The American Attempt on Quebec in 1775-1776*. Boston: Houghton Mifflin, 1979.

Hayden, Horace Edwin. "General Roger Enos, A Lost Chapter of Arnold's Expedition to Canada, 1775". *Magazine of American History*, vol. XIII, 1885: 463-476.

Henderson, Denis L. *General Oliver Hanchett*. www.worldconnect. rootsweb.ancestry.com/cgibin/igen.cgi?op=GET8db=limmeadenis51.

Henry, William Louis, comp. Lineage of John Joseph Henry. Detroit: W.L. Henry, 1909.

"Note on the Heth Journal". *Proceedings of the Virginia Historical Society at the Annual Meeting held Dec. 21-22, 1891*, 1892: 320n.

Hildreth, S.P. *Biographical and Historical Memoirs of the Early Pioneer Settlers of Ohio,* [Chapter on Col. Return Jonathan Meigs]. Cincinnati: H.W. Derby & Co., 1852.

Hines, Ezra Dodge. *Arnold's March From Cambridge to Quebec*. Salem, MA: The Salem Press, 1898.

History of Cumberland and Adams Counties Pennsylvania. Chicago: Warner, Beers & Co., 1886. [Hendricks Family, 8, 276].

Howes, Wright, comp. *U.S.iana (1650-1950)*. New York: The Newberry Library, 1963.

Hubbard, Harlan Page. *One Thousand Years of Hubbard History*. New York: Harlan Page Hubbard, 1895.

Huston, James A. "The Logistics of Arnold's March to Quebec." *Military Affairs*, Dec., 1968: 110-124.

Introductory Note to Squier Journal. *Magazine of American History*, vol. 11, 1878: 685.

Jones, Charles H. *History of the Campaign for the Conquest of Canada*. Philadelphia: Porter & Coates, 1882.

Jones, Electra. *Stockbridge Past and Present, or Records of an Old Mission Station*. Springfield, MA: Samuel Bowles & Co., 1854.

Judd, A. Milne. "Autobiographical Notes of Freeman Judd: A Diversionary Expedition." *Niagara County Genealogical Society*. October 31, 1981.

Knapp, Samuel L. *The Life of Aaron Burr*. New York: Wiley & Long, 1885. Appendix. [Arnold's Journal]

Kapp, James Edward. *Early Perry County People (Prior to 1830)*. The Perry Historians, n.d.

Kerr, Don. "The Gamble for Canada." *The Braver*, Vol. 82, Jan 2003: 8-12.

Kilbourne, James Dwight. *Virtutis Praemium: The Men Who Founded the State Society of the Cincinnati of Pennsylvania.* Rockport, ME: Picton Press, 1998.

Kimball, G.F. *Kimball Family News.*
---"Moses Kimball", Feb. 1903: 69-71.
---"Moses Kimball Again." April 1902: 57-58.

Kingsley, Orson. *Report to Stephen Darley on Major William Goodrich in Middlebury.* Research Center, Henry Sheldon Museum, Middlebury, VT, February 2010.

Lanctot, Gustave. *Canada and the American Revolution.* Cambridge, Mass.: Harvard University Press, 1967.

Laughlin, Jean. *Report to Stephen Darley regarding information on the McCoy Name in various records.* Mifflin County Historical Society, 2010.

Le Moine, Sir James M. "Arnold's Assault on the Sault-au-Matelot Barriers, 31st December, 1775." *Literary and Historical Society of Quebec, Transactions # 12,* 1876-1877: 40-70.

Le Moine, Sir James M. "The Assault of Brigadier-General Richard Montgomery and Colonel Benedict Arnold in Quebec in 1775. A Red Letter Day in the Annals of Canada." *Royal Society of Canada, Proceedings and Transactions,* 1899: 457-466.

Le Moine, Sir James M. *Quebec Past and Present: A History of Quebec, 1608-1876.* Quebec: Augustin Cote & Co., 1876.

Leake, Isaac Q. *Memoir of the Life and Time of General John Lamb.* Glendale, New York: Benchmark Publishing Company, 1970.[Eleazer Oswald, 130,149,168,202-3,209,330,344,359].

Lefkowitz, Arthur S. *Benedict Arnold's Army: The 1775 American Invasion of Canada During the Revolutionary War.* New York and California: Savas Beatie, 2008.

Lincoln, William. *History of Worcester. Massachusetts, From Its Earliest Settlement to September 1836.* Worcester: Charles Hersey, 1862. [Captain Jonas Hubbard, 231-232].

Locke, John Goodwin. *Book of the Lockes: A Genealogical and Historical Record of William Locke of Woburn, Appendix H.* Boston and Cambridge: John Goodwin Locke, 1853.

Ludlum, David. *Early American Winters, 1604-1820.* Boston: American Meteorological Society, 1966.

MacDougall, Walter M. "Arnold's Expedition to Quebec, 1775." *Down East Magazine,* Vol. 22, Sept 1975: 36-40.

MacLean, Allen. "Arnold's Strength at Quebec." *Military Collector and Historian,* Autumn 1977: 137-139.

Marshall, John. *The Life of George Washington Commander in Chief of the American Forces During the War which Established the Independence of His County and First President of the United States,* 2 vols. New York: Walton Book Company, 1930.

Martin, James Kirby. *Benedict Arnold Revolutionary Hero, An American Warrior Reconsidered.* New York and London: New York University Press, 1997.

Mason, Richard A. *The Quiet Patriot: Colonel Return Jonathan Meigs."* Westminster, MD: Heritage Books, 2010.

Matthews, William, comp. *American Diaries: An Annotated Bibliography of American Diaries Written Prior to the Year 1861.* Boston: J.S. Canner & Company, 1959.

"The McCobb Family of Maine." *Genealogy: A Journal of American Ancestry,* vols. I & II, 1912: 244-245

McCoy, Chauncey E. and Raymond M. Bell. *John McCoy, His Children and Grandchildren.* McCoy and Bell, 1990.

McSpadden, Joseph Walker. *The South in the Building of the Nation, vol XI* . [Biography of Charles Porterfield]. Richmond, VA: The Southern Historical Publication Society, 1909.

Mead, Daniel. *A History of Greenwich, Fairfield County, Conn.* New York: Baker & Godwin, Printers, 1857.

Mead, Spencer P. *Ye Historie of Ye Old Town of Greenwich, County of Fairfield and State of Connecticut.* New York: The Knickerbocker Press, 1911.

Meigs Family History & Genealogy. www.meigs.org/rjm90.htm.

Meigs, Rick. *Return Jonathan Meigs 1ˢᵗ.* Meigs Family History and Genealogy, www.meigs.org, n.d.

Mills, William H. "Benedict Arnold's March to Canada." *Magazine of American History, with Notes and Queries*, Feb. 1885: 143-154.

Morgan, Forrest, Editor in Chief. *Connecticut as a Colony and as a State, vol. 2.* Hartford: The Publishing Society of Connecticut, 1904.

Morrison, Leonard Allison and Stephen Paschall Sharples. *History of the Kimball Family in America From 1634 to 1897.* Boston: Damrell & Upham, 1897.

Morrissey, Brendan. *Quebec 1775: The American Invasion of Canada.* Oxford, UK: Osprey Publishing, 2003.

Morse, Jedediah. *Annals of the American Revolution.* Hartford: Jedediah Morse, 1824.

Munn, Charles A. *Rare Americana Including Selections from the Collection of the Late Charles A. Munn.* New York: American Art Association, Inc., January 21 and 22, 1926.

Nelson, James L. *Benedict. Arnold's Navy: The Ragtag Fleet that Lost the Battle of Lake Champlain but Won the American Revolution.* Camden, ME, New York: McGraw Hill, 2006.

Nichols, Charles J. "The March of Benedict Arnold Through the District of Maine." *Sprague's Journal of Maine History, Vol. XI,* 1923: 145-150; 195-208.

Nichols, Francis. *Proceedings of the Delaware County Historical Society,* vol. 1, Sept 29, 1895-Dec. 5, 1901: 26-29.

North, James W. *The History of Augusta from the Earliest Settlement to the Present Times.* Augusta, ME: Clapp and North, 1870.

Noyes, Benjamin Lake. *Deer Isle Pioneers.* Privately Printed, 1908.

Online, Family Treemaker. *Lt. Jeremiah Greenman.* familytreemaker. genealogy.com/users/c/h/a/Lorraine-Chandler/WEBSITE-0001/UHP-0327.html.

Oswald, Ginny. *Eleazer Oswald's Descendants.* June 29, 2001. www.genforum.genealogy.com/oswald/messages/263.html.

Park, Edward. "Could Canada Have Ever Been Our Fourteenth Colony?" *Smithsonian,* December 1987: 40-49.

Pierce, Frederick Clifton. *Pierce Genealogy.* Worcester, MA: Press of Charles Hamilton, 1880.

"Report to Stephen Darley From Dewey Research Center on Major William Goodrich in Sheffield." Sheffield Historical Society, 2010.

Rich, Obadiah. *Bibliotheca Americana Nova; or a Catalogue of Books in Various Languages Relating to America, Printed Since the Year 1700.* 2 vols. New York: Harper and Brothers, 1835.

Rikes, David M. *Report to Stephen Darley regarding Information in the Cumberland Historical Society and Hamilton Library on the William Hendricks Family, including the Hendricks genealogy file.* Cumberland County Historical Society and the Hamilton Library, January 2010.

Robinson, Arthur W. *Sportsmen's and Toutists' Guide Book to the Dead River Region of Maine.* Boston: A.W. Robinson, 1884.

Roger Enos- Revolutionary War General. Eno Family Association. www.enofamily.org.

Rowland, Bob. "Tobias Hendricks: A Family Tradition of Service." *Cumberland County History,* vol. 20, Summer/Winter 2003: 49-55.

Rueger, Bruce F. "Geologic Influences on Benedict Arnold's March to Quebec, 1775." *2006 Philadelphia Annual Meeting, The Gealogical Society of America.* Philadelphia: 2006.

Sabin, Joseph. *Bibliotheca Americana: Dictionary of Books Relating to America from Its Discovery to the Present Time.* 29 vols. New York: J. Sabin's Son, 1879.

Seymour, Keith M. *The Descendants of Thomas Hanchett.* San Francisco: Keith M. Seymour, 1985.

Shain, Charles and Samuella. *The Maine Reader.* Boston and New York: Houghton Mifflin Company, 1991. [Abner Stocking,].

Shelton, Hal T. *General Richard Montgomery and the American Revolution: From Redcoat to Rebel.* New York: New York University Press, 1994.

Shipton, Nathaniel and David Swain, ed. *Rhode Islanders Record the Revolution, The Journals of William Humphrey and Zuriel Waterman.* Providence: Rhode Island Publication Society, 1984.

Simon Fobes Goes to War. The Life of a Revolutionary War Soldier. History Instruction Resource Materials. Washington, D.C.: National Archives and Record Administration, n.d.

Smith, Jonathan. *Peterborough New Hampshire in the American Revolution.* Peterborough: Peterborough Historical Society, 1913. [Captain William Scott, 316-324].

Smith, Jonathan. "Two William Scotts of Peterborough, N.H." *Proceedings of the Massachusetts Historical Society,* vol. XLIV, 1911: 495-502.

Smith, Justin H. *Arnold's March from Cambridge to Quebec; a Critical Study, together with a reprint of Arnold's Journal.* New York: G.P. Putnam's Sons, 1903.
—. *Our Struggle for the Fourteenth Colony: Canada in the American Revolution.* New York: G.P. Putnam's Sons, 1907.

Smith, Justin H. "The Prologue of the American Revolution." *The Century Illustrated Monthly Magazine,* Vol. LXV, Nov. 1902-April 1903: 72-94;351-369; 529-544; 713-731.

Some Charges of a Very High Nature: The Court-Martial of Col. Matthias Ogden, Parts I-XI. Walking the Berkshires, www.greensleeves.com/berkshires, 2010.

Soucier, Daniel S. "News of Provisions Ahead: Accommodation in a Wilderness Borderland during the American Invasion of Quebec, 1775." *Maine History* 47, 1 (2013: 42-67.

Stanley, George Francis Gilman. *Canada Invaded, 1775-1776.* Toronto: Samuel Stevens Hakkert and Co., 1977.

Streeter, Thomas Winthrop. *The Celebrated Collection of Americana Formed by the Late Thomas Winthrop Streeter, Morristown, New Jersey.* New York: Parke-Bernet Galleries, Inc., 1967. [Abner Stocking 1810 journal, 596].

Sullivan, Mark. "The Lost Journal of Private Freeman Judd." *Journal of the American Revolution,* Sept. 25, 2018.

Tobias, Sr. v Tobias, Jr. December 23, 2004. www.sio.midco.net/ltsco/hendricks/toby%20v%20toby.html.

Trask, William B. Genealogy of the Ware Family. *New England Historical and Genealogical Register,* April 1852: 129-145.

Walker, J. Samuel. *The Perils of Patriotism: John Joseph Henry and the American Attack on Quebec, 1775.* Lancaster, PA: Lancaster County Historical Society, 1975.

Ward, Christopher. *The War of the Revolution 2 vols.* New York: The Macmillan Company, 1952.

Wells, Gabriel. *Rare Books from the Estate of the Late Gabriel Wells. Catalogue No. 1.* New York: Charles S. Boesen, n.d. [Arnold Manuscript Journal, 8-13].

Whaples, Meigs H. *An Historical Sketch of Return Jonathan Meigs, A Revolutionary Hero of Connecticut.* Colonel Jeremiah Wadsworth Branch, Connecticut Society, Sons of the American Revolution, 1918.

Wheeler, William Ogden, comp. *The Ogden Family in America, Elizabethtown Branch, and Their English Ancestry.* Philadelphia: J.B. Lippincott Company, 1907.

Whitemore, William H. *The American Genealogist Being a Catalogue of Family Histories and Publications.* [Statement by J.W. Dean regarding journal of Ebenezer Tolman]. Albany, N.Y.: Joel Munsell, 1868. 84-85.

Williams, Stephen W. *The Genealogy and History of the Family of Williams in America.* Greenfield, MA: Merriam & Mirick, 1847.

Winter, Florence Small. *The Kennebec-Chaudiere "Arnold" Trail.* Augusta, ME: RJ Printing, 1978.

Wright, James Osborne, comp. *Catalogue of the American Library of the Late Samuel Latham Mitchell Barlow.* New York: 1889.

Wright, Gen. Marcus J. "Letter From a Revolutionary Officer." [Charles Porterfield]; *Publications of the Southern History Association,* vol. IV, 1900: 254-257.

Wrong, George M. *Canada and the American Revolution: The Disruption of the First British Empire.* New York: Cooper Square Publishers, 1968.

Young, Henry J. "The Spirit of 1775, A Letter of Robert Magaw, Major of the Continental Riflemen." *John & Mary's Journal,* 1975: 6-50.

Zinn, Donna Heller. *Search of Records Report to Stephen Darley on George Morison from Records in Cumberland and Perry County.* The Perry Historians, 2010.

INDEX

Printed in the United States
by Baker & Taylor Publisher Services